The Complete Idiot's Reference Card

Running Start Checklist

"Help! I pulled my kid out of school today; what do we do tomorrow, this week, and this month until we get our act together?" Don't panic—just follow this list to hit the ground running:

➤ Allow for a period of decompression or deschooling. See Chapter 1, "What Is Homeschooling?" and Chapter 5, "Approaches to Home Education," for more about making the transition from school to home.

➤ Encourage your child to pursue his or her own interests while you keep a list or journal of activities. See Chapter 17, "Keeping Records," for ways to keep records, including keeping a journal.

➤ Spend time with your child and determine what he or she would like to do. Let your child tell you what he or she liked and didn't like in school, so you can avoid these pitfalls while you plan his or her learning experiences in the homeschool. See Chapter 9, "Out of the Box: Planning Your Own Curriculum," for more tips.

➤ Determine your child's learning style. Is your child visual ("show me"); linguistic (a bookworm); auditory ("read to me"); kinesthetic (needs to move, touch, and arrange)? See Chapter 7, "So Much to Choose From," for more on determining your child's learning style.

➤ Since what was happening in school wasn't working, try a different approach. Do a relaxed unit study; find some library books on a topic in which your child is interested. Include at least one unit with some projects to try. Take a field trip; visit local museums or historical sites; check your newspaper or community bulletin board for plays, programs, and festivals. Get comfortable being together: Cook and bake, read out loud to your child (or take turns reading with an older child); take a nature walk and collect specimens to identify; do volunteer work in the community. Read Chapter 18, "Getting a Grip: Keeping Burnout at Bay," for more ways to integrate life and learning.

➤ Check your journal entries. What is your child doing that you can count as "school" subjects? Identify his or her activities according to subject areas. Are there areas that need to be addressed? How can you best bring in these areas while using your child's learning strengths and interests? See Chapter 9 for ideas on curriculum planning.

alpha
books

Beginner's Checklist

The following checklist assumes a one- to three-month planning period before you start homeschooling:

➤ Read at least two books on homeschooling that seem to reflect your reason for homeschooling, and one from an entirely different perspective. See Appendix E, "Bibliography," for a list of books on homeschooling and related topics.

➤ If you have Internet access, visit Web sites such as www.Kaleidoscapes.com, www.midnightbeach.com/hs/, www.nhen.org, and www.unschooling.com. See Appendix B, "Curriculum Winners and Selected Resources, Including Dynamite Web Sites," for more.

➤ Obtain a copy of the homeschool law or regulations in your state or province. See Chapter 4, "Getting Legal: Alternatives to Compulsory Attendance."

➤ Purchase sample copies of homeschool publications. Subscribe to at least one homeschooling periodical that supports your vision of homeschooling and one that will stretch your thinking. See Appendix D, "Independent Study Programs and Support Schools, Publications, and Vendors," for a list of homeschooling publications.

➤ Find a local support group. Attend some meetings and activities. Talk to people who are homeschooling. Remember to filter advice through these questions: "Do their kids learn like mine?" "Is this homeschool parent like me?" "Will this approach, method, material work for us?" Some kids need structure, some need to go with the flow, and most are somewhere in between. See Appendix C, "Homeschooling Support Organizations," for a listing of national and state support groups, and Chapter 6, "Finding Support," for suggestions on finding a local group.

➤ Attend a curriculum fair or homeschool conference; attend sessions and browse the vendor hall. Ask questions! Pick up and/or send for some homeschooling catalogs. Compare materials, prices, and approaches. Ask other homeschoolers to show you the materials they like best; borrow materials to try for a few days. Understand your child's learning style and your own teaching style before you make decisions on methods and major purchases of materials. Read Chapter 7 to determine what will work best for you and yours.

➤ Arrange an informative tour of your local library. Find out what is available in the reference section, how to use the card catalog, how to request books through the library's cooperative and/or interlibrary loan, and how to use the Dewey decimal system to find books. Learn to access information efficiently, a vital tool on the homeschooling journey. See Chapter 19, "Self-Directed Learning: The Key to Motivation," for suggestions to directly involve your children in these activities.

➤ Spend time with your child: Cook; do chores; talk about what your child liked and didn't like about school; ask him or her about interests, favorite and least favorite subjects, what he or she would like to learn about; take walks; do projects; and get comfortable together. Read books and watch videos together; discuss what you've learned. Observe your child; discover how he or she learns. Read Part 3, "Choosing/Planning a Curriculum."

➤ Obtain at least one sample scope and sequence (curriculum)—two or more is better! Use it as a guideline while you plan your child's curriculum. Whenever possible, substitute real books, activities, and hands-on projects for textbook learning. Find out more about scope and sequence in Chapter 9.

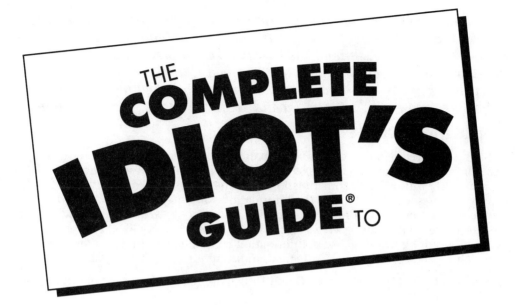

THE COMPLETE IDIOT'S GUIDE® TO

Homeschooling

by Marsha Ransom

alpha books

A Pearson Education Company

To my husband, Dwight, who encouraged me to "go for it" when I was offered the book contract … and who doesn't complain when the laundry becomes "Mount Washmore," dinner is take-out pizza (again!), and the house definitely doesn't qualify for the Good Housekeeping award. And to my children, Ryan, 21, and Aaron, 18, who motivated me to begin home-schooling; and Ervin, 13, and Jacinta, 10, who inspire me to continue.

International Standard Book Number: 0-02-863989-8
Library of Congress Catalog Card Number: Available upon request.

03   02   8   7   6   5   4   3   2

Interpretation of the printing code: The rightmost number of the first series of numbers is the year of the book's printing; the rightmost number of the second series of numbers is the number of the book's printing. For example, a printing code of 01-1 shows that the first printing occurred in 2001.

Printed in the United States of America

Note: This publication contains the opinions and ideas of its author. It is intended to provide helpful and informative material on the subject matter covered. It is sold with the understanding that the author and publisher are not engaged in rendering professional services in the book. If the reader requires personal assistance or advice, a competent professional should be consulted.

The author and publisher specifically disclaim any responsibility for any liability, loss, or risk, personal or otherwise, which is incurred as a consequence, directly or indirectly, of the use and application of any of the contents of this book.

Publisher
Marie Butler-Knight

Product Manager
Phil Kitchel

Managing Editor
Jennifer Chisholm

Acquisitions Editor
Randy Ladenheim-Gil

Development Editor
Lynn Northrup

Production Editor
Billy Fields

Copy Editor
Susan Aufheimer

Illustrator
Jody P. Schaeffer

Cover Designers
Mike Freeland
Kevin Spear

Book Designers
Scott Cook and Amy Adams of DesignLab

Indexer
Lisa Wilson

Layout/Proofreading
Darin Crone
Bob LaRoche

Contents at a Glance

Contents

Appendixes

Foreword

Dr. Frances S. Collins, world-famous leader of the Human Genome project, was home-schooled on a sheep ranch in western Virginia. He followed an "unschooling" regimen where the family studied whatever they found of interest for as long as it remained interesting. There was no science or math concentration at all in this major scientist's background. William F. Buckley, the prominent author, editor, and media personality, took a different route through homeschooling; one heavily involved with classical studies, rigorous training in logic, and endless intellectual debates around the dinner table. And Thomas Edison's education at home was mainly based on first-hand experience. Three different methods, three grand successes. No standardization.

Marsha Ransom, a homeschooling mother of four, has thoroughly examined what education is and how your own kids can get a good one without being locked in a classroom seat—and while building strong family ties through shared learning experiences. She places the methods that create successful individuals like Collins, Buckley, and Edison under a microscope, and concludes that you can do it, too. Anyone can! My long experience as a pretty good schoolteacher tells me she is right.

Every question that can conceivably be asked about the nuts and bolts of home-schooling is taken up and answered in *The Complete Idiot's Guide to Homeschooling*. How to begin, how to define your own philosophy, how to assemble a menu of choices and procedures to make that philosophy happen, where to find curriculum materials, how to connect with others like yourself, how to critique the bewildering world of choices to get what you really want.

Mrs. Ransom rolls up her sleeves and tackles the tough questions that make people nervous, too. She explains how to work within the laws of your state, what to do if you have children with special needs, how to tell if your kids are learning. The question of college is exhaustively considered, and I guarantee you're going to like what she has to say about that (wait until you meet the Colfax family, who sent three sons to Harvard on scholarship from their homeschool on a goat ranch in the mountains of northern California!).

Once upon a time, America was largely a homeschooled nation. We got weaned away from personal approaches by the rise of institutional schooling, which grew up in tandem with the institutional workplace. But over the past 30 to 40 years, an exciting revival of this productive family experience has been gathering steam. Now, at the beginning of the 21st century, as many as two million kids are getting an education outside of school—and the numbers are growing 15 to 20 percent a year.

How fitting, then, to find *The Complete Idiot's Guide to Homeschooling* exactly when we need it to find our own place in this learning revolution. With a lively style that sparkles with insight, common sense, and good humor, Marsha Ransom's book shows you how to be an artist at teaching your own children at home.

Whether you're thinking about making the leap to homeschooling or have already started, let her hold your hand and show you just how easy and right it is.

—John Taylor Gatto

John Taylor Gatto, a retired teacher, was awarded the New York City Teacher of the Year three times and was the 1991 New York State Teacher of the Year. Gatto is the author of four books on education, including his latest monumental investigation of the origins and development of compulsory schooling, The Underground History of American Education. *His Web site, johntaylorgatto.com, offers chapters of his books without cost, and seeks to create a dialogue about education.*

Introduction

I hope you will be motivated to join me, and thousands of others, on the road less traveled—homeschooling. As a new parent, I wanted what was best for my children and thoughtfully made choices about parenting, nutrition, and healthcare. However, I didn't learn about homeschooling until after my two older children had been in institutional school settings for six and four years, respectively. During those years, I did all the things caring parents do: volunteered in the classroom, was a room mother, sat on planning boards, ran incentive programs for the students, and was once asked by a teacher in the hallway, "Do you live here?" I don't regret the years I spent being an involved parent in institutional schools, but I look back on the years of being a homeschool parent with much more satisfaction.

During the years my children were in institutional schools, I helped my children learn how to fit into an environment that wasn't always responsive to them. One of my children struggled because he was a hands-on learner in an academically verbal/linguistic setting. The other was totally unchallenged by his schoolwork, but the school's policy precluded accelerating him into higher-level reading or math classes. My task when I began to homeschool was to excite my kids about learning and find ways for them to learn what they needed to know to grow into capable, independent, self-sufficient young adults.

Our first year of homeschooling was a learning experience for all of us. As I mothered our new baby and our busy toddler, the curriculum I had lovingly planned for the older children was often set aside. My two newly homeschooled sons began to show me what real learning is all about. Self-motivated by their interests, their retention was phenomenal! Although they were only 11 and 8 when we started homeschooling, I have learned much from the boys about how learning happens.

Over the years, I attended homeschool conferences, curriculum fairs, seminars, and support group meetings, talked to homeschoolers, and adapted what I learned to fit my family. I made mistakes and learned from them. I discovered that every homeschool family is unique. I researched many homeschooling approaches, but always ended up picking and choosing elements from a variety of programs to individualize my children's learning.

As you read *The Complete Idiot's Guide to Homeschooling*, you will be empowered to make choices for your family. Whether you choose to homeschool as a lifestyle choice, bring just one child in your family home for his or her education, or begin providing enrichment for your children after school, you will find the basic tools you need to take charge of your family's educational life.

How This Book Is Organized

In this book, I take you step by step through the many aspects of homeschooling you will consider in making thoughtful choices for your family.

Part 1, "Homeschooling in North America Today," gives you a peek into the lives of homeschooling pioneers and discusses how the numbers have grown since the homeschooling revival in the 1960s. I provide thought-provoking commentary on some of the questions most asked of seasoned homeschoolers, and talk about setting homeschooling goals.

Part 2, "First Things First: Getting Started," covers general information about homeschooling laws and regulations, helps you search out legal requirements in your state or province, and provides information about compliance with regulations. I talk about educational philosophy and homeschooling approaches, and lead you to a variety of sources for support and information.

Part 3, "Choosing/Planning a Curriculum," helps you narrow the choices. I encourage you to think about what fits your family, your child, and your goals. I help you think through your choices by reviewing some full-service programs, and show you how to use a planned scope and sequence for a model when planning your own curriculum.

Part 4, "Taking the Plunge: What Do I Do Now?" has separate chapters on working with children of different ages, as well as information on homeschooling kids with special needs. Glimpses into the lives of real homeschooling families and reassurance that mistakes aren't life-threatening help you determine that homeschooling is a workable option.

Part 5, "Keeping Track: Testing/Assessments/Record-Keeping," helps to tame the paper mountain. I talk about the pros and cons of testing as an assessment tool and provide examples of alternative assessments that can be used in conjunction with or instead of testing. I discuss the difference between keeping records for your personal use and keeping records to fulfill legal requirements.

Part 6, "Burnout Prevention," covers ways to keep from being overwhelmed by the additional responsibilities of homeschooling. I provide workable strategies for getting comfortably organized, helping your children become self-directed learners, and helping you deal with doubts. Involvement in the homeschool community and using the Internet to find support for your homeschooling endeavor are encouraged to keep burnout at bay.

There are also five appendixes in which you'll find the names and contact information for national, state, and provincial support groups; as well as independent study programs, support schools, vendors, and publications. You'll also find a glossary, curriculum winners and selected resources, including Web sites, and a bibliography.

Homeschooling Extras

Within each chapter are some special sidebar notes to emphasize things that will help you:

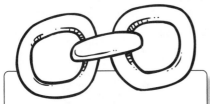

Learning Links

These boxes contain tips to make homeschooling simpler or more cost-effective.

Learning Lookouts

Check these sidebars for warnings and cautions to help you avoid common pitfalls along the homeschooling journey.

Speaking Educationese

These boxes contain definitions of words common to the world of homeschooling.

Spotlight on Education

In these boxes, you get a peek into the lives of real home-schoolers, with explanations of some of the finer points of homeschooling philosophy.

Acknowledgments

This book was made possible by the cooperation and help of many special individuals. My gratitude to my agent, Jeanne Fredericks, for her professionalism and unflagging dedication in helping me through my first book contract. Many thanks to the staff at Pearson Education, especially Randy Ladenheim-Gil, who had the vision to see the possibilities for this book. Very special thanks to Lynn Northrup for working with me to make my book the very best it could be, and to Susan Aufheimer, whose on-target questions and suggestions helped me immeasurably. Thanks also to the illustrator and production team, with whom I didn't work directly, for their contribution to my book; it couldn't have happened without each one of you.

Warmest thanks to Cafi Cohen for giving me the idea, for her valuable suggestions, and encouragement to continue marketing the book after several unsuccessful tries.

My appreciation and love to my brother, Glenn Linderman, and my mother, Martha Linderman, for reading each chapter as it came off the word processor and offering editing suggestions, criticisms, and ideas; and to my husband, Dwight, for listening while I read each chapter out loud.

Special thanks to Louise Haas of the SLD (Specific Language Disability) Center in Kalamazoo, Michigan; Bobbi Otto in Jackie McGeehee's office; and the many other individuals who assisted me with specialized information. You know who you are and I apologize because I don't have room to list you all.

Finally, my thanks to all the homeschoolers (especially the Bemis, Blasco, Cossey, and Drake families) who gave of their time and expertise to help us get started homeschooling; and those who answered questions, shared their experiences, and gave of themselves (the Zamperla, Troutman, Probst, Harthy, Karr, Lambeth, Dobson, and Amos families), for helping me make this book reflect the real story of homeschooling.

Trademarks

All terms mentioned in this book that are known to be or are suspected of being trademarks or service marks have been appropriately capitalized. Alpha Books and Pearson Education, Inc., cannot attest to the accuracy of this information. Use of a term in this book should not be regarded as affecting the validity of any trademark or service mark.

Part 1

Homeschooling in North America Today

What is homeschooling all about? Whatever your reasons for thinking about home-schooling, Part 1 will give you a foundation in the basics. You'll learn not only how all this got started, but how homeschooling grew and changed over the years.

If you're the type who likes to get all your ducks in a row, you'll learn that the statistics on homeschooling can be difficult to gather and corroborate. Meeting real home-schoolers is the best way to learn about them. To help you in your research, I've provided stories about famous homeschoolers past and present, as well as introduced you to some of today's homeschooling advocates—authors and speakers. Finally, I'll discuss possible answers to common homeschooling questions.

Chapter 1

What Is Homeschooling?

In This Chapter

➤ Tracing homeschooling's early roots

➤ Homeschooling over the past century

➤ A rose by any other name: homeschooling, home education, and home-based learning

➤ Why do people homeschool?

➤ Why every homeschool is unique

Homeschooling or home education has been around since the beginning of time. Parents have been teaching their children basic skills and values since time immemorial. Learning at home was the accepted educational norm until the mid-1800s, when compulsory schooling was introduced in Massachusetts.

Even after schooling laws were introduced, there were always a few intrepid souls who, for one reason or another, kept their children home for their education. Remember General Douglas MacArthur? Artist Andrew Wyeth? How about Chief Justice John Marshall? What do they have to do with it? They were all homeschooled!

Today, the annual growth of new homeschoolers is estimated at about 15 percent. New homeschoolers cite such reasons as academic excellence, safety, family togetherness, individualized learning, and the ability to teach their children the values they consider important.

The Good Old Days: Homeschooling's Humble Beginnings

Parents have always taught their children what they need to know to survive in the world. Basic household skills such as cooking, cleaning, laundering, and preserving food were taught to girls, and basic survival skills such as hunting, fishing, farming, and doing business were imparted to boys. Enough reading, writing, and arithmetic were taught to keep records and conduct business. Sometimes these skills crossed gender barriers, but not often.

One's place in society had some bearing on what one needed to know, as well as what one had the opportunity to learn. There were always a few people who pulled themselves up by their bootstraps, found a way to learn things that were unusual for their station in life, and moved up in society. (Consider Abraham Lincoln, for example. He was self-taught, borrowing and reading books whenever he could get his hands on them. These humble beginnings led to a career in politics, and ultimately to the presidency.)

Homeschooling in the Last Century

The first modern wave of homeschoolers happened during the 1960s, with the renewed interest in homesteading. In their quest for meaning, some people sought the simpler life, and purchased land in isolated places in order to live a self-sufficient lifestyle. Living off the land, growing their own crops, preserving the summer's bounty for winter, raising animals and building their own homes, these families often found themselves living too far from the public schools when their children became school age. Others planned to teach their own children from the very beginning, and, using ingenuity and the lessons of life, succeeded in doing exactly that.

During this time period, John Holt, a public school teacher, began to write books pointing out that children learn better without classroom instruction; and Dr. Raymond Moore, a developmental psychologist and educational researcher, decried the early age at which academics were being introduced in the institutional schools.

In the late 1970s, Holt gave up on reforming the educational system and started a newsletter, *Growing Without Schooling,* which became the support system for many homeschoolers of that era. Both Holt and Moore became leading advocates of the early

Learning Lookouts

We can take a lesson from these folks who revived the homestead movement—less is often more. Children learn indelible lessons from the experiences of life; when broken down and analyzed, these experiences often cover all the curriculum areas any curriculum planner might suggest. Real life is an inimitable teacher.

homeschooling movement. Learn more about these visionary men in Chapter 2, "Homeschooling Facts and Figures," and Chapter 5, "Approaches to Home Education."

In the 1980s, new tax regulations forced the closing of many private religious schools. These families, who had chosen to educate their children outside the public sector so they could receive an education based on a Christian world view, suddenly found themselves adrift. Unwilling to send their children to the public schools, these families turned to home education in huge numbers. Christian textbook publishers, losing their large school contracts, began to make some products available to homeschoolers on a limited basis. During this time period, homeschoolers became firmly entrenched in the American public's mind as isolationists. Even today, although it's been proven over and over that homeschooling is successful, socialization is a lingering concern, and one that I'll talk more about later in this chapter and in Chapter 3, "Quick Answers to Beginners' Questions."

During the 1990s, homeschooling numbers swelled as more and more families saw the need to educate their children at home. Homeschooling support groups grew, homeschooling became a marketing niche sought by growing numbers of textbook publishers, new companies sprang up to get a piece of the action, and the media brought homeschooling to everyone's attention on a regular basis. Home education began to be recognized as a mainstream choice.

Homeschoolers today are a very diverse group, coming from every background imaginable—religious and secular; rich, middle class, and poor; rural, suburban, and urban; Republican, Democrat, and Independent. Homeschooling families are headed by doctors, government employees, small business owners, military personnel, factory workers, and even public school teachers.

Learning Lookouts

Remember that with all the resources available today, virtually anyone can homeschool! Being a single parent, not having finished high school, and not understanding algebra are not a problem when video, audio, and Internet sources are available for self-study. Many kids end up teaching their parents some of the hard stuff.

Is There an Easy Definition?

While home education receives increasing media attention, there are still many misconceptions regarding this fast-growing movement—probably due in part to the fact that there are no typical homeschoolers. If we were to ask 100 homeschooling families about their methods and approaches, we would most likely hear 100 different versions of home education.

Homeschool, Home Education, and Home-Based Learning

We know that a rose by any other name is still a rose. And there are hundreds of varieties of roses, so even if you call it a rose, you aren't explaining if it's a climbing rose, a large pink rose, or a tiny white variety. For the purposes of this book, I will use the terms homeschool, home education, and home-based learning interchangeably. However, some homeschoolers have a definite preference for one label or the other. The word *homeschool* usually brings to mind a mother and children around the kitchen table with piles of textbooks, doing school-like assignments, with mother as teacher and, in some circles, father referred to as principal or superintendent of schools. Those who prefer the term *home education* or *home-based learning* tend to feel that true learning occurs outside of school, and without the externally imposed structure and trappings associated with institutional schooling. There are subtle nuances to the terms that you will become more aware of as you learn more about homeschooling.

> **Learning Links**
>
> Both parents of home-educated kids and the kids themselves often refer to themselves as homeschoolers. And while many homeschooling parents will admit they are learning as much as their children, it's usually only the children who are referred to as homeschooled.

> **Speaking Educationese**
>
> **Homeschooling** is a generic term often used to describe any family that has chosen to educate their children at home. While used to describe any such family, the word seems to indicate using the same methodology as is used in an institutional school; classroom, texts, teacher and student, tests, and grades. **Home education** or **home-based learning** is the term preferred by parents who use the home only as a base for learning. They feel the community and world around them is an integral part of their child's education, and consider themselves facilitators or mentors. While these parents may use traditional methods, they prefer real books and real life materials and focus on learning with a purpose.

Although this picture is true in some cases, there are many homeschoolers for whom this picture is totally inaccurate. Some families reach out into the community and the world around them to learn as much as possible from the experiences of life.

Let's look at an example. George, a painting contractor, and Lois, a freelance writer, hike a nature trail with their three children (Jordan, 12; Dale, 9; and Lisa, 5). Accompanying them are Sandra, a single mother who has a cleaning service and lives in a subsidized apartment, and her six-year-old daughter, Alicia. All the children draw specimens in their nature journals. They notice several varieties of birds, using binoculars to see them more clearly. Dad shares his knowledge of various bird species. Later the children use their collection of nature guides to positively identify the birds, leaves, and other flora and fauna they observed that day. Their activities will be noted in their record books under science and art.

Learning Links

Other than the binoculars and nature guidebooks, which many homes will have anyway, this natural science class is very inexpensive. Drawing on the expertise of others, using real books and keeping journals and records in a three-ring binder are thrifty ways to approach homeschooling. And this isn't just an isolated field trip, but a regular part of their science curriculum.

Unschooling? What's That?

Unschooling (or *natural learning*) can be a confusing term. Perhaps your first impression is that it's about taking away what the child has learned. But in reality, what its proponents are determined to take away is the imposed structure of institutional schooling. Families that embrace unschooling feel that children have an internal structure, a natural readiness and zest for learning, which motivates them to learn from every experience in life. Unschoolers may use some of the same materials as other homeschoolers, such as textbooks and cooperative classes, particularly in response to the child's desire to learn in that way. However, most find the larger part of their child's most meaningful learning happens as a result of real life experiences.

Here's an example. Twice a week, Ivano, an artisan who also works part-time for a building contractor, packs his van with handcrafted furniture he's

Speaking Educationese

Unschooling or **natural learning** is learning that happens "outside the box," without the usual structure of schooling. It occurs as a result of participating in the everyday experiences of life. Families that are involved in home business, are active in their communities, or have an interest that the whole family shares find this a workable choice.

made in his woodworking shop, and heads for the open-air market to spend the day displaying his work, talking with potential customers, and taking orders. His wife, Deb, studied art in college but chooses to stay home with their children, sharing the many joys of natural learning and making small projects to sell at the market. Later, after picking bunches of flowers from their garden and gathering a variety of containers to display them in, she and their three children (Harison, 10; Lorenzo, 8; and Ascanio, 3) join Ivano. Mama and Papa take turns tending the booth; the children learn by both watching their parent's example and selling their own wares. Later, they practice their math skills as they total their earnings, keep records, and decide how much to save or spend.

Unschoolers believe that children have an inborn desire to learn and that they can learn from life, in a natural way, many of the lessons that are taught in other ways in institutional settings. Although opponents of this method may look on and say that no learning is happening, unschoolers disagree. And the many unschooled young adults who are presently achieving in colleges, in the workplace, in relationships, and as citizens are living proof that this method does, indeed, work! For an in-depth discussion of unschooling or natural learning, refer to Chapter 5.

What Does Deschooling Mean?

When children are withdrawn from the institutional school setting, there is an adjustment period, often referred to as *deschooling* or decompression. Some parents have brought their children home and jumped straight into a school-at-home program, with all the best intentions, only to lament in a very short time that it isn't working! Veteran homeschoolers have told me that it can take from six weeks to six months for every year a child has been institutionally schooled, for a child to develop an interest in and love for learning.

Speaking Educationese

Deschooling refers to the decompression period for children who are brought out of an institutional school into a homeschooling environment. This can take from six weeks to six months for every year a child has been institutionally schooled.

Don't worry if your child shows no interest in anything when he or she first comes home. Your child may sleep, veg in front of the television, or just follow you around the house; these are normal behaviors for this time period. Quietly start marking your child's activities in a little notebook; this record may provide insight that will help you direct the child as you begin some educational pursuits. Remember to start thinking about each thing your child does (preparing meals, helping a friend repair a motorcycle, watching an educational video, or building a model airplane) in the light of what he or she is learning; this is for your own reassurance, not to be announced to the child! As you begin to figure out some things that your child is interested in, you may want to introduce some related learning activities. However, if your child's institutional school experience has been extremely traumatic, you may want to lean most heavily on project-oriented learning, real life experiences, field trips, and spend time reading together about subjects that interest your child—things that he or she won't relate to school in his or her mind. Follow your child's lead, avoid force and confrontation, and use some reverse psychology for the least stressful transition to homeschooling. Time is a great healer; however, learning can still be happening in alternative ways during the healing time.

Spotlight on Education

I told my son Ryan at the end of fourth grade that we would begin homeschooling in the fall. With the knowledge that we were going to homeschool, my sullen, angry boy gradually morphed into his old self; full of questions, excited about everything new, talkative, and exuberant. We started a fairly structured program in the fall because I didn't have this book to tell me not to! Things didn't go very smoothly, but, thankfully, after the first year of home education, we got only occasional glimpses of the "I can't" kid; most of Ryan's learning after the first year was hands-on or auditory.

The Bottom Line

All those terms with so many different variations of meaning! It boggles the mind! The bottom line is that home educators, whatever they choose to call themselves, and whatever approach or combination of approaches they use, are successfully helping their children receive a good education.

Despite the diversity, nearly all homeschooling families would agree that two points begin to define home education:

1. Most homeschoolers use the home as a base for learning. Some instruct almost entirely at home, using purchased, structured curricula. Others use home as a place for planning and support, moving out into the community for learning resources.

2. In homeschools, parents and children have taken control of education and learning, deciding what to learn, when to learn, and how to learn. Parents and children choose materials and curricula, set their own pace, and learn with games or textbooks or hands-on projects—whichever best meets their needs.

Past that point, it is difficult to define homeschooling exactly because—in practice—there are hundreds of ways to succeed.

Why Homeschool? What's in It for You?

Have you ever wondered why people homeschool? Or considered it yourself? Ever wondered what the benefits would be? Or how it would affect your family? Many, many homeschoolers over the years have pondered the same questions, and there are countless reasons that motivate them. I'm going to mention some of the most common reasons; maybe you'll see yourself in one or more of them.

We Never Settle Down

Folks who enjoy life on an island, or in a remote mountain valley, or w-a-a-a-y off in the Outback of Australia find homeschooling is a perfect solution to the logistics situation. Missionaries and military personnel have chosen home education so their families can remain intact. Families whose sole provider has a job that necessitates transfers across country on a regular basis have found that these moves don't cause near the disruption when education just goes along. Although there's a new house to get settled into and new friends to be made, the adjustments don't include missing a whole unit in the math book, or ending up in a class where everyone is either way ahead or way behind you. Even families with a parent who works shifts or travels frequently have found that homeschooling makes it possible for children to have more time with Mom or Dad. Homeschool schedules can be adjusted so the parent can work with the kids, or read to them, or just enjoy time with them, on a more regular basis than families whose children are locked into an institutional school schedule.

Learning Just Isn't Happening

Some families have chosen to homeschool because their children's needs are simply not being met in the institutional setting. We all know that a classroom with 30 children allows little time for personal interaction between individuals and teacher.

If children have a specific interest, parents can build on that interest to provide an interest-based curriculum (a course of study) or learning experience, allowing for better retention of subject matter. Sometimes distractions caused by disruptive children in a classroom can contribute to the child's lack of ability to excel.

Whether parents want to give an extremely bright child more of a challenge, or provide remedial lessons for a child who is falling behind, home education provides the ideal environment.

Spotlight on Education

Some children who have had learning difficulties in the school setting have blossomed with one-on-one instruction and the ability to work at their own pace (be it faster or slower than in the classroom). Classroom lessons are usually geared to the middle ground, or "average" child. Children who understand the lesson quickly may become bored, which can lead to behavior problems in some cases. Others may be left behind when they miss or don't understand part of the lesson due to inattention or distractibility. Homeschooled children have the advantage of repeating things, having it explained in a different way, or finding a new method to learn it, all generally happening in a timely fashion.

Religious Reasons

Just as homeschoolers come in all shapes and sizes, backgrounds and colors, so religious homeschoolers don't all fit into one homogeneous lump. Lists *of homeschool support groups* include Unitarian Universalists and Humanists, Islamic, Jewish, Wiccan, Adventist, Catholic, Mormon, and a variety of other religious groups. Native American homeschoolers cite being able to preserve their religious and cultural traditions as one of the reasons to choose home education.

Speaking Educationese

A **homeschool support group** may be a national group, a state group, or a local group of homeschoolers banding together to provide support in the form of resources, meetings, and activities.

Some homeschoolers feel that they are specifically called by God to teach their children at home. There are also many religious people who homeschool for reasons other than their religious beliefs; however, their religious beliefs shape their choices in everything in life, including the way they interact with their children. Regardless of motivation, religious persons do agree that homeschooling allows them more time to share their personal convictions, values, and beliefs with their children.

Dangerous School Environments

During the weeks after the 1999 school shootings in Columbine, Colorado, phones rang off the hook across the United States. Homeschooling support groups and contact people received many calls from frantic parents, determined to withdraw their children from institutional schools before their children became victims of the next shooting spree. However, shootings and bombings are not the only things that parents fear in the schools. Some parents have withdrawn their children because of drug problems, personal attacks on their children, and sex-related issues.

As parents, we must protect our children and provide them with a safe environment in which to live and mature. Homeschooling became a safe haven for many children in the 1990s.

Closer Families

We live in a society with a high divorce rate, resulting in many broken families. Many of the activities we engage in don't bring families together. Churches have age-related activities provided in separate classrooms or on different dates. Many heads of families are involved in a plethora of activities that don't allow children. Children have their own set of activities, for which parents drop them off and leave to do their own thing. Families often don't eat meals together, take trips together, or even spend much time talking to each other. Families may live hundreds, even thousands, of miles from extended family, due to job transfers and career moves.

Homeschooling provides a way for families to reconnect, to spend more time together getting to know each other. Older siblings can teach younger ones by reading to them, doing projects with them, and sharing their own discoveries. When extended family members visit, they can share in the homeschool activities, or the homeschool family can take time to enjoy getting reacquainted. Homeschool families do more activities as a family, and logistically have more time to spend together.

The S Word

Socialization is one of the first things I'm asked about when people discover we homeschool. It's one of the biggest worries people have about homeschooling, and one of the things people often bring up as a negative factor in home education. Let me assure you, this is a non-issue.

Speaking Educationese

Socialization is the ability to get along with people of all kinds in a variety of situations.

True socialization involves the ability of a person to interact with others regardless of their age, ethnicity, and status in life. Peer socialization is artificial; it doesn't prepare for the real world. When else in life are we going to find ourselves with 30 others of roughly the same age? Oh, sure, class reunions! Once every five years at the most. Otherwise, whether at work or pursuing leisure activities, we find ourselves with groups of people of disparate backgrounds. Aerobics class, softball team, office staff, sales team, construction crew, or bowling league—seldom a peer group. Homeschoolers are growing up (some even attend the prom and play on sports teams) going to college, getting jobs, dating, getting married, and living very normal lives. Homeschooling provides excellent opportunities for positive socialization. I discuss socialization in more detail in Chapter 3.

Money: The Bottom Line

Although some homeschoolers have had their children in private school in the past, financial considerations have caused some to consider home education as an option. Many families have both parents working to pay tuition, while homeschooling is often pursued on a single income. When money becomes an issue, and parents aren't willing to use the public schools for any of the reasons I talked about earlier, homeschooling can be a cost-effective answer to the dilemma.

Learning Links

Many homeschoolers have found a variety of ways to keep costs down. Using inexpensive or free resources from the government and other sources, using the public library extensively as opposed to purchasing all the books needed, forming teaching cooperatives to share the expertise of several home educators, and making their own learning materials are all good cost-saving measures.

The majority of homeschoolers are one-income families, and most make it work without draining their finances. Homeschooled kids don't need to have as many trendy clothes or the latest fad to hit the school scene. Vacations may be less luxurious, but rich in other ways: visiting historical sites on the way to visit family, or making hands-on museums the highlight of the trip to provide in-depth learning along with family fun. Some families have founded family businesses, which provide an extra income and a built-in learning arena for the children. Some homeschooled children have become entrepreneurs in their own right, learning all the way to the bank.

Defining Your Goal

Suppose you could design an ideal learning environment for your child. What would you include? Challenging academics? A program appropriate to your child's learning style and interests? Cultural activities like music and drama? What type of atmosphere would you specify? Safe, supportive, encouraging, challenging? More than one million families nationwide have asked and answered this question and created their ideal learning situations at home. We call these families and their children homeschoolers.

I Want to Homeschool, But I Can't Right Now

Those families who keep their children in school, but make their home a rich environment for continued learning, also find long-term benefits in spending quality and quantity time with their children. These parents set a positive example of life-long learning, and supplement their children's institutional education with rich experiences outside of school. All parents have been home educators at one time or another. Remember those years when Jimmy just didn't understand math, and you spent almost every evening helping him with his homework? And what about the period in middle school when Angie couldn't seem to get a grip and you found her a tutor for two semesters? Finding the right combination of resources and meeting your children's needs are two key factors in home education. Maybe you have been a part-time homeschooler all along and just didn't know it.

I Want to Homeschool, But Where Do I Start?

Ready to explore homeschooling in more depth? Use this book as a resource to help you find support groups, curricula, and other information you may need in your home education journey. In general, information in the following chapters will help parents, students, and others interested in education who want to ...

Learning Links

If you've just withdrawn your child from school and are in need of instant information, turn to the tearout card in the front of this book for pointers on making a running start.

➤ Explore home education.

➤ Purchase a packaged curriculum.

➤ Research learning styles, materials, and home-schooling approaches before deciding whether to teach their children at home.

➤ Design and implement their own curriculum.

➤ Discover remedial and enrichment ideas to use at home for kids who remain in school.

➤ Use twenty-first century resources, like the Web and computer distance-learning.

One Size Doesn't Fit All: Why Every Homeschool Is Unique

Like all individuals, every family is unique. No one else has the same financial situation, the same sources of income, the same number of kids of the same ages, or the same combination of personalities and learning styles as yours. That's why when a family starts to plan their ideal learning environment, they come up with different answers to the same questions. We can ask advice of seasoned home educators, listen to talks by experienced conference speakers, visit other homeschoolers, and read books and publications about homeschooling. How we interpret what we hear, see, and read will be different from how someone else might understand the same things. In fact, that's one of the greatest beauties of educating your children at home. You can survey the many resources available, and take what appeals to you and leave the rest.

The Least You Need to Know

➤ Although homeschooling has been around since the beginning of time, it has become a popular alternative to compulsory schooling in recent years.

➤ Homeschoolers range from those using the traditional "school-at-home method" to those putting together their own materials (and everything in between)!

➤ Homeschoolers are diverse, creative, and unique; they come from every socio-economic group, political, and religious affiliation, family configuration, and educational background.

➤ Homeschoolers have many reasons for homeschooling, including superior academics, religious motivation, family values, positive socialization, flexibility, and dangerous school situations.

➤ There is no one right way to homeschool, and everyone can do it!

Chapter 2

Homeschooling Facts and Figures

In This Chapter

➤ Getting an idea of how many homeschoolers there are in North America

➤ Rate of growth of home education

➤ Some famous (and not-so-famous) folks who have been homeschooled

➤ Who's who in homeschooling today

Many articles on homeschooling include estimates of the number of homeschoolers or the rate of growth of homeschooling. Figures on homeschooling seem to be most important to the media, school officials, and politicians. New homeschoolers seem to appreciate the fact that there are measurable numbers of others choosing to homeschool; however those who continue to homeschool do so because of the personal benefits their family realizes, not because of the numbers.

In this chapter, you'll learn why we don't really know how many people are already homeschooling their children in North America and read about some famous homeschoolers from the past and the present. Since numbers aren't my thing, I'll try to keep this discussion basic so we can get on to the fun stuff; how many of these famous homeschoolers do you recognize?

How Many Homeschoolers Are There, Really?

A lot of people would like to know exactly how many homeschoolers there really are. Maybe you would, too. Some government officials would like to know for sure; the National Education Association might be interested; so would the marketing folks. With all these people wanting to know, why is it so hard to really know exact numbers? We see numbers quoted in various places, but they don't all match up. Why is that? Read on!

According to the NHERI

The National Home Education Research Institute (NHERI), a nonprofit organization, collects and analyzes original research data on home education, and conducts studies on homeschooling. Its latest finding is that between 700,000 to 1,150,000 United States students in grades K through 12 are currently being home-educated. It also found that the number of homeschoolers is growing at a rate of 15 to 40 percent per year.

NHERI numbers were achieved by collecting information from members of the Home School Legal Defense Association (HSLDA), as discussed in the next section, and by sending questionnaires to homeschooling support groups to be forwarded to homeschoolers in their area.

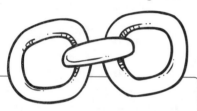

Learning Links

An NHERI study of social and emotional adjustment in home-schoolers found that the home-schooled are as well-adjusted socially and emotionally as their private school counterparts. However, the home-educated are less peer-dependent. (Dehooke, 1986)

What the HSLDA Says

The Home School Legal Defense Association counts about 55,000 homeschooling families in its membership. According to HSLDA's homeschooling FAQs (frequently asked questions) on their Web site, homeschooling is growing at a rate of about 15 percent per year, so it estimates there were about 1.5 million children homeschooled in the 1997–1998 school year.

HSLDA and NHERI have collaborated on studies of homeschoolers in the past. You can find contact information for the two organizations in Appendix C, "Homeschooling Support Organizations," and find information about these studies in Appendix E, "Bibliography."

Other Studies Over the Years

Patricia M. Lines has made several studies of homeschoolers, some as a researcher with the Department of Education, and most recently, as a researcher with a

nonprofit think tank, Discovery Institute. Originally, she based her estimates on three different
sources: data from state education agencies, distri-
bution of curricular packages for homeschoolers,
and state homeschool associations' estimates.
Currently, she relies on homeschooling filing data
provided to her by 32 states and the District of
Columbia. It's important to understand that even
in states where filing is mandated, some homeschoolers do not file. Ms. Lines cites Florida's
annual survey of homeschooling filers as an indica-
tion that the homeschool population is growing at
around 15 to 20 percent per year. She believes that
at the present rate of growth, there will be around
1.5 to 2 million children in homeschooling by the
2000–2001 school year, which is about 3 to 4 percent of school-aged children nationwide. Read her
article online or by requesting a copy of the article
from Discovery Institute. Contact information is
included in Appendix E.

Learning Lookouts

Whether you are researching the
numbers of homeschoolers, legalities, or a homeschooling approach, verify facts and figures
whenever possible. Read, ask
questions, and form your own
educated opinions. Be aware
that some experts have a personal agenda to promote, which
you may or may not agree with.

The latest compiled figures in Canada, documented in an article titled "A Profile of
Home Schooling in Canada," were from the 1995–1996 school year, and estimates
were 17,500 registered homeschoolers in Canada, about 0.4 percent of total student
enrollment. (In British Columbia, students enrolled in E-Bus programs, which provides parents of homeschoolers with a computer and Internet access, are not considered exclusively home-based learning, but are known as alternative-schooling
programs. Thus, they will not be included in compiled homeschooling figures.) Find
contact information to request this article in Appendix E.

As in the States, registration requirements are at the province's discretion, so they
vary from province to province. A couple of surveys suggest 8 to 30 percent non-
compliance in registration. Quebec did not collect any homeschooling figures at all
in the 1995–1996 school year.

This paper states that most provinces are aware that registration figures undercount
home educators. An investigation done by the Canadian Association of Homeschoolers placed homeschooling numbers at 30,000 to 40,000 in 1990, at that time
approximately 1 percent of the total school population. A summary points out that
these estimates do not accurately reflect the total numbers of homeschoolers.

Why These Numbers Are Just Guesstimates

First of all, homeschooling is not under the jurisdiction of the federal government,
but under state or provincial regulation, so no real federal head count is available.

Learning Lookouts

According to the United States Department of Education, there are three states where both homeschoolers and the State Education Agencies believe that filing rates are near 100 percent: Maine, New Mexico, and Wisconsin. Despite officials' beliefs, there are many homeschoolers who do not file with the state due to religious or philosophical disagreement with government requirements.

Speaking Educationese

A **support school** provides legal cover and services for a homeschooler. Some support schools are private schools with a program for homeschoolers, while others exist solely to provide services for homeschoolers. A private school may open some group programs at their campus school to homeschoolers. Typical services provided are record keeping, curriculum counseling, and selling educational materials.

Second, every state and province has its own way of handling home education. Some states and provinces have a system whereby homeschoolers report directly to them; however, in some states and provinces, it is not mandatory. You can easily see why those states and provinces wouldn't have an accurate way to determine how many homeschoolers reside within their borders.

While in some states and provinces homeschoolers are required to report to the local school district, some states and provinces do not have a mechanism in place for the local school district to report to them.

These many studies have tried to determine just how many homeschoolers there are; the media is always digging to find out so they can include it in articles about homeschooling. But, as you can see, it's not easy to determine.

Third, the numbers game is important. Some government and school officials would like to get a vehicle in place to count, register, and regulate homeschoolers. Mandatory filing is seen by many homeschoolers as just the first step in a move to take away their homeschooling freedom. This is why, even in states where filing is mandatory, there are philosophical nonfilers. Such individuals feel that coming generations should be able to choose to home educate, make their own curriculum choices, and teach according to their own values and belief systems, without government interference.

Finally, some homeschoolers don't educate under the auspices of a *support school*, which might be a source for how many homeschoolers are registered there. Other homeschoolers don't report to anyone; their children aren't in school and simply aren't registered anywhere. Some homeschoolers refuse to have their names on any mailing list. No matter which way the number crunchers count it, they will always come up with a different number! After all, if you, your neighbor, and your boss all start homeschooling, there'll be a few more students to add to the numbers!

How the Numbers Have Grown

Based on these theories, it appears that homeschooling has grown from 12,500 in 1978 to 375,000 in 1992. However, as you can see, these figures include a lot of variables, so at best these numbers are simply guesses.

Although homeschooling was revived during the homesteading movement of the 1960s, the first figures available in the States are for 1978, estimating 12.5 thousand homeschoolers, while no figures seem to be available for this time period in Canada.

Available United States figures swelled to 92,500 in 1983, rose again to 183,000 in 1985, and then to 225,000 in 1988. This rapid growth reflects the closing of many private Christian schools due to changes in tax regulations, although there were plenty more people who began homeschooling for reasons such as academic excellence, lifestyle or philosophical reasons, and family closeness. I couldn't find figures for Canada in the 1980s, though an article in the *Education Quarterly Review* states that homeschooling in Canada grew every year since the early 1980s.

Another growth spurt in 1990 brought figures in the States to 301,000 and finally in 1992 homeschooling guesstimates reached 375,000! Since then, reports have shown rapid growth, estimated between 15 and 40 percent, depending on which research you read.

In Canada, there was a 10 percent increase in registered homeschoolers from the 1995–1996 school year to the 1996–1997 school year, when numbers were 19,114.

Learning Links

People are getting the message that homeschooling is a valid education option for the new century. Although it may not really matter to you how many homeschoolers there are; you can see why the numbers are important to others. What's really important to you is figuring out what these folks are doing that works so well!

No one knows how many homeschoolers there have been, nor how many there are today. The only thing anyone can agree on is that home education is growing by leaps and bounds, and will continue to grow as more and more parents realize that home education is an educational option that offers the ability to personalize your child's curriculum, bring your family closer together, encourage positive socialization, and provide a top-quality education for your child.

Famous Homeschoolers: Past and Present

Quick! Tell me the names of three homeschoolers from history! Give up? Oh, yes, we already talked about Honest Abe in the previous chapter; he must have gotten his *values training* at home because he certainly didn't attend school for long.

Speaking Educationese

Values training refers to imparting specific ideals or principles. Many homeschooling families today base their curriculum on specific values or emphasize character training.

I find it fascinating to read biographies and discover how many historical figures were homeschooled or self-educated. Unable or unwilling to attend school, they sought out resources, became detailed observers of humankind, and read avidly. In 1997 a *Home Education* magazine article by Susan McMinn Seefeldt focused on famous women who were educated at home. That article prompted me to find and read every book about or by these women. This eye-opening and enjoyable reading experience lasted for several months. I found many biographies of famous homeschooled women, written for children, to read to my daughter; I also left them lying around for my sons to see and read. (This is one of my many ploys to get my kids to read something I think is important.)

There are lists of famous homeschoolers available on the Internet, on T-shirts marketed by homeschoolers (check Appendix D, "Independent Study Programs and Support Schools, Publications, and Vendors," for the names of some of these vendors), and in the appendixes of some homeschooling books.

Spotlight on Education

Homeschoolers Mac and Nancy Plent have written a wonderful book called *An A in Life: Famous Homeschoolers* (see Appendix E). The Plents homeschooled their children and by 1983 recognized the need to provide some evidence that homeschooling works. So they compiled a list of successful self-taught people who had had little or no formal education. Their list includes some people who never went to school, some who were in and out of school throughout their lives, some who attended school only briefly, and some senior year and college drop-outs.

Here are some past and present homeschoolers whose names you might recognize:

➤ **Ben Franklin.** Franklin attended school for only two years because his father couldn't afford the tuition, then worked in the family business of candlemaking.

He taught himself algebra, geometry, navigation, and grammar, and learned to write by rewriting essays written by others. A printer's apprentice at 12, he was able to get his writings published, albeit anonymously. Ben grew up to be a statesman, scientist, inventor, civic leader, and public servant.

➤ **Pearl S. Buck.** Buck grew up in China, the daughter of missionaries. Schooled at home by correspondence and tutor, she developed a great appreciation for the Chinese culture. She attended college in the United States, later returned to China to teach, and became a prolific writer. Many of her books, set in China, reflect her love for the people of China. In 1938, she won the Nobel Prize for literature at the age of 46.

➤ **Andrew Carnegie.** Carnegie attended school in Scotland until he was 13, when his family emigrated to the United States. He worked to help support his family, obtaining better positions whenever he could. At the age of 24, he became a division manager for a railroad, and had already started making small investments which were the start of his future fortune.

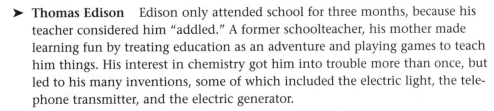

Learning Lookouts

Kids who march to a different drummer are often the same ones who are tested and retested for learning disabilities, have problems remembering to turn in their assignments, and just don't seem to "get it." Seldom motivated externally, these kids can get turned on to something and become so internally motivated that you can't get their attention; and that's when they may get labeled ADD (Attention Deficit Disorder).

➤ **Thomas Edison** Edison only attended school for three months, because his teacher considered him "addled." A former schoolteacher, his mother made learning fun by treating education as an adventure and playing games to teach him things. His interest in chemistry got him into trouble more than once, but led to his many inventions, some of which included the electric light, the telephone transmitter, and the electric generator.

➤ **Charles Dickens.** Dickens attended school on and off until he was about 14; at 12 he worked for a time in a London factory pasting labels on bottles. Most of his education came from his observation of life, especially during the years he worked as a newspaper reporter. He became famous as a writer at age 24 and spent the rest of his life writing, editing, giving dramatic readings, and being active in charities for the poor.

➤ **Sandra Day O'Connor.** Although O'Connor attended private school, she was home-educated during her early years. Even after she attended private school, she spent her happiest times helping with chores, swimming, and riding on her family's isolated ranch. A self-motivated learner, O'Connor graduated from private high school at the age of 16 and was accepted at Stanford University. She was the first woman to be appointed to the Supreme Court.

➤ **LeAnn Rimes.** Rimes, an acclaimed country singer, attended public school through sixth grade, but when singing engagements and travel made attendance difficult, her parents enrolled her in Texas Tech and Texas University for high school extension courses. Because Rimes knew when she was only five that she wanted to be a famous singer and had the drive and ambition to go with it, her parents made it possible for her to follow her interests and achieve her dream.

➤ **Hanson.** This popular rock trio, made up of teenaged brothers Ike, Taylor, and Zach, has been homeschooled since their father's job took them overseas for several years. Homeschooling also helped make it possible for them to devote their time to writing music, traveling to perform, and recording their music. The boys have had a math tutor, but also learn from books, traveling, and life.

Linda Dobson's latest book, *Homeschoolers' Success Stories* (see Appendix E), profiles many more homeschoolers, not so well known, but successful in life in a variety of ways: Jason Taylor, NFL defensive end for the Miami Dolphins; Amber Luvmour, who works as a program leader for the family alternative education and parenting business; Monique Harris, who scored a perfect 1600 on the SAT; and Aaron Fessler, whose home business doing computer networking recently sold for over $55,000,000!

Well-Known Homeschooling Speakers and Authors

Some homeschoolers have found that their knowledge about homeschooling is invaluable to new and seasoned home educators. Some have written books telling about their unique experiences, others have started on the speaking circuit, and still others have done both. We'll explore a few whose writings I have especially appreciated. Many of them I have either heard at a conference or met in person. These are some really special people with an impressive amount of combined knowledge. Be sure to seek out their writings, and if you get a chance to hear them speak, jump at it!

David and Mary Colfax: Homeschooling Pioneers

One of the very first books I ever read on homeschooling was David and Mary Colfax's *Homeschooling for Excellence* (see Appendix E). A small, easily read book crammed with information about their thoughts on education in general and homeschooling in particular, it was especially impressive to me because three of their sons had recently been accepted at Harvard! Today, we know that the Colfax's are just as proud of the accomplishments of the son who didn't attend Harvard. And that's as it should be. Just being accepted into a prestigious university isn't the only measure of a fine human being. More importantly, recent reports tell us that these young men are committed to making a difference in the world in a number of important ways. For example, Reed, their third son, attended Yale Law School after graduating from Harvard. He currently serves as a staff attorney for the Fair Housing Project of the Washington lawyers' Committee for Civil Rights and Urban Affairs. There he litigates cases for victims of housing discrimination in the Washington, D.C., metropolitan area.

Learning Links

Be sure to read David and Mary Colfax's *Hard Times in Paradise: An American Family's Struggle to Carve Out a Homestead in California's Redwood Mountains* (see Appendix E), in conjunction with their homeschooling book, to get a true picture of the life that grew their sons into impressive young men.

I met David and Mary at a homeschooling conference in California two years ago, and found them to be very warm and helpful, as well as forthright in stating their opinions—very much like their books and articles. Mary's answers while speaking during a panel session reminded me very much of the question and answer section of their homeschooling book: down to earth and to the point. David and Mary were pioneers at a time when homeschooling was evolving in North America; having a record of that journey is very valuable today.

David Guterson: The "Why Homeschool?" Advocate

A high school English teacher and published author, David Guterson is the father of four children who are being educated at home. His book *Family Matters: Why Homeschooling Makes Sense* (see Appendix E) recounts the history of education and supplies ample reasons for home education. Guterson doesn't tell you how to homeschool as much as he provides reasons why you should. By pointing out what hasn't worked over the years in public education, he helps us understand what to avoid when educating our children. His book also offers information on the academic success of homeschooled children, education in other societies, and the psychology of learning.

Guterson devotes a lot of time in his book to explaining how children in the past learned from their parents and from life. Many examples are given to show how important it is that learning be directly related and connected to the world around us. Meanwhile, as Guterson correctly points out, today's institutional schooling is nearly always divorced from life. If you are looking for a deeper understanding of today's educational system and are unable to articulate your own gut feelings about home education, you will find words to fit your feelings in *Family Matters*.

Raymond and Dorothy Moore: The Grandparents of Homeschooling

Dr. Raymond and Dorothy Moore's approach to education is based on research and years of working with homeschoolers using their approach. They advocate the use of delayed academics; they are firmly convinced that most children shouldn't be doing intensive academics before age 12. However, that doesn't mean the Moores believe no learning should take place during the early years. Homeschoolers enrolled in the Moore Foundation are encouraged to have their children take a balanced approach to learning, utilizing work, service, and academics with a project-oriented focus.

Dr. Moore, a developmental psychologist, was a member of a task force of leading American educators that determined through studies that academics should be delayed until the child is ready. Dr. and Mrs. Moore (a former teacher and reading specialist) have shared the findings of that research over and over in the many books they have written. They stress that children should help with housework and family service projects or home businesses to learn responsibility. They believe family should be the center of the child's life, and peer interaction should be carefully monitored. Having helped thousands of homeschoolers over the years, the Moores have a proven method worth taking note of.

Materials in their catalog are plainly marked to help you seek out or avoid those with Christian or specific doctrinal content. The Moores have always been happy to help home educators from any background or motivation.

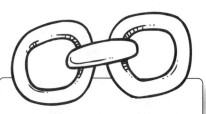

Learning Links

Dr. and Mrs. Moore's seminars include their strongly held doctrinal beliefs regarding nutrition and parenting, as well as their well-researched findings on education. Their religious beliefs are usually presented at the end of their homeschool seminars. However, many homeschoolers have been able to use their educational methods successfully, while still retaining their own beliefs regarding nutrition and parenting.

John Taylor Gatto: 1991 New York State Teacher of the Year

Having been named New York City Teacher of the Year three times and New York State Teacher of the Year in 1991, Mr. Gatto has some hands-on knowledge of what does and doesn't work in the classroom setting. Having left teaching to promote alternatives in education, Mr. Gatto presents insightful talks at speaking engagements across the country. His book *Dumbing Us Down: The Hidden Curriculum of Compulsory Schooling* (see Appendix E) reveals some inside information: Between schooling and television, children don't have time to learn how they connect to the community in which they live or to figure out the lives they might lead if they took a little different road. In his 26 years as a classroom teacher, Mr. Gatto has determined that independent study, community service, apprenticeships, and time to reflect and be a child are important factors in educating children.

Gatto's latest book, *The Underground History of American Education* (see Appendix E), assures us that bringing up children should force us to realize that no child on earth is just like another and that we have no reliable map to tell us what to do. Mr. Gatto says that we should be making it up as we go along or we aren't doing it right. These reflections fit well with what I've learned as a homeschooling parent.

Cathy Duffy: Flexible, Creative, Eclectic Curriculum Designer

Beginning as a structured homeschooler using the *A Beka curriculum* (see contact information in Appendix D) in 1982, when her oldest child was in third grade, Duffy soon began making modifications to their original program. Implementing unit studies, using real books and enriching with hands-on activities, while always considering worldview, the Duffys tailored their program to fit their family. The youngest of Duffy's three children graduated from homeschool high school in 1997.

Well-known for her Christian Curriculum Manuals, and a book called *Government Nannies: The Cradle-to-Grave Agenda of Goals 2000 and Outcome-Based Education* (see Appendix E), Duffy's present focus is to promote a classical approach for older kids, so they will learn to really think and present their ideas well, both orally and in writing. Duffy's workshops include such diverse topics as …

➤ Education in the New Millennium: Child of the State or Separation of School and State.

➤ Life Journey: Real Education and the Search for Truth (for Catholic groups).

➤ Choosing Curriculum to Fit Each Child: Identifying and Applying Learning Styles.

Duffy also provides a session especially for homeschool support group leaders, to address issues they face in counseling members. She is currently looking into the feasibility of using technology to provide a higher quality educational vehicle so more families can find options outside of the institutional schools.

Speaking Educationese

The **A Beka curriculum** uses the same A Beka Book day-by-day teaching curricula that are used in thousands of Christian schools across America, now made available for use by missionaries, evangelists, and Christian parents who choose to teach their own children at home.

Stay tuned, folks! Whatever she comes up with is bound to be worth looking into. Cathy Duffy is a perfect example of the lifelong learner, constantly stretching to reach a new dimension.

Grace Llewellyn: "Rise Out" Advocate Extraordinaire

Grace Llewellyn's first book, *The Teenage Liberation Handbook: How to Quit School and Get a Real Life and Education* (see Appendix E), irreverently and enthusiastically urges teens to take control of their own lives and education by "rising out" (as opposed to dropping out) of school. And this book isn't just theory and philosophy. Although Llewellyn assures teens that she won't hold their hands for the journey unless they want her to, she makes available a very clear road map of ways to do what she advocates; she also makes it clear that there is not one right way to do it. She followed this up with *Real Lives: eleven teenagers who don't go to school* (see Appendix E), which is based on her correspondence with, yes, 11 teenagers who are doing just what her first book suggested. Although Llewellyn's books are aimed at teens, many parents have found her suggestions extremely useful for getting ideas for alternative ways to learn difficult (and not so difficult) subjects.

Llewellyn also sponsors an annual camp called Not Back to School Camp, a retreat experience for unschooled teens, ages 13 through 18. Llewellyn doesn't schedule tightly because she likes things to evolve naturally according to the interests of the campers. She also encourages campers to lead a workshop or coach/teach a game/ sport. Her premise is that even campers who haven't done this before usually have something worthwhile to share with others. Llewellyn also feels that campers don't need to run frenetically from one activity to another; the woods offer the opportunity to commune with nature or enjoy a walk, alone or with friends.

Llewellyn's latest project is called The Dream House, which will be a house where unschooled teens will live and work together, in 10-week sessions, learning by doing, apprenticing, exploring, and living. There will be staff to help with communication, resources, and other details. By the time this book is in your hands, it may be a reality.

Check out all the details about the Not Back to School Camp and The Dream House on the Web site or by requesting brochures. Contact information is included in Appendix B.

Cafi Cohen: The "You-Can-Do-It" Guru of College Admissions

Cafi Cohen and her husband homeschooled two children through middle school and high school using the American School of Correspondence heavily supplemented with interest-directed, real-life experiences. Both of their eclectically homeschooled children were admitted to colleges with sizable scholarships. Cohen has written two books on home education; her book *And What About College?: How Homeschooling Leads to Admissions to the Best Colleges and Universities* (see Appendix E) shares the Cohens' experiences from the get-go, as well as information about how they translated the learning experiences of their children into home-brewed transcripts. It's an excellent handbook for homeschooling parents to refer to from middle school on. Her latest book, *Homeschooling: The Teen Years* (see Appendix E), covers everything about working with teenagers in the homeschool, and includes stories and tips from homeschoolers around the world.

Cohen shares the wisdom gained from her homeschooling years by speaking at homeschool conferences across the country, on such topics as Developing a Writer's Toolkit, Homeschooling an Older Student, Family History, and Putting Together an Eclectic Curriculum. She also writes columns for *Home Education* magazine, *Homeschooling Today,* and *The LINK,* as well as cohosting two Web site discussion boards. Find links to discussion boards in Appendix B.

Learning Links

Discussion boards are good starting points for learning about homeschooling. Two of my favorites are Kaleidoscapes and the *Home Education* magazine boards. Both are in the question-and-answer format, with various topics available. Kaleidoscapes offers an "off-topic" board and a monthly discussion board, with a preselected topic. Post your question. The real homeschooling experts will be glad to give you their two cents' worth!

I met Cohen two years ago at a homeschool conference and was impressed by her no-nonsense delivery of information in the two sessions I attended. She is enthusiastic and straightforward, two traits I admire. Her mission is to give people the information they need to make their own choices about home education.

Patrick Farenga: President of Holt Associates

Carrying on the work of John Holt, Patrick Farenga is today the President of Holt Associates, and publisher of *Growing Without Schooling,* John Holt's original newsletter. Farenga's experience working directly with John Holt, former teacher, education reformer, and homeschool advocate, gave him an excellent insight into Holt's vision of learning. Today, Farenga and his wife Day, general manager at Holt Associates, homeschool their three children.

I first met Farenga 12 years ago at a Clonlara Conference in Toledo, Ohio, when we were still contemplating home education and all it might mean to us as a family. My husband and I visited with Farenga amidst a wealth of hands-on toys and mind-stretching books in the John Holt Book Store display at the conference. I remember we were drawn to the microscopes and the books like children ourselves. The John

Holt Bookstore is still a resource packed with unique and interest-piquing items that aren't often available elsewhere. I've since heard Farenga speak eloquently on a variety of homeschooling issues; he is doing an excellent job of supporting John Holt's dream of a real-life education for every child.

You will discover many more homeschool speakers and writers that will affirm, uplift, and inspire you. Whatever your approach or educational philosophy, there is much to glean from those who have already journeyed on the road less traveled.

Learning Links

Clonlara Campus School, an alternative school in Ann Arbor, Michigan, provides legal cover and services for homeschoolers the world over through their Home Based Education Program (Clonlara HBEP). Their conference each year features speakers on a variety of topics, activities for children, panels, and roundtable discussions. Their unique graduation ceremony, teen prom, and talent show are special features of the conference.

The Least You Need to Know

➤ The number of homeschoolers is an estimate at best.

➤ Homeschooling is presently growing by at least 15 percent per year.

➤ Your children will join an impressive lineup of homeschool alumni from the distant and not-so-distant past.

➤ Homeschool authors and speakers share their wisdom in a variety of forums.

Chapter 3

Quick Answers to Beginners' Questions

This Chapter Box

➤ The true meaning of socialization

➤ Are credentials required?

➤ Can you afford to homeschool?

➤ Extracurricular activities

➤ Assessments and grading

➤ Preparing for college

Some of the questions that come to your mind before you start homeschooling will be answered eventually through your own homeschooling experience. But right now, you probably have burning questions and it seems extremely important to have them answered.

This chapter includes some of the most common questions people have asked about home education during the last few years. My answers are the tip of the iceberg, but Appendix D, "Independent Study Programs and Support Schools, Publications, and Vendors," will help you find even more answers to your questions. You'll also find more in-depth answers to some of these questions in other chapters.

What About Socialization?

When we decided we were going to homeschool, I was surprised to find that the first concern most people expressed to me was about socialization, as I mentioned in Chapter 1, "What Is Homeschooling?" Socialization has three meanings. The first one is to regulate according to the theory of socialism; I don't think that's what we're talking about. The next is to adapt to social needs or uses, and the third is to participate actively in a social gathering. The last two, combined, are what people are asking about.

Learning Lookouts

Homeschooled kids can learn to engage in conversation and activities with people who aren't their own age, in situations that are both structured and unstructured. At first it may not come natural to you to include your children in your own activities; make the effort, and you will all reap the benefits.

I hadn't even given socialization much thought; I was concerned that my oldest son was unhappy and frustrated, and I was trying to determine whether I should purchase a curriculum or design my own, and whether we could even afford this. However, socialization is the number-one concern voiced by others, brought up in the media, and even included negatively in most commentaries by educational experts. As an 11-year veteran homeschooler, I want to assure you that unless you choose to isolate yourself, your child will have ample opportunities for true socialization.

I believe we need to understand what we are talking about: positive socialization or negative socialization? Much of the socialization of children in institutional settings is of the negative kind, characterized by peer dependency and negative self-image. This is one of the reasons more people turn to home education. Most homeschoolers experience positive socialization, evidenced by independent thinking and positive self-image.

Getting Along with Others

When we worry about socialization, are we concerned that Janie is going to know how to get along with people in life, or are we talking about peer dependence? Kids experiencing home-based education can be involved in many more meaningful social experiences than kids who are in school settings. Let's face it, there aren't many times in life (after the school years) when we'll be in a room full of people who are within a year or so of our age, under the direction of one leader, in such a passive environment. "May I be excused to go to the restroom?" "May I please go get a drink of water?"

Homeschooled kids learn to take responsibility for their needs while in the home setting, and interact with people in a variety of experiences: in community service; in work-and hobby-related activities; in play groups; in homeschool groups; and during Scouts, 4-H, and Campfire events.

Will My Child Get to Go to the Prom?

First of all, let's remember that not all institutionally schooled kids go to the prom. Although your kids may feel differently, many adults believe that the prom is an over-rated rite of passage. And with the high cost of buying a dress, renting a tuxedo, getting hair done, perhaps hiring a limousine, and buying dinner for the big event, proms can be major expenses. In some areas parents band together, do fund-raisers, plan and implement a lock-down, no-alcohol, post-prom party to try to prevent their kids from staying out all night, getting drunk or high, and getting into tragic automobile accidents. Yes, kids who agree to attend the post-prom party are actually locked in for the night. Kids can choose from a variety of entertainment through the night and are served breakfast in the morning before they leave. Too often, in areas where there are no lock-down, post-prom parties, we hear about motel-goers who are subjected to private post-prom parties in adjacent motel rooms; kids play loud music, run up and down the halls, set off the fire alarms, and throw up everywhere. Some motels have implemented policies to prevent groups of teens from renting rooms during prom season. Is this really what you want your children caught up in?

Learning Links

Some large homeschool groups sponsor their own proms for high-schooled homeschoolers. Several small groups may collaborate on a celebration. Clonlara's Home Based Education program has a very casual prom as part of their annual conference; entertainment is often provided throughout the evening by various attendees—an impromptu talent show! And quite a few homeschooled teens have attended a prom with a schooled date.

However, if the prom is truly an issue for you and your kids, let me assure you that some home-schoolers have, indeed, gone to the prom at a local school. After all, the majority of kids in this country are institutionally schooled, and homeschoolers usually have schooled friends. Home-educated kids get asked out on dates by schooled kids; taken to games; invited to school shows; and yes, even asked to attend the prom! Some homeschool groups and support schools even put on their own proms. See Chapter 13, "Teenagers in the Homeschool," for more about going to the prom.

Don't I Need Credentials to Homeschool My Kids?

Not only do you *not* need credentials, but having teaching credentials can be the biggest handicap, as I've been told by *former* teachers who homeschool. Unlearning something to learn a new skill is much harder than learning something for the first time.

Most of what is taught in teacher certification programs is geared toward helping an aspiring classroom teacher learn to manage a large group of children; that is, to learn how to deal with the logistics of institutional schooling. Unless you have 30 children at home, you won't need lessons in crowd control.

Studies of homeschoolers have shown that teacher certification or qualification have no direct correlation to student outcome. That's reassuring! Some homeschoolers have never finished high school, and yet are successfully homeschooling their children.

Homeschooling credentials include such things as ...

➤ You are already your child's teacher.

➤ You have a genuine love for your child.

➤ You know your child better than anyone else.

➤ You have a desire to know your child even better.

➤ You want what's best for your child.

➤ You are willing to do whatever is necessary to obtain the best possible education for your child.

Learning Links

An interlibrary loan expands your local library system's resources to include libraries all over the country. Check with your librarian to see if you can request books through the library's computer system, on your own using online database at the library, or even online at home. When the books you've requested come in, it's almost like another birthday (but you're not a whole year older).

Before I started homeschooling I feared that my child wouldn't look up to me as a teacher (as in "that's not the way the teacher said to do it" from the homework-helping days), and that I wouldn't be able to make him do the work. I learned that it's much easier to start from scratch than it is to help a child do homework assignments when I don't have the book and am not sure what the teacher really wants. I also learned that children are self-motivated when they are interested in the topic and when they enjoy the work they do.

How Can We Afford This?

Whether you can afford to homeschool depends on how you intend to do it. The question of affordability is all relative. If you are a single mom running a home business and barely making ends meet, you may use a different program from the one used by someone who has a very large income or is independently wealthy.

However, I can't stress strongly enough or often enough that most of us have a terrific resource at hand that is very affordable: the public library!

Libraries may have everything from wonderful books, videos, and audio tapes, to CDs, reference materials (some libraries even let you check some of them out), helpful personnel, and, quite often, supplemental programs of all sorts.

Some libraries provide online access. If you have to pinch pennies, or even if money is not an object, do check out the library (pun intended)!

Shifting Your Priorities

Homeschoolers often make some sacrifices in order to educate their kids at home, although most would be quick to assure you that, in the long run, it's all worth it. Some families have foregone the annual glitzy vacation—complete with the costs of childcare—in favor of a family camping trip, with stops at historical points of interest. Such trips can prove to be so educational that you realize more learning is taking place than happens at home!

Spotlight on Education

One year we spent two weeks traveling in the East. We rode into Philadelphia, Pennsylvania, by elevated train, toured Independence Hall, the site of Ben Franklin's home, and a museum of Franklin's inventions. We visited Washington Crossing State Park and spoke with re-enactors, toured the fire station in Pennington, New Jersey, where my cousin was fire chief, took a birding trip to Cape May, New Jersey, and enjoyed the exhibits at a nature center. We purchased books about the Revolutionary War, a Colonial cookbook, and other goodies from museum bookstores, hoping to extend our learning experience. For several years afterward, my kids were still making connections to things they had seen and experienced on that trip.

Some parents have pared expenses by cutting back on dinners out. They involve their kids in learning to cook more meals from scratch and enjoy the interaction, the food, and the unplanned lessons learned. (Did you know that doubling Aunt Jane's soup recipe is a good way to practice math fractions?)

Making do with just one car can necessitate careful planning and schedule juggling, but some families manage just fine. Other strategies include carpooling with other homeschoolers to field trips and activities, ordering materials cooperatively to cut down on shipping and handling fees, and sharing materials (bartering, selling, or renting).

More for Less

You can do aerobics at home to a tape, rather than have a health-club membership; give up cable and stick to videos; work a part-time job when your spouse can be home with the kids, or become a Discovery Toys or Usborne Books distributor and earn free books and educational toys to supplement your current home library. The sky's the limit!

Some homeschoolers get together with other locals and hold a swap at the end of each school year to see what they can get from each other before planning the next year's purchases. Sometimes someone is lucky enough to find everything he or she needs this way!

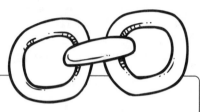

Learning Links

Find out if your library has a used book sale, and plan to attend. Find the used book stores near your home, and don't forget garage sales. It's amazing what people get rid of for small change! There are also used curriculum stores, newsletters, and Web sites available for homeschoolers.

Making your own is the name of the game for some penny pinchers. If you want to play a geography game, involve the kids in helping you find questions and answers. Using a board game with cards as a sample, make your own board, and make up your own cards. If your child has a photographic memory, he may have an easier time with the questions and answers on the cards he made, but hey! If he remembered it, maybe he learned it, and wasn't that the object to begin with? Planning your own curriculum using free or low-cost materials isn't as difficult as it sounds. (See Part 3, "Choosing/Planning a Curriculum," for more suggestions about curriculum planning.)

Many homeschoolers have reported that once they start homeschooling, even their choosiest kids don't need as many fashionable clothes. Finding good quality clothing at consignment or thrift stores, always checking the clearance rack first when shopping, and asking yourself, "Do I need this or do I just want it?" are helpful tools. Saving your best clothes for public appearances, and changing to everyday things for around the house or when doing things that might ruin your clothes is not only thrifty, it just makes sense. Check Appendix B, "Curriculum Winners and Selected Resources, Including Dynamite Web Sites," and Appendix E, "Bibliography." Also, talk to other home educators and find out what they do to make it work for them.

What About Team Sports?

Ah, yes! Team sports. Well, first of all, let's once again remember that of all the kids enrolled in an institutional school, only a small percentage actually play team sports. "But," you say, "Johnny is extremely talented at basketball. He's spent years practicing on his own and getting up games with his friends, and he really wants to play. Besides, it might help him get a scholarship."

Some States Have Homeschool Access

Some states allow homeschoolers access to public school classes or sports on a part-time basis. However, in order to participate, homeschoolers must meet specific requirements. Most states require that a student verify that he or she is passing core subjects. Homeschoolers may have to provide achievement test scores or academic reports even if the state homeschooling law does not require them. In other states, a student may have to contact his or her local superintendent or make a presentation before the local school board to receive permission to play on a team. Check with local homeschoolers in your area to find out what the possibilities are for playing team sports through the schools, or, if that is not an option, what alternatives are available.

Learning Lookouts

Seasoned homeschoolers warn that our homeschooling freedoms were won at a cost. Situations in which homeschoolers voluntarily comply with state regulations so their children can play sports, or participate in program through government schools, could lead to increased regulation of homeschooling. This could cost homeschoolers some of their freedoms.

States that don't have specific equal access laws (providing homeschoolers access to sports or classes on a part-time basis) have different ways of deciding whether homeschooled students may participate in sports. However, quite often, the state and school district have no say about whether homeschooled students may participate in sports. In those states, an athletic association may have the final say, and in most cases, does not allow home educators to participate. Again, even full-time students in the school must take a minimum number of classes and have passing grades to play. If a school decides to let a homeschooler play, the athletic association (being a private organization) has the right to remove the school from the league. Most schools won't take that risk.

Why Most Homeschoolers Aren't Begging to Participate in Team Sports

Home educators, especially those who are looking at the big picture, as opposed to just what they might want for their family today, have always felt that more laws may lead to more regulation. We don't want any more regulation because what we're doing works, and we don't want anybody to mess with it! We want homeschooling to be around for our grandkids and anyone else who wants to homeschool. We need to remember that forcing schools by legislation to do something they don't want to do will not make for a harmonious relationship between schools and homeschoolers.

It's difficult to realize that many homeschooled kids really enjoy participating in family sports activities, unlike many institutionally schooled kids, who often eschew family outings in favor of peer-dominated social activities. Homeschooled kids are generally very aware of the reasons behind the choices their family makes as homeschoolers. Although others may believe that homeschoolers are missing out on something if they can't participate in school sports, homeschoolers know that they are enjoying benefits beyond what such participation might offer: family closeness, independence, freedom, and the ability to study and learn at their own pace, in their own way. Pat Montgomery, Director of Clonlara School Home Based Education Program in Ann Arbor, Michigan, said it very well when she remarked, regarding institutional schooling, "If you want to play in their ballpark, you've got to play by their rules." It applies just as well to homeschoolers playing sports!

Speaking Educationese

Intramural means occurring within the walls or confines of a school or institution. These teams get together to play simply for fun, to hone skills and techniques, and for the joy of the game.

Intramural Sports Teams/Private School Teams

Some homeschoolers have found that although they can't get their kids on the school's sports teams, there are *intramural* sports teams available that their kids can get involved in. Some community education programs offer tennis lessons, swimming classes, weekly volleyball and basketball games, and martial arts.

If the purpose of playing team sports is simply for the experience, the camaraderie, and sheer joy of playing as a team, this may fill the bill.

Some private schools have different regulations about allowing homeschooled team members. It's worth a check to see if local private schools might be willing to work with your student. However, it's very likely that there will be some hoops to jump through!

Homeschool Sports Teams

In some areas, homeschoolers have pulled together their own sports teams and drive great distances to compete with other homeschooled sports teams. They've formed their own leagues, and sell subs at homeschool curriculum fairs and conferences to help pay for their expenses. It's just like being a soccer mom for an institutionally schooled kid!

Check with local homeschoolers to see if there are homeschool sports teams in your area. If not, look into organizing a team if this is what lights your child's fire.

Spotlight on Education

Jo and Tom had two sons who were very interested in playing on a basketball team. However, the state sports association prohibited participation by homeschoolers on public school teams. The local support group had no athletic activities, so this family found a homeschool sports league 30 miles north of them on which their sons could play. For the years that Jo and Tom were involved with the sports association they enjoyed traveling to sporting events and getting to know other homeschoolers while their sons enjoyed being a part of a team, getting acquainted with other homeschooled teens across the state, and honing their basketball skills.

Alternatives: Skiing, Skating, Martial Arts

Many home educating families have found that they can be very involved in personal sports. Some of these sports involve competition in a somewhat different way. If you are a downhill skier, you may be able to get into racing. Ice skating involves competition, and so do martial arts. However, not all homeschoolers are looking for competition with others. If the joy of perfecting your own style is challenging enough for you, taking some private lessons and working on your own speed or form may be all you need. Don't forget your local health club and YMCA/YWCA as sources for physical sports. Remember, too, that sailing, biking, hiking, and other sports make wonderful activities for families or groups of homeschoolers to pursue.

Learning Links

When my oldest son got fairly confident on his downhill skis, he was reluctant to take lessons. Instead, he would ski near someone who was taking a private lesson, or hang out near a group lesson, or just play "follow-the-leader" behind a more experienced skier.

How Can I Tell If My Kids Are Learning?

Some experienced homeschoolers will tell you that you will just know when learning is happening. And although that is true after you've been homeschooling for a while, it doesn't seem likely when you are just starting out. Watch for what I call "a ha" or "light bulb" experiences. This is what happens when a child makes a connection for him- or herself. Something the child has just learned reminds him or her of a fact from another time and place; when this happens, you will get a warm, fuzzy feeling right along with the child! Making connections between new and already known information is part of genuine learning.

Learning Links

Take time every couple of months to read some journal entries (yours and/or your child's), look back over your records, or leaf through each child's portfolio. Make a mental or actual note of the progress being made. This is a simple way to get a quick fix on your child's progress.

Some homeschooling parents use testing regularly. Others totally eschew testing, preferring to use alternative methods of assessment such as observation, evaluation, journals, and portfolios. The largest group falls somewhere in the middle: those homeschoolers who use testing on an occasional basis as well as alternative methods to track activities and progress. (Read Chapter 15, "Testing, Testing, 1, 2, 3," for more on this subject.)

Some states require annual testing, or testing at specific grade levels. Of these, some accept alternative assessments, such as teacher evaluation or submission of a portfolio or other records. Although many states don't require reporting, those parents working with a support school must keep records to submit for the school's purposes. Even homeschooling parents who have no official reason to keep records often do so as a way to monitor their child's progress. Such records may take the form of journals kept by the parents or homeschooled kids, portfolios compiled by the parent or student, or calendar jottings. Chapter 16, "Other Assessments for Measuring Progress," discusses other assessments for measuring your child's progress; and Chapter 17, "Keeping Records," helps you develop ways to keep track of your child's learning journey.

It's very obvious when a nonreader becomes a reader, and then becomes a fluent, avid reader. It's quite apparent when kids master new skills, such as long division or fractions. Although the results of other learning may not be as readily evident, when children are actively involved in a rich, activity-filled environment, learning does happen.

How Can I Teach Subjects I Don't Understand?

You don't have to. However, many parents have found that working through a text together, or taking a class together can be a good way to learn together. One homeschool mother had a daughter who wanted to learn how to rebuild an automobile engine. They purchased a manual, rolled up their sleeves, and tackled the project together. When they got stuck, they consulted others with expertise in automotive technology. Neither of them had ever done any mechanical work before, but they managed to get the job done. Perhaps, though, for very valid reasons, you just can't take this involved hands-on approach right now. Other parents have utilized mentors, private tutors, online classes, CD tutorials or community college classes. There is always more than one way to approach a challenge.

Can I Homeschool Part-Time?

That depends on what you mean by homeschooling part-time. Homeschooling is not always about two parents teaching their children around the kitchen table for a set number of hours, 180 days of the year, using a packaged curriculum. There are endless variations and approaches to homeschooling. This flexibility is part of what makes homeschooling a much more attractive option for mainstream families in this century. Some parents homeschool their kids in some subjects, but use classes or private tutors for other subjects.

Many homeschoolers today prefer to use the home as the base for learning and planning, but implement a variety of other resources to enrich and even cover certain aspects of their children's education. Although they consider themselves full-time homeschoolers, they are not responsible for teaching their children for seven hours a day, five days a week. As children grow up and develop good reading skills and become independent learners, parents find that they don't have to spend as much time working one-on-one with their children.

So if you mean, "Can I teach the basics (reading, math, English, writing) to my kids, and have them take swimming at the Y, private music lessons, and a couple of classes at the homeschool cooperative?" the answer is an unequivocal "Yes!"

If you mean, "Can I teach them a couple days a week and send them to school for three days a week?" there are a couple of states that have programs that might make it possible for you to do that. In other places, you may be able to work out something with the school district you live in. Check with seasoned homeschoolers in your area to find out what the climate is for this possibility.

If you mean, "Can I work part-time outside the home, teach the kids when I'm home, and have my spouse do the rest while I'm working?" ... Hey! You'd better talk to your spouse about that one! Seriously, though, quite a few homeschoolers have tweaked their responsibilities and schedules to make it possible to homeschool as single parents, or when both parents must work outside the home. Creative parents may work opposing shifts or alternate days, or one spouse may work at home. Part-time homeschoolers may also develop strong support networks of daycare providers, extended family, and teen (paid or volunteer) sitters to fill in the gaps when one parent is not at home.

Whatever your situation, approach homeschooling as a challenge, talk to other homeschoolers, keep a positive outlook, and you can figure out a way to make it work.

Spotlight on Education

Jim and Karen have two elementary school-aged children. Karen worked in a bank before the children were born, and continues to do so now. Jim uses the A Bekah program to homeschool the kids in the morning, dropping them off at a daycare provider at about 1:00 in the afternoon, when he heads to his job in advertising at the local radio station. When Karen leaves work between 1:30 and 2:00, she picks up the children. She does the field trips, errand running, library visits, and enrichment activities (baking, reading, and crafts) with the kids.

Should I Give Grades?

This is another one of those questions to which there is no right answer. Some home-schoolers use the school-at-home approach that includes assignments, tests, grades, and the whole nine yards. If that's the approach you choose, you may want to embrace the whole works. However, you can also customize it. Even when I was using a more structured approach, I didn't use grades. My philosophy was that I wanted the kids to do the work to learn the material. If they missed math problems, or put down wrong answers, I lightly marked them with a pencil. Then my child and I would talk about what he was thinking about when he put down that answer. Did he add wrong? Not understand the new math concept? Was he just in a hurry? Did he guess? Could he put down the correct answer now? I put the emphasis more on my child's ability to either know the right answer or know where to go to get the answer. When my child was finished with a paper, he could choose a sticker to put on it, not to indicate that he did a perfect job, but to show that he had stuck with it and understood the concepts on that particular paper. If you work with a support school or have to report to the state, you may have to provide grades. I'll explain in Chapter 16 how you can provide such records without actually giving grades on a daily basis.

How Can My Child Get into College Without a High School Diploma?

First of all, there's no reason your child can't acquire a high school diploma. Depending upon your state's regulations, you may be able to print up a diploma on your computer, using the name of your incorporated nonpublic school, or the name you've assigned to your homeschool. If you are homeschooling under the direction of a private school, your child will probably be issued a diploma from that school. Students working with correspondence schools and other support schools will be issued a diploma from those schools.

Most community colleges don't require a new student to have a diploma to enroll in classes. Requirements vary from one community college to another. Some homeschoolers register their high school students to take some classes at the community college for dual credit. It's a type of *dual enrollment,* but you pay for the classes, instead of paying the school district.

Speaking Educationese

Dual enrollment allows qualified institutional school students to take Advanced Placement classes at a local college, with the local school district footing the bill. Homeschoolers can do the same thing, but generally pay for the classes themselves.

Some home educators use the community college as their children's high school, having them take enough classes to transfer to a four-year school upon high school graduation. Others have their children take some of their classes at the college, while homeschooling other subjects during the high school years.

Many colleges are adopting new policies for homeschooling admissions. Some will accept nontraditional assessments of a child's high school years, such as portfolios, letters of recommendation, and diplomas and transcripts signed by the parents. Some colleges are actively recruiting home-educated students. (See Chapter 13, "Teenagers in the Homeschool," for more on this subject.)

The Least You Need to Know

➤ Homeschoolers are positively socialized by their interactions with others in real-world situations.

➤ The only credentials you need are the same ones you already possess as a parent.

➤ Some public school programs are available to homeschoolers, but there are strings attached.

➤ There are many resources available so you don't have to teach every class yourself.

➤ You can make your own decisions about giving grades and making assessments, unless your state regulations dictate otherwise.

➤ Your student has many options for obtaining a diploma, and can even get into college without one.

Part 2

First Things First: Getting Started

In this section, I will help you gather information about legalities in your area and discuss the importance of understanding the law for yourself. I'll give you tips on how to sift the wheat from the chaff, and make suggestions about complying with regulations.

I'll give you a quick overview of homeschooling approaches, complete with suggestions on how to determine what will work for your family. Lastly, I'll provide tips on how and where to find support.

Chapter 4

Getting Legal: Alternatives to Compulsory Attendance

In This Chapter

➤ Understanding homeschool regulations

➤ Learning about laws in your state or province

➤ Determining your responsibilities to comply with the homeschooling requirements

➤ Complying with state regulations by submitting required documentation

For many years, homeschooling was not legal. However, during that time, there were still some brave souls who taught their children at home. These pioneers, some of whom had a hand in making homeschooling legal, deserve our thanks and recognition for their contribution to homeschooling as we know it today. Many of them were just ordinary people like you and me, doing what seemed best and right for their children. Although we don't know many of their names, we can be thankful for those who, by continuing to homeschool in spite of adversity, harassment, jail time, court proceedings, and (in at least one case) death, paved the way for us today. Because of their sacrifice, we want to ensure that we don't lose any of our homeschooling freedoms.

Be aware that within the homeschooling community there are some who feel that more and better homeschooling laws will make it easier for homeschoolers. Others feel that there are too many laws already, that some existing laws need to be revamped, and that many of the laws now being considered will remove some of the hard-won rights of home educators. Don't depend on the opinions of others. Read, do your research, and form your own opinions.

Many homeschoolers today are active in tracking legislation that might be harmful to home educators. They form grassroots organizations that keep homeschoolers notified of developments. Keeping abreast of changes is important so you know where you stand legally. Letting your representatives in government know your opinion about pending legislation is vital, as well.

Homeschooling and Your Rights

Depending on whether you plan to homeschool for religious, secular, or philosophical reasons, you may find protection in different aspects of constitutional law.

Religious homeschoolers may find protection in the First Amendment—free exercise of religion. To claim this protection, parents must claim sincerely held religious beliefs and be able to show that the state, by regulating homeschooling, has made it difficult for them to exercise those beliefs.

Some states have *waivers* of specific homeschool regulations (such as teacher certification) for those who have deeply felt religious beliefs regarding the education of their children.

Parents who homeschool for philosophical or secular reasons may find protection for their choice in the Free Speech Clause of the First Amendment of the Constitution. Parents have traditionally been primarily responsible for choices regarding the education of their children. There are only two reasons the state may interfere with the sanctity of the family:

Speaking Educationese

A **waiver** is a document containing a declaration to give up a privilege or right. A waiver allows some parents to homeschool their children in spite of state education regulations that are contrary to their beliefs.

1. To protect state interests, such as public health and safety
2. To protect a child in case of abuse or neglect

There are already laws on the books to protect such state interests.

The Ninth and Tenth Amendments to the Constitution provide protection by outlining the powers and rights not delegated to the federal government. These are deemed the business of the states. Education is not specifically mentioned in the Ninth Amendment, but it makes it clear that regulation of education is not a power delegated to the United States government, but rather is the responsibility of the states.

These amendments may also provide protection for homeschoolers who cannot claim religious reasons.

Yes, in Every State and Province

Today, homeschooling is legal in every state and province in North America. The freedoms in some of these states were very hard won. Today, there are still homeschooling laws, regulations, and amendments to codes being brought up for consideration. Homeschool regulations are not static. By the time you read this book, anything I wrote about legalities in your state or province might have changed. Be aware of any legislation regarding education; it might affect you.

Although polls show that nonhomeschoolers feel that homeschools should be more closely regulated, the proof of the pudding is recognizing the successful adult homeschoolers who are making their mark in the world today. Colleges have begun to actively recruit home educated students. A 1993 study by J. Gary Knowles, University of Michigan assistant professor of education, showed that two thirds of 53 adults who were homeschooled were married, which was normal for adults their age, and none were unemployed or on welfare. Over 40 percent had attended college, and of those, 15 percent had graduate degrees. Nearly two thirds were self-employed, but few worked in solitary occupations. Most either provided employment to others or worked in a family business.

Regulations haven't produced dramatic positive changes in government-funded schools; more regulations aren't necessary to make home education more successful, either.

Not All Laws Are Created Equal

Although homeschoolers can legally teach their children in every state and province, there is a lot of variation in the way each state identifies and regulates home educators. Some states have amendments to compulsory school codes, and/or require you to provide an *equivalent* education.

The following states have *equivalency* laws:

➤ Connecticut   ➤ Kansas

➤ Delaware   ➤ Massachusetts

➤ Idaho   ➤ New Jersey

➤ Indiana   ➤ South Dakota

However, parents have the right to provide an education for their children that is compatible with their beliefs and principles.

Even states that require parents to provide a curriculum don't usually dictate a specific methodology that must be followed to teach the children. Some states do require that homeschoolers use a specific curriculum; homeschoolers are often creative in implementing that curriculum.

Some states permit you to homeschool as a private school. These are often considered the easiest states to home educate in, because most states don't regulate private schools. Private schools are exempt, in most states, from teacher certification requirements and have the freedom to choose their own curriculum.

The following states permit private school status for home-based schools:

- ➤ Alabama
- ➤ Alaska
- ➤ California
- ➤ Iowa
- ➤ Illinois
- ➤ Kentucky
- ➤ Michigan
- ➤ Nebraska
- ➤ Oklahoma
- ➤ Texas

Other states have specific homeschool laws, and even these vary greatly from one state to another. In some of these states, there is a great deal of regulation, while in others there is not.

These states have home education laws or amendments:

- ➤ Arizona
- ➤ Arkansas
- ➤ Colorado
- ➤ Florida
- ➤ Georgia
- ➤ Hawaii
- ➤ Louisiana
- ➤ Maine
- ➤ Maryland
- ➤ Michigan
- ➤ Minnesota
- ➤ Missouri
- ➤ Mississippi
- ➤ Montana
- ➤ Nevada
- ➤ New Hampshire
- ➤ New Mexico
- ➤ New York
- ➤ North Carolina
- ➤ North Dakota
- ➤ Ohio
- ➤ Oregon
- ➤ Pennsylvania
- ➤ Rhode Island
- ➤ South Carolina
- ➤ Tennessee
- ➤ Utah
- ➤ Vermont
- ➤ Virginia
- ➤ Washington
- ➤ West Virginia
- ➤ Wisconsin
- ➤ Wyoming

In Michigan, you can choose to homeschool under the private school exemption or the home education amendment, or both! You are not required to report your decision to anyone unless requested to do so because of an investigation into your homeschool. In California, there are four different options under which you may implement a homeschool plan. Alaska has five different options. Several other states have a two or more options to choose from, as well. In Florida and Utah, groups of homeschoolers can band together to comply with legal requirements. In Florida, you can incorporate as a private school. In Utah, members of a homeschool support group can qualify as a private school.

Learning Links

Some states have specific reporting requirements. However, in states that require reporting, but don't require specific forms, your records may be kept very simply. A calendar with large blocks and/or a spiral or three-ring notebook with journal entries may be all you need. (See Chapter 17, "Keeping Records," for more tips.)

Some states require parents to report to the state department of education, the local school superintendent, or some other school official. Others suggest reporting, but don't enforce it.

Some states require proof, such as records, test scores, or reports, while others don't require anything. Some states require the homeschool program to be approved by a school official; others don't. Similar variation exists in the Canadian provinces, with regulations and reporting being specific to each province. As you can see, you must do your research and find out what is required in your state or province.

How Do I Know What the Laws Are in My State?

Good question! It's really important, first of all, to get a copy of the law, amendment, or code regarding home education in your state or province. Having obtained it, you will find that it may be difficult to understand. Some homeschool regulations are so couched in legalese that it's hard to know what is expected of you, the new home-based learner. Some laws seem to be deliberately vague, which sometimes makes it easier for parents to implement diverse learning experiences for their children, based on their abilities and needs. Unfortunately, this same vagueness can be used to the advantage of some officials who may choose to make things difficult for home educators.

Where to Go for Advice

There are homeschool support groups at the national, state, and local level; most will provide you with information regarding legality in your state or province. Your best bet is to find a state organization that maintains a legal and legislative watch and

Learning Links

Home Education magazine, the National Home Education Network, and The Home School Legal Defense Association all provide links to state regulations on their Web sites. Always check to see if these are the actual laws or just summaries. You'll find contact information in Appendix C.

Learning Lookouts

At one time, most support groups were inclusive, meaning homeschoolers banded together regardless of background, philosophy, or religion. Today, however, some groups require members to adhere to specific beliefs. These groups are sometimes called exclusive. If you don't share those beliefs, you may need to find an inclusive group, or start one of your own.

keeps its members informed on a regular basis. Determine whether this organization is one that will provide you with the data to make informed choices, or if it is trying to tell you what to think and do. If you can't find a state group, look for a regional or local group that provides the same services.

Check Appendix C, "Homeschooling Support Organizations," for support groups and organizations that you can contact for information about laws in your state.

Obtain and Read the Statutes for Yourself

If you have Internet access, you can go to several Web sites that post the actual amendments, homeschool laws, or regulations. Or you can request that information from a variety of homeschooling advocacy or support groups.

Once you've learned about the legalities, you will probably have more questions. Quite a few of these laws are interpreted in different ways. Your local or state support group may make that information available, and may even have a handout that explains the legal aspects in layman's language.

Speak with Knowledgeable Home Educators

If you haven't met any veteran homeschoolers yet, be sure to seek out a support group and attend some meetings. If there is more than one support group in your area, attend at least a meeting or two of each one. Homeschoolers are a very diverse group of people; in some areas you will find several groups that reflect different home education philosophies. One group may fit your needs more than another, or you may get something different from each group.

If you're not comfortable with any group, you may want to start your own support group. Quite often, there are other homeschoolers who would like to get together with like-minded people, but don't fit in with the existing homeschooling group. We need more support groups that are truly inclusive, supporting home-schoolers of every background, religion, and ethnicity simply because we are all homeschoolers.

Seasoned home educators often have opinions about legal issues; be sure your reasons for homeschooling are similar to theirs before you depend entirely on their interpretation and implementation of the homeschool law. What may be true for religious homeschoolers may not be true for secular or philosophical homeschoolers. Homeschoolers are a good source of information if you are careful to understand the worldview from which they have formed their opinions.

It's very important to do your homework; you have the right to read and interpret the law as it pertains to you. It's your responsibility to make the final decision about how you will educate your children. No one else can do it for you.

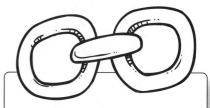

Learning Links

When veteran homeschoolers offer advice, always ask if they can point you to further information about it. This is especially true when it comes to legal advice. Although people mean to be helpful, sometimes they don't understand all the nuances of the law. Ask for the name of a book, publication, or a Web site where you can learn more.

Evaluating the Research

You've gathered a lot of information. You've read the state statutes, gotten some opinions about what homeschoolers must do in order to legally homeschool where you live, and subscribed to a couple of helpful newsletters or other publications. Now you need to consider some of the circumstances around your own personal homeschooling decision and determine what you need to do.

Compulsory attendance age is one factor to consider. Some states don't require children to attend school until age six or eight. Others don't require attendance after age 16. If this is the case in your state, you don't have to include in your report children who are not of compulsory attendance age.

Speaking Educationese

State **compulsory attendance** laws may require attendance in an educational program between certain ages, for example, between 6 and 16. However, these ages vary from state to state.

If your child has been in an institutional school, and you have decided to home educate, there are a couple of ways you can handle it. If you live in a state that requires you to file a statement of intent (notify the school district that you intend to homeschool) or to report in some other way, simply fill out and file the form as required. If your state doesn't have filing requirements, speak with homeschoolers in your area to find out what the climate is for interaction between homeschoolers and the institutional school.

Learning Lookouts

Start a file for legal information. Keep copies of everything you send to and receive from school officials. Send important communications return receipt requested. When making telephone calls to school officials, note the date, time, and name of the person you spoke with, as well as the information he or she gave you.

Speaking Educationese

A **support school** may be a private school with a homeschool program, an organization that exists solely to provide legal cover (or an umbrella) for homeschoolers, or a school that provides distance learning, curriculum, and other services for homeschoolers. Affiliation with a support school makes life simpler when dealing with uncooperative school districts.

If you find that other homeschoolers have simply written letters to the school principal notifying the principal of their intent to homeschool, this may be a good option for you.

If you find out that relations between homeschoolers and the institutional school have been strained, you may want to enroll your child in a *support school*. Your child's withdrawal from the school can be handled as a transfer to a private school, with the support school requesting the child's records. See Appendix B for a list of support schools.

Exactly What Do I Have to Do?

Talk to people who have been home educating for a number of years; speak with homeschoolers from a variety of philosophies. Consider all the information and advice you're given and the books and articles you've read, and make the choice you are comfortable with. Keep it all in perspective by remembering that as you go along, you will learn more about home education, and can make changes in the way you do things.

Give Officials Only What They Ask For

If you live in a state where reporting or requesting permission is required, get the necessary forms and take care of those steps. Be sure to meet the required deadlines. Don't volunteer information that is not required; give only the information that is specifically requested. Some school districts have sent forms to homeschoolers requesting information that is not required by state regulations or laws. Know the law, be aware of your rights, and ask a veteran homeschooler if you have any doubts about forms you receive from the state or from school districts. Remember that although the state requires you, the homeschooler, to obey the law, school and state officials must also follow the law as it stands.

Spotlight on Education

When we began homeschooling, we enrolled our children with a support school, which requested their records from the public school. Although homeschoolers who were not using a support school were being contacted by local school districts during this time period, we were never contacted by the public school or by the state. When Ryan wanted to take classes at the county intermediate school district level during his high school years, we consulted with our support school and with a counselor at the local public high school to establish what the requirements were at that time. We had to register with the public schools and file a form with the Michigan Department of Education. It pays to know the law, be informed, and take appropriate steps to prevent problems.

Seasoned homeschoolers have learned that sometimes when we give more information than is required, it can later become required information. States with legal requirements regarding homeschoolers vary as to what is actually required.

Here are examples of the types of reports that states require:

➤ Notification of intent to homeschool

➤ Curriculum plans

➤ Periodic reports

➤ Evaluation by a certified teacher

➤ Test results

➤ Any combination of the above

Keeping detailed records for yourself is an excellent idea; however, you don't have to share every intimate detail of your personal homeschooling life with state officials.

Complying with State Regulations

If you've learned that your state has specific reporting regulations, you still may have some flexibility in complying with the requirements. Talk to homeschoolers in your area and find out how they handle the various components of the reporting requirements.

Curriculum Requirements

Most states do not specify a particular curriculum; some do require specific subject areas to be covered. There is no required federal core curriculum, and even institutional schools aren't required to adhere to a universal curriculum. Many school districts have curriculum planners on staff, and adjustments are made periodically. As a homeschooler, you have the right to adjust your curriculum, too. After you have filed your curriculum, you may find that it takes longer than you thought to cover certain concepts. Other areas may be a breeze for your child, or you may decide to supplement learning in a different area. You may need to flex the curriculum (and your goals) to accommodate a burning interest exhibited by one of your children. When writing your curriculum plan, you can insert a phrase that indicates you will periodically assess your curriculum and make adjustments according to the learning needs of your children.

Many parents find out what subject areas are covered in a school curriculum, and plan to cover those general areas. Homeschoolers often plan experiential, hands-on, project-oriented activities to teach subjects that might otherwise be taught using a textbook or workbook.

Spotlight on Education

Your children may need a different approach from the textbooks and worksheets you're familiar with from your years of institutional schooling. If your children have struggled with the institutional school curriculum, you need to research learning styles, and make that stretch to accommodate the learning differences of your children. Some homeschoolers have discovered that a textbook or a grade-level-appropriate curriculum is a helpful tool they can use as a guideline. They then use books from the library or bookstore, hands-on projects, and field trips to cover the same subjects. Being aware of a child's learning strengths and weaknesses makes it easier to design learning experiences that reach the child and are retained.

Filing a curriculum doesn't mean you are obligated to duplicate the typical textbook/workbook style curriculum used in institutional school when working with a child who needs a hands-on or auditory-kinesthetic method. Use creativity to fulfill the legal requirements while providing your kids with a program that is exciting, interesting, and meaningful.

Find out exactly what is required before filing your curriculum. If you are required to list the texts and materials you plan to use, and your child requires lots of hands-on support, you can supplement those texts with real-life projects to meet the learning needs of your child. Many homeschoolers use texts as resource materials, covering the same material in much more interesting ways.

See Chapter 5, "Approaches to Home Education," to learn more about the various homeschooling methods; and Part 3, "Choosing/Planning a Curriculum," for more on curriculum planning.

Reports

Some states require homeschoolers to submit reports at established times during the school year. It may be just a list of subjects and grades. If you are doing a fairly structured program and use grades, this may be a simple thing to do. Although it may be more complicated if you are unschooling (using natural learning as the basis for your child's education) it's still not impossible. Programs that are based on real-life experience or hands-on projects tend to overlap in the subject areas, but careful record keeping can keep things manageable. Many homeschoolers journal their activities, using some sort of code to keep track of the subject areas being covered.

You will not want to turn in your journal, since it is probably more than is required, and is a good record for you to keep to document your homeschooling journey. You can use your journal as a resource for making a report that education officials can understand and accept. Read more about record keeping in Chapter 17.

Evaluations

Some states require *evaluation* by an outside party. Often, this person must be a state-certified teacher. Although this may sound ominous, especially if you have deeply held convictions about being required to use a certified teacher, relax!

Talk to local homeschoolers about finding a teacher in the area who understands homeschooling and is

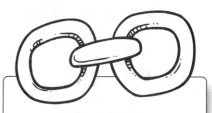

Learning Links

Coding your journal can be as simple as assigning letters to subject areas. (S) in the margin beside an activity or project in the journal can indicate science. (ES) can stand for earth sciences, (LS) for lab sciences, and (BS) for biological sciences. By checking the codes at the time you make up your report, it will be easy to note what subjects were covered.

Speaking Educationese

During an **evaluation,** the evaluator will usually look over a portfolio or collection of materials provided by the homeschooler and provide a report to the necessary officials. In most cases, this evaluation includes speaking with the homeschooled child and the parent.

sympathetic to any alternatives that you may employ in providing your child with the best possible education. Many states set specific criteria for evaluators (such as state certification) but leave the actual choice of an evaluator up to the parents.

Some states require evaluation once a year, while others may require it more often. The best thing you can do is keep your focus on providing a quality education for your child, know what is required for evaluation, keep good records, and provide only what is required.

Testing

In some states, mandatory testing is carried out in schools or testing centers specified by the state. In others, required testing may be done in the home by a certified teacher. In some states, testing may be waived by homeschoolers, and alternative assessments, such as portfolio evaluation, may be substituted.

Learning Lookouts

Studies have shown that testing shouldn't be used as the only assessment of a student's education, since there are too many variables that can make test results inconclusive.

This is one of the really sticky wickets for compliance. Sometimes testing is one of the reasons homeschoolers are teaching their kids at home. Perhaps their children retain the material just fine, and can narrate the information, or provide it when there is no stress, but become overwhelmed in a timed test situation. This is not an uncommon problem, and it's one that educators see in their classrooms regularly. Sometimes it's just a matter of maturity, and later on the child handles testing just fine. However, some children—and even some adults—have a problem with testing and need alternative assessments. Some homeschoolers have a deeply held conviction against testing; they simply won't subject their children to it. Some homeschoolers have moved to another state with more lenient homeschooling regulations. Others simply go underground. States with extremely restrictive homeschooling laws are likely to have the most underground homeschoolers—those who don't comply with regulations or report to officials. Check with other homeschoolers in your area to find out if there are any alternatives to testing, or what they have done regarding compliance when they have children who don't test well. (See Chapter 15, "Testing, Testing, 1, 2, 3," for more on this subject.)

Homeschooling is about taking responsibility for your child's education. It all begins when you take responsibility for learning what is legally required in order to do so. See Appendix C for a listing of national and state organizations and support groups to help you get started on your research.

The Least You Need to Know

➤ Homeschooling is legal in every state and province in North America, although homeschool laws differ among states.

➤ Homeschoolers need to be familiar with regulations in their own state or province. Obtain a copy of the law, read it for yourself, and talk to local homeschoolers about understanding the law.

➤ Reporting requirements vary from state to state. While some states require testing, regular evaluations, and reporting, others have no mandatory requirements at all.

➤ Comply with regulations by doing only what is required. Being familiar with the law prevents you from reporting information that is not required.

Chapter 5

Approaches to Home Education

In This Chapter

➤ Defining your educational philosophy

➤ A look at the different homeschool approaches

➤ Using programs from institutional schools

➤ Finding tutors and mentors to enrich your program

Homeschoolers have choices galore when it comes to deciding which approach to use. The initial choices you make regarding philosophy, approach, and materials are important; however, keeping your children's needs, learning differences, and personalities in the forefront will help you keep things in perspective.

This chapter will help you learn about some of the most popular and basic approaches. You'll also learn how homeschoolers adapt some of the approaches to make them work better for their families. You'll find out how some homeschoolers borrow what they feel are the best or most workable elements from several approaches to develop a personalized program, tailored to fit the needs of their children. Finally, you'll learn how you can enlist help and support from individuals and institutions so you don't have to do it all yourself.

What's Your Educational Philosophy?

Educational philosophy sounds like quite a mouthful, doesn't it? It's simple, really—you determine your educational philosophy by considering your family's values, beliefs, and priorities, and the needs of your children. Remember that your philosophy of education may change and flex as your family grows and has different needs.

Educating your children can be a wonderful learning experience for your entire family. You can learn, grow, expand your horizons, and experience the wonders of life together in a way you never dreamed was possible! Perhaps your philosophy of education will change even as you explore homeschooling. You will begin to know your children better, understand them and their learning styles, as well as knowing yourself better. All of this contributes to a constantly evolving growing and learning experience.

An Overview of Homeschooling Approaches

Each homeschooling family eventually develops its own unique style. In considering what you want to use to begin your home-based learning odyssey, it is helpful to understand a few of the major approaches being used today.

From school-at-home to unschooling, unit studies to living books, there are a variety of methods being used across the board. But no matter what you call it or how you do it, it's still homeschooling. You'll find some of the basic approaches addressed in the following sections of this chapter. You may feel quite overwhelmed with the vast amount of information available about the approaches already in use today by home educators. Don't be! Having a general understanding of the various approaches will make your decisions easier in the long run. Each approach has its pros and cons. Most approaches can be tweaked to provide a workable solution to your family's needs. Be sure to check the appendixes for resources that will help you research these and other approaches in depth.

The basic homeschooling approaches include …

➤ School-at-home.

➤ Unit studies.

➤ Charlotte Mason or the Living Books approach.

➤ Unschooling or natural learning.

➤ Classical, Waldorf, Montessori, and Eclectic.

Let's take a closer look at each of these homeschooling approaches.

School-at-Home: The Traditional Approach

The *school-at-home* method is also called the textbook approach, the traditional approach, or the school model. Many homeschoolers begin with this approach simply because it is familiar. Most of us have been institutionally schooled and understand the way it works. Each subject has a textbook or consumable workbook while the parent has a teacher's manual or teacher's guide.

School-at-home method is usually based on a scope-and-sequence approach (basically, who learns what when). The scope is the body of knowledge that someone believes should be taught. The sequence is the increments someone has divided this body of knowledge into, usually 12 grade levels and 180 daily lessons.

Students read a chapter at a time, answer questions at the end of the chapter, do an assignment based on the information in the chapter, and may have a chapter test. The parent checks the students' work, reviews areas that were incorrect, and assigns grades. The parent may keep an attendance record, have a plan book, and chart out the lessons for the year just as it is done in an institutional school.

Speaking Educationese

The **school-at-home** approach, the closest to the method used in most institutional schools, includes both secular and religious approaches such as the Classical approach (we'll talk about this later in the chapter).

Some parents like the school-at-home approach because everything is planned for them and most textbooks follow a planned scope-and-sequence approach. These parents like the fact that everything is cut-and-dried and feel that they can be sure everything is covered and there will be no learning gaps. Tests are usually supplied by or are available from the textbook publisher. When the student is doing well on the daily assignments and making good grades on the tests, parents feel that their homeschool is successful. If that's the case, and if your children are retaining the large share of the material being covered, this may well be the approach for you. However, be aware that one of the major weaknesses of the school-at-home approach is the tendency of children to learn for the test, commonly referred to as short-term learning.

I've spoken with college graduates with Master's degrees and doctorates who have shared with me that despite the degrees they've earned, they don't feel that they have a large body of knowledge under their belts. What is happening, when students can spend years and years of their lives studying and still feel woefully undereducated?

Some possible reasons follow:

➤ The school model doesn't consider individuality or personal interests. Most textbooks are geared to the average child; however, all children are unique and have individual gifts, interests, and learning styles. Where are the "average" children that these textbooks are geared to? They don't exist! And being locked into the

textbook regime regardless of a child's natural interests causes many learning opportunities to be lost.

➤ Textbooks "dumb down" the information, presenting it in an unconnected way, as a series of facts to be learned, rather than making connections and relating the material to life. Consequently, much of the meat of the material is lost, as well as the wonder.

➤ Textbooks build from year to year, so that if you compare the texts from three successive grade levels in the same subject, you will find that they contain much the same material, simply adding a few details to each successive level. Such redundancy can lead to boredom and apathy.

➤ Most textbooks are also *teacher directed*. Many homeschoolers have found that materials that allow the children to discover and learn at their own pace are more useful, especially once the children are able to read on their own.

➤ Purchasing textbooks for a large family is very expensive, and checking papers and following up on incorrect answers for several children can lead to burnout.

Spotlight on Education

I compared the seventh- and eighth-grade scope and sequence when Aaron wanted to skip seventh grade because he was bored with it. I was amazed to discover that, barring a few details, the requirements were the same for both grades. To ensure that Aaron was capable of doing the work, I used some chapter tests from an eighth-grade math book. He not only understood the work, but actually "tested through" half of the book before he came to material for which he needed to read the explanations. It seemed pointless to require him to do the same work he already understood for two years in a row, not only in math, but in every subject area. Why not just do the eighth-grade work and be done with it? We did, and it worked just fine!

Some folks have homeschooled for a year using the school-at-home approach because they weren't aware of any other method. By the end of the year, regardless of their original motivation, they were ready to throw in the towel. Others, just visualizing what it would be like to run a school-at-home on their own, simply don't begin. These are the people who say, "I could never homeschool. I don't have the temperament, patience, training …."

However, despite its drawbacks, many homeschoolers are happy with some variation of the school-at-home approach. Perhaps the ones who use it most successfully are those who personalize the program to fit their children's needs. Some alternate days of textbook learning with hands-on projects. Others enrich their children's learning with reading assignments from real books, or develop writing assignments that necessitate research. Still others do school-at-home four days of the week and have a project or field day the fifth day. Some families use a textbook approach for six weeks, and alternate with a unit study (see the following section) for six weeks. As you continue to learn about the various approaches, you will find an approach, or combination of approaches, that will work for you and your family.

Unit Studies: Concentrating on a Theme

Unit studies have become a very popular homeschooling option and one that works well for many families. A unit study can be as simple as a child reading an interesting library book, discussing it with the family around the dining room table, and being motivated to do a project that relates to the book.

Rather than teaching the many subject areas abstractly and in an unrelated way, a unit study covers all the curriculum areas, connecting and interconnecting in a way that makes children understand why they need to learn this. Since everything relates to the common theme and connects naturally, studying the various subjects makes more sense. Choose a unit study that your children are interested in, and you can be sure of better retention of the material.

Speaking Educationese

Doing a **unit study** means basing all studies on a chosen topic of interest or a particular theme. This method is based on the idea that learning should be integrated instead of segmented.

Here's an example of a very simple unit study on dogs:

➤ Find three books on dogs: a nonfiction book on the breeds of dogs; a nonfiction book on dog care and training; and a collection of dog stories.

➤ Collect pictures of dogs and articles about dogs found in magazines.

➤ Learn to spell the names of several breeds of dogs. Keep lists of your spelling words on notebook paper.

➤ Make word cards of new vocabulary and meanings encountered while reading.

➤ Make a graph or chart about dogs.

➤ Write a short essay about how dogs have been important to humans throughout history.

➤ Write a short essay about types of dogs typically related to geographic regions of the world.

➤ Combine your graph, vocabulary words, spelling lists, essays, pictures, and collected articles into a notebook. Include a list with the names of the books you read. Be sure to include your name and the date you compiled your information.

Some purchased unit studies are planned to take about six weeks. Many home-based learners have discovered that once interest is sparked, their studies expand and grow, taking on a life of their own, and research has shown retention to be 40 percent better than that achieved through traditional methods.

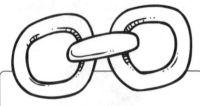

Learning Links

Be sure to strongly consider children's input, because they often learn more readily when it's their idea. Coming to the end of a planned unit study doesn't mean the learning will stop. If one or more of your children continues to spot programs, library books, or other materials that will continue the learning experience, by all means, go for it! Motivation is more than half the battle in education.

The unit study approach is excellent for families with children of varying ages, because all ages can study the same topic, with adjustments made for the ability level of the children. Shared family interests, such as bird watching, sailing, or softball, can be made into a unit study for a fun way to do a trial run.

Using a unit study helps children get the big picture and promotes independent thinking. Children often come up with excellent ideas for expanding on a purchased or family-planned unit study.

Planning your own unit study is not complicated. Making a list of the various subject areas and plugging in the activities, books, programs, and field trips that you could use may be all you need to do before getting off to a running start!

Don't be fearful of learning gaps. Everyone has learning gaps caused by lack of interest in presented material, absence from school, or for no apparent reason. No one knows everything. However, teaching your child good research skills, how to think, and how to learn is much more important than trying to cover every tidbit of information that someone else has laid out as important. Prioritize! And begin to make note of the areas your child is being exposed to serendipitously while following an interest. If you don't feel that your child is getting enough math during a given unit study, you can supplement with additional math to keep your child's math skills honed.

Although it may seem difficult to determine a grade for the work your child is doing while pursuing a unit study, it's not hard to decide whether learning is happening. When those "a ha" or "light bulb" moments occur, there will be no doubt. You may question how you will keep records. If you truly need a list of subjects and grades for a support school, you can certainly use an evaluation system and come up with some grades, but many homeschoolers have found that keeping a journal of activities is a perfectly acceptable method of record keeping for their own purposes. Coming up with a coding system to mark which subject areas are being covered works well for those who feel the need to break things down in that way. See Chapter 16, "Other Assessments for Measuring Progress," for suggestions and ideas for record keeping and evaluations.

A Student's Sample Journal Entries During a Unit Study

➤ Read *Where Do You Think You're Going, Christopher Columbus?* by Jean Fritz. (Language Arts/Reading/History)

➤ Started a journal with entries telling of the voyage as if written by Columbus. (Language Arts/Writing/History)

➤ Traced the route Columbus took on a world map. (Geography/Map Skills/History)

➤ Drew Columbus's ships and pasted them on cardboard cut them out and made a diorama of the ocean in a shoe box. (Art/History)

➤ Went on the Internet with Mom to find out when and where the Tall Ships are coming to a harbor near us. (Research Skills/Computer Skills)

➤ Sent away for information on the Tall Ships schedule. (Language Arts/Writing)

➤ Played "Made for Trade," a game about Colonial life with my brothers and sister. (Math/History/Economics)

Some homeschoolers have said that they can't keep up with doing project-based unit studies all the time. Home educators, regardless of which approach they are using, need to pace themselves and remember that tomorrow is another day. There's absolutely nothing wrong with taking a break from whatever approach you are using. Some home educators use unit studies to enrich a school-at-home approach; six weeks of traditional methods and then six weeks doing a unit study. If a slump hits, take a nature walk, sit by the fire and read out loud, or bake and decorate cookies together to revitalize everyone. Be sure to check Appendix B for Web sites and other resources, and Appendix E for books on planning unit studies.

The Living Books Approach: Twaddle-Free Learning

The *Living Books* approach is based on the writings of an early twentieth-century British educator, Charlotte Mason, whose methods flew in the face of educational trends of the day. Home-educated by her parents and orphaned at the age of 16, Mason devoted her life to teaching children. According to Mason, living books are real books (as opposed to textbooks) that make the subject seem real and alive. Mason coined the term "twaddle" to describe books that contained secondhand, distilled information. Measuring books by her standard provides a homeschool with a treasury of material that is worth reading. Her ideas have been said to be a way of life rather than a curriculum.

Speaking Educationese

The **Living Books** approach, or real books method of home-schooling, is based on the writings of British educator Charlotte Mason. It teaches good habits, the basics (reading, writing, and math), and exposes children to real-life learning through such experiences as nature walks, touring art museums, reading good literature, and attending concerts.

Charlotte Mason didn't believe in the educational philosophies of her day that treated children as if they were empty containers just waiting to be filled up with isolated bits of information. She treated her students, instead, as human beings in whom a zest and love for learning could be nurtured. She also disdained manufactured learning experiences.

Home educators who follow Mason's approach encourage their children to use their curiosity and creativity, which help them continue to love learning. Lessons are kept short and don't include busywork. There is a purpose for the tasks included in a lesson, and the child's ability and developmental level is always taken into consideration. Developing good character and habits are integral to the Mason approach, which will stand a student in good stead later in life. Parents model these traits and snatch the teachable moments during the day's activities to talk about these things.

The Charlotte Mason approach is an excellent approach to use as a guideline when planning studies for a child who has been failing in an institutional school. Short, sweet academic lessons and an abundance of living books and real-life experiences can re-spark a child's love of learning. Reading out loud to a child who has lost (or never learned) a love for good books can allow for re-bonding of the parent/child relationship, give the parent a chance to teach some values serendipitously through the stories, and spark an interest in reading. Participation in day trips and hands-on experiences on a regular basis will help bring an interest in learning new things to the fore again.

Unschooling: Interest-Oriented, Real-Life Learning

John Holt based his writings about children on his own observations of children as they learned. Through his experiences as a public school teacher and interacting with children elsewhere, he observed the way children learned and felt that the classroom situation could be improved to facilitate learning for children. After years of attempting education reform within the system, John became an advocate of home education.

When John Holt first coined the word *unschooling*, he may have been trying to provide a word to use to describe the type of learning he had seen happening when the child was interested and self-motivated to discover knowledge. There are many homeschoolers who call themselves unschoolers; their styles range widely. I would venture to say that if you visited 99 different unschooling families, you would see 99 unique versions of unschooling. One of the beauties of homeschooling is that whatever approach you choose can be individualized to suit your family.

Unschooling is based on the belief that children have an insatiable desire to learn and when allowed to follow their interests and share in real-life experiences, will learn much more, with greater retention, than through many other methods. Unschooling does not mean that children are provided with no guidance or structure in the home. Rather, such parents plan learning experiences based on their child's inner timetable, readiness, and interests. These parents teach more by example and modeling than by externally structured lesson plans.

Learning Links

Here's an example of a teachable moment: A child does something kind for another family member; the parent notices the child being good, and praises the child for the behavior. The child learns because the lesson is positive, he or she has been recognized for the behavior and will be motivated to repeat the experience. Over time, the positively reinforced behavior becomes a habit.

Speaking Educationese

The term **unschooling** indicates a way of learning that differs broadly from the traditional textbook method with its linguistic emphasis. Many unschoolers tune in to their children's interests and abilities, providing them with materials, resources, and experiences that will enhance their understanding of a topic.

Unschooling can be very cost effective, necessitating no more than the materials normally found in most homes. Unschooled kids learn from life, supplemented by good books, which can be found at the library. Cooking, budgeting, pet care, hobbies, chores, and communicating with other family members are the base; the community provides mentors, tutors, and expanded social opportunities.

Sample Journal Entries of an Unschooler

March 4

➤ 9:00 A.M. Led a tour of senior citizens through the Chris Craft Exhibit at the Maritime Museum. (Speech)

➤ 10:00. Did research in the museum library for a presentation to be given in a gifted and talented class. Wrote up headings for displays for the presentation. (Language Arts/State History)

➤ 12:00 P.M. Home for lunch.

➤ 1:00. Read several *National Geographic* articles. (Science) Continued reading a biography of Andrew Carnegie. (American History)

➤ 3:30. Doubled recipes and baked cookies, then cooked dinner. (Math/Living Skills)

➤ 6:00. Lifted weights and listened to audio tape about John Phillip Sousa. (Physical Education/Music Appreciation)

➤ 7:00. Checked bank balances on the Internet. Figured out what percentage of my paycheck needs to go into a fund to pay for my car insurance. (Computer Skills/Math)

Many unschooling parents teach children without appearing to provide any structure or lessons by modeling behaviors they want their children to learn. Some parents who choose unschooling are self-employed and use their home-based business as a learning ground for their children. Math, budgeting, economics, supply-and-demand, handwriting, typing, English grammar, social skills, and many other subjects can be learned while placing orders, estimating costs and needs for stocking, filling out forms, answering phone calls, writing business letters, and doing other activities related to the business. Other unschoolers do volunteer work in which they involve their children, supplying opportunities to enhance social skills, as well as a variety of skills similar to those taught by working in home-based businesses. Sometimes parents begin homeschooling in a more structured mode and their children's interests, learning styles, and needs or the circumstances of life lead them to unschooling as a more practical approach.

Spotlight on Education

My son Ryan always liked taking things apart and putting them back together again. When he decided, at 12, to purchase a small engine repair manual, we weren't terribly surprised. His first project was rebuilding the rototiller, which ran at the first pull! When he talked to another homeschooler who had taken a small engine repair course by correspondence and had his own business, we knew what was coming next! After Ryan completed the course, the correspondence school sent him business cards and everything he needed to set up a small business for himself. Soon his hand-lettered sign was hanging by the road and Ryan had more customers than he knew what to do with.

Beyond modeling, parents with children who have had the *square peg in a round hole* experience in an institutional school, are well advised to take a hands-off approach during the first few days, weeks, and sometimes even months, after bringing the child home.

Unschooling can provide a good transition from an institutional school experience until you find the approach that works best for you and yours.

Other Approaches: Classical, Waldorf, Montessori, and Eclectic

I'm fascinated with the wide variety of approaches used by homeschoolers. I've found it helpful to read and learn about many approaches; I've borrowed techniques and tips from nearly every approach I've learned about. Some other approaches worth mentioning include the following:

Learning Lookouts

Square peg in a round hole is an expression used to describe children with learning styles different from the verbal/linguistic approach often used in institutional schools. Hands-on kids, kinesthetic learners, and kids with a combination of learning styles may encounter difficulties in the classroom setting that aren't a problem in the homeschool.

➤ **The Classical approach.** This form of education used in the Middle Ages produced many great thinkers and philosophers. The Classical approach uses a curriculum that is structured around three stages of childhood development called the Trivium. Verbal and written expression are emphasized, as well as ancient disciplines and the study of the Classics and Latin.

➤ **The Waldorf approach.** Based on the educational philosophy of Rudolph Steiner, this holistic approach to education is used by many alternative Waldorf schools in North America. It is based on the changing developmental stages of the child. Because Steiner attempted to achieve a homelike setting in his schools, his methods are easily adapted for the homeschool. The creative use of classic literature, well-written children's stories, and nonfiction books for children—instead of textbooks—can make learning the same material much more engrossing.

➤ **The Montessori method.** Based on the work of Dr. Maria Montessori, this method promotes preparing a natural and life-supporting environment for the child, observing the child living freely in this environment, and continually adapting the environment so the child may fulfill his or her greatest potential—physically, mentally, emotionally, and spiritually. Dr. Montessori believed each child is born with a unique potential, rather than as a blank slate waiting to be written upon by others. Her work with poor slum children in Rome produced phenomenal results and changed the education of young children forever.

➤ **The Eclectic approach.** If you still haven't found one approach that seems to fit every facet of your unique family, looking at all the approaches like a giant smorgasbord, picking and choosing what seems best from each approach, may help you arrive at a solution. The Eclectic approach allows families to tailor a program to fit their needs and remain flexible enough to bend with changes, which ensures a low-stress and high-retention style of learning.

You Don't Have to Do It Alone!

If you need some help implementing a homeschooling program, you're not alone. Support schools and other resources exist to make life easier for you. You may be able to work with local institutional schools, or find community resources to expand your children's learning opportunities.

Support Schools

There are many schools and programs available that provide services of all kinds: correspondence schools with diploma programs, schools that turn the responsibility back to the parent, and local umbrellas (private schools with a homeschool program). It's possible that the homeschooling requirements and laws in your state or province make using a support school a necessity. Some parents simply want someone else to keep the records (remember, you still have to provide them) or want a diploma for their child from a recognized school.

Sometimes the safety net of a support school helps new homeschoolers start out with confidence; then over time they gain the assurance they need to do it themselves. Whether or not you enlist the services of a support school is a personal issue. Some schools provide partial programs, as well as full-service programs. These schools may oversee your child in one or two subject areas, leaving you to handle the rest. Some schools provide services such as curriculum planning and record keeping, allow you to order materials and report to or confer with them occasionally. Read carefully and be sure you know exactly what is included in the price you pay. Some support schools have an annual fee that covers everything, while some have a base registration and tuition fee and provide counseling, curriculum planning, and other services for additional fees. Some have plans for working with special needs students, as well. Be a careful shopper and ask lots of questions!

Learning Lookouts

Be sure you know exactly what services and materials a particular school will provide and what you have to supply yourself. Find out what return policies are, in case you are not satisfied with the program. Get as much information in writing as you can.

Chapter 6, "Finding Support," and Chapter 8, "Sixth Grade in a Box: Using a Full-Service Program," give you more information about support schools of all kinds. Also check Appendix D for contact information. Look for other programs in homeschooling publications, on the Internet, and through local support groups.

Part-Time School Attendance

Some homeschooling families homeschool their children part-time and have them attend an institutional school part-time. Some states make provision for this option in their homeschooling regulations. Be aware of state or provincial regulations in order to know what is possible in your area (see Chapter 4, "Getting Legal: Alternatives to Compulsory Attendance"). Ask local homeschoolers about possible options in your area.

Perhaps your child is very musical and can take choir, band, or orchestra at the local public school. Some private schools welcome part-time students in a variety of classes. Some *charter schools* offer programs in which children attend for two days and learn at home with their parents for the other three. Visit www.edreform.com for statistics on funding, implementation, and success of charter schools.

Speaking Educationese

Charter schools are public schools funded by state monies which may be sponsored by private institutions to provide an alternative to the regular public or private schools available in an area. Laws regulating charters vary from state to state.

You will find that speaking to veteran homeschoolers in your area, as well as seeking out new and creative ways to work with institutional schools, will lead to a variety of possibilities. Remember that situations often change because of policy or personnel revisions. Some institutional schools are set up to work with homeschoolers, complete with registration forms that let you check off such choices as …

➤ Transferring from another public school.

➤ Transferring from private school.

➤ Transferring from homeschool.

Other schools will need to be encouraged to walk through the process step by step, while still others will simply refuse to work with you. Be prepared for anything and be flexible yourself. Remember that you have many options to choose from and that a closed door today may turn into an open door later. If you can't get your child into the program you want most, find another option that will work.

In general, there are two basic ways to work through the public schools. The first is to use a state-mandated homeschooling program that is available through the public schools. Check with local homeschooling support groups to see if your state or province has such a program.

The second is to customize a program, with homeschoolers and public schools working together to accommodate the learning needs of each child. Depending upon where you live, there may be a good rapport with the local school district, or you may be the person who begins the process of establishing such rapport. Remember the reasons why you are home educating your child in the first place. If your child had difficulty with the structure and keeping up the pace, a public school program may not be the answer at this time. However, if you have other reasons for home educating, and simply want to enrich your child's home studies with music or art or other subjects, taking a class or two through an institutional school may be a workable option.

You have to decide for yourself whether the program you are pursuing for your child is worth the time and effort you may have to devote to getting your child into it. Another thing to consider is that until homeschooling is truly accepted as a mainstream option, we have to be careful that we aren't trading homeschoolers' future freedoms for a semester of convenience now. In other words, the more we as homeschoolers rely on institutions, the more likely homeschoolers will be regulated by the state.

Weigh the pros and cons, seek out a variety of possibilities, and make the best choice for your child and the future of home education.

Tutors, Mentors, and Apprenticeships

It's usually high school students who use tutors, mentors, and apprenticeships, but parents of children of all ages should consider these options. We're all used to the idea of our children having private teachers for such things as piano or guitar lessons. Homeschoolers have been expanding on this concept very successfully to provide expanded learning opportunities to their children.

A mentor can be a paid tutor, or a friend, relative, or neighbor who is thrilled to share his or her expertise. He or she can provide a little guidance, help the student plan projects, work together with the student, or give advice over the phone or via e-mail. You are limited only by your imagination in finding people to work with and teach your child in areas that might require specific expertise. See Chapter 13, "Teenagers in the Homeschool," for more discussion of tutors, mentors, and apprenticeships.

When you need to look beyond your own circle of family, friends, and neighbors, network on a homeschool e-mail list for ideas, resources, or the names of folks who have specific skills. Attend fairs, conferences, or shows sponsored by groups involved in the skill your child wants to learn. Speak with vendors and exhibitors to find folks who might provide opportunities for your child. Let friends, neighbors, family, and other homeschoolers know that you are looking for someone to teach a specific skill to your child. Finding others to enhance your child's education may be time-consuming, but many homeschoolers have found it well worth the effort.

Learning Lookouts

Considering our choices in the light of homeschoolers' future freedoms is important because most of us want homeschooling to be available, without undue restrictions, for our children and grandchildren. Making choices today that will keep our freedoms intact will ensure having those freedoms in the future.

Learning Lookouts

Choose your child's mentors carefully. Be sure you have recommendations for, or personal knowledge of, the person who will be mentoring your child. Special care should be taken with very young children. Suggest that the mentor spend some time with your family first, or invite the mentor to work with your child at your home until you know the mentor better.

When negotiating with a potential mentor, remember to suggest a trial period. Some potential mentors may be hesitant or even negative at first. They may not be used to working with young children, or may have had previous bad experiences teaching children who didn't have a real interest. The mentor will appreciate your consideration and you will be able to call things off if it isn't working out. Keep in mind the personalities of the mentor and child, and decide when, where, and for how long they will be meeting.

These are just suggestions to get the thought processes flowing. Some mentors just appear serendipitously. Others will require more background work on your part. The bottom line is to keep an open mind and not to overlook any possibilities.

The Least You Need to Know

➤ Keep your child's personality, interests, and learning style in mind when deciding on a homeschool approach.

➤ Unschooling can help you make the transition from an institutional school to the approach you decide on.

➤ You can combine approaches for a custom fit.

➤ Enrich your child's learning program with resources found outside the home.

Finding Support

In This Chapter

➤ Umbrellas are for more than rain showers

➤ Why local support is important

➤ What state support means to you

➤ National support networks

➤ Books, magazines, and more: almost too much good stuff to list!

Finding support from other homeschoolers is important, especially if family and friends greet your intentions to homeschool with incredulity. You may not realize just how important finding support is until you embark on the sea of homeschooling.

Never fear—there is plenty of support out there for any new homeschooler. In fact, wading through all the options in the support arena may seem overwhelming at first. In this chapter, I'll give you an idea of what support options are out there for home-schoolers. There's a lot to talk about, so let's get started!

What's an Umbrella School?

Nope, it doesn't have anything to do with rain, but, like the umbrella we're all famil-iar with, it does protect you. Umbrellas (the term as well as the institution) came to be during the 1970s and 1980s when homeschooling wasn't legal in every state.

Speaking Educationese

Umbrellas, sometimes called **cover schools,** permitted homeschoolers to educate their children "under the umbrella," or protection, of an institutional school.

Speaking Educationese

An **independent study school** is an institution that provides services to individuals who wish to homeschool or study on their own. Some, but not all, independent study schools have a campus school. These programs serve as umbrellas or covers to help homeschoolers meet legal requirements.

To help parents comply with laws that require such things as teacher certification and testing requirements, some private and alternative schools allow homeschoolers to enroll and then provide varying degrees of oversight. Sometimes such schools are called *umbrella* or *cover schools*. Some private and alternative schools still have home-based education programs available; check with homeschoolers to see if this is the case in your area. Such programs generally provide materials, oversight, curriculum guidance, testing, and other services for a fee, while the actual learning is done at home.

Would an Independent Study School Be Helpful?

Independent study schools provide everything from curriculum planning, counseling, materials, teacher consultation, testing, evaluation of students' work, individual education plans (IEPs) for special needs students, to diplomas and certificates. Many homeschoolers have found using an independent study school to be easier than doing it entirely on their own.

Some homeschoolers use such a school for a while until they become confident enough to do it on their own. Others stay with the program right through their child's high school graduation. As with everything else in home education, there are many individual choices to be made, based on the needs of the family.

Check Appendix D, "Independent Study Programs and Support Schools, Publications, and Vendors," for a list of schools to start your search. Be sure to talk to other homeschoolers, especially those who have a similar educational philosophy, to get some feedback about working with particular schools.

Request and read all materials available from the independent study school, ask lots of questions, and obtain satisfactory answers. You want to choose a school that understands your needs and is prepared to meet them.

Checking Out Local Support Groups

Support groups can range from groups that have mothers-night-out meetings once a month to groups that coordinate field trips, have a home-school cooperative offering a large variety of classes, and have a drama club, choir, and sports teams. If your group doesn't do the things you are looking for, take a little time to get acquainted, then get involved in planning some activities that meet your needs.

How Do I Find One?

The local library is a good place to check. Quite often librarians know the homeschoolers in the community. (Homeschoolers are the ones who check out so many books!) Depending on local homeschoolers, librarians may keep materials about homeschooling in a vertical file, including contact names of local home-schoolers, or they may take your name and number and promise to contact a local homeschooler, who, in turn, will contact you. If your local library subscribes to a homeschooling publication, check to see if any of the issues have a listing of state support groups. State support groups may be able to lead you to a local group.

Learning Lookouts

When shopping for an independent study school, find out exactly what is included in the fees charged. Is there a flat yearly tuition fee that covers all services? Are there charges for extra services? Does the school make the materials available? If not, do they require certain materials or a specific curriculum?

Spotlight on Education

I found my local support group by getting acquainted with a local homeschooler. My sister-in-law who gives piano lessons was teaching three children from a family that home-schools. I called the homeschooler, and she invited me to her house and to a field trip the homeschool group had planned. What a great way to get a feel for homeschooling! I also attended the end-of-the-year pizza party with this homeschool group and got ac-quainted with more homeschoolers. Several people let me visit them on a homeschool day to talk to their children and observe their learning style.

Will It Fit My Educational Philosophy?

There are lots of homeschooling groups out there with many different philosophies. In a densely populated metropolitan area, you may find several Christian groups, groups for a number of other religious beliefs, and a group that supports homeschoolers of any religious or philosophical motivation. In a sparsely populated rural area, you may find your choices more limited.

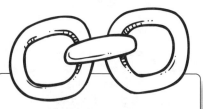

Learning Links

You may find a couple of like-minded families in your support group with whom you can plan field trips and learning activities. Although membership in a local group provides some planned activities, it doesn't need to limit your creativity in providing more learning experiences for your child.

Some homeschoolers like being part of a group that has a religious focus, in which prayer is the starting point of every meeting. Others prefer a homeschooling group that helps them with their home education questions, without the focus on religion.

Some homeschoolers have found that local homeschool group meetings are open to parents only, with no child care provided. For some homeschool families whose focus is on the family, this may not fit their needs. They may be looking for a group that focuses more on family activities, and less on parent meetings. Each of us has different needs and hopefully will find a group that will support those needs. If you can't find what you need, perhaps it's time to get involved in the planning activities of the existing group, or to start a new group! Read Chapter 21, "Involvement in the Homeschooling Community," for information on revitalizing an old group or starting a new one.

Does It Offer Cooperative Classes?

More and more homeschooling groups are starting to realize that within a group of families you have a lot of untapped talent and excitement. In some states, there is an option in the law that allows a group of homeschoolers to incorporate or function as a private school. Providing services cooperatively seems like a natural result of such a liaison.

Learning Links

Working cooperatively with other families is a good way to save money as well as time. In our group, one family has a chemistry lab and provides classes (for a consumable materials fee) for our homeschool cooperative. Imagine the costs if everyone had to purchase these materials!

Some homeschooling groups already have programs in place that provide core classes as well as the arts and sports. To start such a program or add a new one, talk to other homeschoolers in your group. Brainstorm about the things you each like to do. See Chapter 21 for more detailed information about involvement in the homeschooling community.

National Support Organizations

There are many national groups out there that support homeschooling. Some are specific groups that hinge on religious belief, educational philosophy, ethnic background, or educational handicaps. Other groups focus on alternatives in education, and some provide just plain homeschooling support. Check Appendix C, "Homeschooling Support Organizations," and Appendix D for a list of support groups and publications to help you in your search.

Check with each individual group to see what it offers, whether it's a nonprofit or for-profit group, and what you are required to do to become a member. Enclose a self-addressed stamped envelope with your mail requests because many of these groups are run on volunteer time or very small budgets. If there is no membership fee, remember that making a small donation now and then may ensure that the group is able to continue to support you in the future.

Be aware of the overall purpose of each group. Request information from the group to familiarize yourself with its background, current issues it is involved with, and financial status. Some groups have very specific goals totally related to home education, while others have a broader focus involving issues unrelated to homeschooling. Support the group or groups that provide you with the information and support you need, while spending your dues on issues that you are happy to support.

Every nonprofit group must submit Form 990 (Return of Organization Exempt from Income Taxes) to the Internal Revenue Service. The information on this form is made public to help people decide whether or not to financially support a specific nonprofit organization based on its performance. To obtain a Public Inspection Copy of Form 990 for any nonprofit group, write to: Internal Revenue Service, Department of the Treasury, PO Box 9941, Ogden, UT 84409. Include your name, address, and phone number (so the IRS can contact you with the fee amount) and the name, address, and EIN (Employer Identification Number) of the group. To locate the EIN of a nonprofit group, ask someone in the group for the number or do a search on one of these Web sites:

➤ www.guidestar.org

➤ www.nccs.urban.org

State Support Organizations

Most states have at least one or two state homeschooling organizations. Others have several. Just as the national groups do, state groups cover a broad scope of philosophies. Most states have at least one Christian group and one or more other groups. Check Appendix C for a listing of groups in your state.

Some state groups are affiliated with national organizations. Others are simply standalone state groups. Many homeschoolers have found that grass roots volunteer

Learning Links

The National Home Education Network (NHEN) Web site (www.nhen.org) has an ongoing project encouraging support groups to register online. It has liaisons for almost every state and will help you find a support group in your area. NHEN's listing includes information about the purpose of the group, as well as contact information. Both *Growing Without Schooling* and *Home Education* magazines publish a yearly listing of support groups.

groups—which operate at the local or state level rather than being a part of the centers of political leadership—can be very effective in keeping their members apprised of legislative action and other issues that are important to them.

Be aware of the different purposes of the state groups and support the one that gives you the information and support you need. As you learn and research, you may find out that another group provides services that are more in keeping with your educational philosophy. By all means, support that group.

Other Resources You Can Turn to for Support

Besides local, state, and national support groups, there are many other resources from which to get advice, help, and ideas. Just to give you an idea, here's a list of a few other sources of support and information:

➤ Magazines and periodicals

➤ Books

➤ Vendors

➤ Newsletters

➤ Homeschool conferences and curriculum fairs

Let's take a closer look at each.

Magazines and Periodicals

Magazines! I love them! I have subscribed to several homeschooling magazines over the years and read still more by swapping with friends. Here are a few of my favorites. (Check Appendix D for a more complete listing of periodicals.)

➤ *Home Education* magazine provides articles that support homeschoolers regardless of motivation. Like some homeschool support groups, this magazine's focus is on getting the information out there, supporting homeschoolers where they are, providing services, and empowering homeschoolers to think for themselves. Real-life homeschoolers write most of these articles. They've been there, done that, and they tell it like it is.

➤ *Growing Without Schooling* is the oldest home-schooling periodical around. Started by John Holt, written by subscribers, the magazine focuses on natural learning, otherwise known as unschooling.

➤ *Homeschooling Today* is a unit study magazine from a Christian perspective. If you are considering using the unit study approach (see Chapter 5, "Approaches to Home Education"), this magazine comes with lots of ideas, plus some built-in unit studies.

➤ *The Link* is a free homeschooling newspaper. Look up the address in Appendix D and get one coming your way!

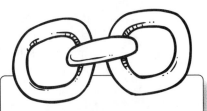

Learning Links

Some libraries subscribe to homeschooling magazines. You may be able to request others through interlibrary loan. Speak with a friend about sharing a subscription. Or talk to others in your support group about each of you subscribing to different magazines and swapping.

Books

I'm a bookaholic, as my husband (who has to keep building and buying bookshelves) will attest, and am nearly always reading more than one book at any given time. Homeschoolers and books just seem to go together like pancakes and syrup. There have been many, many books published about homeschooling. Quite a few are written by homeschoolers who recount their personal experiences. Some include the responses of many homeschoolers to specific issues or questions. Many are rich with resources and bibliographies, which will lead you to more information. Most homeschooling books are written from a particular bias or opinion. As you read, try to be aware of where the author is coming from, what the author's worldview is, and whether the author's opinions coincide with yours.

Here are some of my favorites. (See Appendix E, "Bibliography," for details on these and other books you might enjoy.)

Learning Lookouts

Don't limit yourself by reading just one type of homeschool book. Every book on home education that I've read has taught me something, regardless of worldview, background, homeschooling style, or bias. We promote divisiveness in the homeschooling community by choosing to understand only certain types of homeschoolers.

➤ *I Learn Better by Teaching Myself* and *Still Teaching Ourselves,* by Agnes Leistico, a former La Leche League Leader and home education advocate, are among my favorite books about home education. Originally published as two separate titles, they are now available in one volume. Leistico chronicles her homeschooling journey candidly. She doesn't gloss over her negative feelings and fears, with which I could certainly identify, especially during those early years of homeschooling. If you are homeschooling a child who has had difficult school experiences, take heart, as I did, at what a healing experience homeschooling can be.

➤ *The Home School Source Book: A Comprehensive Catalog and Directory of Learning Materials That Are Challenging, Constructive, and Fun; with Commentaries, Notes, and Essays About a "Liberal Arts" Education at Home, from Birth Through Adulthood,* by Donn Reed, was my favorite resource during the early years of homeschooling. Donn's title says it all. I appreciated the individual attention Donn gave to a new, thoroughly befuddled homeschooler. Although Donn has since passed away, his wife, Jean, continues to keep his book, an invaluable resource, updated.

➤ *The Art of Education: Reclaiming Your Family, Community, and Self,* by Linda Dobson, is the most mind-stretching book about educational choices that I have read. Comparing public education with natural learning and compelling you to think through the issues, this book opens up a whole world of new thoughts on education. What is education? Are the institutional schools achieving it? Are we, as homeschoolers, able to do better? How? And why should we? Linda doesn't try to give you all the answers, but certainly seeks to empower you to think through the issues for yourself.

Learning Links

Two companies that publish beautifully illustrated, informative, and interactive books are Dorling Kindersley Family Learning, Inc., and Educational Development Corporation, the publisher of Usborne Books. Books from both companies are often available at homeschool conferences and curriculum fairs.

Vendors

Vendors fall into various categories. Many, run by homeschoolers, consider their businesses a ministry to home educators. Others are simply sellers of top-quality resources. Some companies make their materials available at homeschool conferences, by mail, or at parties sponsored by distributors. There are also several used-curriculum newsletters and Web sites, some of which are also run by homeschooling families. Check Appendix D for a complete listing of these and other vendors.

Some homeschoolers have opted to sell products of a particular company as a way to build their personal/homeschool library while providing employment and extra income for themselves and their children.

I'll list some of my personal catalog favorites here and let you discover the rest by checking Appendix D, reading ads in homeschooling magazines and newsletters, and talking to local home educators. I'm not getting any kickbacks or incentives to push these companies, but simply feel their catalogs are topnotch resources.

➤ **The Elijah Company** rightly calls its catalog more than a catalog; it's full of teaching tips, helpful hints, and a wonderful selection of books and materials tested by the owners and their friends.

➤ **The Genius Tribe** is Grace Llewellyn's catalog of totally mind-bending books and materials, some of which I have not seen offered elsewhere. Llewellyn offers her unique catalog for three dollars, and it comes with a three-dollar coupon redeemable upon your order.

➤ **John Holt's Bookstore** makes available many of the writings of John Holt and other leading homeschool advocates, plus back issues of *Growing Without Schooling* magazine.

➤ **The Sycamore Tree Center for Home Education** selects their materials for academic excellence, spiritual influence, and value per dollar. A nice balance of Christian and secular materials is provided in this well-organized catalog. The Sycamore Tree also provides a full-service homeschool program.

➤ **Dover Publications** is a resource for affordable books and educational materials you won't find anywhere else. Dover has specialty catalogs in these and other categories, as well as seasonal catalogs featuring all fields of interest, including math and science; children's books; antiques and photography; social science; literature and language; and crafts, needlework, and cooking.

They are a very inexpensive source for classics, themed activities, puzzle and coloring books, audio tapes, paper dolls, posters, and much, much more. Be sure to request Dover's whole line of catalogs.

Learning Lookouts

Browsing catalogs of homeschooling materials can be dangerous to the budget! If money is a major issue (as it is for many homeschooling families), don't forget to attend local used-curriculum swaps, used-book stores, and garage sales before you buy new. Then use your materials budget for the items you can't beg for, borrow, or buy thriftily elsewhere. Don't forget the library as a terrific way to supplement your homeschool curriculum.

Learning Links

If you're fortunate enough to have a homeschool resource store in your community or within driving distance, be supportive of its endeavor to support you. Even if you have to pay a dollar or two more for an item, it's worth the convenience of being able to inspect the materials before buying.

Newsletters

Newsletters abound in the homeschooling community. Your local support group probably publishes the accomplishments, planned activities, and other items of interest regarding local homeschoolers. State groups use newsletters to keep homeschoolers within their state informed of conferences, legislation, and other activities statewide. National groups have newsletters about specific issues, such as homeschooling children with learning differences, unschooling, or homeschooling from a particular perspective. Some support schools publish newsletters to keep enrollees abreast of changes, improvements, and additions to their programs.

There are also newsletters for homeschoolers who are interested in a particular homeschooling approach; and newsletters about other areas of interest to homeschoolers, such as homeschooling on a budget, monthly cooking, or simplifying life. Check Appendix D for a more complete list of homeschooling publications.

Homeschool Conferences and Curriculum Fairs

Some support schools put on a *homeschool conference* or a *curriculum fair* every year to give enrollees a boost. A typical program will include a keynote address by the director of the school, workshops by support teachers and enrollees of the program, and activities for the kids. Some include graduation ceremonies. Conferences typically have a vendor hall where you can see, hear, and touch some of the things you've been reading and hearing about.

Quite a few conferences have sessions or workshops put on by the vendors, to explain and demonstrate their wares. Vendor halls can be fun, because sometimes there are drawings for free products, lots of handouts and catalogs, as well as a chance to talk to someone who probably knows the answers to some of your curriculum and materials questions.

Some conferences have workshops that are not directly related to curriculum or other resource materials. These sessions are intended to encourage, inspire, and support homeschoolers. There is usually a question-and-answer period at the end of most workshops.

You'll find lots of other homeschoolers at conferences. Be sure to get acquainted with some of the workshop attendees before and after (but not during) sessions. Some of my most valuable insights have been gained while just talking with other conference-goers.

Speaking Educationese

A **homeschool conference** is a gathering sponsored by a support school, support group, or individual to bring together homeschoolers for mutual support, discussion, networking, and workshops. Some conferences include sessions especially for kids. A **curriculum fair** is a homeschool conference on a smaller scale, usually including workshops, a vendor hall, and sometimes a used-curriculum swap.

Try to attend a conference before you start home-schooling. You will learn a lot, get to know some other homeschoolers, and have the opportunity to see what is available in the way of support and re-sources. Once you start homeschooling, try to get to a homeschool conference regularly, even if it's just a small one. It's always helpful to listen to oth-ers speak about homeschooling, and to get ac-quainted with others who are taking the road less traveled. Some homeschoolers call attending a conference their annual booster shot.

Online Support

Virtually everything that you can find elsewhere is present in some form online. Almost everything, except actual human contact, is out there in cyber-space. I receive a lot of support from several e-mail lists of homeschoolers, as well as my local support group. I also visit Kaleidoscapes' and *Home Educa-tion* magazine's online bulletin boards frequently, to touch bases on the issues that are coming up in the homeschooling community nationwide.

Bulletin Boards

Quite a bit more interesting than the bulletin boards we usually see, homeschooling online boards run in the question-and-answer format. Someone logs on to a bulletin board with a specific question, to which they may receive several varied responses. Someone else, trying to locate a resource or a Web site, posts his or her question. It's always interesting to read what other posters come up with; bulletin boards can be a great way to get information. Check Appendix B, "Curriculum Winners and Selected Resources, Including Dyna-mite Web Sites," for some great bulletin boards.

Learning Lookouts

Some conferences are not kid-friendly, and not only don't have sessions for kids, but directly pro-hibit kids from attending. Make sure you know the conference's stance on kids before you pack up the car and head for a con-ference.

Learning Lookouts

Most bulletin boards and e-mail lists have specific policies pro-hibiting the posting of flames (derogatory messages). If you plan to participate on bulletin boards and e-mail lists, read the FAQs (frequently asked ques-tions) and respect others as you want to be respected. Flaming can result in being asked to un-subscribe or discontinue posting.

Chats

Chats are a little closer to personal contact than are e-mail lists or bulletin boards. Comments fly fast and furious (literally) and someone, usually a moderator, tries to keep things in order and soothe any ruffled feathers. Chats provide homeschoolers with another way to exchange opinions about products, publications, and other resources, as well as a place to share personal stories that encourage, affirm, and support others. Some Web sites have archived chats that you can read later at your leisure.

Web Sites

Homeschooling Web sites abound! Here are a few of my favorites:

➤ Chart and Compass for Homeschoolers (www.ChartnCompass.com)

➤ Family Unschoolers Network (www.unschooling.org/index.htm)

➤ Jon's Homeschool Resource Page (www.midnightbeach.com/hs/)

➤ Learn in Freedom (www.learninfreedom.org/readbook.html)

There are also Web sites for checking state homeschooling laws, and Web sites for many support schools. National and state organizations often have a Web presence. Use a metasearch engine (see Chapter 22, "Cyber Learning") to find lots of Web sites pertaining to the topic you are interested in:

➤ C4Search (www.c4.com)

➤ Dogpile (www.dogpile.com)

➤ Starting Point (www.stpt.com)

Appendix C includes information on Web sites that address many homeschooling approaches and other home education information.

Online Vendors

Many vendors have made their products readily available for order online. Quite a few curriculum publishers have Web sites, where you can learn about their products and order them directly. There are many used-curriculum vendors with Web sites, too.

Some vendors include informative articles and support of various types along with their product listings. Check Appendix D for a listing of homeschooling vendors whose products are available online.

The Least You Need to Know

➤ A wide variety of services are available from "umbrellas," independent study schools, and support schools.

➤ National, state and local support groups vary in focus and services provided.

➤ If you can arrange to attend a homeschool conference or curriculum fair, do so!

➤ Browse the catalogs, check out the vendors at conferences, see what your library offers, and talk to other homeschoolers before investing a lot of money in curriculum.

Part 3

Choosing/Planning a Curriculum

Although there are a myriad of choices available to homeschoolers today, I'll help you learn to weigh and evaluate materials and programs, using an understanding of your family's needs as a rule of thumb. You'll learn how considering your child's learning style, abilities, interests, and goals can make choosing or planning a curriculum much simpler than you'd think.

Whether you want to use a prepackaged curriculum or create your own program, I will show you ways to tweak an existing program or start from scratch.

Chapter 7

So Much to Choose From

In This Chapter

➤ What curriculum and materials are best for your family?

➤ Understanding the role that your family's worldview plays

➤ Considering the different learning styles

➤ How money can be a major factor

➤ What to do when the materials don't work out

Now that you've decided to look further into home education, the question looms: "How do I decide on curriculum and materials?" Whether you are considering using a school-at-home approach, a very relaxed approach, a combination of approaches, or writing your own curriculum, it's a good idea to consider some basic factors when choosing curriculum and materials.

When choosing materials for your homeschool, it helps to understand how your children learn. This chapter shares insights from research on learning styles, and some resources to help you determine the kind of learners you have in your family. I'll also talk about using your kids' interests and goals as a starting point in choosing learning materials, budget considerations, and what to do if you invest in materials that don't work well for you.

Finding Out What Suits Your Family

Your individual family members are the most important clues you have to work with in planning your homeschool program. Taking your children's learning styles, interests, strengths, and weaknesses into consideration will provide the biggest payoffs in the end. Don't panic if you really don't know how your kids learn. There are some excellent resources to help you learn about your kids. It will take some time, but remember that you don't have to make all the decisions immediately. Refer to the Running Start and Beginner's Checklists on the tearcard in the front of this book for a quick overview to help you relax and begin homeschooling even if you don't have all your ducks in a row.

Speaking Educationese

Your **worldview** is based on your traditional sociocultural patterns. Your beliefs, the way you were raised, the experiences you've gone through, and your value system all contribute to your worldview.

Your Family's Worldview

I've mentioned the word *worldview* in several places, and it simply refers to traditional sociocultural patterns. Your family's worldview is based on your family's beliefs and value systems.

Your worldview may differ from that of other homeschoolers. Considering your beliefs and how important they are to you will be the controlling factors in what you decide about home education. Worldview affects the way you interact with others including your children; homeschooling will intensify that interaction in the parent/child relationship.

Rethinking Your Educational Philosophy

Do you still think that all children must be exposed to a classroom setting, a structured program, and a specific curriculum to learn? Many have found that, removed from the environment of an institutional school, homeschooled children develop an internal motivation that far exceeds any external factors that were present in the institutional setting.

Some homeschoolers make it very clear that, while school-at-home activities worked for some of their children, their other children needed something different. Speak to homeschoolers who have been doing this for a while; they may be able to share some insights that will help you develop your educational philosophy. Although your thoughts on education may not change as you go along, it's rare for homeschoolers not to do some mental stretching and learning right along with their kids. There's a reason why homeschooling is often referred to as a journey.

Spotlight on Education

Stephen, an avid reader, tested as gifted and talented in the public schools. He was seldom challenged, finding many school projects boring. Diagnosed with both ADD and Tourette's syndrome, he was teased by peers and had low self-esteem in the institutional setting. Beginning a home-based learning program, having input into his course of study, and starting a home-based business made a huge difference in Stephen's outlook and feelings about himself. He and his brother David found it very beneficial to be able to measure progress by personal gains rather than by being compared to others. As a result of homeschooling, the boys have become much closer and developed a willingness to help others less fortunate.

If you are planning your homeschool from a Christian worldview, you will find Cathy Duffy's curriculum manuals very helpful. Duffy, an author and speaker who homeschooled her own now-grown children, has done a lot of research on learning styles and personality types and has incorporated much of this into the planning sections of her manuals. She categorizes learners into four basic groups with names to lend easy understanding to the traits that help identify each group. Wiggly Willy, Perfect Paula, Competent Carl, and Sociable Sue provide starting points to understanding learning styles of both adults and children, as well as identifying the preferable learning situations for each type. Understanding the way you learn, as well as the way your children learn, is invaluable in planning curriculum and making resource choices.

Another excellent book written from a Christian perspective is *The Way They Learn,* by Cynthia Tobias. Of course, many of the suggestions are valid for secular homeschoolers as well. Two good secular resources are *In Their Own Way: Discovering and Encouraging Your Child's Multiple Intelligences* by Thomas Armstrong and *Discover Your Child's Learning Style* by Mariaemma Willis, M.S., and Victoria Kindle Hodson, M.A. The latter book includes a questionnaire for your child to fill out so you can work directly from your child's input. See Appendix E, "Bibliography," for more on these books and others about learning styles.

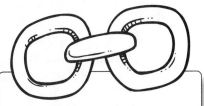

Learning Links

It's never too late to learn. In fact, after 10 years of homeschooling, my two younger children (aged 13 and 9) are taking the assessments in *Discover Your Child's Learning Style* to discover where we can breathe new life into our home-based learning program.

Evaluating Materials

Whether you attend a curriculum fair or spend time browsing through some catalogs, it won't take long to realize that there is almost too much to choose from. Unless you are very sure about the type of learner your child is, or have decided already that you are buying a packaged curriculum no matter what anyone says, it won't take long until you are totally overwhelmed with the choices. That's why it's important to take a step back and put off purchasing decisions until you have given some thought to all the issues and have done a little research on all the factors that affect learning, including ...

➤ Learning style

➤ Personality

➤ Interests and goals

Learning Styles: How Do Your Children (and You) Learn?

Howard Gardner of Harvard University advanced a theory of multiple intelligences that has become a touchstone for many researchers and educators today. He identified nine intelligences:

1. **Verbal/linguistic** children display strength in the language arts: speaking, writing, reading, and listening. These students usually do well with school-at-home (traditional) homeschooling. A prepackaged or home-brewed curriculum may work fine with these children. Supplement with such activities as word games, reading aloud or listening to audio recordings, using the computer, and participating in discussions.

2. **Mathematical/logical** children demonstrate an aptitude for numbers, problem solving, and reasoning. These children usually succeed with a program where teaching is logically sequenced. School-at-home featuring structured unit studies, a prepackaged or well-planned, home-brewed curriculum will work well with such children. Supplement with puzzles, number and logic games, and activities that require sequencing and classifying.

3. **Visual/spatial** children learn well visually and organize things spatially. They need to see what you are talking about in order to understand. Project-oriented programs and unit studies with lots of visual/spatial activities will suit these children. Use charts, graphs, maps, tables, illustrations, art, puzzles, and even costumes to provide the dimension these children need to learn.

4. **Musical/rhythmical** children learn best through songs, patterns, rhythms, instruments, and musical expression. Children with this intelligence are often left

behind in traditional education, but it doesn't need to be so in home education. There are many resources for teaching every subject area musically; learning the parts of speech, math facts, and the periodic table of the elements set to music are possibilities. Having a private music tutor may be important to this child. Singing, dancing, composing, playing and conducting music, and playing games to rhythm or music will make learning easier for these children.

5. **Bodily/kinesthetic** children learn best through activity: games, movement, hands-on tasks, and building things. Search out resources that involve activity, and add movement and hands-on projects to as many of your child's learning experiences as possible. Provide construction toys and materials and encourage imaginative play. These children learn well by putting on plays, dancing, playing sports, and using manipulatives (real objects to represent abstract concepts) to solve problems.

6. **Naturalist** children love the outdoors, animals, and field trips. More than this, though, these students pick up on subtle differences in meanings. The traditional classroom has not been accommodating to these children, but you can be! Charlotte Mason's nature walks, nature journals, and narration work well with these children. Caring for pets, growing houseplants, volunteering at the nature center, and caring for a garden are all excellent activities for naturalist children.

7. **Interpersonal** children are noticeably people-oriented and outgoing, and do their best learning cooperatively in groups or with a partner. In the traditional setting, these children are often labeled "too talkative" or

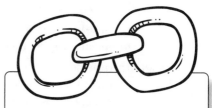

Learning Links

Modeling with clay, experimenting with the graphic arts, solving mazes, and imaginative play (playing dress-up, putting on a play, or imagining pictures in the clouds) are all ways to support visual/spatial children.

Learning Lookouts

A bodily/kinesthetic child is often labeled ADHD (attention deficit hyperactivity disorder) or LD (learning disabled) because of the child's seeming inability to sit still. If your child has been diagnosed with a learning disability, finding out his learning style may provide a whole different perception of your child. For example, once you know that movement is part of your child's learning process, he may seem intelligent and capable instead of disabled.

"distractible." Field trips, cooperative classes, and other group activities are important to these children. These children often blossom under the tutelage of an understanding mentor.

8. **Intrapersonal** children are especially in touch with their own feelings, values, and ideas. Often reserved, they are quite intuitive about what they learn and how it relates to themselves. Seeking input during curriculum planning and choosing resources is especially important with these children, no matter how young. You may be amazed at how definitely they will choose one resource over another. When an activity is their idea they buy into it whole-heartedly and are extremely self-motivated.

9. **Existential** children learn from the context of where they fit into the "big picture." If your child is already asking you "Why am I here?" and seeking ways to help others in the world, you have a child who needs purpose to his or her learning. Many of the philosophers were, no doubt, existential learners, constantly questioning and trying to understand the purpose of life. A holistic approach, such as Waldorf (see Chapter 5, "Approaches to Home Education"), will suit this child well.

Remember that your children will not fit neatly into just one of these categories. Everyone has all the intelligences to varying degrees; thus, we all have multiple intelligences.

Learning Links

Print out a Multiple Intelligences (M.I.) Survey at surfaquarium.com/MIinvent.htm and/or send a check for $10 to Walter McKenzie, c/o Creative Classroom Consulting, 10808 Seven Oaks Court, Spotsylvania, PA 22553, to see where you and your child fit in the scheme of things. There is no right or wrong to the results of the Multiple Intelligences Survey. It's simply a tool to help you understand learning styles. Remember that everyone has some combination of all the intelligences, and M.I. theory is meant to empower, not label, people.

If your children are preschoolers and you are considering home education, good for you! You can begin to observe them and learn about their learning styles and their abilities as they play and learn around the house. You can have their learning styles figured out before you need to worry about making major curriculum decisions. You don't need to plan an intensive academic program for your little ones. This is a wonderful age for being excited about learning; children learn naturally from all their experiences. Provide an environment rich in resources and spend time with them reading, playing games, and doing chores and projects. They'll need little else.

Does one of your children find it difficult to sit still? He or she may be a bodily/kinesthetic learner for whom it would be most helpful to focus on project-oriented materials and real-life experiences. Does another like to copy you when you sit down to pay the bills, insisting on having a pencil and paper and maybe an old checkbook to work on, just like you? She may be verbal/linguistic and visual/spatial. Perhaps she will enjoy doing some workbooks and seat work (things done at a desk or table, similar to traditional schoolwork) activities. Begin to make some mental notes, or start a notebook with jottings of your observations. They will help you make some decisions about materials later on.

Your Child's Emerging Personality

When considering materials for your children, keep their personalities in mind. Will your busy boy be happy sitting and filling out pages in a phonics workbook, or does his activity level and short attention span make you realize it would make more sense to postpone such activities? Can you make learning the letter sounds more *tactile*, involving large and small motor skills and engaging his interest for a little longer? For example, to teach the shapes and sounds of the letters, have your child say the letter while tracing it in a large pan of rice or sand. Draw giant letters on your child's back with your finger while saying the sound. Cut large letter shapes from sandpaper so your child can trace them while you say the letters together. Keep word games short and stop before they get tedious.

Speaking Educationese

Tactile materials reinforce concepts by allowing the child to learn through the sense of touch.

Can you make an active game of learning? Toss a ball back and forth while singing a phonics song with an audio tape? Have your child jump on the trampoline while reciting some math facts? Do some research on what's available for early learners, and make your choices based on what you've learned about your children.

If your children have already been in institutional schools, and are failing miserably or just don't seem to be learning much, talk to them. What are the areas in which they have the most problems? What do they hate the most about school? What do they enjoy? Ask for their feedback about school and the positive and negative experiences they have had. If your son tells you that he is sick of doing pages and pages of worksheets, use that as a clue not to purchase a workbook-based program or to download all those great worksheets you found on a homeschooling Web site.

If your daughter's favorite thing was a woman's talk about her culture, involving the entire class in preparation of an ethnic dish, she may be giving you clues to an interest (learning about other cultures) and her learning style (visual/kinesthetic). Consider a *multicultural* unit study, with emphasis on learning about and preparing a special dish or meal from each country.

What if your children have been in institutional school and make great grades, love doing schoolwork (even homework), but you aren't happy with the safety issues, drug problems, negative socialization, peer pressure, or other factors of the school experience? Maybe you feel that there is not enough emphasis on character and values in the school curriculum or would prefer your children receive a religious-based education. Whatever your motivation, your kids are probably some combination of verbal/linguistic, visual/spatial, and/or mathematical/logical. They may thrive using a packaged curriculum based on the school-at-home approach. For those desiring a religious-based or character-based curriculum, there are many available, including some with a unit study approach. (Check Appendix B, "Curriculum Winners and Selected Resources, Including Dynamite Web Sites," for resources.) Even with these children, remember that a break in routine for some field trips, hands-on projects, and variation in activities keep life more interesting.

What about you? Were you happy filling out worksheets when you were in school? Was reading the chapter and answering the questions just part of the territory and no big deal? Or was school a stomach-clenching environment, full of seemingly impossible goals and assignments you never understood and couldn't keep up with? Was school easy or boring or just plain horrible?

How do *you* learn now? Do you take classes when you want to learn new skills? Do you find a book to teach you? Or do you research the Internet to find out how to approach a new project? Have you ever thought about it? Take time now to consider your own learning preferences. It's important to consider your learning style, and how it will affect your planning, interaction with your children as they learn, and record keeping. Use the Multiple Intelligences Survey, or the assessment in *Discover Your Child's Learning Style* (there's one in there for parents), and do some reading about learning styles.

Becoming Aware of Interests and Goals

Most parents fall somewhere in between extremely involved and uninvolved with their children. By choosing homeschooling you will get to know your children better than you ever have before. Assuming you have been very involved, volunteering in the classroom, helping with homework, and perhaps having your child tested, you may already know some of his or her strengths and weaknesses.

For example, you've observed that your child's behind in math and struggling in reading, but loves science, art, and gym. The teacher complains that your son doesn't pay attention in class and probably has a learning disability, but you know your son is all ears, eyes, and concentration when Grandpa takes him fishing or shows him how to tie flies. Your son has also been getting in trouble at school for fighting. He explains that all the kids call him dumb; however, you know that he can name all the fishing flies he and his grandpa use and can identify which fish the flies will attract to the hook.

Perhaps you haven't been involved much with your children's education because academically everything seemed to be going okay. The kids make good grades, although when you ask them what they learned today they usually say, "Nothing." Just a month ago there was a bomb threat at your children's school and since then a student was expelled for having a gun. Your kids are fearful about going to school, have frequent nightmares, and are developing negative attitudes about life in general.

Spotlight on Education

Kevin and Jennifer went to a small public high school where drugs and violence were commonplace. Their older brother had dropped out and, although he finally got his GED, didn't seem to have any focus in life. The kids were scared and asked their parents if they could homeschool. Their parents agreed and, after a couple of false starts, they settled on the American School of Correspondence. During his studies, Kevin started working part-time at a retail store, moved into a full-time position, graduated, and is presently working in store security. Jennifer also holds down a full-time position in retail while completing her high school credits. Both kids appreciate being able to take charge of their own lives and education.

Or maybe you're beginning to realize that your child has interests outside of school that are providing true learning; however, the hours spent in school prevent him or her from spending enough time to pursue those interests in depth. You wonder how far your child might go with horseback riding, figure skating, or graphic design if given the opportunity to complete school requirements more efficiently. If your child has expressed frustration with the limited time available to practice or work at his or her interests, you now know that there is something you can do about it.

Homeschooling uses time so much more efficiently, allowing students to either integrate school subjects into their interests, or streamline completion of academic subjects, allowing more time for pursuing interests.

Even if you aren't a list maker by nature, now is a good time to make some lists. Mark down the things your children are interested in, your own interests and activities, and some clues to the kind of learners your children are. As you continue to think about home education, you can jot down additions to the list. Talk to your kids and get their input. All these factors are important, and getting them down on paper will help you begin to make some order out of the whirl of thoughts that are going through your mind. Once you have written the list, consider whether your child's current passion covers some of the subject areas required in institutional school. Likewise, think about whether connecting academic subjects to that interest would make learning academic subjects more appealing or pertinent to your child.

Stretching the Family Budget

If you're the organized sort who already knows exactly what your income and outgo are, you're in luck. You already know exactly how much (or how little) can be spared to cover home education expenses.

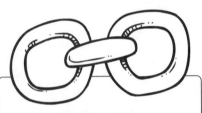

Learning Links

In *Homeschooling on a Shoestring: A Jam-Packed Guide* (see Appendix E), Melissa L. Morgan and Judith Waite Allee suggest dividing a page into three categories: Why are you working? Would your wallet allow you to quit? Do you have the will to make it happen? Within each category make two columns: Reasons for Keeping My Job and Reasons for Leaving My Job. The authors also include in-depth discussion of thinking through these issues.

However, if you aren't sure, now is a good time to find out where you stand financially. If you are presently depending on two incomes, what can you cut out in the way of expenses to make it possible for one of you to stay home with the kids? Or will you be able to work different shifts, so someone is always home with the kids?

If you've always been a one-income family, you're probably already used to making ends meet. With some creativity, many families have learned to stretch their incomes to cover the necessary expenses, and to prioritize to allow for fun without jeopardizing the budget. The long-term benefits are well worth any sacrifice.

Remember that many homeschoolers don't spend a lot of money for materials. Using the library, stocking your own home library with used books from a variety of sources, and making your own materials are thrifty ways to have it all without the expense. Searching for free and almost-free resources, bartering services, trading books with other homeschoolers, and starting a family business to employ the stay-at-home parents and the homeschooled children are all ways homeschoolers have managed to meet the financial challenge.

Stress due to financial difficulties can affect the learning environment. Keeping your expenditures reasonable, finding some ways to supplement your income, and teaching frugality and thriftiness as part of your homeschooling curriculum are ways to reduce such stress.

What If These Materials Don't Work Out?

Another stress that potential homeschoolers have is spending megabucks on materials that don't work out. That's why it's so important to take the time to do your homework before spending a large amount of money! Read through this chapter once more and take the time to obtain some more information about identifying learning styles and use this knowledge to make informed decisions. Despite the most careful planning, every homeschooler has made some major purchasing blunders. This is especially easy to do when you have no way to preview the materials because you purchase them through a catalog.

Look for the key words that help you identify the product regarding the type of learning it supports. Remember, copywriters sometimes use buzzwords that could be misleading to sell products, so if "hands-on" means there are cards to pick up, read, and sort, it probably won't be a thrill for your bodily/kinesthetic learner. If you have questions, most vendors will try to answer them. Some have hotlines that you can call specifically for curriculum questions.

When purchasing materials, always check with the vendor regarding the return policy. Some vendors advertise satisfaction guaranteed on all but consumable products. Return policies vary widely, so be sure you know what they are before ordering.

Finally, if you do your best to purchase appropriate materials and it just doesn't work out, there are a few things you can do:

Learning Lookouts

If you're given personal attention from a vendor at a curriculum fair or store, please don't go home and order the same product from a discount catalog. Small vendors and store owners can't always compete with catalogs dollarwise, but they offset this by providing answers to your questions and the ability to see and handle the materials. Reward their efforts with the sale!

➤ Put the materials away and see if they will work with another child or at a later time.

➤ Save them for the next curriculum swap or sale.

➤ Advertise them in a used-curriculum newsletter or on a Web site.

If you purchased a prepackaged, school-at-home curriculum that is not returnable, but you now realize it doesn't fit your children's learning style, don't despair. Use the curriculum as a guide for what you need to cover, and plug in activities and learning experiences that better fit your children's learning styles, abilities, and personalities. After you've gotten the year's worth out of the material as a guideline, implement one of the previous suggestions.

It's possible to salvage a textbook that has turned out to be dry and impossible to work with. Open it to the table of contents and use that as a guide in selecting twaddle-free books and materials to teach the same concepts that are dumbed down in the textbook.

Most clouds have a silver lining. Even your curriculum mistakes can teach you something: what *doesn't* work with your child!

The Least You Need to Know

➤ Your homeschooling program should reflect your family's worldview.

➤ Understanding your family's learning styles and your children's personalities and interests are key factors in planning learning experiences and purchasing materials for your children.

➤ Howard Gardner's theory of Multiple Intelligences shows that everyone can learn in a variety of different ways.

➤ Stresses like budget woes and making major mistakes choosing curriculum materials can be alleviated by careful planning.

Chapter 8

Sixth Grade in a Box: Using a Full-Service Program

You've decided that, at least for the first year of homeschooling, you want to find a full-service program to get through the adjustment period. There are many such programs available. It's important to choose a program that fits your family's needs in every way.

Each program has unique features, making it hard to compare one against the other. The best way to get a perfect fit is to determine if a program includes the services you need, fits your budget, has a workable schedule, and spells out its policies in the event that it simply doesn't work out for you despite your best efforts.

Full-Service Programs from A to Z

Full-service programs provide everything from school-at-home in a box to programs that turn all the learning decisions back to you. In between, you will find programs that provide variations on both themes, with unique features that may be just the thing for you. Types of full-service programs include …

➤ **Correspondence schools** provide course work, which enrollees complete and return for grading.

➤ **Independent study programs** provide courses by mail or online. Unlike most correspondence schools, many independent study programs help students design specialized studies. Some independent study programs are standalone programs; others are offered through universities, private schools, and learning centers.

➤ **Home-based programs** are usually associated with an institutional school, but may be stand-alone programs. They provide services for homeschoolers, such as curriculum planning, evaluation, record keeping, transcripts, and diplomas. In some cases, grading of course work may be provided; more often, parents are responsible for grading papers and reporting to the school.

➤ **Online programs** may be one part of a correspondence course, independent study program, or home-based program, or affiliated with a distance-learning program at a learning center or university.

➤ **Multimedia: video and CD-ROM programs** may offer video classes available mostly as individual classes, although A Beka has a complete K-12 video program. CD-ROM curriculum is available through some full-service providers and vendors.

In looking over the many programs available, you'll find that it's hard to put them into tidy little slots that correspond with these categories. For instance, some distance-learning programs are affiliated with colleges, some with private schools, and others are standalone programs. Correspondence courses are available as standalone programs, but also through private schools and some colleges. You will have to look at each program carefully, because you are not comparing apples with apples. There is a lot of variability in what is offered from one program to another. There are many unique programs; finding the one to fit your family is the challenge. The information in the following sections should help you narrow your choice. Check Appendix D, "Independent Study Programs and Support Schools, Publications and Vendors," for a listing of full-service programs.

Correspondence Schools

Most correspondence schools supply core courses plus electives which are mailed to students. Students receive textbooks, tests, and possibly some equipment required to supplement the texts, and mail their completed work back for grading. Prices range from $150 to over $1,000 per year. These schools issue transcripts and diplomas based on completed course work.

Correspondence schools offer courses ranging from elementary to high school level. Some provide both a general course and a college preparatory course for high school students. Others also provide online courses via the Internet. College-level courses are available from correspondence schools, as well, which is a good option for advanced study for high-schoolers. Some correspondence schools are standalone entities, while others are affiliated with a university or private school.

Learning Lookouts

Beware of diploma mills—shady businesses that require a fee and little more to issue a diploma and transcript. Ask for references and plenty of information about a program before signing on the dotted line. If it sounds too good to be true, it probably is.

Independent Study Programs

Many independent study programs provide courses by mail or online. Some offer more flexibility than others in designing a personalized or unique study based on needs or interests. Services vary widely from one program to another, but often include teacher support, curriculum design, record keeping, transcripts, and diplomas.

Home-Based Education Programs

Home-based programs affiliated with private schools (sometimes called umbrellas or satellites), and standalone programs (institutions that provide legal cover for home-schoolers but don't actually have a campus school), are available locally, statewide, or nationally. Some provide services for international students. These programs vary from structured to extremely flexible. Home-based program affiliates typically keep student records, help with curriculum planning and locating resources, and provide transcripts and grant diplomas. Fees vary. Some home-based programs charge an annual enrollment and tuition fee that covers all the children and all the services. Others charge a nominal enrollment and record-keeping fee, and then charge for services on an "as used" basis. Since there is quite a bit of overlap and variation in services, it's important to do your homework carefully when researching such programs.

Online Programs

Online programs can be one part of a distance-learning program offered by a correspondence school, independent study program, or home-based program. Online programs also exist through affiliation with a distance-learning program at a learning center or university. You can pick and choose online courses to supplement a purchased or self-planned curriculum or pursue all studies online. Pennsylvania Homeschoolers, the family business of the Richman family of Kittanning, Pennsylvania, makes *advanced placement (AP)* college courses available through online access via its Web site. These courses can be used for high school credit. Check Appendix B, "Curriculum Winners and Selected Resources, Including Dynamite Web Sites," for contact information.

Speaking Educationese

Advanced placement (AP) courses are college-level courses that are available to high school students for dual credit (both high school and college credit).

Multimedia: Video and CD-ROM

A Beka School Services, a full-service provider, has a complete video course package, enabling families to implement a Christian school program via the VCR. Alpha-Omega Publications offers the Switched-On Schoolhouse program for CD-ROM, and the Robinson Self-Teaching Curriculum is based on CD-ROMs supplemented by other materials. Other full-service providers have supplemental programs available on video or CD-ROM. You'll find contact information for these and other multimedia resources in Appendixes B and D.

Texts, Worksheets, and Record Keeping

By choosing to work with a full-service provider, you are agreeing to make yourself accountable in some way to that provider. Each school and program has a different criteria that you, as the homeschooler, must meet. Most full-service providers are relatively structured and have clear-cut guidelines for you to follow in implementing their programs. Many require certain texts; some provide them for a fee while others include course materials in their tuition. Be sure you determine which way the providers you are considering structure their fee scale, so you know what the total cost will be.

For those providers that include course work, you will receive materials either in the mail or online. Those providers that recommend certain materials, but do not provide them in the enrollment fee, often make them available by mail order. Some providers sell grade-level packages. It's important to know whether your child is reading at the level required for a specific grade, and whether the provider will let you make up a package according to your child's abilities. If your child is ahead in some areas and behind in others, choose a provider that will help you customize a package for your child. Many grade-specific programs have some deficiencies in meeting the needs of your child. School-in-a-box isn't the answer for everyone.

Some programs offer an *assessment test* to help determine your child's skill level. Find out if there is a prepurchase assessment that your child can take before you buy the program, to help you determine your child's grade level. If not, obtain an assessment test (see Appendix B) or compare your child's skills to a preplanned grade level curriculum to help you determine this yourself.

Speaking Educationese

An **assessment test** evaluates your child's readiness for certain grade-level specific materials.

Worksheets and workbooks are used by some full-service providers. Be sure your child's learning styles are verbal/linguistic and mathematical/logical (see Chapter 7, "So Much to Choose From," for a discussion of learning styles) before buying a program requiring a whole year of workbooks. Find out if you can get some samples to try with your child before buying a program. Some programs have samples available to download from their Web sites. Get them in the grade level that you believe your child is working at, and use them for a few days to see if the program suits your child.

Record keeping also varies from one full-service program to another. Most have specific record-keeping requirements. Plan to get with the program from the beginning, because procrastination only makes the job more difficult. Some schools, such as Clonlara Home Based Education Program (which I talk more about later in this chapter), are very flexible in their record-keeping requirements, encouraging parents and students to develop their own way of keeping records. However, even Clonlara expects high school records to be reported in a certain format, so whatever you have developed still needs to be translated into a form that is easy for Clonlara to deal with in developing transcripts for graduation. Be sure you understand record-keeping requirements from the get-go, so you aren't scrambling madly around at the last minute trying to resurrect clues to piece together forgotten learning activities.

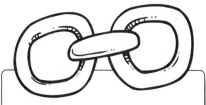

Learning Links

Ask how much time the average student spends doing course work each day in order to meet the requirements of the program. Consider what you know about your child to determine if it may take him more or less time to complete assignments.

Will We Have Time to Do Hands-On Projects?

If you've already determined that you have a bodily/kinesthetic or musical/ rhythmical learner, it won't take long in looking over the course work required by many full-service providers to realize that their programs may require quite a bit of seat work.

If your child is a reluctant reader and writer, an intensively academic program may not be in his or her best interest. Some programs are available that take these aspects into consideration. Even if your child is mathematical/logical or verbal/linguistic, a program that doesn't allow for some hands-on and interactive activity is soon going to pall. In her book *And What About College?* (see Appendix E, "Bibliography"), Cafi Cohen notes that the traditional school-at-home approach is associated with a high burnout rate. Beat the averages and plan for a program that will be exciting, joyful, and fun to implement right from the start.

Determine how flexible the program is. Some encourage input from parents. Some programs permit you to purchase their materials and specified services while opting out of school enrollment.

Spotlight on Education

Making a full-service program work for you may require some tweaking. For example, some parents purchase program materials but use them without provider oversight, and instead arrange for curricular evaluation through a local teacher. For another example, students can take two years to complete a specific grade level, doing half the course work each day and spending the other half of the day doing project-oriented activities and field trips, reading classics, and tending to chores on the farm, in the yard, and in the house.

Remember, the bottom line is to provide a rich educational experience for your child. Be sure you purchase a program that will work for all of you.

How Can I Tell If This Program Will Work for Us?

You can address this issue by looking at several programs side-by-side and comparing them to each other. Let's envision an imaginary student, Evan, who will be entering sixth grade in the fall. You've already determined that his learning style is a combination of mathematical/logical, musical/rhythmical, and bodily/kinesthetic. While he was in an institutional school, teachers variously told you that he may have a learning disability, is gifted, and doesn't pay attention. You also have a limited budget. With these clues, let's look at the following programs (which I chose because they are widely used and represent divergent philosophies) and decide which would best fit your family:

➤ A Beka Correspondence School's program is based on textbooks used in Christian schools and promotes a Christian worldview in all studies.

➤ Calvert School's program is drawn from the Calvert Day School Curriculum. Calvert's home instruction courses have been used to educate children since 1906.

➤ Clonlara Home Based Education Program provides a suggested curriculum as "working papers" and encourages enrollees to plan an individualized program.

➤ Laurel Springs School focuses on a student's abilities and learning styles, allowing students to work at their own pace.

➤ Moore Academy encourages use of the Moore Formula: balancing work, service, and study, while taking children's interests and abilities into consideration.

Your Family's Worldview

Although Evan's family is religious, that isn't their motivation for deciding to educate him at home. Evan, though obviously bright, has developed a very poor opinion of both learning and himself. Although they would strongly consider a Bible-based curriculum, that won't limit them in choosing a program. They know that they can teach him their values very clearly by modeling them in the home, attending worship services together, and living a life of service to others (see more about defining your family's worldview in Chapter 7). Most importantly, they want to find a program that will re-install a love and interest in learning.

Here's how each of these programs stacks up on worldview:

➤ **A Beka Correspondence School:** This school is a branch of the Pensacola Christian Academy. Christian textbooks are published by A Beka Books, an affiliate of Pensacola Christian College. This program is designed to provide a Christian education for English-speaking children.

➤ **Calvert School:** Calvert education follows very closely the Core Knowledge Sequence, a detailed outline of specific knowledge to be taught in grades K–8, developed by the Core Knowledge Foundation. It emphasizes study of the Classics, language arts (especially composition), and social studies.

Learning Links

Learn more about the Core Knowledge Sequence by visiting www.coreknowledge.org/ or reading *Cultural Literacy: What Every American Needs to Know,* by E. D. Hirsch (see Appendix E).

➤ **Clonlara Home Based Education Program:** In this program, children are encouraged to learn by doing real-life chores, determining the solutions to real-life problems, working with people who love and respect them, and having good, working adult models to imitate. Internal motivation rather than coercive external structure is strongly recommended. Living is learning.

➤ **Laurel Springs School:** This school's founders believe every child is a living treasure, has the ability to demonstrate genius, and needs a loving and supportive environment to enhance learning. The school honors the uniqueness of all students and appreciates the many learning styles children present.

➤ **Moore Academy:** This program has a three-part formula: Part 1) Study from a few minutes to several hours a day, depending on the child's maturity; 2) perform manual work at least as much as study; and 3) perform home and/or community service an hour or so each day.

Which program do you think fits Evan's family's worldview the best? It's a hard choice, isn't it? Remember, most of all they want a program that will help Evan love to learn again.

Your Maturing Educational Philosophy

It's rather difficult to separate worldview from educational philosophy (see Chapter 6, "Finding Support"), and some "experts" will tell you that worldview should take precedence over, or totally negate, educational philosophy or choice. However, many homeschoolers have proven that regardless of which educational philosophy you choose, you can still retain your intrinsic beliefs and values, modeling them for your children on a daily basis.

Comparing the choices by educational philosophy, determine which one would be most helpful to Evan's family:

➤ **A Beka Correspondence School:** This program provides you with Christian textbooks and workbooks which are designed to combat humanism and secularism. Minimum and maximum time frames are outlined and a fee is charged for extensions. Evaluations are performed by certified teachers every nine weeks.

➤ **Calvert School:** Calvert education is solidly grounded in the basics, using traditional methodology to teach strong skills and an important body of knowledge.

Preplacement tests are required. Enrollment is open and study may begin at any time of the year. Courses are planned for a nine-month school year, but children may progress at their own pace. To receive a certificate, a pupil must complete a course within two years under supervision of a Calvert advisory teacher.

➤ **Clonlara Home Based Education Program:** Families are encouraged to choose what is appropriate for them. Although textbooks are not recommended, Clonlara will respect and support you if textbooks are the right choice for you. Curriculum guides are provided for ideas, but enrollees may choose to substitute in any area and work at their own pace. Support teachers are available as needed by enrollees.

➤ **Laurel Springs School:** Homeschool families work with Laurel Springs staff to design their children's curriculum and correspond with support teachers on a monthly basis. Laurel Springs' curriculum can be adjusted to meet your child's interests and intellectual development; you can, for instance, order Fifth Grade English, Sixth Grade Math, and Seventh Grade Science for your sixth-grader.

➤ **Moore Academy:** Parents are advised to focus on kids' interests and needs and to model consistency, curiosity, and patience. Formal, scheduled study before the ages of 8 to 12 (depending on the child) is discouraged. Materials recommended are free-exploring and largely multilevel and self-teaching. Parents who follow the Moore approach have a very low level of burnout.

Now what do you think? Which program would work best for Evan's family?

Considering Learning Style and Strengths

Evan needs to move, touch, and feel the beat (indicating that his learning style is a combination of bodily/kinesthetic and musical/rhythmical) but he's also a whiz at figuring out math problems in his head. When he does a page of math, he misses some of the problems (his teachers say he's easily distracted), but when posed a verbal math problem, he gazes at the ceiling while talking himself through a complicated process, arriving at the correct answer almost every time! Since one of Evan's strengths lies in mental math, let's look at what each of the programs offers for math:

➤ **A Beka Correspondence School:** Courses cover the basic fundamentals on each grade level. No alterations can be made to the course when done for credit. The math program approaches math from a traditional Christian perspective which stresses the absolutes of God's creation, trains the mental ability of the student, and gives the student concrete facts upon which to build later mathematical understanding. Materials used include a math text, speed drills and tests, and flash cards.

➤ **Calvert School:** A placement test is required for grade six. Math materials include a math text, a mathematics manual, and reteaching worksheets.

➤ **Clonlara Home Based Education Program:** Recommendations include hands-on exploration and activities with concrete materials *(manipulatives)* in order to understand the abstract concepts and symbols of math. Clonlara also recommends multi-age non-textbooks about math.

➤ **Laurel Springs School:** Parents may choose from a basic math text at the level their child needs or a project-based curriculum for students who need a more concrete approach and a chance to apply math skills to the real world. Enrollment with an *IEP* is another option.

➤ **Moore Academy:** The Moore Foundation suggests drilling (but only for short periods daily) to develop math skills when children are ready in senses, brain, and reasoning, and learning math by earning money and accounting for it. Moore's catalog includes several choices that will appeal to various learning styles and interests.

Are you getting closer to choosing a full-service provider for Evan's family? Have you narrowed it to two or three possibilities yet? Let's look at the programs from another angle.

Interests and Goals

Evan is a little young to be making final choices about his future. However, most kids his age have a couple of ideas about what they want to be when they grow up. Most will change their minds several times before they graduate from high school.

Do the goals of these full-service providers take children's interests and goals into consideration?

➤ **A Beka Correspondence School:** The primary focus of this provider is to provide a curriculum that has a Christian worldview.

➤ **Calvert School:** This program's philosophy is that thorough instruction in the basics and the knowledge acquired through traditional methodologies will serve the student well in future endeavors.

➤ **Clonlara Home Based Education Program:** This provider's goals include maintaining the strength of the child's curiosity, self-esteem, self-confidence, and feeling of self-worth; that self-reliance, self-control, and a sense of responsibility to self and others grow to appropriate proportions; that the child gain the basic skills to manage his or her own affairs in the world; that the child become intimately familiar with the tools of learning and the many methods of acquiring knowledge; and that the child be supported in the developmental years on the route toward his or her highest possible human potential.

➤ **Laurel Springs School:** This school's stated goal is to provide a wide variety of options to best support your child's intellectual, emotional, and physical growth. Since learning takes place in all environments, Laurel Springs wants to work with parents to develop various opportunities and choose the ones that are appropriate for their child.

➤ **Moore Academy:** The Moore formula advises parents to open the door wide to knowledge, whatever their children's interests. Parents are encouraged to avoid textbooks and workbooks, instead providing biographies, nature books, and character-building literature.

Is it getting easier to decide which school Evan's parents should choose? You still have a couple more categories to consider before making a final decision.

The Bottom Line: Dollars and Sense

Some of these options look pretty interesting, don't you think? If you send away for information on these and other full-service providers, you will find even more possibilities. Let's take a look at the varying costs of these providers.

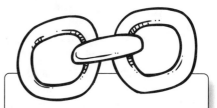

Learning Links

A sixth-grader shouldn't feel pressure to make career decisions at this age. His or her full-time job is being the best child he or she can be. If, on the other hand, a child has already exhibited interest in a specific field it can be helpful to nurture that interest by focusing curricular choices in related areas. Focused interest is a powerful motivation.

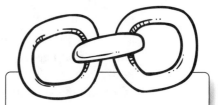

Learning Links

An interest in cars can lead to the study of chemistry and physics (internal combustion engines); economics (comparison shopping); math (figuring gas mileage, saving to buy a car); history (of automobiles or motorcycles); geography (mapping travel routes); languages (spoken in countries where cars or motorcycles are designed and built); cultures (study of countries where cars are designed and built); and development of manual skills (during apprenticeships or in home business).

What does it cost to enroll and what do the fees include?

➤ **A Beka Correspondence School:** Grade Six Basic Course fee is $600, with an optional fee of $3.75 for mailing envelopes to return student's work. Course materials are packaged and sent as a complete set. Correspondence instructors evaluate students' work every nine weeks. Tuition fee includes shipping charges for UPS delivery only within the contiguous Unites States. Additional fees are assessed for students living elsewhere, but reimbursement is made if actual shipping fees are less.

➤ **Calvert School:** Grade Six Basic Course is $595, which covers all books, workbooks, required supplies (protractors, crayons, for example), and teaching manual. The total fee is due upon enrollment. Calvert courses are shipped UPS ground service, U.S. parcel post, or foreign surface mail, at no additional cost. You must include additional shipping fees with enrollment if you select air shipment.

➤ **Clonlara:** The enrollment fee is $550 per year for families with one student enrolled in the United States, Canada, or Mexico. Enrolling two or three children is $575, and four or more is $600. The fee for overseas families with one student enrolled is $625 per year, two to three children is $650, and four or more is $675. There is a substantial discount for re-enrollment in subsequent years. Prorated tuition fees are available for those who enroll later in the school year.

Tuition includes enrollment, a contact teacher/mentor, contact with school authorities if needed, a suggested curriculum with order form, Math Skills guidebook, Communications Skills guidebook, newsletter, contact with other Clonlara families (on request), pen pals for students (on request) and postage/phone costs that originate in the Clonlara office. Tuition does not include textbooks and supplies or their shipping and handling costs, postage and telephone costs that originate with the family, or Standard Achievement Test costs.

Learning Lookouts

Full-service providers have different ways of structuring their fees. Be sure you request a full disclosure of what each fee covers and ask for clarification if you aren't sure what is included.

➤ **Laurel Springs School:** Enrollment begins on the day Laurel Springs receives your enrollment and book order form. One enrollment fee covers the entire family and is valid for one year. Partial (six month) enrollments are also available. You may choose from a variety of courses, Web-based or textbook-based. Depending on the program you choose, materials may include a syllabus (study guide), workbooks, tests, answer books, and CD-ROMs. Web-based, supplemental courses are available for either program.

Used textbook materials may be available; Laurel Springs buys back materials in good condition (except used or opened software).

Annual tuition includes teacher support, which varies with the type of program. Tuition may be paid annually, by semester, or in 10 monthly auto drafts or credit-card payments. Students who need more than 10 months to complete their work may have a two-month grade period at no charge, but then must file for extensions for an additional $25 per each two and one-half month extension.

➤ **Moore Academy:** Full-service program enrollment (required the first year) is $595, and may be paid with $211 down payment, with the balance of $384 due in four $96 payments made two, three, four, and five months from the date of the down payment. Student enrollment price includes a required $30 MFA (Moore Foundation Associate) fee and $15 for a "Moore Report International" newsletter subscription. Enrollment includes counseling from experienced educators. Beyond the first year you may choose the less-expensive independent study program.

What If We Don't Like the Program?

It's a little scary to think of investing hundreds of dollars into a full-service program, especially when you are buying materials by mail and haven't had an opportunity to review them. I know homeschoolers who have purchased three different programs before they found one they were satisfied with. Find out as much about the program and materials as you can ahead of time. Ask other homeschoolers to let you look at their materials, if they are using a program that you're considering. Attend a home-school conference where schools you are considering will be exhibiting.

These are the refund policies for the programs we're reviewing:

➤ **A Beka Correspondence School:** No refunds are available for partially completed or canceled courses. A reinstatement fee of $20 will be assessed to the account of a student whose work is not received within four months of beginning the course of study or who is placed on the inactive roll and then wishes to resume his or her course of study. Enrollment may be terminated at any time at the discretion of the administration. Noncompliance with guidelines will automatically result in termination.

➤ **Calvert School:** A refund of tuition fee will be issued if the complete course (books and supplies) is returned to Calvert unused; refunds must be requested within 90 days of enrollment. The teaching manual is leased and remains the property of Calvert School. All textbooks and supplies become the property of the pupil. Cancellations and withdrawals prior to enrollment are refunded in

117

full. Deductions will be made for postage and handling, and when appropriate, for testing and evaluation.

➤ **Clonlara Home Based Education Program:** If a family cancels enrollment, Clonlara must be notified within 10 days of a family's receipt of Clonlara material, (shipping records will be used to determine date of receipt). Refund will be made minus a $75 processing fee. Before a refund is issued, Clonlara must receive all materials and a written explanation of the reason for cancellation. If a refund is requested after 10 days, and Clonlara approves the special circumstances cited, the $75 processing fee will be charged, plus $50 for each two-week period that the materials are in the possession of the family.

➤ **Laurel Springs School:** If you are not fully satisfied, return the complete curriculum (or individual books) within 30 days for a refund. A $15 restocking fee will be assessed. The amount of refund will depend upon the condition of the materials. There is no refund on shipping costs or bank fees incurred from processing your credit card. If enrollment is canceled within 30 days, all of the enrollment fee (less a $50 registration fee) will be refunded. After 30 days no money will be refunded.

➤ **Moore Academy:** According to Dorothy Moore, they will work with families on a case-by-case basis. She adds that they haven't had many requests for refunds.

Finally! We've covered all the bases. Which program do you think will work best for Evan? And which will work for you and yours?

Learning Lookouts

Send away for information from full-service providers and do your homework, so you know exactly what is provided and how flexible or inflexible each program is. You'll find contact information in Appendix D.

The Pros and Cons of Using a Full-Service Program

Some families report that they like having a planned curriculum and materials, as well as a contact teacher readily available. Some families say that using a full-service school helps keep them accountable. Others families like a program because it doesn't require reports to be filed by a certain date. These families opt for a more flexible program. The full-service programs discussed in this chapter vary quite a bit in structure and flexibility. Most families who wish to use a full-service program should be able to find one that is structured enough or flexible enough to meet their needs. Some homeschool families find it objectionable that some programs don't have specific requirements, while others object to requirements they find too stringent.

If choosing a program that runs parallel to your beliefs would be important to you, be sure the program you choose also fits your other criteria (flexibility, adaptability to your child's learning style, and so on). Lack of flexibility is an issue with some programs; however, some programs are extremely flexible. Cost is a big issue for many homeschoolers. If all the dollar amounts made you flinch and gasp, it's time to start thinking about planning your own curriculum. Continue on to the next chapter for complete information on writing your own curriculum.

The Least You Need to Know

➤ If you are considering a full-service program, do your homework!

➤ Full-service providers vary from extremely inflexible to very flexible.

➤ Be sure the full-service provider you choose fits your family's needs before you take the plunge.

➤ Have the refund policies in writing, in case, despite every precaution, you have to cancel.

➤ If you decide against a full-service provider, the research you have done on the many options will stand you in good stead as you plan your own curriculum.

Out of the Box: Planning Your Own Curriculum

The most important element in planning your own curriculum is your child. While putting together an educational plan, be sure to keep his or her needs uppermost as choices are made. Planning and writing a curriculum for your child should be a labor of love, motivated by a desire to provide the best learning experience for that particular child.

Whether the plan you write turns out to be detailed and professional in appearance or is simply a list of goals and possibilities in a loose-leaf binder is immaterial. The important thing is whether the plan you've made is right for your child.

Using One or Several Scope and Sequences as Models

Begin by obtaining one or more sample scope and sequences to use as you plan your curriculum. Pat Montgomery, Director of Clonlara School, suggests that enrollees use

Learning Lookouts

Notice how much repetition and review there is within the 13 years of a scope and sequence. Homeschoolers have found that with one-on-one tutorial learning along with interest-led learning, retention is so much higher that excessive repetition and review soon become frustrating. By cutting back unnecessary review, you will have more time to pursue other studies.

Learning Links

If you have three children at different grade levels, and the scope and sequence you are looking at has each grade doing a different type of social studies, for example, consider taking world history one year, American history the next, and state history the third year, rather than juggling all three every year.

the sample curriculum provided by the school as a working paper. This is a good way to look at any sample curriculum or scope and sequence from any source. There is no one right or perfect scope and sequence. When you look at the samples you will soon see that many elements are similar from one to another.

Scoping Out a Scope and Sequence

As I mentioned in Chapter 5, "Approaches to Home Education," scope and sequence or curriculum is, first of all, simply a listing of subject areas. Each one has been put together to fit someone's idea of the areas that should be covered and in what order they should be covered. A typical scope and sequence will be broken down into grade levels, Grade 1, Grade 2, and so on. Most sample scope and sequences will go from Kindergarten through Grade 12.

Within each grade level is a listing of subject areas, such as mathematics, social studies, and language arts. Subheadings under language arts can include reading, literature and poetry, penmanship, and spelling.

Who Learns What When?

Your scope and sequence can be a flexible plan, outlining who in your homeschool will learn what subjects and when they will learn them. You can also include ideas of how they will learn them, as well as specific books, materials, and projects. Don't be surprised if everything doesn't work out the way you planned. And you don't have to do everything that's listed in all the curricula you see, either. Remember, these are working papers.

If you plan to cover a topic in three weeks and at the end of that time your children are clamoring for more, more, more on that topic, *now* is the time to cover it. Build on that interest while it is there. There will be time to cover the other areas another time. Some things will take less time than you planned for, as well.

Finding a Scope and Sequence

Many full-service providers make their scope and sequence available on their Web sites. Some even list the books and materials they use to cover those subject areas. If you request materials from some of the full-service providers discussed in Chapter 8, "Sixth Grade in a Box: Using a Full-Service Program," you will receive some scope and sequence materials built right into their catalogs.

An excellent book that gives you a step-by-step plan for designing your own curriculum according to your child's needs and your values and beliefs is *How to Write a Low-Cost/No-Cost Curriculum for Your Home-School Child* by Borg Hendrickson (see Appendix E, "Bibliography"). This is the perfect resource if you need to submit a sample curriculum to fulfill requirements. Remember, submit only what is required! Even if you aren't apt to actually make up the lists and do all the steps, read through this book. It's chock full of good ideas and thought-provoking comments.

Learning Links

World Book Encyclopedia will mail you one copy of its "Typical Course of Study" free of charge. Call 1-800-WORLDBK. It's also available from its Web site at www.worldbook.com/ptrc/html/curr.htm.

Cathy Duffy's books on planning curriculum take the mystery out of curriculum planning with reviews, recommendations, information on learning styles, and tips on teaching, planning, and record keeping. Remember to use these, and other books, as tools, not as something you have to live up to, imitate, or follow rigidly. Any curriculum planning book, from any perspective, is a potential tool in your quest to plan your child's educational experience. Take the parts that are useful to you and leave the rest. Check Appendix E for information on Duffy's books and for more books on curriculum planning.

Homeschool catalogs are also useful resources for planning a curriculum. Some have essays that explain various points about the materials or homeschool approaches. Many are divided up by age levels or subject areas. Check the index, make a list of the subject areas, find the materials that pertain to the ages or skill levels of your children, and pick and choose likely materials. Some catalogs have toll-free numbers you can call to ask questions about specific materials. A couple of catalogs have consultants that will help you plan a curriculum.

Can I Write My Own Scope and Sequence?

Of course you can, if you want to! Homeschool parents have been doing this for a long, long time. Children once learned from their parents what their parents had learned from their parents before them. Skills, trades, and crafts were handed down easily and naturally; children learned by observation, experience, and practice.

Homeschooling can be much the same. You may not need to do anything more than keep a couple of preplanned curricula in the file to refer to now and then. If that works for you, great!

If you do plan a scope and sequence around the academic subjects, be sure to plan time for the children to work with you around the house. If you do chores together and teach your children step-by-step, eventually you'll have some excellent helpers. Children like to feel needed, and many homeschool kids are very aware that in order for them to continue to homeschool, everyone has to help Mom. Cook together and practice fractions by doubling recipes or cutting them in half, learn about biology by gardening, experiment with crafts, and live joyously.

Spotlight on Education

My son Ryan was having a hard time grasping fractions, so I asked him to help me in the kitchen. We started by talking about the measuring cups and spoons and how important it is to understand which is which. We set up all the measuring cups and looked at the markings. We poured four sets of the ¼-cup measure into the 1-cup measure. We poured two sets of the ½-cup measure into the 1-cup measure. We measured lots of rice just to understand the measuring cups and spoons, and then we baked brownies. Ryan had a much clearer understanding of fractions after that.

Don't allow yourself to be caught up in a rat race. Academic learning is only a part of the learning we do in life. Children need to learn from life, as well as from academic resources. Many of the things we learn from books can be learned better from hands-on experience.

Children will need to be able to run a household, balance a checkbook, figure their gas mileage, and budget for groceries. Yes! You can write your own scope and sequence, and you can incorporate joy into it. If your child loves to help in the kitchen, by all means, start there.

If your child's forte is the workshop or the garage, find ways to bring the child into those areas to learn. Stretch your thinking to discover ways to light the fire of learning for your child.

Start with Your Kids

If your children are very young, ask them simple questions to get their input. If you are planning nature studies for science, ask them if they like cats or dogs better, insects or birds, land animals or ocean animals. Rather than asking them an open-ended question that can be answered with yes or no, ask them something that requires a choice. You can then assure them that you will be studying things they like best; the other areas can be touched on as they relate to the chosen topic.

Older children can be very involved with, and quite decisive about, curriculum planning. The more involved the child, the more interest is usually shown when it's time to start studying. If your children are aware that you are planning to begin homeschooling in a couple of months, and are champing at the bit to begin, get some books from the library on subjects that interest them and let them begin. Learning does not have to be compartmentalized. You may discover that learning from living books is a good way to engage your students. Save the money you would have spent on texts or other materials by checking out books from the library, and then plan for some day trips or other educational outings. Be creative. The sky's the limit!

Learning Links

Usborne Books has a little gem of a book called *Science in the Kitchen*. There are lots of fun, messy projects full of squishing, tasting, and smelling, plus a project that results in yummy dinner rolls, while teaching about yeast forming a gas that makes bubbles in the dough!

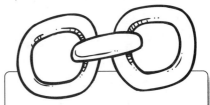

Learning Links

Visit a museum and observe your children's reactions to exhibits. Use their interests as a starting point in choosing materials and books to study.

What Are My Kids' Interests?

If you don't know, don't ask yourself, ask your kids. Ask them questions that can't be answered with yes or no. If your kids don't give you definitive answers, narrow the questioning. For instance, if you begin by asking, "Do you like history?" and get "I don't know" or "No" for an answer, ask your kids, "Would you prefer learning about how the United States became a country, or about the ancient Romans and Greeks?" If the answer is "I don't know" or "Neither," try asking the children if they would like to study real people in history. Many homeschoolers have their children read biographies and historical fiction to get them interested in history. Many children think of history as a boring set of unrelated, unconnected facts, names, and dates. Making the connections is the important part.

Ask your children if they would like to learn about their own family's history. Homeschoolers have found that studying genealogy is a very interesting way to learn about the history of their country and the world, along with their family history. Young children will enjoy making a book about themselves. Help them find snapshots of themselves, siblings, pets, parents, grandparents, cousins, aunts, and uncles. Let the youngsters arrange the pictures and label them. Older children may enjoy researching the family tree by tracing genealogical records, interviewing elderly (and not so elderly) parents and other relatives, visiting courthouses, and sending away for vital records. Once an interest is sparked, it's a quick jump to learning about the time periods of the various generations. Start with the child, his or her close family, and then branch out, until eventually the child can make a time line of his or her family tree.

Your Goals and Priorities

It's easy to become so involved with the logistics of planning for the year ahead that you forget the long-term goals and priorities you have for your children. As you learn more about homeschooling and get to know your children better, your goals and priorities may change. Use the following list as a starting point for making your own list of goals.

I want my child to …

➤ Be capable and self-reliant.

➤ Respect cultural and ethnic differences.

➤ Be a contributing citizen.

➤ Know how to cooperate with others.

➤ Be a lifelong learner.

➤ Learn skills for the sake of the skill, not because someone else is learning it, or because he or she *should.*

➤ Be physically fit.

➤ Find work he or she loves.

➤ Be happy.

➤ Realize life is education and education is life.

➤ Be creative or inventive.

➤ Be able to sustain relationships.

➤ Appreciate music and art.

These are just a few of the goals homeschoolers have for their children. Your list may include others.

Where Do I Find Resources?

Everywhere! Your kitchen, workshop, garage, the library, toy stores, computer stores, homeschool vendors, publishers, bookstores, yard sales, specialty shops, Grandma's attic, and the community. The list is endless. Homeschoolers are learning in every way from school-in-a-box to life itself. Many homeschoolers seek a middle ground, and blend ideas from traditional and not-so-conventional educational methods to find the right combination of activities to suit their philosophy, worldview, and their kids' abilities and learning styles. Check Appendix B, "Curriculum Winners and Selected Resources, Including Dynamite Web Sites," for materials and products that homeschoolers have been using successfully.

Make sure you look at any potential resource—whether it's a book, a text, workbook, or packaged unit study—with the needs of your child uppermost in your mind. Besides the learning abilities and differences of your child, consider whether it

Learning Lookouts

Does your child thrive on verbal/ linguistic materials such as worksheets and texts with study guides? Or is he or she auditory and might retain more by listening to books on audio tape or hearing you read the book out loud? Does your child need movement? Does the material being considered incorporate action projects and tactile activities?

will fit your educational philosophy (see Chapter 6, "Finding Support"). Does it teach from a worldview you are comfortable with, or will you need to adapt it to your own use? Remember, you don't have to find something that is perfect just as it is. On the other hand, why make yourself work if you *can* find something that you can use as is? You have to set your priorities. Finally, can you afford it? Is it something you can reuse with other children for several years, making it worth paying a little more for it? Can you make something similar for much less money? The choice is yours.

Real Life as the Curriculum

Once upon a time homeschoolers learned from life; most people didn't go to school. Nearly everyone learned that way, and everyone had their parents as their first teachers, then branched out to learn from grandparents, neighbors, mentors, and employers. It was during the Industrial Revolution that compulsory schooling came into being and people began to equate schooling with education. Despite that, some successful and famous people had little or no formal schooling, and learned enough from life to invent new products (Wilbur and Orville Wright and Alexander Graham Bell), discover new concepts (Pierre Curie and Blaise Pascal), amass fortunes (Andrew Carnegie and Jimmy Lai, founder of Giordano International), or perform feats that attracted acclaim (George Rogers Clark and Tamara McKinney, World Cup skier).

Many homeschoolers learn as much or more from everyday experiences of life as from their academic studies. Sometimes their education happens serendipitously, as the result of the desire to earn some money, or because of their pursuit of an interest. Others have deliberately entered into an experience because of the possibility of learning something new and have learned not only what they set out to learn, but much, much more!

Consider these examples of real-life learning:

➤ Ryan was 12 when he acquired a lawn mower and began mowing for one of his father's painting customers. Through word of mouth he got more customers and soon his nine-year-old brother became his partner. From the beginning they saved a percentage for college, and a portion for maintenance of their equipment. Later Ryan acquired a used lawn tractor in trade for painting a farm tractor for a friend, and the boys purchased a string trimmer. Ryan took a correspondence course in small engine repair and did all the maintenance and repairs on their equipment. His brother Aaron took over the bookkeeping, billed the customers, and kept a record of earnings, savings, maintenance fund, and expenses.

➤ Logan, 14, enjoyed hands-on activity and wasn't inspired to do academic work. When his mom was elected to the community water board, she found a volunteer position for Logan with the water master. The board's need for an excavator led Logan's parents to purchase a tractor with several attachments, which Logan leased with his earnings. Logan began to do excavating for the community and for private customers. As demand for Logan's services grew, Logan fielded phone inquiries, learned new skills, and recently won a two-year contract as sole excavator for the community. Logan, now 15, has discovered a reason to study and the importance of learning. Logan plans to attend college and major in construction management.

➤ Andrea, 15, raised a puppy for Guide Dogs for the Blind. She named the puppy Faraday and took him anywhere a blind person might want to go. When she was tempted to allow him to do something that was forbidden, she thought about how it would affect the blind person who would get Faraday as a guide dog. At the end of the year, Faraday, her friend and confidante, left to continue his training. She discovered, through her heartache, that self-sacrifice has made her a better, kinder, more thoughtful person. Andrea recently completed a summer internship at Guide Dogs for the Blind.

➤ Growing up on a farm, John built a greenhouse when he started high school, for the fun of the experience and to conduct some growing experiments. After two years, John had accumulated enough plants to sell about $200 worth at a fund-raising sale. Impressed, he began to grow plants for profit, selling them at the local farmer's market. During his second year of college, John built another, bigger greenhouse. Although he makes only about $5,000 to $7,000 per year on the venture, he will continue after college graduation. He plans to buy into his father's farm, and keep the garden/greenhouse business on the side.

Learning from life imprints indelible lessons on the mind and heart. Immersion learning is an accepted way to enable foreign language majors to not only be able to read and understand a language, but to communicate with native speakers of that language. Immersion in life is one way that homeschoolers provide a well-rounded education for their children, one that enables them to function in the real world before they reach an age where they must.

Translating Real-Life Experience into Educationese

Families keep records that can vary from photos and videotapes of large projects or experiences to portfolios with essays, contest entries, and artwork. They write in journals and diaries, or they save notebooks with jottings, calendars with entries, and shoe boxes full of memorabilia such as ribbons from the fair and certificates from swimming class, the summer reading program, and the homeschool science fair.

Speaking Educationese

Educationese is a unique language used by teachers who perform evaluations, college recruiters, and admissions officers. As a homeschooler, you must take real-life learning experiences and translate them into a form that is easily understood by people in the academic community.

Figuring out how these activities all fit into curriculum areas can seem daunting, but with a little practice most homeschoolers become very adept at knowing what to call the activities their children participate in. Translating such activities into *educationese* for school officials and assessors becomes easier with practice.

If you are required to keep records for your state, or work with a support school or umbrella and need authentic-looking records to submit, or if you simply want to prepare a decent transcript for your child, how can you assign curricular names to real-life activities?

Here are some examples drawn from my own family's experience, as well as other homeschoolers I've met or corresponded with:

➤ Mow grass using a push mower: physical education

➤ Keep books for a mowing business: math

➤ Write to a pen pal: language arts

➤ Practice calligraphy: handwriting/art

➤ Read *Time* or *Newsweek:* social studies/current events

➤ Play Yahtzee: math

➤ Do genealogy research: history/language arts

➤ Make a scrapbook: art

➤ Garden: science/physical education

➤ Play Monopoly: Economics/consumer math

➤ Cook dinner or bake cookies: science/math/life skills

➤ Paint T-shirts: art

➤ Snowboard/skateboard/ski: physical education

➤ Research Grandma's health condition on the Internet: health studies

As you can see, nearly all these activities are things children might do without having them assigned. Most are everyday things that people do for fun, relaxation, or because it needs to be done. Yet all are real-life, educational activities; all are learning experiences; all can be categorized into curriculum areas.

Compliance with State Homeschool Requirements

Many homeschoolers live in states that have requirements, such as equivalent education or the submission of a curriculum. How can you be in compliance with these requirements if you choose to use an eclectic approach with your children? Observe your children's everyday activities during a break from school or over summer vacation. How many of the things they do during their free time give you clues, not only to curricular areas you could slot them into, but to your children's interests?

Look over the requirements. If your state requires you to submit a curriculum, list resource materials you plan to use for each subject area. Because you list a textbook you don't have to read every word and cover every chapter.

You can also use the textbook in the usual way, supplementing with some of the suggestions mentioned in the previous sidebar.

If your state requires an equivalent education, that means the state wants a homeschooler to learn the same things as would be presented in the public schools. The state isn't saying you have to do it in exactly the same way. Obviously children who are working one-on-one with their parent as teacher will not be taught in the same way that a class full of 20 to 30 students will be taught. Even if you have several children at home, you will still have more time to spend interacting individually with your children than the typical public school teacher could spend. Homeschooling is extremely efficient. You can use methods, resources, and techniques that simply will not work in an institutional school setting, and achieve excellent results. Your child can receive not only an equivalent education, but a superior one.

Spotlight on Education

You can use a textbook as a guide for determining what areas to cover, teaching from living books from the library, from the bookstore, or from your own bookshelves. You can read aloud to your children from those books or give them the books to read themselves. You can discuss the books with your kids or have them narrate the stories to you. Some homeschool kids get creative and make posters advertising the book as it would be advertised if it were a play. Others make dioramas in a shoe box to illustrate a favorite part of a book.

Covering All the Subjects

Choosing topics to study from a book is a way to expand the curricular impact of a book-driven curriculum. While reading the Laura Ingalls Wilder's *Little House* series to my children, I kept a notebook beside me. In it I kept a list of the various animals and plants mentioned in the stories. We checked out books from the library to continue our studies across the curriculum. We also kept a map of the United States on the wall to mark the many places the Ingalls and Wilder families lived. Thus, by using a set of historical fiction books, we covered every subject area except math. You can do the same thing with any book or series of books. Here's how we did it:

➤ Social studies: We read the *Little House* series and discussed why the family moved so much, the differences in the way they did everyday chores, the lack of labor-saving devices, and what they did to entertain themselves.

➤ Geography: We traced their journey on a map, using map pins to mark the places they lived. We looked up the states they lived in and read about the states in the encyclopedia.

➤ Science: We studied the plants and animals mentioned in the books.

➤ Language arts: We made a scrapbook with short essays and pictures about the states where the Ingalls and Wilder family lived, and the plants and animals they encountered along the way.

➤ Life skills: We prepared foods from the *Little House Cookbook: Frontier Foods from Laura Ingalls Wilder's Classic Stories* by Barbara M. Walker (HarperCollins, 1985), and made butter the old-fashioned way.

When a topic of interest to your child comes up, begin to make mental notes of the various curriculum areas that are being covered as he or she pursues that interest. Facilitate learning by helping your child find materials, books, programs, and other resources. Make suggestions and help implement those that are accepted eagerly. Don't push, but be available to help your children plan.

You can teach independence, creative thinking, research skills, and much more by taking a hands-off approach. Your hands are still on the reins, providing a certain amount of guidance but the child has the thrill of planning, researching, and following up on his or her interest.

Finding Resources Within Your Community

You've already heard about using the library, searching for the used book stores in your area, and checking out yard sales and Grandma's attic. Your community is a rich source of materials; most of us just aren't used to looking at our area through the eyes of a homeschooler. Many homeschoolers use 4-H, Scouts, Campfire, and similar groups as a source of learning and social experience. While schooled parents may look on many of these activities as *extracurricular*, homeschoolers realize that these groups are rich in educational experience.

Some areas have special homeschool troops or 4-H groups that work on their merit badges or projects as part of their curriculum. Even if you don't have a purely homeschool group, check out the projects with new eyes. Learning wilderness safety is social studies. Doing a crafts project is art. Learning animal husbandry (raising sheep, pigs, or rabbits, or learning to show cats, horses, or steers) is science. Woodworking projects, baking, canning, sewing … the list is endless.

For those whose children aren't interested in doing group activities, most cooperative extension services will make materials available for your child to pursue such projects on his or her own. When my daughter wanted to learn about goats and rabbits, I requested materials through the cooperative extension service, as well as the library. Many libraries also have Boy Scout and Girl Scout manuals available, so your child can duplicate the projects done for merit badges. The learning experience is the same, and if your children prefer working on their own, at their own speed, why not?

Check the Yellow Pages for museums, and visit the local ones. Call on your Chamber of Commerce for information about what visitors to the area are told to visit. Play tourist in your own town, and visit the local scenic points, overlooks, and historical spots. Attend town hall or city hall meetings. Plan field trips to businesses in the area. Attend local health fairs, festivals, church programs that are open to the public, open-air music concerts, or whatever catches your eye. Sometimes an area of interest that you wouldn't have known about is sparked simply by doing something a little different. If you have a quilter's club, an antique engines club, a motorcycle club, or a community orchestra, contact a member and find out about visiting and talking to members about their interests. People who have a love and passion are usually happy to share it with others.

Many homeschoolers have learned to use the word "curriculum" very loosely. Simply put, curriculum means "who learns what when?" Although you may have to provide your state with a list of subject areas and the resources and materials you plan to use to educate your children, remember that much of what your children learn may be learned from life. The world can be their classroom. We aren't limited to learning about the world while sitting at a desk, being presented with small bits of unconnected information for specific periods of time during the day. We can live it, experience it, see it, taste it, feel it, while drinking in and soaking up the myriad lessons that are there for the taking. Go ahead! Reach out and try it.

The Least You Need to Know

➤ A scope and sequence, also known as a curriculum, is someone's idea of who should learn what when.

➤ You can write your own curriculum; use a scope and sequence for a game plan, model your own after someone else's, or make up your own plan according to your child's interests and needs.

➤ The world around you is a treasure trove of resources which you can use to enrich your curriculum: Living books, museums, clubs, programs, projects, jobs, community service, and field trips make the list of curricular objectives come to life.

➤ Real life as the curriculum translates very nicely into educationese, complies with homeschool regulations, and covers all the subject areas.

Part 4

Taking the Plunge: What Do I Do Now?

Once you're ready to jump in, you'll learn that homeschooling can be structured or flexible, depending upon which will work best for your family's needs. Considering the ages and learning styles of your children, you can create and personalize a program to suit every individual in your family.

Whatever the age of your child, whether he or she needs an extra challenge, has learning difficulties or special needs, this part is full of information that will give you the confidence to make informed choices for your family's learning program.

Chapter 10

Learning at Home with Three- to Five-Year-Olds

In This Chapter

➤ Considering the many ways three- to five-year-olds learn

➤ Providing a safe environment, interaction with family members, and interactive toys

➤ Deciding whether a playgroup, a cooperative preschool, or home-based learning better fits your young child

➤ Creating your own preschool curriculum

Lucky you! Homeschooling has become a mainstream choice, homeschoolers are everywhere, and you've learned about homeschooling in time to make a decision before sending your children off to school. The years since your toddlers were born have flown by and you can't imagine sending them off to all-day kindergarten yet. They still love their snuggles with you in the morning, taking walks before lunch, having you read to them and sing with them, and they still need an afternoon nap!

Children are so innocent and precious at this age, and you'd like to preserve that just a little longer. You can. Insulating your kids, providing them with positive socialization when they are ready for it, and teaching them yourself are important ways to nurture your three- to five-year-olds.

You Are Your Child's First Teacher

Safety, security, interactive toys, and plenty of your time and attention are the most valuable commodities to a *preschooler* (a child under the age of five). Just watch those little ones! They pretend to talk on the phone, stir up something in a bowl, sweep the floor with the little broom and dustpan, and "read" a book upside down. They are learning by imitating everything you do. It's one of the ways in which they learn.

Speaking Educationese

Preschooler is the institutional designation for a child under the age of five.

Exciting, but a little scary, isn't it? You are your child's first teacher; always have been, always will be. These early years, from birth to five, are the most impressionable, and children learn a larger body of knowledge during this time period than they ever will again. Realize that almost none of it will come from books. It's learned by observation, imitation, playing, helping, talking, and listening.

Please Read to Me

Studies have shown that parents who read to their children and are avid readers themselves model a behavior that is extremely important to their children's development. Occasionally, but rarely, readers have children who are nonreaders. The best way to develop children who are readers is to read to them—early and often.

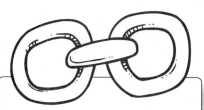

Learning Links

The Read-Aloud Handbook, by Jim Trelease (Penguin USA, 1995) and *Honey for a Child's Heart,* by Gladys Hunt (Zondervan Publishing House, 1989) both suggest books to use in a read-aloud program for children of all ages. For more ideas and tips, check out these resources from your local library.

Some people begin reading to their children while they are still in the womb! Studies have proven that babies recognize their parents' voices immediately after birth. Some babies have recognized music that their parents played repeatedly while their children were still in the womb! So, go ahead, read Dr. Suess and other children's books to your child before he or she is born. It's good practice for all the stories you're going to read to him or her after birth.

Using a Purchased Curriculum

Yes, there are homeschool programs available for teaching your preschooler at home. Most preschoolers don't need a packaged curriculum to learn; however, if you're interested in using one, turn to Appendix B, "Curriculum Winners and Selected Resources, Including Dynamite Web Sites," for a list of some available preschool programs. Just remember that little ones have short attention spans and need your attention, love, and care more than they need academics. Choose programs that are weighted towards hands-on, project- and activity-based experiential learning.

Preschool-at-Home: The Traditional Approach

Traditional institutional preschool programs typically include hands-on activities: coloring, cutting, pasting, playing with clay, counting, singing, learning rhymes and games, playing in the playground, and learning to get along with others. You can find the materials at your local discount department store to create learning centers for your three- to five-year-old. From tubs of counting bears to crayons, from special safety scissors to nontoxic clay and little workbooks to teach shapes and colors, it's all there. Sampling such activities for short spurts on a daily basis can be fun, and your child will enjoy the interaction and undivided attention if you keep activities relaxed and nonstressful.

Using a packaged program such as Before Five In A Row (FIAR), available from Five-In-A-Row Publishing, or Preschool Plus, published by Hewitt Homeschooling Resources, can provide you with some ideas if you don't know where to start. A large bookstore or your public library can provide a number of books with preschool activities. However, try not to get overwhelmed or carried away with doing everything suggested in every program or book. Use the program; don't let it use you.

Learning Lookouts

Some preschools have become miniature academies to prepare tots for extremely competitive, academically oriented kindergartens. Worksheets and drills prevail, with eye-hand coordination and large motor skills taking a secondary position. Beware of emulating these programs in your home.

Using the Unit Study Method

If you're intrigued with the idea of unit studies and want to begin now, just choose a topic. Let's use farms as an example. Purchase or borrow from the library some books about farms, farm animals, tractors, and related topics such as …

➤ *Farming* by Gail Gibbons (Holiday House, 1990)

➤ *If It Weren't for Farmers* by Allan Fowler (Children's Press, 1994)

➤ *Drive a Tractor* by Lara Tankel Holtz (DK Publishing, 1999)

➤ *The Silly Sheepdog* by Heather Amery and Stephen Cartwright (EDC Publications, 1992)

➤ *Picking Apples & Pumpkins* by Amy Hutchings (Cartwheel Books, 1994)

Read a story or two to your child; then talk to him about the story you read. What does he remember? What did he like? Can he point at items in the pictures as you name them?

Have your child draw a picture and tell you what it's about; print the information on the page. Talk about the picture with her; point at parts of the picture and ask her to explain it. Don't label the picture with words for your child; ask *her* what it is. Save the pictures and after a week or two involve your child in putting them together into a book. Have her draw a picture for the cover. Print her name lightly on the cover so she can trace it with a crayon.

Count the number of objects in pictures. For example, show your child a picture of a field with haystacks and ask him how many haystacks are in the picture. Point and count; then, have your child point and count. Find shapes in pictures: the triangle in the gable end of the farmhouse, the square of the house itself, the circles of the tractor wheels. Compare things: the picture of the big cow versus the little dog, the large barn versus the small shed. Name the colors: a red barn, a green tractor, a brown cow, and a yellow flower.

Arrange to visit a farm near your community. Point out the things you have seen in the stories you've read. Talk about them with your child while you're there. Talk about the people who live and work on the farm. Reread the stories and talk about the things you saw during the farm visit.

Explain how we get our food from farms all over the country. When you visit the grocery store, show your child the products that come from the farm. At mealtime, talk about the milk you are drinking and how it came from a cow on a farm.

Spotlight on Education

Tie-ins to your relaxed unit study will pop up everywhere you go. We learned two farm riddles at day camp recently:

> You throw away the outside and cook the inside, then eat the outside and throw away the inside. What is it? *Corn on the cob!*

> A big green house has a smaller white house inside. The white house has a smaller red house inside. The red house has lots of black and white babies inside. What is it? *Watermelon!*

Corn on the cob and watermelon are both grown on a farm. There you go! A unit study, across the curriculum. Something just that simple can spark an interest: Children notice the smallest events and most minute details and form connections between what has already been learned and the new information.

Creating Your Own Curriculum

Depending on the abilities and interest level of your three- to five-year-old, you can create a curriculum specifically for him or her. Your time and attention are more valuable than any educational toys. Many children's story books are based on learning various concepts, such as shapes, colors, numbers, counting, and other languages and cultures. A visit to the library or bookstore will prove to you that you can provide a rich education with books as a starting point for ideas.

Start with the basics and branch out from there:

➤ **Reading:** Read to your child regularly and provide a variety of books for the child to "read" to him- or herself. Let your child arrange magnetic letters on the refrigerator.

➤ **Writing:** Provide crayons, washable markers, and several different types of paper; let your child scribble to his or her heart's content. Provide colorful workbooks with letters to trace, and a big chalkboard for tracing big letters and numbers.

Learning Lookouts

Many young children like to put things in their mouths. Make sure your children don't put magnetic letters, shells, or other small objects that could be a choking hazard into their mouths.

➤ **Arithmetic:** Provide counting manipulatives (beans, shells, plastic bears), magnetic numbers for the refrigerator, a tape measure, rulers, and an oversize calculator (kids like real tools).

➤ **Science:** Plant seeds together, take walks and bring home leaves and other items to identify, do crayon rubbings of leaves, notice birds, butterflies, and animals. Read stories about animals, plants, colors, the Earth and the sky.

➤ **Social studies:** Read about other countries, other cultures, small towns, farms, big cities, careers (police officer, firefighter, nurse, doctor, and newspaper reporter), visit city hall, a farm, the police station, fire station, a doctor's or dentist's office, a newspaper office. Attend cultural festivals, try ethnic foods, play music from our country and others.

➤ **Music:** Play classical music, children's songs, your favorite music, polkas; learn finger plays (remember "Here is the church, here is the steeple, open the doors and see all the people"?); attend concerts (outdoor ones are usually a favorite with this age group and their parents); provide rhythm instruments, a toy xylophone, or piano; march, clap, and dance to the music.

➤ **Art:** Provide a wide variety of materials: paint and brushes, markers, clay, many kinds of paper, stencils, safety scissors, pencils, colored pencils, finger paints, old magazines to cut up, paste, glitter, colored sand, and found objects. Supervision for safety's sake is important, and doing your own project while your child creates can be fun for both of you.

➤ **Health:** Talk about good food choices, use visits to the dentist and doctor for regular checkups as learning experiences, promote exercise (walking, jumping on the jogger, running) and good sleep habits. Teach good hygiene: hand washing, bathroom habits, brushing teeth correctly.

Hands-On Projects

Three- to five-year-olds are generally busy, active, and interested in doing things. Hands-on projects are the learning experiences of choice. Going places, participating, handling, tasting, and observing are all important parts of learning for this age group. Involve your children in simple food preparation. (A low table to work at during food preparation is safer than a stool to stand on.) Have them help you with the new baby's bath, with pet care (feeding, brushing, learning to handle the pet properly), with gardening, and with whatever you are doing.

Provide three- to five-year-olds with real tools so they can help. Child-sized brooms, dust mops, and bins for sorting their toys at pick-up time promote good cleanup habits. While you're dusting, give your child a duster or rag and have him or her dust the things that are within reach. If you're sweeping the floor, provide a small broom or handheld vacuum cleaner. While folding laundry, throw the socks into two small clothes baskets (light and dark) to be mated and folded together by your child. Have 20-minute pick-ups set to lively music, in which you and your child put away everything that's out of place.

While you're sewing, give your children buttons to sort, and thread or scraps of fabric to play with. My daughter used to stand on the chair behind me and style my hair while I sewed! Although it seems to take longer to accomplish things with a three- to five-year-old helper, it takes no longer than trying to keep the child busy and occupied with something else while you're working on your project.

Learning Lookouts

Supplies that are potentially dangerous, could damage things, and need to be used with supervision should be stored in a safe place out of the reach of your three- to five-year-old.

Arts and Crafts

Provide a shelf or table with art supplies that your child can use safely without supervision. Safety scissors, old magazines, lots of paper, crayons, and washable markers can be kept in a couple of bins near a low table where the child can work when the idea strikes.

Working with Play-Doh or clay may be a supervised activity if you have carpet and don't want to face the cleanup. A large plastic tablecloth under the work table can solve this problem, if your child stays in the work area with the clay. Some families provide sandboxes full of rice for a really fun play activity. Again, this will depend on the age of your child and his or her ability to keep the messy materials within a designated area, or your tolerance for having such materials strewn from one end of the house to the other.

Pretend Play

Imagination is the largest nation in the world. Pretend play is one of the best learning experiences for children of this age group. Remember watching your child imitate everything you do? Jabbering into the toy phone, putting a naughty doll on a chair for a time-out, and mixing up who knows what in a plastic bowl? Children love to make houses with blankets over a table or clothes line, or draped from the top mattress of a bunk bed.

Spotlight on Education

My daughter Jacinta and her friends delight in dressing up in each other's clothes. They also love trying on my dress shoes. Having Jacinta style their hair is another fun activity, due to the sheer number of hair clips and barrettes she has on hand! Once suitably coifed and garbed, this motley assortment of budding beauties loves to put on a show accompanied by favorite music on the tape player. Playing store is another favorite activity, especially in summer when the picnic table and benches on the screened porch can be used as store counters and displays for clothing, toys, and books.

A bin of dress-up clothes and costumes, bandannas, hats, scarves and shawls, high-heeled shoes, and costume jewelry can provide hours of interactive fun. Playing store, having tea parties, acting out stories, and putting on shows can involve children in hours of imaginative play. Note the detail in the play and marvel at the observation powers of this age group!

The Real-Life Approach

This is the easiest approach of all: simply being there for—and with—your child, and involving your child in the experiences of everyday life. From the time the child awakens until he or she is tucked into bed for a story at night, your child soaks up life's lessons from everyday events.

Learning Links

For a special thank-you note, take some of your child's artwork and fold it to fit into an envelope. Lightly write the words "Thank You" on the front and the child's name inside for the child to trace in marker or crayon. Have your child affix a stamp, and put the thank-you note in the mailbox. Several motor skills are involved, as well as showing responsibility and gratitude—important character traits.

Learning Lookouts

Don't become impatient with your child's endless questioning; this is natural learning at its best. If it's too distracting because you are driving in heavy traffic, for example, tell your child that this is not a good time, but when you can, you will answer his or her question.

Learning experiences abound in the busy household of a three- to five-year-old. A child this age is still excited about learning and notices everything. Without turning everything into a school-type lesson, parents can use everyday experiences as ways to teach many of the lessons contained in a packaged curriculum.

After a birthday, the three- to five-year-old can make thank-you notes for the people that sent gifts. Going through this process each time it's appropriate to thank someone will form a lifelong good habit.

When company is expected, the three- to five-year-old can help with readying the house, setting the table, arranging the pickles in a dish, and putting rolls in a basket for the meal. The importance of observing good hygiene while working in the kitchen and preparing food can be taught, along with life skills such as simple food preparation and setting the table. To teach table setting make a place mat out of a piece of construction paper, trace a place setting (plate, silverware, cup, and napkin) onto it and have your child use it as a sample.

Emptying the dishwasher? Sorting is a good skill for children this age; have them put away the silverware (after you have removed the sharp items). If you haven't already rethought your kitchen cupboards, it's time to consider having a lower cabinet with unbreakable plasticware that your child can get out and put away on his or her own.

Three- to five-year-olds are quick to learn to put away canned goods in the right places, deciding which are fruits and vegetables at the same time. My children started using the pictures but gradually learned to read the labels by matching the pictures with the sounds they could pick out from the letters on the label. They began to recognize some words by sight, as well.

Involving your child in everything you do can be a challenge. But that's what most children of this age enjoy the most. Finding a related activity for your three- to five-year-old while you are working around the house can reap endless benefits. Children need to be needed. Our society today removes children from the center of productivity, rather than preparing them for life by involving them.

A mother with a new baby and a preschooler will naturally include the older child in the care of the baby. Story time with the older child may occur while the baby is sleeping or breastfeeding. An older child who is already used to helping with small kitchen chores, cleaning up his or her own toys while listening to a song tape with Mommy, and helping fold the towels and socks while Mommy does laundry will usually fit into the new regimen quite readily. He or she already feels an integral part of whatever is going on. The three- to five-year-old enjoys walks to the park, pushing the new baby in the stroller, and showing Mommy and the new baby how high he or she can swing and how far he or she can climb on the monkey bars.

The family with several homeschooled children, all older than the three- to five-year-old, has several built-in helpers for educating the little one. The oldest sister might take over some of the reading out loud of stories, which helps her practice her vocal reading skills, while giving the mother time to work with another child on his or her math. Another older sibling may play games with the three- to five-year-old, while the oldest sister is helping mother in the kitchen. Balancing the educational needs of all the members of the family with the chores and responsibilities of the household can actually be easier with several children than it is with one or two.

Eclectic Preschool

The eclectic approach takes the best parts of all the possible approaches to teaching the three- to five-year-old at home, and tailors the experience to the child's needs and abilities.

Purchasing Select Materials

Although most homes will already have many appropriate toys, tools, and books to use in engaging the learning of a three- to five-year-old, you may want to consider what you already know about your child's learning style and select some special materials that will pique his or her interest and provide a new perspective. Once again, multi-age materials, and those that will provide more than a short-term interest engagement are to be recommended.

Building toys, small versions of real tools, and things that preschoolers can use now with supervision and later by themselves are suggested, including ...

➤ **Simple cookbooks.** Cookbooks of the step-by-step variety, with simple recipes, lots of pictures, and large print, are best for beginners.

➤ **Craft books and materials.** Craft books with colorful illustrations to spark interest, with a box or bag of materials to complete several projects, will come in handy on rainy days.

➤ **Phonics book or program.** A phonics program can be a book, such as *Alpha-Phonics* by Samuel Blumenfeld (Paradigm Company, 1986) or *Teach Your Child to Read in 100 Easy Lessons* by Siegfried Engelmann, Phyllis Haddox, and Elaine Bruner (Simon & Schuster, 1986); or a reading program in a box, such as *Sing, Spell, Read and Write*, available from many homeschool vendors.

➤ **Math manipulatives.** Math manipulatives range from buckets of plastic items for counting practice to those designed to teach math concepts. Experience has taught many homeschoolers that providing manipulatives for free play and exploration removes the mystique. That is, when concepts are taught using manipulatives, children are ready to learn with them, as opposed to wanting to play with them. Check Appendix B for a suggested list of materials.

Using the Community as a Resource

Children aged three to five enjoy exploring their world. Walks to the park, playtime with other youngsters, and weekly errands with a parent can all be great learning experiences. Rather than leaving little ones home with the other parent or a sitter, include them in the process. Find out if there are programs for youngsters at local museums, library, or community education. See if your health club or the YMCA has programs for preschoolers or homeschoolers. Visits to the doctor or dentist to tour the facilities, or a peek behind the scenes at the post office, fast food restaurant, newspaper, radio station, or print shop can be exciting for the three- to five-year-old.

Don't forget once-a-year experiences like the county or state fair, the circus, Christmas caroling, local festivals, art shows, and craft fairs.

You know your child best and can plan activities that are appropriate for his or her interests and attention span. Remember, planning short and sweet activities is usually the key to keeping experiences fun.

Speaking Educationese

A **playgroup** is an informal gathering of young children and their parents for the purpose of nurturing interaction between the children and providing the parents with company and support.

Playgroup

Many homeschoolers have started *playgroups* as a branch of a parenting group or church group, or by meeting other homeschoolers elsewhere and planning a playgroup from scratch. Meet other homeschoolers interested in forming a playgroup at library story hours, fast food play areas, La Leche League meetings, Mothers of Twins meetings, or at the park. Some homeschoolers put ads on grocery store or community bulletin boards, or run ads in the newspaper to get like-minded people together to brainstorm. Quite often, the homeschoolers need an outlet and an understanding ear, and their children reap the benefit of developing friendships with others their own age. Smaller is usually better at this age level, and less rather than more structure is recommended.

Organizing a Cooperative Preschool

If you really want to involve yourself and your child in a preschool experience but can't find a preschool program that you like, consider expanding on the playgroup concept and organizing a cooperative preschool. In *Playful Learning: An Alternate Approach to Preschool,* (La Leche League International, 1986), Anne Engelhardt and Cheryl Sullivan tell you everything you need to know about doing this on your own, from how to find other interested parents, to organizing and implementing a program, even including activities to use during preschool sessions. If you decide not to organize such a program, the book includes a wealth of information, such as developmental skills scales, recipes, and suggestions for day trips and activities.

A preschool-at-home developed by like-minded parents has many advantages, including the ability of the parents to plan for the actual needs and abilities of the children involved, to provide a secure and comfortable environment for the children as well as a higher adult-to-child ratio, and to allow for a closer bond between the parent and child.

Hand-Me-Down Education

Do your children wear hand-me-downs? Many parents pass like-new clothing on to younger siblings or gratefully accept such offerings from their children's cousins or friends. Although hand-me-downs may be anathema to you in the clothing or toys field, *hand-me-down education* is a fact of life that's unavoidable. Most parents have noticed that, whether homeschooled or not, younger siblings tend to catch on to, or pick up on, certain behaviors and abilities from watching their older sisters and brothers.

Speaking Educationese

Hand-me-down education is the body of information that is specifically learned by younger siblings from older ones.

Learning from Older Siblings

While you are working with the older children in the family, younger siblings are usually underfoot, trying to get a piece of the action. Providing them with similar materials and activities usually brings peace and a certain amount of satisfaction on the part of the younger children. Being like the older ones, or like Mom and Dad, are major goals at this age. Since this is so, why not take advantage of this interest and build on it?

While your older children are doing an art project, provide similar nontoxic materials for your three- to five-year-old. If you have a very busy, active three- to five-year-old, you may want to do art projects with the older kids during the younger ones' nap time. However, if you are prepared for the mess, being a part of what the older ones are doing is an excellent learning experience for the littler one.

Whenever possible, have your younger children quietly involved nearby when working with older children. Don't tell them that you want them to listen; mention that you are working with the older children and need them to keep busy and quiet nearby so they don't distract the older ones. This tactic almost ensures that they will be all ears to find out what you are doing with the older children! While you are reading out loud from a book that is appropriate for the older children, a three- to five-year-old can be busily occupied in the same room playing with toy dishes or trucks, or working on a puzzle. Or provide art supplies such as paper and crayons, and let your youngsters illustrate the story as you read. It's surprising how much the preschooler will pick up from the story, as may be evidenced when you discuss it later.

Learning by Doing: Being a Helper

By now you know that little children want to be needed, to feel important, and to be an essential part of the family. If your little one is constantly amused by videos while you do the work, essentially separating you even though you are right in the home, it's not too late to make some changes. I guarantee that your child will enjoy helping you, if you give him or her the opportunity. You will be spending 50 to 100 percent more time together by making this one simple change. Over time, you will also know your child better, and you will have a better relationship.

I have heard so many parents talking about feeling guilty for not playing with their children. Others comment that that's just the way it has to be because adults have so many things they have to do, and children just have to learn to amuse themselves. Well, I'm here to tell you that you don't have to feel guilty about not spending time with your children: Spend time with them, starting today. Children enjoy you playing with them, but they also enjoy doing real-life things, sharing in the adult activities, and being a productive human being, just like you.

Helpers grow up to be contributing adults with strong values and a commitment to helping others. Don't cheat your child out of an opportunity to be all he or she can be.

The Least You Need to Know

➤ Three- to five-year-olds learn a lot from watching the adults in their lives.

➤ Play is learning, and helping around the house develops positive self-worth and other important character traits.

➤ Resources for preschoolers abound in the home and community.

➤ Creating a curriculum can simply be a natural extension of the everyday discoveries of a three- to five-year-old.

➤ Capitalize on the three- to five-year-old's natural curiosity and zest for life.

Chapter 11

Homeschooling Six- to Eight-Year-Olds

> ### In This Chapter
>
> ➤ The advantages of teaching six- to eight-year-olds at home
>
> ➤ Building on the basics learned in the early years, or re-building a shaky foundation
>
> ➤ Homeschooler's homework; teaching kids to help out at home, and basic values and character training
>
> ➤ Deciding which approach to use for six- to eight-year-olds
>
> ➤ Focusing on six- to eight-year-olds' unique abilities
>
> ➤ Keeping the lessons short and sweet

Six- to eight-year-olds who haven't been to institutional school are, almost without exception, still excited about learning. You can do many of the same things I recommended in Chapter 10, "Learning at Home with Three- to Five-Year-Olds," adjusting upward for age and ability.

If your six- to eight-year-old has had a difficult experience with institutional school, be sure to allow time for him or her to decompress or deschool. Veteran homeschoolers often suggest doing things that don't remind the child of school activities. Textbooks, worksheets, assignments, or the mention of subjects by name (social studies, math, English) may receive a negative reaction. On the other hand, nearly all six- to eight-year-olds will respond much more readily to participating in read-aloud times, helping out around the house, taking day trips to places of interest, and spending time exploring the outdoors.

Start with the Basics

Whether your child has always been at home or has come home from institutional school, concentrate on teaching the basics. Remember, though, that teaching the basics can vary from one homeschool to another, and doesn't have to duplicate what you remember from institutional school. Children who are predominately verbal/linguistic and mathematical/logical may respond readily to school-at-home lessons, especially when the lessons are kept short and upbeat. For these children, little workbooks or a packaged curriculum at their level used for a couple of hours total each day and supplemented with hands-on and real-life activities will be sufficient. Examples of supplementing can include …

Learning Links

Simple, colorful workbooks are available at discount department stores nationwide. Some homeschool parents simply make up their own practice sheets: Write the alphabet and short words to be copied by the student, write math problems to be worked by the student, and teach phonics using real books. Dating and keeping these home-generated school papers in a file folder or binder provides a record of work completed.

➤ **Verbal/linguistic:** Memorize and recite the math facts for math, keep a journal (beginning readers can draw pictures and narrate captions) for language arts.

➤ **Logical/mathematical:** Use Tangrams (math manipulatives that aid in the development of shape concepts, problem solving, perception of equivalents and spatial relationships, eye-hand and fine motor coordination, visual discrimination and visual memory, and thinking skills) or Geo-boards (a board with pins for use with rubber bands that teaches shape, design, spatial relationships, angles, fractions, area, perimeter, symmetry, and coordinates) for math; put a story in proper sequence for language arts. For more on these resources, see Appendix B, "Curriculum Winners and Selected Resources, Including Dynamite Web Sites."

For other types of learners you may need to create activities that match their learning styles while still teaching the same basics. For example …

➤ **Visual/spatial:** Use Learning Wrap-Ups (self correcting math puzzles) for math; paint the alphabet in rainbow colors with watercolor paints for language arts.

➤ **Bodily/kinesthetic:** For math, stand before a large chalkboard and write numbers and math problems very large, using whole body movement; for language arts, write the alphabet and spelling words, using whole body movement, and act out stories.

➤ **Musical/rhythmic:** Tap out number patterns and problems for math; sing the sounds of letters and spell words to music for language arts.

➤ **Intrapersonal:** Set personal goals for learning the math facts; keep a journal (beginning readers may draw pictures and narrate captions) of books read for language arts.

➤ **Interpersonal:** Provide as much group learning as is practical, such as a cooperative math class, tutoring by an older sibling, or a reading/discussion group for language arts.

➤ **Naturalist:** Use natural items, such as sea shells, acorns, and leaves for math manipulatives; point out subtle differences in letter sounds, and ways to print letters and pronounce words for language arts.

➤ **Existentialist:** Provide reasons for learning math and language arts, including field trips to visit people who use these skills in their work.

Reading Out Loud Is Fundamental

Whether or not your child has begun to read, reading out loud is the base for homeschooling six- to eight-year-olds. This may be the most important thing you can do for a child in this age group. Beginning readers and nonreaders are interested in many things that are beyond their reading ability. Experiment with reading to your six- to eight-year-old a variety of books, including classics, adventure stories, nonfiction, fantasy, poetry, and popular fiction.

Even if your child has started to sound out words or to read short stories to him- or herself, don't cut back on the amount of time you spend reading out loud together. John Taylor Gatto, author, homeschool advocate, and former New York City and State Teacher of the Year, recounts that his mother held him on her lap and ran her finger under the words as she read; a classic picture of at-home reading instruction. My mother gifted my brother and I in the same way. We didn't have many children's books but the ones we had were well-loved and Mother read them to us so many times that we memorized them.

Learning Links

Let your children see you reading often. Have them help you read the instructions to the bookshelf you are assembling. Read them captions in the newspaper or magazine you are reading. Stop and read the signs in store windows together. Look things up in the encyclopedia. Share tidbits from the things you read. Show by example that reading is fun and important.

We were able to "read" them well before we had begun to decode the words. My brother and I both read before we started public school at the age of six.

Spotlight on Education

I read everything to my son Ervin from books on space exploration to historical fiction until he was almost nine. When he was seven I introduced some phonics tapes and read-along books, played games with letter sounds while reading billboards and signs on stores, and used tips gleaned from phonics books and programs. I wrote letters and blends (combinations of sounds such as *bl, thr, ow,* and *oy*) on the chalkboard and had him trace them and say the sounds. A phonics book we tried was soon discarded. We continued reading out loud frequently and doing casual phonics activities. When Ervin was almost nine he suddenly began reading. Within six weeks he was picking up newspapers, magazines, and adult fiction, reading fluently with excellent comprehension and retention.

Don't worry if your child is not yet an independent reader at the age of six to eight. Many children don't become independent readers until much later, even those who are institutionally schooled. Once your child begins to recognize some letters or words you can consider him or her a beginning reader. At that point, it's just a matter of time; more reading out loud, relaxed reinforcement, and review are helpful during this time period. Studies have shown that it's impossible to detect, among adult readers, which ones were early readers and which began at a later age.

Reading Instruction: Make It Fun and Nonthreatening

It's important with this age group to provide plenty of time for reading out loud together and for learning the basic letter sounds and phonics rules, and to keep such instruction fun and positive. Don't shame the child if he or she isn't learning the sounds quickly and easily. If the child isn't exhibiting readiness, it's best to concentrate more time on reading out loud than on drilling. Purchase a basic phonics book or program so you can learn the sounds yourself. Many of us weren't taught to read *phonetically.* To help your child learn to use this tool you have to learn it, too. Then it is much easier to implement casual lessons and tips so your child will pick up tips serendipitously.

Phonics is not a crutch but an important tool. Some children learn to read well without phonics, but many more children learn to read well because of learning to decode words by sound. It's not imperative that a child learn to read by a certain age unless the child is in public school. Homeschoolers are able to provide flexibility and alternate methods to help nonreaders compensate. If your children have been institutionally schooled and haven't learned to read, don't feel as if you must get them caught up in six weeks. Take your time, provide positive support, spend time reading out loud together, and wait for things to click.

Speaking Educationese

Someone who learns to read **phonetically** learns the sounds made by the letters when they are spoken.

Writing: Parent as Scribe, Child as Artist

Six- to eight-year-olds often have wonderful ideas and can tell stories that go on and on and on. However, getting them to write down their stories on paper may be more difficult. Borrow a page from Charlotte Mason's book and try narration. Get pencil and paper or sit at the computer or typewriter and have your child tell you the story. You write it down or type it out. Divide the story up on several pages and have your child draw pictures to go along with the words. Bind their efforts into a book. Such stories are excellent tools to use when teaching reading. It's more fun to read your own book than it is to read a purchased one. Plus, many children's books include much harder words than the ones in basal readers. Many children age six to eight don't have the small motor control necessary to do lots of writing; don't force it. Putting words together is the important skill here; getting them down on paper can be your job for now.

Let's Talk About Language: Narration

Narration is also an excellent way to help your child learn language skills. Read a story to your child and have her retell the story in her own words. Prompt her if she forgets parts: "And then what happened after Robbie saw the puppy?" Ask questions, make statements, and give feedback to see just how much the child remembers. Help him with sentence structure by repeating in correct syntax some of the incorrect things she says. If Junior says, "He goed over the hill to find the billy goats," you can respond, "Oh, Simon went over

Speaking Educationese

Narration, having a child retell a story that has been read to him or her, teaches a child to recall details of a story in order, and is a way to find out whether the child remembers and understands what has been taught or read.

the hill hoping to find them?" Narration can be used to determine what the child is retaining, and to teach language skills.

Arithmetic: Hands-On Is Important

At this age, most children enjoy using manipulatives to understand abstract concepts. Occasionally a child aged six to eight has a real talent for mathematics, making instruction almost superfluous. Let such a child progress at his or her own speed. You will find that most children of this age will benefit from real-life experiential learning and the use of a manipulative-based program, such as Math-U-See or Miquon. Real-life experience can include counting money, baking and cooking, measuring, and learning to tell time.

Science: Natural Is Best

Getting down and dirty is the best way to teach science to this age group. Grubbing in a garden, collecting specimens while taking walks in the woods or on the beach or while hiking in the mountains, and doing hands-on experiments are all terrific ways to teach the basics of science. Janice Van Cleave has authored some neat books on a variety of science topics, as well as one on math. I call them unit studies in book form. You can pick and choose activities and use these books for several years. Most homeschool vendors will include other books that are excellent for teaching science to this age group. Check Appendix B for resources for teaching science.

Responsibility/Accountability: Helping Out at Home

Children aged six to eight are able to become very capable little people. They are old enough to keep their own space clean and help out in many ways around the house. Being aware that their contribution is important and that they are needed is important for children to know. However, if helping out is a new concept because you haven't had them do chores or help out before, it may take a little planning to get cooperation. You may need to have a family meeting, make some assignment charts, and follow up on assignments for a while before things fall into place.

In his book *How to Really Love Your Child*, Dr. Ross Campbell talks about a child's need to have his or her love tank filled before the child can handle negative input or correction. Many ideas for teaching your child to help at home are included in the book *401 Ways to Get Your Kids to Work at Home,* by Bonnie Runyan McCullough and Susan Walker Monson. How to teach basic values and character traits for helping a child achieve are included in the book *Megaskills: Building Children's Achievement for the Information Age*, by Dorothy Rich. Although these books are written with institutionally schooled children in mind, many of the suggestions can be easily adapted for your homeschooled child. Check Appendix E, "Bibliography," for details on these books.

Learning Lookouts

Positive feedback should outweigh and precede negative comments. When critiquing a completed task, look carefully for as many positive things to say as you can, even when you have to say something negative. Saying "You really worked hard cleaning up your room! Your bed is made, all the toys and books are put away, and the fish bowl has been cleaned. Do you think you could put all the shoes away in the closet, too?" will make your child feel much better than, "Good grief! How many times do I have to tell you to put away your shoes when you clean your room?"

Using a Purchased Curriculum

With care and understanding of your child's learning style, personality, interests, and abilities, you can purchase a curriculum that can form the base for an educational program for six- to eight-year-olds. Reread Chapter 8, "Sixth Grade in a Box: Using a Full-Service Program," for a review of the things to consider in choosing such a program.

School-at-Home: the Traditional Approach

Some homeschoolers duplicate school in their homes. Since studies have shown that children aged six to eight shouldn't be doing intensive academic work for long periods of time, choose a packaged curriculum that is appropriate for their attention span. Look for programs that have short lessons, allow for individualization, and provide alternatives to seat work. If possible, use a packaged curriculum as a guideline and provide substitutes for some of the seat work yourself.

Using the Unit Study Method

Packaged or preplanned unit studies are often a hit with six- to eight-year-olds, especially unit studies that lean more heavily on activities and less heavily on linguistic activities, such as writing papers and filling out worksheets. Have your child choose a topic for a unit study and then have fun exploring and learning together. If you are homeschooling other children, you may be able to use the same unit study for all of them; adjust activities and assignments to reflect each child's abilities.

Speaking Educationese

A **literature-based approach** is a homeschooling curriculum planned around a specific body of literature.

Living Books

A *literature-based approach* works well with this age group, especially for children who aren't yet fluent readers.

Reading out loud from specially chosen books can reinforce or teach a love for books, introduce many new concepts, and help bring parent and child closer together. A number of programs are literature-based, and many homeschool catalogs carry books that would be a good base for a homegrown literature-based program. Remember, although it's good to begin accumulating your own reference and reading library at home, the library is a good place to find books. Some of the books will be keepers, and those you'll want to buy at a bookstore.

Creating Your Own Curriculum

Many homeschoolers have decided that although there are a lot of well-planned packaged programs available, most of them require quite a bit of tweaking to be useful. Therefore, planning an individualized program for homeschooled kids is something many homeschooling parents do. As you've already learned, it's not as difficult as you might think at first.

Hands-On Reading, 'Riting, and 'Rithmetic

Children aged six to eight need to learn the basics, but they don't need to be drilled, regimented, forced to sit still, or burned out on intensive academics in order to do so. Reading, language arts, and mathematics can be covered with short, simple lessons similar to those used in the traditional institutional schools, but supplemented with lots of hands-on, real-life experiences that will help this age group connect the lessons to something concrete. If you don't feel imaginative, browse some homeschool catalogs or bookstores to find books with ideas to get you started.

For activities to promote reading, Jill Frankel Hauser's *Growing Up Reading: Learning to Read Through Creative Play* has many good ideas for fun projects, encourages reading out loud, and includes lists of suggested read-aloud books. It's also an excellent resource to help you design the language arts portion of your curriculum.

Math for the Very Young: A Handbook of Activities for Parents and Teachers, by Lydia Polonsky, Dorothy Freedman, Susan Lesher, and Kate Morrison (John Wiley & Sons, Inc., 1995), includes a number of projects to teach math while doing everyday things around the house and visiting places in the community. One section is all about animal facts and figures ("How Many Feet?", "Which Animals Are Smallest?", "And Who

Eats More, You or a Masked Shrew?"). Math-oriented crafts, making a personal record book (including body measurements and counting teeth), playing math games, and learning counting rhymes and stories are included. Concepts taught are patterns, numbers, collecting and understanding data, geometry, and measurement.

Do you see how purchasing a single multi-age book such as *Math for the Very Young* can cover the whole curriculum? Watch for books that cross the curriculum even though their main focus is one particular subject area, and are appropriate for many age brackets. Such books will be your best buys; the ones you will reach for again and again.

The Kids' Nature Book: 365 Indoor/Outdoor Activities and Experiences and *Hands Around the World: 365 Creative Ways to Build Cultural Awareness and Global Respect*, both by Susan Milord, are excellent resources that provide an activity per day to use as your science and social studies starting points. Build on the suggestions in these and similar books by finding more books to read on topics of interest, by creating your own related craft projects, or by making a scrapbook of articles and pictures.

Learning Lookouts

Because many children aged six to eight are nonreaders or beginning readers, many books and programs labeled for these ages will be too advanced. Scan through materials and determine whether the activities are appropriate based on what you know about your own child.

Involve Kids in Making Learning Materials

Many homeschooling families create their own learning games, flash cards, and manipulatives for learning particular skills. Get ideas from books and catalogs, but don't burn the midnight oil making the learning materials for your child. Involve your child in making games as part of his or her learning; many homeschooled children have learned new information while working on such projects. Making a game often turns out to be more than half the fun. Use board and card games you already own as springboards for ideas in creating your own geography, history, or math games. You can borrow markers and spinners from existing games, or make your own. Keep your ears open for helpful suggestions from your homeschooled kids as you work on such projects; quite often children can help you solve your dilemma when you don't think there's a solution to your problem.

Making scrapbooks or portfolios relating to your studies is a fun way to reinforce learning and provide a lasting record of the learning that is happening. Your child can draw pictures while you read out loud; or your child can cut out magazine pictures that reflect the terrain, animals, and plants in the area being studied; or your child can clip or copy recipes and poems, or write essays (using narration, if needed). Photographs of your child making related craft projects, attending pertinent programs, and drawing, cutting, or pasting can be included.

Spotlight on Education

My daughter Jacinta loved being read to from the *American Girls* series stories by Pleasant Company and leafing through the American Girl doll catalogs. We cut out pictures of the dolls to hang on her bedroom wall. We also cut up enough catalogs to make a scrapbook, including the various accessories, learning about them as we went along. Jacinta learned about furniture and home styles, fashions (including nightwear, hats, and undergarments), types of lighting, birthday and Christmas celebrations, forms of entertainment, needlework, variations in schooling, and much more during this project. We still have the scrapbook to remind us of the fun we had making it together.

Imaginative Play Counts!

If your child likes to dress up as a knight of old and conquer the dark dangers in his or her imagination, spends time with imaginary companions, or loves to pretend he or she is capable of going back in time to live in the past, don't despair! These imaginative kids may find an outlet in historical re-enacting, involvement with a local theater group, or simply learning about and re-enacting historical time periods for a select audience such as immediate family, grandparents, aunts, and uncles.

Learning Links

Studies have shown that children with imaginary playmates develop excellent social skills; their relationship with their imaginary friend prepares them well for interacting with real friends later.

Don't pressure your children to turn their imaginary play into a school lesson. If they are interested in exploring the time period they fantasize about and learning about the customs, traditions, and perhaps the cookery of that era, you may have found the key to their cooperation in learning. You can develop some structured or relaxed unit studies based on their interests.

Homeschooled families have put on medieval fests—complete with costumes, music, and foods—and sponsored ethnic festivities from countries that sparked their child's interest. Combining research with craft projects to produce costumes, foods, reports, place settings, home decorations, music, and a short program can be a fun incentive for learning about a new country or time period. Using your child's imaginative play as a starting point can help you reap enormous benefits in gaining your child's interest in study.

Avoid Comparisons: Some Learners Blossom Later!

If you've met homeschoolers whose children seem to be prodigies or have unique talents in music, art, or some other area, it's easy to begin to make comparisons.

I've heard some homeschoolers comment that their kids are just average. They are often responding to the news of another homeschooled child being accepted into a prestigious college, or statistics about homeschoolers scoring high on standardized tests, or winning a spelling or geography bee. While such accomplishments are special and give homeschooling positive press, such achievements aren't the reason most of us homeschool. If our children choose to persevere to attain such goals, we will do our best to support them. However, many homeschooled children become successful, productive, happy adults without taking a standardized test, winning a national competition, or attending an Ivy League school (or any college at all). Sometimes homeschoolers have moments when they feel concern about delays or worry that their child will never "catch up." Are they focusing on their child's personal accomplishments, or how he or she measures up to someone else? Such concern is part of the transition from being somewhat involved to being totally responsible for your children's education.

Remind yourself often that every child is unique, that each one develops at individual rates, that no curriculum or scope and sequence is going to fit every child (or even any child), and that you will learn right along with your child. It's okay if your child struggles with a concept: In fact, that may be a clue to tell you that he or she is not yet ready for that concept.

Don't compare your own children with each other, either. Your auditory/kinesthetic learner has strengths and weaknesses different from those of your logical/musical learner. Each child has his or her own gifts and own struggles. Teach to your children's strengths and provide reinforcement in the areas where they are weaker. Honor your children for their strengths, encourage them in the areas where they struggle, and avoid comparing your children to other children.

Learning Lookouts

Comparing your children to each other or to other homeschoolers can create feelings of rivalry and dislike. Rather than comparing your children's accomplishments to others, be sure to comment when they improve their skills or learn something new. Some children enjoy seeing a graph or chart that shows their progress.

Keep Lessons Short and Sweet

Six- to eight-year-olds are often wiggly, have short attention spans, and still manifest a lot of excitement about learning. Capitalize on the positive aspects of these attributes by feeding that excitement with varied and interesting projects and lessons.

Capture their imagination while you keep lessons concise, and you won't have to worry as much about their short attention span. Stopping before you've lost their interest is often the key to cooperation as you pick up where you left off another day. If they're still excited about the project, it'll be a simple matter; however, if they became bored and restless yesterday, getting them to start on it again today may be an uphill battle. Wiggliness won't be a problem if you plan for lessons that provide for movement and participation and don't involve lots of seat work. Keep the academic lessons (worksheets and written work) to a minimum, devoting more of your teaching time to projects, games, and activities.

The Least You Need to Know

➤ Teaching the basics to six- to eight-year-olds can involve all the modalities.

➤ Play and imagination are an integral part of learning for six- to eight-year-olds.

➤ You can tailor your six- to eight-year-old's education to his or her needs and abilities.

➤ Six- to eight-year-olds develop reading, writing, arithmetic, and other skills according to their own individual internal time table.

➤ Keep lessons short and sweet to maintain a six- to eight-year-old's interest.

Chapter 12

Homeschooling Nine- to Twelve-Year-Olds

In This Chapter

➤ Why homeschool your nine- to twelve-year-old?

➤ Getting an understanding of your youngster's abilities and interests

➤ Deciding whether to purchase a curriculum or design your own

➤ Using your community as a resource: how time with others can revitalize uninterested learners

---

Some things are universal about nine- to twelve-year-olds. Most still enjoy being read to, although they often won't admit it! Nine- to twelve-year-olds also need you to be there for them, although they don't usually let you know that either. Although the media has recently made much of the early adolescent years as a time in which kids have a burning need to be just like their peers, there is no reason to buy into this pop culture theory.

It wasn't that long ago that the term "teen" came into being, along with certain expectations, including peer dependency. The age at which our culture expects peer dependency gets younger and younger. As a result, kids who need more nurturing at this age tend to hide it or minimize it, causing parents to feel shut out or that their children are more independent than is true. Eye contact, positive interaction, sustained attention, and personal communication with parents are still extremely important with most nine- to twelve-year-olds. As kids get closer to the teen years, they often do begin to separate from their parents, but deep down they need the approval and nurturing only a parent can provide. Keep these thoughts in mind as you homeschool your nine- to twelve-year-old.

Accentuating the Positive and Alleviating the Negative

If you've been homeschooling all along, your child's social development is already rooted in the family, supplemented with occasional forays into the community. Your nine- to twelve-year-old's identity and self-worth is flourishing without the constant pressure of peers, and your child already gets along well with people of all ages and from all backgrounds because he or she accompanies you on errands, visits the library, and participates in community service and group activities. Your child's skills have been developing according to his or her own timetable, and your child identifies with his or her parents more than with his or her peers. Your child can have all questions, important or silly, answered without fear of ridicule or teasing from peers, and is not being pressured to achieve according to society's norms. You've been designing your child's program according to your child's interests, abilities, and learning style.

If you are just beginning to homeschool, your child's social development may already be rooted in values that you aren't comfortable with. Your nine- to twelve-year-old may already be caught up in the *preteen* culture that dominates the world of middle school. Such labels tend to assume that people of certain ages behave in predictable ways; actually, the labels tend to encourage predictable behaviors instead. It's an old story: Kids live up to our expectations.

It may take time for your child to re-identify with your values, but you can encourage this by consistently modeling appropriate behavior for your child. How you live teaches your child far more than anything you say to him or her. Your child may have low self worth and identity at this point, but acceptance, reassurance and love without condemnation will help your child develop positive feelings. He or she may be uncooperative and sulky, or make constant comparisons to the institutional environment left behind. This is normal. Remember that your child has probably experienced negative reinforcement from which he or she may need to decompress and is experiencing uncertainty based on adjusting to a new situation. Over time, your child's attitude will improve.

Speaking Educationese

A **preteen** is a boy or girl who is not yet 13 years old, especially one between the ages of 10 and 13.

Learning Lookouts

If your nine- to twelve-year-old has a negative attitude toward learning, be patient! This attitude didn't appear overnight, and it won't disappear overnight. Encourage your child by keeping criticism constructive, outweighing negative comments with positive ones, and eliminating as much pressure as possible.

Once your child settles down, he or she will be able to develop skills according to his or her own developmental timetable. Don't expect to get up to "grade level" in a short time or compare your child to anyone else, within or outside the family. Allow this first year of homeschooling to be an adjustment and learning period for both of you. Your child will begin to identify more with family than with peers, and will begin to ask questions, explore for him- or herself, and show interest in learning.

Keep activities appropriate to your child's abilities, interests, personality, and learning style, and don't be concerned with whether activities are age or *grade-appropriate*.

Speaking Educationese

Grade-appropriate activities and materials are those that are planned specifically for a particular grade level.

Short, hands-on activities and real-life experiences will be tolerated better than institutional-type academic lessons, particularly during the initial decompression period.

Advantages for Your Child

Your child will reap the benefits of homeschooling in many obvious and not-so-obvious ways, including …

➤ Social development within the family rather than among peers

➤ Skills development according to the child's internal timetable

➤ Learning in a safe, secure environment without fear of ridicule

Advantages for You and Your Family

Homeschooling your nine- to twelve-year-old can benefit you and your family, too. For example …

➤ You get to know your preteen and can better understand, accept, and deal with his or her strengths and weaknesses.

➤ You have more influence on your child's values as you guide his or her attitudes and concepts of life on a daily basis.

➤ Family bonds are strengthened because your nine- to twelve-year-old's emotional needs are being met in a relaxed setting with plenty of care, interest, acceptance, and love.

➤ A stronger parent/child relationship is forged through frequent interaction.

➤ You develop confidence as a parent while giving of yourself to your preteen in such an important way.

➤ Your family develops a closer relationship as a result of shared experiences and interaction while learning together.

Involve This Age Group in Curriculum Planning

A preteen doesn't always want to show a need for parents. But the nine- to twelve-year-old is also young enough to need guidance and feedback from parents to reassure him or her that all's well with the world. When dealing with your nine- to twelve-year-old be aware of the mixed emotions, changing feelings, and hormones that are coming into play. Provide nurturing when your child needs it and give him or her space when it's indicated. Keep priorities and values consistent to provide a strong base for your child to build on as he or she grows up.

Nine- to twelve-year-olds often have definite opinions about what they want to do and what they do and don't like. Encourage participation and discussion as you read and research about homeschooling methods. Encouraging your preteen's input into the program will encourage participation from your child when it's time to begin.

Building on the Basics

If you've been homeschooling your nine- to twelve-year-old from the start, your child may already have a fairly firm foundation of basics in place. If not, or if this is your first year homeschooling a previously institutionally schooled child, be aware of your child's skills or lack thereof. Perhaps you have withdrawn your child from institutional school because you are well aware of a lack. Some time will be profitably spent in determining your child's capabilities. A simple assessment test might be helpful, not to label or discourage, but to give you tools to work with.

Learning Links

Read a book out loud together, then discuss it, to determine your child's ability to read and comprehend. Keep it a positive experience by calmly correcting or coaching when your child has a problem with a word. Use numbers to figure out a real-life problem to see if your child knows which math concepts to apply and how to get to the answer. Ask your child to write something, such as a thank-you note, or a list of things he or she would like to study, to provide you with some clues about your child's writing and spelling ability. Keep your feedback to your child casual to ensure continued cooperation.

If testing is difficult for your child, just spend time doing things together while you make mental notes of areas that need reinforcement or review. Use these conclusions as a starting point for your homeschooling program.

If your child needs help with reading or basic math skills, provide help in those areas. Sometimes reading improves dramatically when easy-to-read materials in the child's area of interest are provided, or when a specific interest requires the reading of manuals or instructions. If decoding words is a problem, purchase a basic phonics program or book to work through with your child.

Many parents have found that children of this age enjoy having a reason for learning. Look for opportunities to use needed skills to perform everyday tasks rather than inventing assignments that may be perceived as busywork.

Language Arts: Letters to the Editor

Nine- to twelve-year-olds often have strong opinions about events and situations. Learning to write letters to inform, persuade, or complain is a valuable skill that can be taught at this young age. Rather than writing imaginary assignments, youngsters can write letters to the editors of newspapers to give their opinions on local or national situations and events. Writing letters to customer service departments to explain problems with merchandise purchased or services rendered helps children build confidence while learning to handle frustrating situations capably.

Letters of commendation can also be written to local or national heroes. One homeschooled child wrote a letter and sent a small handmade gift of appreciation to the mother of a local firefighter who lost his life while trying to rescue someone from a burning house. He treasures the letter he received from the firefighter's mother in response to his efforts.

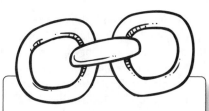

Learning Links

If a child purchases an item that proves to be defective or faulty, have him or her write a letter to the manufacturer, a constructive way to handle the situation. Occasionally, such letters reap benefits beyond rectifying the situation, such as coupons for future purchases or gifts of products from the manufacturer.

Math: Graph Allowance or Earnings

Numbers and money can be abstract concepts to youngsters. Some preteens are already earning money doing such jobs as baby sitting, lawn care, or walking pets. Many children enjoy counting their money and planning what they will purchase.

Parents can take this opportunity to teach values about money, explaining their personal stance on such issues as savings, tithing, and giving to charity. Some families set guidelines that are followed in managing money. For instance, in one family, once children are earning their own money, at least 20 percent is earmarked for continuing education.

Children can use graphs to show how much money they have or to set goals for savings and show progress towards that goal. Learning to budget is a valuable skill that can be learned early.

Science: Experiments and Bug Collections

Reading a science textbook is a dry way to learn science when compared with the joys involved in performing experiments and identifying specimens from nature. Many interesting books are available with science experiments that require only items found around the house or in the local stores. Nature guides are helpful when identifying specimens acquired on walks and hikes in the woods, along the shore, or on the plains. Grasses, wildflowers, seedpods, abandoned bird's nests, shells, and other specimens can form the basis for a nature display or collection, as well as spark an interest in botany.

Responsibility and Accountability: Daily/Weekly Chores

The child who has no responsibilities around the house will not feel as much an integral part of the family as the child who knows he or she is needed and important in the overall scheme of things. This doesn't mean your child will never groan or complain of being overworked! After all, don't you sometimes feel that way yourself?

Every family has its own way of including children in chores around the house. If your child has been helping since toddlerhood, you can build on the foundation already in place. If you are just starting

Learning Lookouts

Be sure you aren't picking endangered or protected wildflowers or grasses. You may want to take a camera along on your roamings to "pick by click" those items you want to identify later.

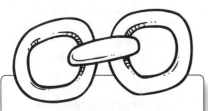

Learning Links

Chore charts, chore spinners, job jars, family meetings, negotiations, chore swapping, and 20-minute pick-up (in which everyone in the family stops what he or she is doing and spends 20 minutes picking up out-of-place items throughout the house) are just a few of the tools that homeschoolers use to motivate their kids to keep accountable.

to homeschool and have never had your child help out around the house, now is the time to make some changes. This may prove to be a shock to your child's sensibilities, but stick to your guns! The rewards you reap in the future will far outweigh the inconvenience of being consistent now. Check Appendix E, "Bibliography," for books about parenting, getting organized, and involving children in chores.

Selecting a Curriculum

Whether you decide to purchase a packaged curriculum or plan to follow a preplanned homeschooling method you've researched or read about in a book, you need to consider your nine- to twelve-year-old's learning style, personality, and interests, as well as your budget and teaching style. Think about the basic homeschooling methods (see Chapter 5, "Approaches to Home Education") and how they relate to your child and family, as discussed in the following sections.

School-at-Home

This approach is often used in its entirety (textbooks, workbooks, worksheets, tests, and grades) by beginning homeschoolers. It's also a frequent choice of parents whose preteen children were doing well academically in institutional school but who want to provide an education based on their values or religious beliefs.

If your nine- to twelve-year-old was having major difficulties with academics and you want to try a traditional approach, you will probably want to supplement the traditional lessons with a variety of activities, kinesthetic projects, and field trips.

Learning Links

To provide a varied structure for a beginning program teach reading, writing, and math using traditional methods and use projects and experiments to teach social studies and science. Observe which methods are most successful with your child and adjust the program accordingly.

Unit Studies

Take your youngster's interests and use them as a basis for a unit study. Whether it's *Star Wars*, sailing, or antique dolls, you can build a unit study around it and cover all the curriculum areas. Many preplanned unit studies are available through homeschool vendors or on Web sites. Books are available to help you plan your own unit study based on your child's interest if you can't find a preplanned unit or simply want to do it yourself.

If your preteen seems to be allergic to anything that resembles school, keep units relaxed and unstructured. Focus on your child's learning style when planning activities and ask him or her to complete a project in a way he or she will enjoy. Most nine- to twelve-year-olds can readily choose their preferred method of learning from several acceptable choices.

169

Spotlight on Education

Let's pick a broad topic, such as "the ocean," and see how different learning styles gravitate toward certain interests and ways of learning. A logical/mathematical learner or a visual/spatial learner may enjoy charting the ocean's food chain. A musical/rhythmical learner may enjoy learning the names of the oceans to music. A naturalist may want to learn all about the habits and habitats of ocean animals. An interpersonal learner may enjoy working with others in a cooperative class, while an intrapersonal learner may like individual reading and planning his or her own ocean projects. Holistic learners can figure out how the oceans affect human life and ways in which we depend on the ocean. Bodily/kinesthetic learners may enjoy a trip to the aquarium, while verbal/linguistic learners may like writing a report about the ocean.

Themed units generally cross most curriculum areas, providing a good balance of activities. Sometimes it's difficult to cover some areas, specifically math, when using unit studies so you may want to provide math separately. Including your preteen in planning a unit study (choosing materials, projects, and field trips) will almost guarantee willing participation.

Living Books

You learned in Chapter 5 that Charlotte Mason coined the terms "living books" and "twaddle"; many of her theories are alive and well today in the homes of preteen homeschoolers. A literature-based curriculum uses living books as opposed to textbooks, eliminating most twaddle in one fell swoop! A textbook may be used as a reference or a guide to help you cover a specific body of knowledge. Use the chapter headings as suggestions for locating living books, those that bring the concepts covered to life, which can provide the base for student learning. Discussion, narration, journals, and drawings can be used by students to show what they've learned.

Use searches on www.amazon.com, www.barnesandnoble.com, www.borders.com, or in the card catalog at your library to find real books to teach textbook concepts in a rich, interesting, and vital way.

Unschooling

Learn to know and trust your preteen's interests and instincts, provide an environment rich in example and resources, and use the experiences of life as a resource for learning. All are part of unschooling. Children aged nine to twelve have already begun to learn from the adults they encounter in their everyday lives. Grandparents share hobbies and skills. Neighbors become mentors and offer part-time apprenticeships to provide a way for children to learn skills they might never learn if they were sitting in a classroom for seven or more hours a day. Visits to career fairs, festivals, concerts, and anywhere people are sharing their skills and interests, can be a starting point for your nine- to twelve-year-old. Preteens who have been institutionally schooled and are turned off to learning often blossom when offered the opportunity to participate in and be responsible for things they consider adult activities, such as community service, real jobs, and mentorships.

An Eclectic Program

If you think that each homeschooling program you've read about has its good points and bad points, but none of them seem to fit your family's and preteen's particular needs, you may want to choose an eclectic program. A well-planned eclectic curriculum is the basis for many successful homeschool programs. Follow your nine- to twelve-year-old's interests (borrowed from unschooling) to choose a theme for a planned unit, and find a mentor to teach some parts of it. Use lessons from a correspondence or support school for part of the time and do hands-on, real-life projects and field trips for the rest of the time.

Learning Lookouts

Remember that your child's interests grow and change as he or she gets older. Be flexible—don't be afraid to change horses in midstream and go with the flow.

These are all just suggestions of ways to implement an eclectic approach to homeschooling. Doing whatever works to provide a rich, balanced education in a modality that fits your child is often the way to go.

Designing Your Own Curriculum

Children learn by doing, as do many adults. Most nine- to twelve-year-olds do very well with a program that is more heavily weighted with hands-on and experiential activities, balanced with a smaller proportion of academic seat work. Your homeschool program will be much more efficient than any institutional program can be, since you won't need to spend time on roll call, dealing with many children at a time, or administrative duties. Many of your everyday activities will reinforce or teach academic concepts, as well.

Keeping Your Goals in Mind

Are you hoping to reinstate a love for learning in a preteen who has been in institutional school? Provide a character or values-based curriculum for your nine- to twelve-year-old? Do you want your preteen to learn the basics of reading, writing, and math that he or she missed out on somewhere along the way? Make a list of the things that are most important to you and refer to the list when you feel yourself becoming sidetracked by someone else's ideas of why you should be homeschooling, or which materials you should choose to homeschool.

Focus on Strengths

Think about your preteen's strong points. If you already know your child is a good reader, design and implement a program that is literature-based, knowing that your child reads fluently with excellent comprehension. If writing is a strength, find varied writing activities to nurture and encourage this ability. If your nine- to twelve-year-old is a math whiz, provide a variety of interesting materials for him or her to experiment with while learning new math concepts. Don't limit your math program to a textbook or workbook, but introduce manipulatives or one of the multi-age math books that include family projects.

Spotlight on Education

My son Ervin is detail-oriented, spending inordinate amounts of time completing a project to his satisfaction. Whether building a Lego structure, drawing an X-Wing ship, signing his name on a card, or totaling up a mail order, every tiny detail must be exact. When he spent hours using a computer drawing program to enlarge detailed sketches using a graph chart system, I wondered if this patience and attention to detail might be helpful in some future career. Since then, Ervin, now 13, has expressed an interest in a career in graphic design, for which these traits will be beneficial.

Find Fun Ways to Work on Weaker Areas

When talking about his theory of multiple intelligences (see Chapter 7, "So Much to Choose From"), Howard Gardner states that all of us possess traits of each type of intelligence in varying degrees. Some traits are dominant and others play a lesser role in our learning ability. We can, however, strengthen the weaker areas. One way to do this with your nine- to twelve-year-old is to encourage learning in the weaker area with projects that are fun and catch your child's interest.

For example, if reading is a weak point with your child, spend time reading together. Read books that spark his or her interest, as well as funny books. Find books that teach subjects your child needs to cover in an interesting and lively way. Spend as much time reading to your child as you can spare. Find books to read that are not difficult for your child, books that he or she can read without embarrassment or a lot of stumbling over difficult words. Work up from there as your child gains confidence. If math is a problem, use hands-on experiences such as baking or woodworking to teach difficult concepts such as measurement and fractions. Use manipulatives and multi-age math books with interesting projects.

If writing is a weak point, use narration and dictation, allowing your preteen to illustrate his or her dictated prose. If small motor control is the problem, let your child type instead of write by hand.

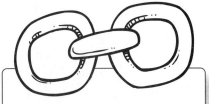

Learning Links

Games like Yahtzee and Monopoly are not only fun, they're great for building math skills! Encourage your nine- to twelve-year-old to use math for real-life purposes, so he or she will begin to understand the need to learn the basics. Double or halve recipes, keep a budget, or draw up an elaborate plan for saving for a special toy or event.

Use the Community as a Resource

Although you can probably implement a complete homeschool program without ever leaving the house, most homeschool families have learned that this is impractical, because a wealth of learning experiences exist right outside your door! Whether you live in a small town, rural area, or metropolis you can glean educational experiences everywhere. Check community education programs, museums, libraries, and art centers for homeschool programming. If no special programs are available for homeschoolers, suggest that they consider starting some. Find out if they have any daytime programming and attend some of their offerings to get a feeling for what is available. Call your local chamber of commerce to find out if they have a brochure, map, or flier of activities and points of interest for your area.

Many times it's easy to overlook what is right under your nose. Remember that children of all ages enjoy day trips to community resources such as fast food restaurants, dentist's and doctor's offices, the police station, the fire station, and city hall for a behind-the-scenes tour of how things work at these everyday places. Call ahead and make an appointment at a time when someone can conduct a tour for your family or a group of homeschoolers. Some preteens are already looking forward to driving, getting a job, and other milestones of the upcoming teen years; consider such tours an early look at career planning! Look in the Yellow Pages of your local or nearby city phone book for more ideas.

The Least You Need to Know

➤ Involve your nine- to twelve-year-old in planning his or her curriculum and learning activities.

➤ Advantages to nine- to twelve-year-olds and their families include deeper relationships, time to pursue shared interests, and the ability to work at their own speeds.

➤ There are many ways to teach the basics; preteens often enjoy hands-on projects and appreciate a reason for learning.

➤ You can design your own curriculum to teach preteens responsibility and accountability, strengthen weak areas, and reinforce strengths.

Teenagers in the Homeschool

Some teens have been homeschooled from the very beginning, others have been homeschooled for a number of years, and some begin learning at home as high school students. Whatever your situation, homeschooling a teen can be very different from homeschooling a younger child. Some teens have a goal in view already, providing a catalyst for curriculum planning. Others are very aware of their learning strengths and weaknesses and are able to provide feedback during goal setting and curriculum planning.

Some homeschool providers prefer to work directly with teens in curriculum planning and record keeping which helps provide built-in accountability. Many teens are capable of self-study and self-monitoring. Consider these variables when thinking about homeschooling your teen.

Speaking Educationese

GED stands for general educational development testing. The diploma is granted after the student has successfully passed a GED test. Classes and study guides are available to prepare students for the test.

Learning Lookouts

Don't let the term "equivalent education" intimidate you into using only traditional methods for your teen. Community service, employment, and projects that reflect your teen's interests and learning style work, too.

What's Your Goal?

Are you homeschooling your teen because you are committed to educating your child all the way through high school? Is your teen learning at home because of a learning disability or difference? Or because of religious or philosophical differences with the institutional school's curriculum? Is it because your child is so brilliant that you feel he or she would be better served with an individually planned program of academics? Or because your child was physically unsafe or suffering emotionally in an institutional school? Your reason will affect your goals for your child's high school education.

Do you want your child to have a public school high school diploma? A private school diploma? Is a *GED diploma* okay with you? Is your child planning to attend college, seminary, or technical school? Do his or her plans include military service, mission work, or learning a trade? Your answers to these questions will affect the choices you and your teen make regarding his or her high school curriculum.

The College Question

When you begin homeschooling a teen, people will start questioning you again. Many homeschoolers begin questioning themselves even when they've homeschooled their child up to this point! "Can you really homeschool through high school?" "What about hard subjects?" Perhaps you failed Algebra II (I almost did!) and wonder how you will ever teach algebra to your child, since he or she wants to attend college.

If your child plans to attend college, it's a good idea to consider the colleges that he or she may choose to attend, and request their admissions requirements. If you're not sure which colleges your child may want to attend, find out what several colleges are looking for and go for the requirements of the one that requires the most. In following those requirements, your child will be prepared for nearly any college he or she may apply to. Another option is for your teen to attend community college, either for high school credit or after completing most of his or her high school courses. Most community colleges will let students without a high school diploma take classes. Your teen may then transfer to the four-year school of his or her choice at a later time. (Refer to Part 3, "Choosing/Planning a Curriculum," for tips on planning curriculum.)

College Requirements

All colleges want to ensure that their students will succeed. Besides specific courses that they would like to see on a high school transcript, most colleges also look at awards, essays, extracurricular activities, grade point average, interviews, and recommendations.

You and your teen need to keep a file or a continuously updated portfolio containing certificates and awards, evidence of activities that would be considered extracurricular, and copies of any letters of recommendation that are written for your teen. Some activities that you may choose to count for high school credit and are also good to list for extracurricular activities include …

➤ Membership in Scouts, 4-H, Campfire

➤ Community service

➤ Participation in local music, drama, and arts productions

➤ Playing on sports teams; participating in other sports such as martial arts, skiing, and sailing

➤ Coaching sports teams

➤ Teaching classes, tutoring, or mentoring in areas of expertise

➤ Working in a family business, self-employment, or outside employment

Learning Links

Some schools list their suggested courses of study on their Web sites. You can find others in their brochures, or in Barron's *Profiles of American Colleges*. Many support schools and correspondence schools have a college preparatory track. *Homeschooling the High Schooler* (see Appendix E), by Diana McAlister and Candice Oneschak, contains typical graduation requirements for a general, community college prep, or college prep program. Research; then plan.

Whenever your teen works with a mentor, coach, teacher, employer, or trainer other than yourself, have your teen ask for a letter of recommendation at the conclusion of his or her association with each one. These can be included in portfolios or college applications.

Alternatives to College

College is just one of many options open to teens today. If your child has a specific interest, hobby, or pastime, is there any way it could be turned into a career? Would it best be learned by attending college, by apprenticeship, by on-the-job training, or by some other form of education?

177

Have your teen research career options, job-shadow
(spend a day following someone as that person goes
about his or her job duties), and do volunteer work in
his or her area of interest. Your teen should talk to
people who work in areas that interest him or her and
ask them specific questions:

➤ Why did you choose this career?

➤ How did you get your training?

➤ Are there required training programs or certifi-
cations?

➤ May I spend a day watching what you do?

➤ May I work as a volunteer helping you?

Some teens start businesses based on their interests, or find a need that they can fill
as a way to earn money, and turn their small enterprise into a real money-making career. This is a very real possibility in today's world. More and more people with impressive educational credentials and lucrative careers are becoming entrepreneurs and
working from home. Does your teen need a college degree to pursue the career that
interests him or her? Together you can do the research and find the correct path.
Check Appendix E for some books to get you started.

Analyzing Diploma Programs

Some teens who've been homeschooled through a specific support school or correspondence program since the early grades just continue on that track. Others who are
homeschooling for the first time try such a program as a way of duplicating what
they're used to in an institutional setting. Still others choose to enroll in a correspondence program as the base for their program, completing lessons in two to three
hours a day and enriching their curriculum with other activities, such as volunteer
work, paid employment, and the pursuit of various interests.

Do You Need One?

Depending on your state's requirements and what you are comfortable with, you may
or may not choose to use a diploma program.

There is no right answer for all homeschooling families; each family has to make
what seems to be the most appropriate choice, try it, and decide if that's what they
want to continue doing in the future. The bottom line is, you don't have to use a
diploma program, but many homeschooling families use one for a variety of reasons.
If it's important to your family that your children possess diplomas from an accred-
ited school, you will want to find a program that provides one. If you need or want

curriculum counseling, support services, or a preplanned program, find a program that provides these things. See Appendix D, "Independent Study Programs and Support Schools, Publications, and Vendors," for a listing of independent study programs and support schools.

Checking Out Other Options

If you decide you don't want to use the services of a full-service program, you can purchase a book outlining how to homeschool teenagers through the high school years. Or obtain a sample high school curriculum and plan your teen's studies together. You may or may not choose to use textbooks. You might decide on textbooks for certain subjects but implement real-life experiences and real books to provide learning in other areas. Many homeschooled teens use selected correspondence courses in specific areas of interest, or take classes at community colleges, through community education programs, through homeschool cooperatives, or through the Internet. The options are endless. Read on for an in-depth discussion of working with your teen to develop his or her individualized curriculum.

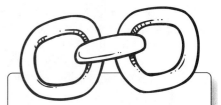

Learning Links

Go through the process outlined in Chapter 8, "Sixth Grade in a Box: Using a Full-Service Program," to determine what each program offers, its cost, how flexible or structured it is, and whether it fits your teen's personality, learning style, and interests, and your family's budget and educational philosophy.

Do-It-Yourself Academics

Some people call it unschooling, because to them unschooling is about pursuing their interests, using the world around them as a resource, using whatever materials work (including textbooks), and learning things as they need them. Others call it eclectic homeschooling—tailoring a program to fit their needs. Whatever you call it, many homeschooled teens are planning their own curriculum around their interests, tailoring their learning experiences to their own abilities and strengths, and focusing on getting a real-life education.

Attacking Difficult Subjects

Whether you design a structured program similar to what you might obtain from a support school or correspondence school, or take a more relaxed approach to learning, one thing is sure. At some point in your teen's high school years, he or she is going to need to learn something that is beyond your knowledge.

After doing some research at the library, surfing the Net, and exhausting all the possibilities you can think of, you may determine that a given subject is something for which you need to reach beyond your own resources. Whether your child is interested in flying, automotive training, or becoming an emergency medical technician, some things just require finding a mentor, tutor, or special course.

Some students take advanced placement courses online or by mail, use county intermediate school district programs, or attend community education classes. If your child is gifted in the arts, you may find classes at a center for the arts, a mentor in community theater while your teen pursues a role in a production, or private classes as ways to provide intensive learning experiences for your teen.

Learning Links

If homeschooling advanced math such as algebra, geometry, or trigonometry seems daunting to you, you might enlist the aid of a tutor, have your teen take the class through a community college, online, or by video or CD-ROM. Similar strategies work well for other classes that may seem intimidating, such as biology or chemistry. Check to see if anyone in your homeschooling support group has suggestions. Some parents have found that studying the difficult class right along with their student is very rewarding. Many parents find out they remember more than they had imagined, and it isn't quite as difficult the second time around. Parent and teen often end up learning from each other!

Preparing the Homeschooled Teen for College

Many unschooled, self-schooled, and eclectic homeschoolers have been accepted to colleges and universities all over the country. If college is your teen's goal, peruse college brochures, talk to homeschoolers who are attending college, speak to college admissions officers, and read books about homeschoolers who have gone to college. The most important thing students can do is learn how to learn. Teens can learn important research skills by searching for information on topics that interest them. Whether it's skydiving, silk-screening, or repairing a diesel engine, teens can obtain useful information by knowing how to use the research tools at the library, chatting with the research librarian, surfing the Internet, and using bibliographies and endnotes in books for additional resources.

If your teen is working toward college admissions, have him or her prepare for taking the *PSAT, SATs,* and *ACTs*. SAT is the name for a test that used to be called Scholastic Aptitude Test. ACT stands for American College Testing Assessment. The PSAT is a preliminary SAT test, given only in October, to prepare students for the SAT. Merit scholarships are available based on scores on the PSAT. For details about the SAT and ACT, call your local high school counseling office or check out www.collegeboard.org and www.act.org/aboutact/history.html on the Web.

There are books available that provide sample tests, test-taking tips, and other information that will be helpful to your homeschooled student. Some high school students may be able to get college credit for home-based studies by taking the CLEP (College Level Examination Program). Some CLEP credit is not transferrable, so it's good to discuss this issue with college counselors. (See Appendix B, "Curriculum Winners and Selected Resources, Including Dynamite Web Sites," for information about college testing; and Appendix E for helpful books for preparing for college testing.) Check with local homeschool support groups about having

Speaking Educationese

The **ACT** (American College Testing Assessment) and **SAT** (formerly Scholastic Aptitude Test) are used as assessment tools to determine the readiness of high schoolers for college. The **PSAT** is a preliminary SAT.

your homeschooler take the PSAT, SAT, and ACT at the public high school. Or call your local high school counseling office and ask for yourself; you don't have to give your name if the climate toward homeschoolers is iffy in your area.

Remember, too, that performing community service, being involved in an organized sport, participating in a group (such as Scouts, 4-H, or Habitat for Humanity), being self-employed, or working for the family business or an outside employer all help to create a well-rounded person who will appeal to college admissions officers.

Whether your teen uses traditional or offbeat methods to approach learning, the love of learning, ability to find the information your teen needs, and interaction with others are important pieces of the puzzle.

Mentorships, Apprenticeships, and On-the-Job Training

Mentorships, apprenticeships, and on-the-job training, are important parts of learning a skill or trade. This valuable experience can lead to certification in a specific area, as well as provide the experience to go along with the piece of paper that says the training has been completed. How often have you heard someone newly graduated from college describe job hunting this way? "I have the degree but no experience. They tell me to come back when I've gotten some experience, but no one will hire me." It's frustrating and disheartening to spend all that money and time and not be able to find a job to pay off the college loans! More and more colleges are offering apprenticeships as part of the final semesters of schooling, which is helping to alleviate this conundrum.

Your teen's apprenticeship may be an official one, or your teen may find an unofficial mentor who will teach him or her valuable skills and tricks of the trade. A letter of recommendation from that mentor may help your teen find employment in that field later. Offering to work without pay or for low pay for a short trial period may also help your teen get a foot in the door with a company that employs people in his or her area of interest.

College Admissions

If your teen's goal is to attend college, plan a curriculum that includes what most colleges are looking for. It's possible for your teen to do some unique things that can then be included on his or her transcript under the most mundane of headings, worded in such as way that they are easily understood by college admissions officers. Your state may have graduation requirements you must follow, or that you can use as a guideline. A typical college prep high school curriculum will generally include the following number of credits:

➤ English: 4 credits

➤ Math: 3 or more credits

➤ Social science: 3 credits

➤ Science: 3 or 4 credits

➤ Physical education/health: 2 credits

➤ Fine arts: 1 credit

➤ Foreign language: 2 or more credits

➤ Electives to equal 22 or more total credits

Learning Links

Have your teen take his or her portfolio along to a college admissions interview. Seeing the scope of a homeschooler's accomplishments written down in black and white on a neatly completed transcript backed up by the impressive record compiled in a portfolio will help the admissions officer understand the educational background of your homeschooled applicant.

English, math, science, and social studies are considered core classes. Physical education, languages, and fine arts are also required subjects to round out the core education. Electives go beyond the core classes, and for college prep students may include such things as advanced mathematics and advanced placement classes in English, science, or foreign language taken at colleges, or via distance education.

To provide an equivalent education you may choose to use a support school that uses traditional materials and methods, or write your own curriculum using real-life experiences, community service, mentorships, and other unorthodox methods to obtain the same end. Careful documentation of what the student has learned, letters of recommendation from mentors and tutors, and a portfolio of completed projects, awards, certificates, and photographs of the student will be helpful in developing transcripts that college admissions officers can understand.

Preparation for the World of Work

If college isn't in the plan, there are a variety of ways to prepare teens for the realities of the working world that awaits them after high school. Put simply, the best preparation is work. Your teen might start his or her own business that reflects current interests, work for the family business, apprentice in a field he or she is considering, or obtain a job just to earn some money and gain the experience of working for someone else.

Spotlight on Education

When my older children were 14 and 11, I formed a small renovation business, retaining my painting contractor and remodeling expert husband as a consultant. With my children as my employees, I purchased neglected but structurally sound houses in good neighborhoods and we set to work to improve them for resale. My motives: to provide employment for our children who were too young to do such work for anyone but us, to teach our children a good work ethic and the skills they would someday need to maintain a home of their own, and to make a profit. The kids learned the basics of plumbing, electrical, drywall finishing, painting, landscaping, figuring for materials, financial skills, and much more on the job.

There is no substitute for the pleasure gained from doing an honest day's work and reaping the material benefits. Learning to use one's earnings responsibly is another benefit of earning one's own money. Teens learn responsibility because they have to schedule time for work in addition to their other activities. To learn to work for someone else, get along with other employees and customers, be responsible for getting the job done right, and take pride in one's work are all stepping stones on the path to independence.

The Socialization Question

As I first mentioned in Chapter 3, "Quick Answers to Beginners' Questions," just when you are feeling comfortable with the idea of homeschooling your teen, inevitably someone comes along and starts talking about socialization. One parent minces no words as she asks naysayers to visit a public high school, observe the masses of kids, and let her know just what they think her kids are missing. On the other hand, many homeschooled teens have both institutionally schooled friends and relatives as well as homeschooled friends. Quite a few are involved in family activities that provide natural socialization as they work, play, study, and relax together.

Learning Lookouts

Don't underrate your ability to provide appropriate social experiences for your child by tapping into your own extended family and social circle. Many educational experts point to the family as the most influential component leading to successful students.

Most are involved in a variety of activities, including employment, which ensure that they are positively socialized, articulate, and already able to function in the so-called "real world."

Community Service

Homeschoolers are doing community service in towns across the nation. Some train as docents (tour guides, teachers, or lecturers) at museums, pick up litter, learn to rehabilitate injured and ill wild animals through nature center programs, help build homes for Habitat for Humanity, participate in walk/jogathons for shelters for battered women and children, clean cages and feed the animals at an animal shelter, and visit the elderly in nursing homes. Homeschooled teens collect canned goods for shelters, make quilts and afghans for children with AIDS, and hold yard sales and car washes for flood victims. Some teens volunteer in areas in which they are interested to decide if they would enjoy a career in that field: These kids help out in a veterinarian's or dentist's office, clean tools and change oil for an independent mechanic, or provide tutoring for an after-school program.

Some parents and support schools make volunteer work a non-negotiable part of their children's curriculum. There has been some discussion about the validity of volunteer work if the child is obligated to perform it. Teens of this age are old enough to understand the value of doing community service, and to realize that volunteering their time is not a one-way street; they will be benefiting from the experience as well as performing a vital service for others. As long as the child understands the purpose of a parent or school requiring volunteer service this shouldn't be considered a coercive arrangement. The key to your child having a satisfying experience volunteering (versus getting paid) requires that your child enjoy and understand the value of his or her efforts.

Spotlight on Education

Ryan was extremely interested in maritime history. He replied to the maritime museum's ad for interns to work as docents, only to be told that the museum had never had a high school student apply before. I suggested that he go in for an interview so the director could meet him. Upon seeing Ryan's interest and enthusiasm for the museum exhibits, as well as learning that he was also trained in small engine repair and had his own business, the director gave Ryan the opportunity. Ryan started out doing research for new exhibits, took the training to become a docent, and was soon giving tours to groups of senior citizens, elementary school students, and college kids.

Volunteer work can be counted toward high school credits as well: My son Ryan used his research time at the maritime museum toward a state history credit and his docent training and experience as his speech credit.

Sports

A very small minority of public school students actually plays on the teams at institutional schools. Playing on sports teams is an extracurricular activity that has become extremely overrated in our society today. Although sports teams were originally formed to provide good clean fun and to teach sportsmanship and team spirit, many of the teams today leave a lot to be desired. Reports of coaches who emphasize winning at any cost, parents who engage in violence as a result of miscalls by umpires, and kids being allowed or encouraged to use steroids to enhance their abilities have caused some parents to discourage participation by their children who are institutionally schooled. For this and other reasons many homeschoolers are not interested in involving their children in the world of institutional sports. In most states homeschoolers may not play on public school teams. Some homeschoolers have found spots on private school teams, and occasionally homeschoolers play on public school teams where it is legal to do so. See Chapter 3 for more discussion about playing team sports.

Homeschoolers in some areas have formed leagues and travel for state tournaments, duplicating in many ways the sports scene found in the public schools. Other homeschoolers encourage their teen's participation in such competitive sports as martial arts, downhill ski racing, diving, and tennis. Intramural and private teams can be found in some areas. Still other homeschoolers enjoy a variety of sports simply for the joy of participating—competing with themselves to become more proficient without being involved in any organized competition.

The Prom

Imagine that after much soul searching and agonizing over whether you can do it, whether it will work, and whether it will help with the problems your teen has been experiencing, you decide to homeschool your teen. Then imagine that the first question your neighbor asks you is, "Will she be able to go to the prom?" Has this been one of your major concerns in making the choice to homeschool? Probably not. However, since it does come up now and then, consider this: Most—yes, the majority—of high school students do not attend the prom! Think about it. Remember when you were in high school? It's not that different now. So remember, first, that if your homeschooled teen doesn't attend the prom, he or she might not have attended even if he or she were in public school. Second, be assured that homeschooled teens do get invited to school dances and the prom, because most homeschooled teens don't totally disassociate themselves from their schooled friends—although some do, especially when peer dependence was the major reason for homeschooling. If your homeschooled teen is still dating schooled teens, chances are your teen may attend the prom as well. Finally, ask yourself: Is the prom a big issue with your teen, or is it your issue? There's more on this topic in Chapter 3.

Learning Links

Whether your teen attends a graduation ceremony, initiates a new family tradition, or receives his or her diploma in the mail, consider hosting an open house for friends, neighbors, relatives, and mentors to share in this special milestone.

Graduation

If your teen is just beginning to homeschool after spending 10 years in the institutional school track, you are most apt to feel a sense of loss when thinking about graduation. Commencement exercises are a tradition that many parents think about when they look ahead to the milestones in their child's life. Sometimes when parents begin to homeschool, such traditions become an unimportant ritual, and some teens' high school and college years blend together so there is no clear point of demarcation. Some support schools and umbrella schools sponsor a commencement ceremony in which your teen may participate. Other homeschoolers attend graduation ceremonies planned by local support groups, or plan a special family celebration to mark the event.

The Least You Need to Know

➤ Having a goal in mind makes high school planning easier.

➤ You can use a diploma program or write your own curriculum that is tailored to your teen's needs.

➤ To simplify the college admissions process, carefully document your teen's activities and learning experiences.

➤ Employment is a valuable learning tool, providing experience and confidence.

➤ Homeschooled students have many opportunities for positive socialization, including community service and playing sports.

Chapter 14

Homeschooling Kids with Special Needs

In This Chapter

➤ How homeschooling can help special-needs children

➤ Establishing your own support network

➤ Finding assistance through books, periodicals, groups, and researching online

➤ Using an umbrella school that works with special needs

➤ Designing a tailor-made program that meets your child's needs

➤ Developing a positive attitude and celebrating any and all progress

Homeschool a child who has special needs? Yes! More and more parents are motivated to homeschool because of their children's special needs. Special-needs children benefit from homeschooling whether they exhibit specific language disability or mathematical dysfunction, need behavior modification or emotional support, are medically fragile, are academically gifted, or are hearing- or vision-impaired.

If you are considering homeschooling a child with special needs, you're not alone! Parents of such children stress the importance of finding support, learning what your child needs, and keeping a positive attitude. This chapter will help you by providing resources and suggestions for planning for your child with special needs.

How Homeschooling Can Help Your Child with Special Needs

Unless you opened this book immediately to this chapter, you've already learned a lot of what you need to know about researching the homeschool laws in your state, the climate for homeschooling in your community and school district, and how to choose a support school or design your own curriculum.

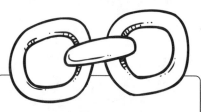

Learning Links

If you used the index or table of contents to find this chapter, read Part 3, "Choosing/Planning a Curriculum," for help researching home education. Find help in planning a program for your child in Part 4, "Taking the Plunge: What Do I Do Now?" Much of the information can be adapted to fit your child with special needs.

The most important thing you need to know about providing an educational program for your child with special needs is to know your child. Use him or her as the benchmark in choosing materials, support programs, and learning experiences. Consider his or her interests, abilities, personality, and needs when choosing materials or curriculum. It doesn't really matter what worked for another homeschooler, because that family's situation, the child's disability, and the child's temperament and needs will differ from yours. What matters is whether it will work for *your* child.

Find out what homeschool support groups, umbrella schools, or consulting services in your area provide support for specific special educational needs. If there aren't any local resources available, you will have to go further afield to locate the information you need. Check Appendix C, "Homeschooling Support Organizations," for national, state, and provincial organizations to help you in your research. Appendix D, "Independent Study Programs and Support Schools, Publications, and Vendors," includes distance-learning programs that offer IEPs and other services for children with special needs.

Focusing on Your Child's Special Needs

It's important that you learn as much about your child's diagnosis as you can. Having a working knowledge of your child's learning differences, physical and neurological disabilities, or behavioral problems will enable you to plan a learning program that will meet his or her specific needs.

Seek Out Others in Similar Situations

Whenever we encounter a new situation in life there is something comforting about talking to someone else who has already walked the same road. Parents of special-needs children are no exception. Many organizations exist to help parents cope with the new experiences they will encounter in parenting a child with special needs. However, whether you have been advocating for your child in an institutional school or just recently received a diagnosis, your special-needs support network may not consider it wise for you to homeschool. Although there are many programs available through public schools, more and more parents are choosing to provide an individualized program for their special-needs children at home. Remember that *you* are the one most qualified and responsible for making the final choice for your child.

You are not the first person to consider homeschooling a special-needs child; remind those who would discourage you that you are aware of many parents who are successfully providing a home-based education for children with special needs.

In the past few years a proliferation of Web sites, bulletin boards, e-mail lists, and chat rooms have sprung up to encourage and support those who are homeschooling special-needs children. The Internet is also a good resource for locating support groups and parents in your area who are homeschooling children with special needs (see Appendix B, "Curriculum Winners and Selected Resources, Including Dynamite Web Sites").

Finding someone else whose children have similar needs can speed up your own search for resources and programs, and spark ideas for working with your own child.

Support Groups for Special Needs

If your child has been tested and diagnosed with a special need, chances are that you have been given some reports and other material to read. Some testing centers also provide reading lists, local support group information, and some contact names so you can speak with others who have children with similar disabilities. Make as many contacts as you can; you will learn something new from each person you talk to. A good understanding of your child's special needs will help you make the best choices regarding homeschooling that child.

Learning Lookouts

Health professionals, your family, friends, and the parents you meet at support group meetings may discourage you from homeschooling, citing your lack of experience with both the child's special needs and homeschooling. Most homeschoolers learn as they go, and although it is wise to have a general plan, you and your child can learn the ABCs of homeschooling together.

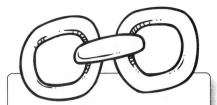

Learning Links

Always ask each person you contact to recommend a favorite book on the special-needs topic and the name of any resources he or she has found helpful. In the case of parents, ask them what they wish they had known when they first got their child's diagnosis.

Here are a few support groups listed by type of educational special need:

➤ **Down syndrome:** National Down Syndrome Society, 666 Broadway, New York, NY 10012; 1-800-221-4602 or 212-460-9330; www.ndsccenter.org

Speaking Educationese

Dyslexia, a specific language disability, is a severe difficulty in understanding or using one or more areas of language, including listening, speaking, reading, writing, and spelling, while skills in the other areas are age-appropriate.

➤ **Dyslexia:** International Dyslexia Association, Chester Building, 8600 LaSalle Road, Suite 382, Baltimore, MD 21286-2044; 410-296-0232; www.interdys.org

➤ **Gifted:** The National Research Center on the Gifted and Talented, University of Connecticut, 2131 Hillside Road, U-7, Storrs, CT 06269-3007; 860-486-4676; www.gifted.uconn.edu/nrcgt. html

➤ **Specific language disability and communication disorders:** LDA (The Learning Disabilities Association), 4156 Library Road, Pittsburgh, PA 15234-1349; 412-341-1515; www.ldanatl.org; also, American Speech-Language Hearing Association, 10801 Rockville Pike, Rockville, MD 20852; 1-888-321-ASHA or 301-897-5700; www.asha.org/professionals/convention/convention.htm

Other children may have special needs that are more behaviorally specific, but respond well to tutorial instruction, immediate positive reinforcement, and individualized curriculum planning. Here are some examples:

➤ **ADD/ADHD (attention deficit disorder/attention deficit hyperactivity disorder):** CHADD (Children and Adults with Attention Deficit Disorder), 8181 Professional Place, Suite 201, Landover, MD 20785; 1-800-233-4050 or 301-306-7070; www.chadd.org

➤ **Autism (the full spectrum includes Asperger's disorder, pervasive developmental disorder, Rett's disorder, childhood disintegrative disorder, and fragile X syndrome):** Autism Society of America, 7910 Woodmont Avenue, Suite 300, Bethesda, MD 20814-3015; 1-800-3AUTISM, extension 150, or 301-657-0881; www.autism-society.org

➤ **Dysfunction in sensory integration:** Sensory Integration International, P.O. Box 9013, Torrance, CA 90508; 310-320-9986; home.earthlink.net/~sensoryint

➤ **Obsessive-compulsive disorder:** Obsessive-Compulsive Foundation, Inc., 337 Notch Hill Road, North Branford, CT 06471; 203-315-2190; www.healthtechsys.com/ocfound.html

➤ **Tourette syndrome:** Tourette Syndrome Association, 42-40 Bell Blvd., Bayside, NY 11361; 718-224-2999; www.tsa-usa.org

➤ **Traumatic brain injury:** The Brain Injury Association Inc., 105 North Alfred Street, Alexandria, VA 22314; 703-236-6000; www.biausa.org

Spotlight on Education

Amy, 11, has always been homeschooled but exhibited little interest in learning to read, which concerned Laura, her mother. Although she was never tested, samples of her work indicated dyslexia. The program at the school was ruled out due to its high activity level; Amy prefers quiet learning pursuits. Instead, Amy has been working with an Orton-Gillingham trained tutor from a specific language disability center, and is doing great with her reading progress. The Orton-Gillingham method of tutoring is language–based, multi-sensory, and focuses on the student's (usually) strong thinking skills. Amy's tutor gives Laura lists of words with which to help Amy between tutoring sessions. Amy and her mother use *Explode the Code*, a phonics workbook series, as part of her daily reading instruction.

Some physical challenges may necessitate very personal attention to physical accommodations as well as individualized curriculum planning. Many homeschoolers are successfully educating children with these special needs, as well as medically fragile children and children with multiple special needs:

➤ **Hearing impaired/deaf:** Deafness Research Foundation, 15 West 39th Street, 6th Floor, New York, NY 10018-3806; 1-800-535-3323 (voice) or 212-768-1181 (voice/TDD); www.healthy.net/pan/cso/cioi/DRF.HTM

➤ **Orthopedic impairment:** The National Easter Seals Society, 70 East Lake Street, Chicago, IL 60601-5907; 312-726-6200; www.easter-seals.org/; also, National Multiple Sclerosis Society, 205 East 42nd Street, New York, NY 10010; 1-800-344-4867; www.nmss.org; also, Spina Bifida Association of America, 4590 MacArthur Blvd. NW, Suite 250, Washington, DC 20007-4226; 1-800-621-3141 or 202-944-3285; www.sbaa.org; also, United Cerebral Palsy Association, Inc., 1522 K Street NW, Suite 1112, Washington, DC 20005; 203-842-1266; www.ucpa.org

➤ **Vision impaired/blind:** American Foundation for the Blind, Inc., 15 West 16th Street, New York, NY 10011; 1-800-232-5463 or 212-620-2020; www.afb.org

National groups, such as those previously listed, can often point you to a local support group, newsletters, workshops, and conferences. You may also receive referrals to such groups from doctors, health clinics, therapists, and other health professionals. If you live in an urban area you may be able to locate such a support group in the telephone directory. If there are no local groups, obtain information from a national group about starting a chapter in your area.

Attend special-needs support group meetings as soon as you can. The support and feedback you will get from members will be invaluable in helping you adjust to the diagnosis, support your child, handle doubts and questions from well-meaning family members and friends, and cope with life with a child with special needs. It's possible that support group members may discourage you from homeschooling, just as many parents of normally abled children discourage their peers from homeschooling. Get what support you can from special-needs support groups; then look for support from other homeschoolers with special-needs children, from within yourself as you follow your gut instincts, and from literature on homeschooling kids with special needs. Homeschoolers often play the role of pioneer; breaking trails for others. When you succeed at homeschooling, others may be encouraged to try it with their children.

Homeschool Support Groups

Make contact with a local homeschool support group for information about legal issues and leads to sources for materials and curriculum—and, of course, for support. (Chapter 6, "Finding Support," contains tips on locating homeschool support groups.) Even if you don't find any other homeschoolers who are teaching children with specific special needs, you will find homeschoolers who will be happy to help you by sharing catalogs, making resource recommendations, and talking to you about homeschooling regulations in your state of residence. Although your specific needs may be somewhat different than the average homeschooler's, many home-based learners adapt materials to their children's needs, use trial and error, and work through insecurity and doubt on a regular basis. Local home educators may also be able to lead you to resources that would be difficult to learn about otherwise, such as local homeschool curriculum consultants, umbrella programs that work with special needs, and tutors and evaluators.

Consider Community Resources

Depending on the nature of your child's special needs, you may find support within the community. Some parents homeschool their child while using programs through the local department of mental health, the local school district, or private programs at colleges, tutoring centers, and specific language disability centers.

The intermediate school district in some states provides services for homeschoolers. It may provide evaluation, consultation, special programs and services, and referrals to other helping agencies. The school district's programs may include such things as special education classrooms, speech and language therapy, psychological and social work services, occupational and physical therapy, and services for the visually impaired and hearing impaired, among others. Even infants, toddlers, and other preschoolers may be eligible for services. Be sure you know your rights and responsibilities under the existing homeschooling law before contacting the school district.

Community education classes, museum and library programs, and church outreach programs are all sources worth checking into. Talk to people you know about what you are planning to do. Don't let them talk you out of your purpose to homeschool, but do ask them for suggestions and help. Although you may not agree with or pursue all suggestions, networking sometimes reaps the most interesting benefits; someone you speak to may have a neighbor or cousin or friend who is homeschooling a child with special needs. Such tips often lead you to a resource that will work for you and your child.

Talking about the challenges you face may pay off in respite care, home-cooked meals, books, educational materials, and other special gifts from an acquaintance or neighbor you would never have asked to help. If people aren't aware of what you are doing they won't know how to help. Many times people want to help if they only knew what to do. Accept all help, gifts, and kind gestures graciously, in the spirit with which they are given.

> **Learning Links**
>
> If you are considering home-schooling but want to continue to receive services from the local public school, contact Pete (a special education attorney) and Pam Wright (a psychotherapist) about your homeschooling rights. Reach them c/o The Special Ed Advocate, P.O. Box 1008, Delta-ville, VA 23043; 804-257-0857. To subscribe to their free online newsletter, visit their Web site at www.wrightslaw.com, or e-mail them at webmaster@wrightslaw.com.

Where Else Can I Find Support?

The possibilities are ever growing and changing. As I write this, there are probably new Web sites and bulletin boards being created online to better serve the needs of parents of children with special needs. Let's take a look at what's available.

Newsletters and Magazines

Publications such as newsletters and magazines are available from national support groups, specific disability centers, parents who are homeschooling kids with special needs, and online entities. The use of the Internet makes locating such resources very simple; go to a multi-search engine and key in the name of your child's diagnosis to receive a long list of matches. If you don't have access to the Internet, you can often use a computer in your public library. You can also ask your child's pediatrician, family practitioner, occupational therapist, support group members, library's research librarian, and anyone else you think might be able to lead you to periodicals that will help you. Check Appendix B for a list of special-needs publications.

Books

There are many, many books written to assist parents in parenting their child with specific disabilities (see Appendix E, "Bibliography"). Many of these books are rich in tips to help you parent; these same tips may prove very useful in working with your child in the homeschool setting.

Don't overlook any resource that is specific to your child's special needs. If the title or author's approach seems at odds with what you already know about your child's learning differences, at least scan the book's table of contents, bibliography, index, and appendixes for the names of support groups, publications, books, and other resources to help you in your quest for knowledge to help your child. Although you may not totally embrace an alternative approach now, you may still get valuable insights, tips, and resources from such writings. Given time and experience, you may find that alternative methods are exactly what you and your child need to optimize his or her learning program.

Learning Lookouts

Some researchers have connected environmental issues such as pollutants, pesticides, and other contaminants to some specific disabilities. If you are interested in following the research on this issue, contact Environmental Research Foundation, P.O. Box 5036, Annapolis, MD 21403; www.rachel.org. The foundation also offers a free newsletter.

Online

Online support is stupendous! If you have Internet access, your first challenge will be to sift through the mountains of information available. Make your first search effort as specific as possible to eliminate frustration! You will find support for your child's specific disability, as well as support for homeschooling children with special educational needs.

Online resources include informational Web sites with names of national and local support groups, e-mail lists, Web rings, bulletin boards where you may read archived messages and post questions for other parents and experts to answer, and chats. See Appendix B for more information.

Umbrella Schools That Offer Special-Needs Support

Depending on your child's special needs, on homeschooling legal requirements in your state, and on your own feelings of confidence or inadequacy, you may choose to use an umbrella school or full-service program. If your child has been enrolled in a special education program in a public school, it may be simpler to transfer your child to a private school program which offers a homeschool program with *IEPs* than it would be to simply withdraw your child to be homeschooled. Some homeschooling umbrellas and support programs will work with you to develop an IEP for your child with special needs. Be sure you have carefully researched your options before initiating a plan of action.

Consider your child's educational needs when comparing umbrella schools and full-service programs. Will your child's needs be adequately met by simply tailoring the program to his or her needs, or does your child need an IEP? Some programs are flexible enough to allow for a wide variety of learning differences, while others just simply wouldn't work. Other programs are available that provide curriculum counseling and planning, help develop IEPs, and support you through every phase of your child's educational journey.

If monetary concerns make the use of such a program impossible, you will have to continue to educate yourself and become extremely creative to provide the individualized program your child needs. Remind yourself often that you were your child's first teacher, you know your child best, you understand your child's needs, and since you love your child more than anyone else in the world, you are imminently qualified to continue your child's education. Another advantage of homeschooling without program oversight is that you won't have to schedule an IEP meeting every time you want to make a curriculum change!

Speaking Educationese

IEPs, or individual education programs, are the blueprints for your child's special education. They include the specific classroom setup, curricula, support services, and program and educational goals.

Design Your Own Learning Program

Rather than replicating what wasn't working in the institutional setting, don't plan on doing "school-at-home." This is especially true if your child has been in special education. Deschool yourself and your child. Decide what is really important—time with your child, basic skills, or regaining a love for learning—and plan your days

Learning Links

When the going gets tough, the tough get going! Take some time off. Go for a walk or do something else physical. Keep your sense of humor; read a funny book or the comics with your child. Trade kids with another parent, or get together for a play date or park day. Take a trip to a hands-on museum or the zoo. Get up, get out, refocus, and recharge.

accordingly. Don't be surprised if things don't always go smoothly. You are both on a new learning curve.

Focus on the positive side of your child's special needs. If your child gets immersed in a project to the exclusion of all else, encourage him or her! Be sure your child gets plenty of rest, fluids, and remembers to eat, and let your child go with his or her interest. It's called following interests, and many homeschoolers use it on a regular basis. Give it a try.

Be aware of your child's learning style and the idiosyncrasies of his or her special-needs diagnosis. When your child is acting angry or annoyed, it may be because the activity doesn't work for him or her. Don't take it personally; ask nonthreatening questions such as …

➤ Is this too easy for you? Are you bored?

➤ Is this too hard for you? Are you frustrated?

➤ How would you like to learn this?

➤ If you could change this, how would you plan it?

Listen to your child's answers. Children can be amazingly insightful about their own learning style especially when their frustration is being accepted.

Don't allow a focus on schooling to keep your child from experiencing real life. Find mentors, tutors, special programs, and resources. Use educational television, videos, real books, community classes, and real-life experiences like camping, traveling, and community service. Allow your child to dream, to set seemingly impossible goals, and to work toward them.

Honor Differences and Focus on the Positive

It's easy to become overwhelmed with the negative aspects of your child's learning disabilities or physical challenges. Some things cannot be changed, but your attitude can. Accepting that your child's differences are a very real part of that child, and realizing that your own attitude is going to shape your child's attitude about him- or herself is often a very large step toward understanding your own capabilities and limitations in helping your child. Focus on the things that you can help with or improve, and take things one step at a time. Although progress may be slow, celebrate the baby steps that are made toward a preplanned goal. Whenever possible, consider your child's disabilities in a positive light, allowing your child to see that you perceive him or her as a whole person, not just a person with a disability.

Children who have been labeled *LD* shouldn't have to hear terminology with negative implications (such as dysfunction, disability, deficit, or disorder) constantly applied to them, or used as a crutch or excuse. Acceptance is part of the adjustment process but using negative terminology on a regular basis can be debilitating. Perhaps you can substitute the term "learning differences" as a way of honoring your child.

According to the theory of multiple intelligences (see Chapter 7, "So Much to Choose From"), everyone learns differently, and although most institutional schools address only a couple of these—notably the verbal/linguistic and mathematical/logical models—many of us learn in other ways. How many of the children who bear the label learning disabled simply learn in ways that are not recognized and celebrated in our culture today? Many parents who homeschool children labeled learning disabled in the institutional setting find that their children flourish with an individualized curriculum, a focus on strengths, the removal of pressure, and the use of interest-oriented learning projects. In some cases the disabilities either disappear or diminish and learning progresses much better than expected. Some children begin to find a renewed interest in learning when removed from an environment in which their learning style is not understood, and where peers mock and belittle anyone who is minutely different from the norm.

Parents of children with other disabilities such as autism, auditory hypersensitivity, Down syndrome, and sensory integration dysfunction find that one-on-one time, individualized learning experiences, and positive reinforcement of progress are the keys to success in maximizing learning for their children. Whatever your child's disabilities or learning differences, you can maximize his or her learning potential by providing a unique home-based program.

Speaking Educationese

LD, or learning disabled, encompasses a variety of special needs, including but not limited to attention deficit disorder, hyperactivity, dyslexia, dyscalculia, dysgraphia, dysnomia, and dyspraxia.

Learning Lookouts

Children live up to our expectations. Using the word "disabled" can cause a child to perceive him- or herself negatively. Focus on the child's ability: Help your child to realize that although he or she is differently abled, he or she also has specific abilities. Uniqueness isn't always valued in our society; at home we can celebrate differences and be proud of accomplishments.

Spotlight on Education

Tammy homeschools her daughter Pamela, who is autistic. Not all autistic children learn in the same way: Pamela is visual and kinesthetic, needing concrete, sequential approaches. Although many autistic children seem to prefer doing the same schedule every day, trial and error has shown that Pamela finds variation much more enjoyable. When Pamela is stimulated by jingles from television commercials, Tammy helps her turn annoying phrases into something useful, a fun way to practice language skills. Since Pamela loses abstract thinking skills for about three days when she doesn't stick to her gluten-free, casein-free diet, Tammy always encourages parents of children with special needs to check into alternative therapies to enhance educational and behavioral ability.

The Least You Need to Know

➤ The first step toward successfully homeschooling your special-needs child is understanding his or her special needs.

➤ Keep your purpose to homeschool foremost in your mind as you gather information, network, consult with others, and plan.

➤ Look at resources, programs, and activities in a different light: How can I adapt it? What will my child learn from it? Will it help him or her build self-confidence, learn a new skill, or encourage independence?

➤ All children have learning preferences, personalities, interests, and needs that will help you plan the optimal learning program.

➤ You *can* homeschool your child with special needs!

Part 5

Keeping Track: Testing/Assessments/ Record-Keeping

How do I know my child is learning? What if he or she has difficulty taking tests? Do I need to keep records? You'll learn about the many issues involved in the areas of testing, assessments, and record-keeping.

You'll determine your stance on testing and other assessments. In the chapter on record-keeping, you'll learn how to decide what to keep, how to file it, and how to present records in compliance with regulations without jeopardizing homeschoolers' freedoms.

Testing, Testing, 1, 2, 3

Does testing go along with schooling in your mind? Testing is the one method most used by institutional schools to determine whether students are learning. However, more and more people are questioning whether one specific test is an accurate measuring tool for all students.

Studies of homeschoolers usually include statistics regarding how homeschooled students who are tested measure up to their institutionally schooled counterparts. It's a fact that tested homeschoolers consistently score higher than their peers in the institutional school setting. However, not all homeschoolers are comfortable with testing, and not all homeschoolers use testing. In fact some homeschoolers refuse to use testing as an accountability measure for a variety of reasons, which we'll explore in this chapter.

To Test or Not to Test? That Is the Question

Institutional schools use tests as a way to determine whether students are learning a specific body of knowledge. Perhaps that's the first issue we should look at: What is being tested? Obviously, a test contains questions about a specific body of informa-

tion. To score well on such a test children need to be prepared by learning the information covered on the test. Therefore, many institutional schools spend an inordinate amount of time teaching just that. Most parents have read articles deploring the practice of *teaching to the test,* and are aware of this technique being used in their children's schools. This practice focuses attention on covering the material to be included on a specific test while neglecting other areas of the curriculum that should be covered.

Studies have shown that classrooms that focus on teaching to the test tend to be less creative. They spend less time on group projects, don't promote learning that fosters thinking and problem solving, and often fail to engage and challenge students. Homeschoolers who use testing need to consider these realities when deciding whether to devote time to preparing for standardized testing.

Speaking Educationese

Teaching to the test is the practice of covering material that is to be included on a specific test while neglecting other areas of the curriculum. This practice is often criticized not only by parents, but by the teachers who are required to implement the practice.

When money is tied to test scores, as is often the case with state mandated tests and tests that are tied to federal funding, the pressure is even higher on the administration of school districts to get teachers to teach to the test.

Spotlight on Education

Many states have a state-mandated curriculum in place, and about 18 states require proficiency tests in order for students to be promoted to the next grade or to graduate. Politicians have focused on educational issues as a way of getting the vote, with the Democratic party calling for a system of accountability for every student, school, and state, while the Republicans state that raising the standards without accountability is meaningless. With politicians calling for higher standards, what means are being implemented to determine whether children are being educated? Tests. Is testing the best way to determine if children have learned? Absolutely not! A valid evaluation will always consider the overall performance of the student, not just a test score.

A study in 1998 by the National Research Council concluded that a single test score should not be the sole or automatic basis of an educational decision that will have a major impact on a test taker.

What the Studies Show

Studies of tests have raised many questions about what purpose is served by testing. First, we need to understand that the primary purpose of many standardized tests is to rank students, determining those who will be successes, failures, and mediocre (the majority). *Norm-referenced tests* are designed to rank students, while *criterion-referenced tests*, which are not designed to rank students, still serve the same purpose. Standardized tests are biased in favor of white middle-class males who live in metropolitan areas and echo the background, cultures, and upbringing of typical test designers. Thus, such tests are biased against females, children of color, rural children, and children from lower socioeconomic backgrounds. Children whose test scores are low in the early grades may be sentenced to spending the rest of their school years doing remedial practice in lower-level groups or in special classes.

Because teachers spend a lot of time going over material that will be on the test, practicing test-taking skills, and preparing for the test, the scope of material covered in the classroom narrows. Teachers and students have less time to spend on real, meaningful, and important learning. Standardized tests tend to be negatively oriented, focusing on students' inability and what they don't know, while not providing the information really needed to design an individualized learning program.

Speaking Educationese

In a **norm-referenced test,** the score is derived by comparing the number of items answered correctly with the average performance of others. In a **criterion-referenced test,** the score is based on whether or not one can perform up to a set standard.

What does all of this have to do with you, the potential homeschooler? There is a big push on for more accountability among homeschoolers. Some states already have standardized testing requirements in place for homeschoolers, though most will accept an alternative assessment. As a homeschooler you must decide whether or not to submit your students for standardized testing, to whom you will allow testing results to be released, and how much time you will spend preparing your child for testing. To find out whether testing is required in your state or province, obtain a copy of the regulations and check with local homeschoolers to find out how such regulations are enforced. See Appendix C, "Homeschooling Support Organizations."

Why Is So Much Emphasis Put on Test Results?

In the institutional school setting, the bottom line is money. Many tests have large amounts of money tied to them in the form of national or state funding. Teachers are pressured, and children in the classroom bear the brunt of that pressure. Children endure weeks or months of test preparation, including taking timed sample tests, and enduring drill and rote learning in the areas that are deemed weakest. Participation in group learning projects, art, creative writing, and other interesting classroom activities take second place to preparing for and taking standardized tests.

As is true any time money is involved, people get greedy and there have been reports of cheating on tests. In New York City a scandal implicating dozens of teachers and two principals involved erasure and correction of wrong answers on students' tests. In Austin, Texas, school employees have been charged with invalidating students' low scores to achieve better overall results. Several other states have been involved in similar scandals. When school funding and administrator's promotions, raises, and jobs are tied to test scores, the picture gets increasingly ugly.

Assessing Your Child's Learning

Is it necessary to test homeschooled kids? While some homeschoolers use a school-at-home approach, implementing testing with nary a thought of doing otherwise, some home-based learners don't use testing at all. When living and learning together on a day-to-day, hour-by-hour basis, 24-7, parents become attuned to whether or not their child is learning. Some homeschoolers eschew the use of testing as inappropriate to their learning philosophy and don't use testing at all. Somewhere in the middle of the road are homeschoolers who use testing occasionally, for specific purposes, but not on a regular basis.

Homeschoolers who don't use tests on a regular basis are often able to assess whether their children are learning in very simple ways. If a child is excited and interested in continuing to pursue a specific interest or line of study, learning is happening. Interactive discussions between parent and child regarding the results of experiments, projects, and the content of books being read are another form of unstructured assessment.

Diagnostic tests are available that may be helpful in determining grade level if you are planning to use a school-at-home approach. If you are planning to use unit studies, an interest-driven approach, or a living-books approach, it isn't really necessary to determine

Learning Lookouts

Most standardized tests focus on comparing your child to other children. What's the point? Determine whether learning is happening by asking yourself some questions. Is the child happy about learning? Can your child do things he or she couldn't do before? Has your child mastered any new concepts? Look over your journal to remind yourself where your child has come from and the progress that's been made.

an exact grade level. Such testing has its place, but once again it's important to understand that using one form of assessment—a test—is not very accurate.

Spotlight on Education

Many homeschoolers don't really think much about grade level, other than to keep their kids oriented so they can answer the typical questions from people making conversation: "And where do you go to school? Oh, homeschool! Aren't you lucky? My sister-in-law homeschools! What grade are you in? Don't know? Hmmm. Do you like school? You do? Do you like your teacher? Ha ha ha!" After a few such situations, parents sometimes make a point of reminding their children what grade they're in, just to prevent embarrassment. Grade level, designed to track children and make record keeping efficient, has become an identity criteria among school children. Homeschoolers have the privilege of learning at their individual level, at their own speed, regardless of grade level.

Should You Test Your Child?

While homeschooling parents who use a traditional school-type approach may use testing regularly without a qualm, parents who have looked into the deeper implications of testing may either refuse to use tests, or use testing sparingly and only under certain conditions. Consider your student's abilities and goals, and educate yourself regarding the concept of testing and all it means before making a decision regarding testing. Although requiring institutional students to pass a proficiency test to prove they are ready for the next grade may seem like a positive move toward accountability of the school system, there are a number of reasons why such tests should not be used as the sole measure of performance for students. You'll find some of these reasons later in this chapter, when I discuss why some children do better with alternate assessments. Test scores alone do not prove that a student is learning anything except test-taking skills.

Homeschoolers who use standardized testing can hire someone to administer the test at home in a familiar environment or use a test that can be administered by the parent. In some states, testing is required; tests must be administered at a designated testing center or by a certified teacher to comply with regulations. Check with local homeschoolers to find out how to find approved test administrators. Other homeschoolers refuse to use standardized testing, realizing that such tests don't measure the kind of learning their children are experiencing.

As homeschooled children reach high school age, they may need to learn test-taking skills. For example, students who want to take the usual route into college may want to learn to take the SAT or ACT test. Study guides, Web sites, and programs are available to coach such students in test-taking skills and outline the type of material they will encounter on the tests. If you're going to play in that ballpark, you are more likely to win if you play by the prevailing rules. For another example, some career paths, such as automotive technician, teacher, nurse, doctor, or attorney require students to pass certification or board tests in order to seek employment. Although it's important that students be adequately prepared to take such examinations, there is no need for students to take such tests annually from kindergarten through high school to succeed at test taking in high school or as young adults.

Learning Links

Many seasoned test takers will tell you that there are all sorts of tips and tricks to test taking. If test taking is an important part of your child's career path, he or she must do the research and learn the skills needed to jump through this societal hoop. *Becoming a Master Student: Tools, Techniques, Hints, Ideas, Illustrations, Examples, Methods, Procedures, Processes, Skills, Resources, and Suggestions for Success,* by David Ellis (Houghton Mifflin College, 2000) includes an excellent section on test-taking strategies.

Some Do, Some Don't, and Why

Institutional schools realize that research on learning and education far outpaces the assessment tools available. Although much is understood about the importance of students having opportunities to connect new knowledge to what they already know, high-stakes assessment tests, such as state-wide tests that tie scores to school district funding, still continue to focus on memorization of disconnected facts retained only for the test. Recent legislation in some states also ties scholarships to high scores, in an attempt to encourage wider voluntary participation in state-wide testing by homeschoolers. Such material remains in the child's short-term memory during the test and is soon forgotten. This, folks, is not real learning!

Most homeschoolers and many institutional teachers realize that standardized tests, are not an accurate measure of learning, nor do such tests provide accurate feedback on why the student didn't score well and what to do to improve his or her score. A student who makes a low score on the reading portion of a standardized test may be subjected to remedial tutoring in the form of more worksheets and more drills, when what the child really needs is more exposure to real books and someone to take the time to read to the child about topics he or she is interested in.

Alternate assessments would be much more appropriate for students in the following situations:

➤ The bright child who can answer orally but freezes in a written test situation

➤ The student who understands the overall picture but has a hard time detailing facts

➤ The child who reads slowly and comprehends well but cannot finish a timed test

➤ The smart child with attention deficit disorder or other disabilities that make taking a long test difficult but don't warrant accommodation under testing law

➤ A student whose strengths are in the creative, kinesthetic, mechanical, or musical modalities

➤ A child who is basically capable but has great difficulty in one particular area

➤ A student who isn't used to an institutional setting but is required by law to take a standardized test in an institutional setting, surrounded by strangers and administered by a stranger

➤ The student whose family objects to standardized testing on religious or philosophical grounds

I'll discuss a number of ways to implement alternate assessments, as well as ways to keep tangible records of these assessments, in Chapter 16, "Other Assessments for Measuring Progress."

Standardized Testing

Standardized tests are a very real component of institutional school; public schools administer more than 100 million standardized tests every year. Children are tested and retested ad nauseum: readiness tests for kindergarten; screening tests for learning disabilities or for admission to gifted and talented programs; IQ tests that supposedly measure intellectual ability; and achievement tests that measure a narrow range of skills and content. And for what? We hear constantly that scores are declining and schools are losing funding. Meantime, employers and colleges complain of employees and students who can't do basic mathematics computations, read, write, or spell!

Many standardized tests are multiple choice, which gives a false impression of equal opportunity and fairness. However, according to The National Center for Fair & Open Testing (FairTest), an advocacy organization working to end the abuses, misuses, and flaws of standardized testing and ensure that evaluation of students and workers is

Speaking Educationese

Objective testing deals with facts without distortion by personal feelings or prejudices. **Subjective** testing is based on personal feelings or prejudices in contrast to the factual.

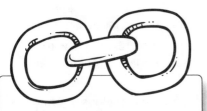

Learning Links

For more information about the pros and cons of standardized testing, contact FairTest at The National Center for Fair & Open Testing, 342 Broadway, Cambridge, MA 02139; 617–864–4810; www.fairtest.org. The Web site offers links to related sites, an online catalog of publications, information about testing reform, and articles about testing.

fair, open, and educationally sound, the only *objective* part of standardized testing is the scoring, which is done by machine. All the decisions made in developing the tests (wording and content of items, what will count as correct answers, how the test is administered, and the uses of the results) are made by *subjective* human beings.

How Can I Prepare My Child?

If state homeschooling regulations require your child to take a standardized test, you may prepare him or her for the test just as institutional schools do. Materials are available to prepare kids for specific tests. Most states that require testing do allow for alternative assessments. If you are uncomfortable with testing, or feel your child does not or will not test well for some reason, look into alternative assessments as an option. You'll find suggestions and tips in Chapter 16.

Young children who are not reading yet will obviously have difficulty taking a standardized test. Children who freeze under stressful conditions, have difficulty staying on task, or have specific learning difficulties will usually fare better with alternative assessments. Such assessments should focus on the child's progress and achievements since the last assessment, rather than comparing the child unfavorably with other children.

Reasons to Use Standardized Tests

Sometimes homeschoolers use standardized tests as a way of proving to doubting grandparents and neighbors that their homeschool program is successful. Although this seems like a good tool to use to get others off your back, it may backfire if your child, for whatever reason, does not do well on the test.

You may choose to have your child take a standardized test to fulfill legal requirements in your state. Some homeschoolers want such testing results on file in case their homeschool ever comes under fire from an official source, such as a school district or child welfare department, or in case of a custody suit.

Although these all seem like valid arguments for standardized testing, bear in mind that such scores don't really prove all that they seem to prove. Some homeschoolers suggest having your child take the test to determine your child's weak areas, so you can emphasize those areas during the next school year. Even this may be a flawed concept. Perhaps your child did poorly on that section of the test because he or she didn't understand it, or because of circumstances such as the following …

Learning Links

Scoring High is a test-specific resource available in book or software form. Spectrum test preparation materials have grade-level appropriate prep for any of the five major standardized tests available in books or software. Test Ready test prep provides a variety of preparation resources. See Appendix B, "Curriculum Winners and Selected Resources, Including Dynamite Web Sites," for details.

➤ Your child needed to use the restroom and had forgotten his glasses, but knew the test was timed and he wasn't allowed to talk, so he waited miserably, squirming, managing to fill in only a few answers, until that section of the test was over, before asking to use the restroom and getting his glasses.

➤ The test became boring, and being a dreamy child with no real concept of the relative importance of a test score, your child was simply using the answer sheet to make a dot design.

➤ Your child lost her place in the answer sheet and every answer was off by one.

➤ The test administrator inadvertently hurt your child's feelings while giving the instructions (he was being wiggly and was asked twice to sit still during the instruction period). So your child was embarrassed, which made it hard to concentrate, and he just filled in any answer to keep from getting in more trouble for not filling out the answer sheet.

All of these examples actually happened to homeschooled youngsters I know, either while they were still in institutional school, or during required testing sessions as homeschoolers. None of the children was trying to blow off the test; each was just being a typical child in a stressful situation. However, a standardized test being a once-a-year, one-chance deal, each situation affected a test score, which in turn may have made the difference between regular or gifted and talented classroom placement, or the ability to continue to homeschool (depending on homeschool regulations). Testing under such stressful conditions should never be used as the only indicator for success.

And although test scores are constantly invoked as a way to prove that homeschooling works, keep in mind that data from states that require testing and homeschooling associations is usually from a select group of homeschoolers who have volunteered to participate in testing. Even in states where testing is a requirement, not all home-schoolers cooperate in submitting their children to standardized testing by govern-mental edict. So, although it's tempting to use test scores to your advantage when talking about homeschooling, it only perpetuates the myth that standardized testing is an accurate assessment of real learning.

College Entrance Testing

Taking the PSAT (Preliminary Scholastic Aptitude Test), SAT, and ACT tests are be-coming rites of passage for institutionally schooled high schoolers. Some home-schooled teens have also used these test scores to help with college entrance, winning scholarships, and attending the college of their choice. (See the discussion on college admissions in Chapter 13, "Teenagers In the Homeschool.") Is it necessary for home-schoolers to take these tests? And if they don't, are there other options if they want to attend college. Read on!

Do Entrance Exam Scores Tell the Whole Story?

As colleges learn more about homeschoolers, many have changed their entrance requirements accordingly. For a while, homeschoolers were required to take extra subject-specific college entrance exams in addition to the SAT or ACT. Some were required to submit extra assessments as well. More and more colleges are actively recruiting homeschooled students because colleges have learned that many home-schooled students are succeeding beyond expectations, and colleges want more of these innovative, intuitive, excited, self-motivated learners on their campuses. Some colleges have different criteria for admitting homeschoolers, using alternative assess-ments such as portfolios in addition to or in place of test scores.

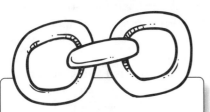

Learning Links

Your child can take the SAT (also called the SAT I; the basic col-lege admissions test) more than once, with only the best score being sent to the colleges of your choice. Some colleges also require scores from the SAT II (subject) tests.

For high-school age homeschoolers planning to take the usual route to college entrance, taking the SAT or ACT may be a good game plan. Possibilities include earning a scholarship based on their test scores. But don't go into this experience cold.

It's interesting to note that although the SAT is con-sidered an essential component for college admissions, the average scores of males and females show a gap of 42 points, with males scoring higher than females. However, even the test's sponsor agrees that females consistently outperform males in both high school and college. This seems rather odd when the stated purpose of the test is to determine college perform-ance.

Spotlight on Education

FairTest's public education director states that colleges and agencies that determine admissions and award scholarships based on the SAT's biased measure are putting themselves at legal risk by denying females equal educational opportunity. In 1998 FairTest initiated a lawsuit that struck down New York's use of SAT scores as the sole factor in awarding state scholarships, and successfully challenged the PSAT based on its role in choosing National Merit Scholarship semifinalists.

There is much more to the testing issue than meets the eye. More and more, parents, teachers, and administrators realize that assessors should look at the whole student, not just at test scores.

Alternatives to Entrance Exams

Homeschooled students can get into college in other ways. For the student who decides at the last minute to attend college, having never considered attending, it will be too late to take the SAT and ACT tests. Since most community colleges don't even require a high school diploma for applicants, applying at a community college and transferring to a four-year school later is one workable option. Some homeschoolers take community college classes for high school credit all through high school, or during their last two years of high school, accumulating credits that will enable them to enroll as a part- or full-time student when they graduate from high school. Students who enroll for classes at a community college must usually pass an assessment test or entrance examination in English, mathematics, and reading skills.

What does all this mean to you, the homeschooling parent? It makes you aware that government-mandated high-stakes testing is flawed. Although

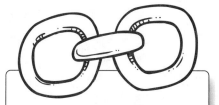

Learning Links

Can't pass the assessment, or failed one portion of it? No sweat! Most community colleges provide tutoring services to help you prepare to take the test. They also offer special classes to teach you the basics you need to be considered capable of taking college-level courses at their institutions. These classes don't count for college credit, but can be used for high school homeschool credit.

your child may need to participate in such testing to some degree, you will be aware that his or her score on such a test is not the end of the world if it's low, nor does it mean you have a child prodigy because the score is high. The testing system itself is intrinsically flawed, and you need to look at participating in testing as a challenge you can master if it's important to the end goal. If you can find an alternate route to reach the same goal, go for it! Model creative thinking for your child. The world needs more people who are willing to forego the status quo and take the path less traveled.

The Least You Need to Know

➤ Testing is just one type of assessment that can be used to determine your child's progress.

➤ Some homeschoolers use tests as a tool while others totally eschew the use of tests.

➤ Some homeschoolers use tests as a means to an end, preparing their students ahead of time.

➤ Alternative assessments are often an option, even when homeschooling regulations state that testing is required.

Chapter 16

Other Assessments for Measuring Progress

In This Chapter

➤ Formal or informal assessment?

➤ Why communication is vital when determining progress

➤ Journals: invaluable tools to measure progress

➤ Why grading isn't essential except in certain situations

➤ Scrapbooking, creating portfolios, and other assessment methods

---

Whatever you've decided about testing, other assessments are important as well to give you and outside assessors an overall picture of your child's progress. Testing is only one method, and as you learned in the previous chapter, it has its drawbacks.

Whether you're using a school-at-home approach, unit studies, natural learning, or a combination of approaches, you will probably want to keep some records. Even casual records kept simply for your own satisfaction and enjoyment can be turned into something more formal if need dictates. Homeschoolers have found some exciting ways to prove to themselves and others that their children are learning. Well-documented projects can provide fodder for the assessor or evaluator. A casual way for a parent or assessor to determine what has been learned by the student is through discussion or conversation. More tangible indicators include awards, journals, formal or informal evaluations, portfolios, and letters of recommendation.

Projects: A Real Learning Experience

Whether building a model to illustrate a science concept, doing a chemistry experiment, making paper dolls of the characters in a biography, building a three-dimensional model of a historic building, or making a poster of musical notes and concepts, homeschoolers are constantly reinforcing learning with hands-on projects. No matter what your child's learning style, some subjects just lend themselves to a project. It can be difficult to accurately assess the value of a learning project, but as a homeschooler you will learn the skill.

Learning Links

Quite often, the project itself is the learning experience. Hands-on projects really stick in the student's mind, enhancing retention of material, because of the use of several modalities in completing the project.

What to do with all these projects, short of keeping them forever, and carrying them around to show them off? If you can't bear to throw them away, is there some way to record them for posterity? Many homeschoolers have become masters at recycling artwork, keeping especially important papers in scrapbooks or portfolios, and recording three-dimensional projects with photos. Other homeschool families use their video camera to keep such records. Paintings and one-dimensional artwork can be framed to decorate walls or given as gifts, used as wrapping paper for gifts, folded and recycled into greeting cards, cut into strips for bookmarks, or used as the cover for books created by the child.

Spotlight on Education

Long ago, when my children were in institutional school, I began saving their school papers and art projects. Soon we had several cardboard cartons full! Once my child invested his or her time and energy into a project, it was very difficult for me to just arbitrarily decide to throw it away. So, a little family tradition was born. Every so often, we'd spread out several favorite art creations on the floor and take a photo of each of them. Once a picture was snapped, the child chose one creation to keep, and we recycled or threw away the rest. When we began homeschooling, we continued the process, placing the photos in our ongoing annual portfolios.

Discussions: Open Communication Is the Key

Talk with your child to get a feel for what he or she has learned from a particular experience or learning activity. Parents who don't need to provide reports for assessors, a support school, or the state find that communicating with their child is one of the key ways to assess his or her progress.

As your child tells you about a field trip or hands-on project, he or she provides clues that will help you determine whether connections to previously learned information have been made, whether something new has been learned, or whether there is still confusion about certain concepts. Keep such discussions casual, make questions open-ended so they require more than a yes or no answer, and listen, making eye contact, to what your child has to say about the subject. Respect your child's opinion and keep your comments nonjudgmental and positive. Be open to new ideas and willing to help your child dig deeper if he or she expresses an interest in continuing to learn more about a certain concept.

Learning Lookouts

Record your child's observations on audiotape or videotape or in a journal to keep an ongoing record of his or her progress. Some children may be inhibited by the presence of a videotape or audiotape, especially if they are aware of its use as an assessment tool. Make it a habit to use video or audio regularly, and your child will loosen up.

Project-oriented learning presents a challenge as parents try to determine what subject areas are being covered, and what the child has actually learned. Some parents develop a code to identify subject areas covered in journal entries. Thus, a paragraph about the science experiment a child has done and the little booklet he or she has written about the project, may include codes to indicate that the project covered skills for science, English, art, and creative thinking.

Awards: Proof Positive of Achievement

Children who are involved with Scouts, 4-H, community service, or homeschool group and community education programs will end up with some certificates of achievement. Libraries present such certificates at the end of summer reading programs; certificates of achievement usually accompany the end of swimming lessons and other activities; and children who perform community service may also be thanked with a certificate of appreciation. These commendations should be preserved for posterity and proof that your child is learning through doing.

A certificate of award is tangible evidence that someone besides yourself values your child's accomplishments or that your child has achieved something special. Such certificates are extremely positive, enhance a child's feelings of self-worth, and make a

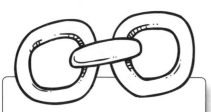

Learning Links

A simple three-ring binder with see-through sleeves and dividers by subject area makes a good starting point for keeping a record of your child's achievements. Awards can be slipped into a sleeve, and any photographs or accompanying papers, ribbons, or letters of recommendation can be slipped into adjacent sleeves.

Learning Lookouts

Put corrections on a sticky note rather than writing them right in the child's journal. Children have a sense of possession about their writing, just as we all do, and although children may accept positive criticism, they usually appreciate being able to keep their work free of red marks and corrections.

very nice statement about your child. Some home-schoolers keep an ongoing portfolio for each child every school year, similar to a yearbook. Particularly prized certificates can be photocopied, so a copy can go into the portfolio, and the original can be framed along with a corresponding photograph.

Journals: A Barometer of Progress

Many parents have never kept a journal and find beginning such an activity very intimidating. Remember, it's your choice to keep your journal private or share it, so you don't have to feel embarrassed about sentence fragments, incorrect usage, or spelling errors. Your journal can be your own record of your home-schooling journey with your child. You might use it to help your child pull together a portfolio, or refer to it now and then to jog your memory to recall, for example, when your child learned the nine times tables, which states you visited when you took that trip to the East Coast, or which children were involved in a specific project.

When children are in the earliest learning stages, keep a journal of their learning milestones. It's really fun to have a record of children who aren't yet school age; kids this age are constantly learning new things, doing and saying amusing things, or amazing you with their precocity. Although some early elementary-age children enjoy keeping their own journals, many parents simultaneously keep a journal with their own comments and observations about their child's learning journey. Such journals can be as detailed or general as is comfortable or as is necessary because of legalities.

Kids' Thoughts and Memories

Once children have developed some writing skills, they might enjoy keeping their own journal. Some parents have their children write daily in a journal, and then the parents write back to them, making comments, asking questions, and occasionally including notes about usage or making corrections. But remember, whether your child's journal is a homeschool assignment or a private effort, it's important to respect privacy. Don't read your child's journal without his or her permission!

Teens' Journals for Record-Keeping Purposes

When a child is old enough to begin keeping his or her own records, a journal is a great way to keep a record of activities, whether academic, community service hours, or hours spent working for pay. Many homeschooled students don't begin keeping their own records until they reach the high school years, but if you have a child who wants to begin before then, go for it! Some parents and students work together to keep records for a specific diploma program. See Chapter 17, "Keeping Records," for more.

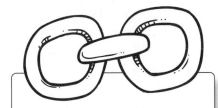

Teens may also enjoy keeping a private journal for recording their thoughts and feelings. During the developmental years, feelings and emotions often keep teens in a turmoil; writing can provide an outlet. If your teens keep private journals, remember to respect their privacy just as you expect them to respect yours. Don't read their private journals without their permission!

Learning Links

If your child wants to keep his or her own records but you aren't ready to totally let go of the reins, keep your own records, too, until you are sure your child is capable of doing a thorough job.

Evaluation: Looking at Learning from All Angles

If you do a loosely structured program geared around your child's learning style you may wonder how you can present his or her activities in a format that will be understood by an assessor. Children are constantly learning through their experiences, whether planned or serendipitous. If you don't grade your children's work but are required to provide grades for a support school or want to provide a transcript for transfer into a private or other institutional school, there are ways to do so after the fact.

Determining Grades for Nontraditional Learners

What do grades indicate? Ideally, they indicate how well a student has learned a specific body of knowledge:

➤ An **A** should indicate that the child has learned all the material very well.

➤ A **B** might indicate that the child understands most of the material.

➤ A **C** may show that the child has an average grasp of the subject.

➤ A **D** should indicate that the child missed something somewhere and needs improvement.

➤ An **E** or **F** usually indicates a total failure to grasp the material.

In many cases grades are poor indicators of a child's actual retention of the material on which he or she was graded. Instead, sometimes the A indicates that the child has the ability to remember a lot of information long enough to regurgitate it for the test, the B that the child has a harder time remembering all of it, but remembers enough to correctly answer 90 percent of the material, a C might show that the child doesn't have an easy time retaining information for the test, although the child's parents will tell you that he or she can explain that information orally, a D, E, or F might simply indicate that the child freezes up at the thought of a test.

Learning Lookouts

Some children get high grades in institutional school and don't have an iota of common sense or hands-on ability, while other children barely pass academically but can tear down a motorcycle engine and rebuild it, or are already selling their artwork in local galleries. Still others tend to be overlooked because they don't shine academically or otherwise. Because they aren't behavior problems and tread the middle of the road in the classroom setting they are virtually ignored throughout school. All children will benefit from an individualized program that considers their strengths and weaknesses.

Speaking Educationese

Mastery is possession or display of skill or knowledge.

If you are required to supply grades, what should you do? Let's hypothesize that you are teaching math using the *mastery* concept.

Your child completes a page of math, you will correct it, penciling an X beside the incorrect answers. First, you will congratulate your child on the number of correct problems, then you will look at the missed problems with your child, determining if the problems were missed due to a lack of understanding of a concept or due to a simple computational error. The child will review and relearn any concepts he or she didn't understand and tackle those problems again. Any simple mathematical errors will also be corrected. Then the paper is perfect! No missed answers. How do you grade that? In my book, if an arbitrary grade must be assigned, it's an A.

Although this same paper would merit a lower grade in an institutional school, and the student may or may not relearn that missed concept or understand why he or she got the problems wrong, in the homeschool, math done the mastery way always merits an A.

In another example, if your child is doing a hands-on project for history, based on a literature selection, a grade can be based on the child's understanding of the material, his or her contribution to the project at hand, and your collaborative discussion of what grade would be appropriate given the effort and interest your child supplied to the project.

A Little Self-Analysis

If your child wants to get the highest grade, he or she must contribute his or her best effort to the project. Consider your child's abilities when determining best effort. The child who writes effortlessly because his or her small motor skills are finely developed isn't contributing the same effort as his or her sibling who struggles along because he or she has difficulty with small motor skills. Although the first child's paper will be much more attractive and neat, the second child's effort was much higher. Do you see why grading can be so unfair?

Student, teacher, and mentor (see the following section) can work together to collaborate on a fair grade by evaluation. Consider such things as effort expended, learning achieved, and the finished project. If the child was doing community service under someone else's supervision, enlist that person's input into the evaluation process. Some homeschoolers develop a checklist of considerations to help with project evaluation. The child can provide input by practicing self-analysis:

➤ Did I give the project my best effort?

➤ Did I learn the new material well, and do I have a good understanding of it?

➤ Is my finished project as neat as I can do it; does it cover the material I studied; is it a good example of my best handwriting, study skills, and artwork?

If the teacher's observation has been that the student deserves 90 percent for his or her effort, 100 percent for learning the material, and 90 percent for the finished project, while the child comes up with 100 percent, 80 percent, and 90 percent respectively, what grade is assigned? Add up the percentages for a total of 550, then divide 550 by 6 to get an average. Rounding up the grade would be 92 percent. Notice that the parent and the child perceived the effort expended differently. This is why it is important to include the child's evaluation into the grading system. When the child knows that, the child will have to give an honest evaluation of the effort he or she put into a project and the child will be motivated to try harder to do his or her best.

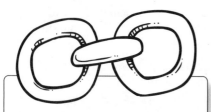

Learning Links

Involve your child in the grading process. A child should understand that a grade that truly indicates a child's progress is not given by the teacher, but is earned.

The parent can judge only by what he or she sees, unable to know, in many cases, whether the child is putting forth his or her best effort or merely skimming by.

Institutional GPAs (grade point averages) seldom reflect the real learning that has been achieved, the effort put into studying or completing an assignment, or input from the child regarding such things. Instead, most institutional GPAs reflect the teacher's evaluation of the finished project. If the homework paper is sloppy, the teacher may not know that the student was up all night with a sick sibling, because his or her parents were also ill, and that said student completed the paper between applying cold compresses to a feverish sibling. By contrast, a homeschool parent is aware of the circumstances surrounding the learning that happens in the homeschool. Homeschools are able to flex when illness hits, temporarily postponing projects in favor of necessary interruptions, allowing for completing of a project under more favorable circumstances.

What Does Your Child's Mentor Think?

When your homeschool student is working with a mentor, coach, or tutor in a specific learning situation, involve the outside person in the grading process. Introduce your grading method and have the outside person give you input for the period of time he or she worked with your student. Schedule conferences from time to time to discuss your child's progress. Or give the person an evaluation form to complete at various points in the learning process. Even a final evaluation, including room for thoughts on the progress made since the beginning of the collaboration, will help you to come up with a final grade for a class. Whether your student is taking music lessons, working as an apprentice in small engine repair, or working with the elderly in a nursing home as a volunteer, getting the input of private tutors, mentors, and supervisors is extremely beneficial.

Portfolios: Whatever You Want to Present

There are many types of portfolios. A student may assemble a portfolio to reflect a specific area of study, a burgeoning interest, a trip or experience, or include the best samples of his or her work from an entire school year. If your child pursues a specific activity, such as dance, horsemanship, or a sport, assembling a portfolio with video clips can be a valuable asset at a later date. Some homeschoolers assemble a portfolio from their high school years, which is presented for college admissions or during a job interview.

Photographs, line drawings completed by the student, essays, awards and certificates, excerpts from journal entries, newspaper clippings, and evaluation forms can all be part of an interesting portfolio. If the portfolio is to be presented at a job or college admissions interview, you will want it to have a professional appearance, be easy to understand, and be neatly organized. Even if you're compiling your portfolio just for your own record-keeping purposes, make it as good as it can be. The portfolio will become a record of one important phase of your homeschooler's life.

Learning Links

Creating a portfolio is an across-the-curriculum project, providing experience in writing, artistic expression, organization, and thinking skills as well as education in the specific curriculum areas included in the portfolio.

Take a Scrapbooking Class for Inspiration

Scrapbooking has taken the craft world by storm, even hooking people who claim to be unable to draw a straight line, and involving folks who have never done any type of crafts. Genealogists, new parents, dog trainers, race car enthusiasts, and photographers, among others, have found scrapbooking an excellent way to provide a tangible memento of their passion. Homeschoolers have discovered that scrapbooking techniques have sparked an enthusiasm for pulling together a portfolio. Some scrapbooking stores host occasional free workshops. Most provide classes for a fee; such a class can be a part of your student's curriculum while providing the skills needed to develop an outstanding portfolio. Schedule a "Mom's Night Out" workshop for your support group as a way to get together as well as learn new skills. By taking workshops or classes, you will learn many tricks of the trade, and the confidence to develop more economical ways to implement many of the skills learned.

Speaking Educationese

Scrapbooking is a hobby in which collections of photos and related mementos are combined with attractive lettering, coordinating papers, stamping, and stickers to form pages in a memory book.

What a Memento!

If your homeschool support group hosts an end-of-the-year project fair, take your children's portfolios along as part of their exhibit. Some homeschool parents consider annual portfolios the homeschool equivalent of yearbooks, and include pages with photos from homeschool events for other homeschoolers to sign, and pictures of the student's homeschool teachers, tutors, and mentors. Get out your old yearbook and look it over to get ideas for things to include in your child's "yearbook."

Whatever form your child's portfolio takes, the finished project will be an invaluable memento of the year's learning experiences, projects, trips, and activities. Some portfolios include reading lists, photocopies of the contents pages of books used for subject area studies, photocopies or original sample pages from math books and other workbooks, bibliographies of recommended reading for homeschool cooperative classes, shark's teeth, museum brochures, photos of students performing community service, baking Christmas cookies with Grandma, and sailing with Dad.

Some parents keep a file and set aside the last couple of weeks of the school year to pull together a portfolio with their students. Others start at the beginning of the year and compile the portfolio as they go. At the end of the year some weeding out may be necessary for the latter type, but it may be the easier method in the long run. Whatever your homeschooling schedule, you may want to set an arbitrary beginning and ending time for your record-keeping purposes; for example, late August through mid-June or early September through late May, depending on vacations and holidays.

At the end of a field trip to the natural history museum, brochures, tickets, completed worksheets, and other mementos can be slipped into see-through sleeves and added to the three-ring binder in the natural history section. When the film comes back from the developer, photos of the student can be added. When photographing field trips, be sure to include the following:

➤ A group photo of all participants

➤ A photo by the entrance including the name of the place being visited

➤ A variety of photos of the student near exhibits that directly pertain to a specific interest or study

➤ A photo of the student standing by any special exhibits, such as the entrance of the planetarium, the mummy exhibit, or the traveling exhibits

➤ If your child is chosen by the tour guide to demonstrate or participate, a photo or two of the event

➤ A photo of your child with the interactive kits and books you purchased in the museum store

➤ A photo of you with your child (ask an employee or bystander to snap this one if you aren't with a group)

While it is left largely up to the individual to determine how to develop his or her portfolio, there are a few instances in which personal taste needs to be set aside in favor of presenting material to the best advantage. For example:

➤ Students who are required by state or provincial homeschooling law or regulations to provide a portfolio for evaluation should follow any existing guidelines in creating their portfolios. Provide only what is required by law or regulations; what is volunteered today may be mandatory tomorrow.

➤ High school students desiring to showcase their years of academic, athletic, community service, and work-related achievements to potential employers or college admissions officers should develop a professional-quality portfolio.

➤ Students whose chosen careers (model, artist, photographer, or dancer, for instance) require a professional portfolio will want to research the specific guidelines for presenting the materials to the best advantage.

Perfect for College Interviews

Once you've narrowed your college choices to a manageable few, your college applicant will want to schedule a portfolio review and interview. Why is it important for a homeschooler to take the time to do the college interview? Many college admissions officers have become used to homeschooled applicants, but some still have doubts and questions. Meeting your homeschooled applicant, reviewing his or her accomplishments via the portfolio, and putting a face to the name on the application can mean the difference between acceptance or rejection.

Spotlight on Education

Your college applicant should be prepared to field questions about homeschooling in general, his or her homeschool experience (including why homeschooling was chosen, whether or not he or she enjoyed homeschooling, and what he or she studied), and extracurricular activities. Although your child's participation in martial arts may have been considered physical education in your homeschool, it may be perceived as extracurricular by a college admissions officer. Your college applicant can opt to go with the flow or to explain why martial arts is both physical education and an avidly pursued hobby or extracurricular activity.

Portfolios make it possible for the college admissions officer to see beyond the test scores, letters of recommendation, essays, and other usual tools and get a picture of the person behind the paperwork.

Letters of Recommendation

Whenever your child is working with tutors, coaches, or mentors, ask them for a letter of recommendation. These may be included in portfolios year by year and provide an outside, unbiased opinion of your student's ability to complete a task, work with others, set goals and accomplish them, and cite progress in a specific area.

Here are some other reasons why letters of recommendation are useful:

➤ **College applications.** Letters of recommendation are a required part of most college application packets. Students who are in the habit of acquiring letters of recommendation from their tutors, mentors, and coaches may have some that are appropriate to use in college applications. In most cases, however, college applications require very current letters of recommendation, and collecting these will be an important part of preparing the college application packet. Keep in mind that students may ask for letters of recommendation from any adults that they have worked with, such as the pastor of their church, choir director, youth group sponsor, employers, supervisors, and leaders of community service and volunteer entities.

➤ **Job interviews.** When a student has had his or her own business, letters of recommendation from customers can be helpful to prove to a prospective employer that the student is capable of completing a task, providing a service, or delivering a product in a timely manner. If the student has done volunteer work or community service, a letter from supervisors will assure the potential employer that your homeschooled student is ambitious, caring, and capable of doing a good job, even without the added incentive of a paycheck. Letters from clients for whom the homeschooled student has provided daycare or babysitting services, lawn care, pet walking, house sitting, or other services can be useful in demonstrating the ability to do a good job.

➤ **Part of a portfolio.** Be sure to include several letters of recommendation in a portfolio. Either include an entire section of such letters, or scatter them throughout the portfolio in appropriate areas. If the portfolio includes pictures of the many animals for whom your student provided pet services when their owners were on vacation, include letters of recommendation from the owners in the same section. A section on physical education can include letters of recommendation from the martial arts instructor, dance teacher, and tennis coach.

Don't miss any opportunity to showcase your student with words of praise and commendation from others. Most of the people with whom your student comes in contact will be happy to provide such a letter. Remember that job and college admissions interviewers may have preconceived notions of homeschoolers, not all of which will be positive. Your child's well-balanced life portrayed via portfolio, including positive words from his or her mentors, employers, and tutors, and his or her ability to converse easily and openly with the interviewer will help to dispel any negative misconceptions.

The Least You Need to Know

➤ Informal assessment is adequate unless you are required to provide assessment for legal reasons.

➤ Grading isn't essential unless required by a support school or legal requirements.

➤ Assessments can be casual (based on conversation or discussion) or formal (a certified teacher's required evaluation of portfolios and/or journals).

➤ It's helpful to file or assemble components for portfolios as you go.

➤ Awards, newspaper clippings, photographs, and letters of recommendation are valuable components of portfolio design.

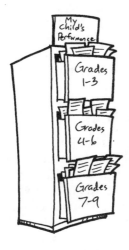

Chapter 17

Keeping Records

In This Chapter

➤ Determining the kind of records you need to keep

➤ Getting your records organized: what to keep and what to throw away

➤ Keeping records for government agencies and support schools

➤ Different types of record keeping

➤ Tips for making your record keeping easier

Most homeschoolers keep records of some kind. These records often reflect the home-schooler's lifestyle, varying from very structured to extremely laid back. The traditional homeschooler may have a planner set up for a semester or several weeks, he or she may check off activities as they occur or keep a separate record of actual events. Unschoolers may or may not keep daily records, but often have photo collages or albums of their children doing a variety of activities, which can lead to an after-the-fact transcript or report of learning when it is needed.

If you live in a state or province that requires you to provide documentation of your homeschooled student's educational activities in report form or for evaluation, you will have guidelines to follow in gathering and submitting the information. Most support schools and distance-learning institutions also provide guidelines to help homeschoolers submit information in a specific format. It's also proven helpful for homeschooled high school students to compile a portfolio documenting their academic, athletic, community service, and working experiences. Providing such proof of a well-rounded lifestyle is valuable in both job and college interviews.

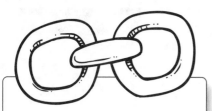

Learning Links

Look at back issues of local homeschool support group newsletters for scheduled events, check your church newsletter, the pile of papers on the kitchen counter, and ask your mom, spouse, and best friend for clues to help you resurrect information about activities your child participated in.

Learning Lookouts

If you're keeping records for a support school or other entity, make sure you understand reporting requirements and adhere to them. Keep a copy of reporting requirements with your record-keeping materials. When keeping records for the state or school district, follow reporting guidelines as closely as possible; don't provide any more than what's required by law. When you provide extra, you may encourage requests for extra documentation or legislation of new reporting requirements.

Whether you relish pulling together a detail-by-detail record of your child's education, find it a crashing bore, or hate even thinking about it, you will find tips here that will help you decide how much is necessary and what kind of records you need to keep.

Where Do I Start?

If you are considering homeschooling or just getting started, I suggest you start keeping records immediately. It's much easier to keep records from the get-go than it is to reconstruct a record later. However, if you've been homeschooling and not keeping records, and now have a reason to want or need a record, don't despair. Chances are you've kept a record of some kind, however informal it may be. For example, most families have a calendar that they use to keep track of appointments, field trips, and other important events (more about using a calendar for this purpose later in the chapter). Also, if your child has been doing traditional schoolwork (workbooks, worksheets, writing essays, and the like), he or she has a collection of schoolwork. Anything you can check to jog your memory will be helpful; look in your checkbook if you purchased items at the museum bookstore after a field trip, paid tutoring bills, or wrote a check for any other educational expenses.

K.I.S.S.—Keep It Simple, Sweetie!

Simple is best. If, however, you have the desire, time, and willingness to keep elaborate records, go for it. My suggestions are just starting points and ideas; most families have their own way to keep records, whether it's tax records, gas mileage, or expenses. How you choose to keep homeschooling records is a personal decision—except if you're keeping records for someone else, such as a support school, umbrella, or the state. Then you'll have to conform to their requirements for record keeping (as I'll discuss a little later).

I'm a Piler, Not a Filer!

If this describes you, that's okay! If you pile things, you will find them eventually, if not readily. Most pilers have a pretty good idea where to find a particular document—in which pile, and how deep in the pile! Occasionally, extra effort is needed to find a document in a pile, but many homeschoolers create wonderful portfolios and transcripts from records kept in piles, stacks, and cardboard cartons. Many homeschoolers use file drawers, but not all! If you have several children, keep a separate pile or file for each child. Have your children put their names and the date on their papers and creations, and enlist their aid in keeping their records. Even the youngest children can punch their work with a three-hole paper punch so they can slip it into a three-ring binder, or put their finished work on a certain pile to be corrected and, perhaps, filed later.

What Should You Include in Your Records?

It's always hard to know what to save and what to throw away. How much is too much? That's your call. I can't help you with that one because I'm an inveterate pack rat, and I always err on the side of keeping more than I need! That trait has helped when my kids are pulling together last-minute pages for portfolios for the end of the year project fair. Having extra museum brochures, stacks of completed school papers, and duplicate photos comes in very handy at such times. At other times, such as when I'm looking through half a dozen cardboard cartons stacked in my front closet, I vow that I'm going to get rid of all this stuff. (It hasn't happened yet!)

So, how do you decide what to keep and what to throw away? Consider the following:

1. **Who's it for?** To determine what to keep and what to throw away, think about for whom you are keeping records. Is this for your own personal records? Are you keeping records for an outside entity, such as a support or umbrella school? Does your state require you to turn in records or have them reviewed by an assessor? Knowing the answers to these questions will help you determine what to keep and what to throw away.

2. **What's its purpose?** Do you want to make portfolios for each child, or a yearbook scrapbook for the whole family? Will you need duplicates to turn in to an outside entity? Do you want to send copies to grandparents?

Keeping Outside Records

Keeping records for someone other than yourself is simpler in one way and more complicated in another. Simpler because most support schools and umbrella schools will outline what they want to see in the records. Perhaps you need to provide only subjects and grades so the umbrella can provide transcripts. Or maybe the support school wants to see details, such as samples of work, photos, or other documentation. If you are working with a support school that grades your children's work, it will keep records on its end, and may send copies of such records to you.

Since there are so many variations on what is required from an outside entity, be sure to check carefully with your support school to determine what documentation it expects you to provide. However, if you live in a state that requires detailed documentation of the subjects and implementation of your homeschool, things get more complicated. Use a preplanned, grade-level appropriate curriculum for inspiration and ease. Keep explanations of what you plan to do as open-ended as possible. List several resources that you plan to use, rather than just one, which allows you more flexibility.

Spotlight on Education

For Claire's first-grade year, her mom Terri must fill out 13 subject pages (arithmetic, reading, spelling, writing, English language, science, U.S. history, geography, music, visual arts, health, bilingual education, and physical education) and send them to the school district. Each subject page is divided into 4 quarters, and Terri has to describe in advance what Claire will be studying each quarter for all 13 subjects. The information need not be extremely detailed, but it also can't be simply a list of books she intends to use. At the time each quarterly report is due Claire must have covered at least 80 percent of the material, and the report must include how many hours she was instructed and her grade.

Umbrella School Records

Some umbrella schools are local institutional schools that have a home-based education program. Local homeschoolers use the same textbooks, follow the same basic schedule, send in work to be corrected, and test their children at the same times as the institutional school. Such schools generally keep records and provide report cards to the homeschooled students at the same time the schools issue report cards to their institutional students. Other umbrella schools may make different arrangements with the homeschoolers they cover under the umbrella of their program. Check with local private and alternative schools to determine whether they work with homeschoolers, and what policies are in place regarding record keeping.

Other umbrellas may or may not have an institutional campus school, and have various policies regarding working with homeschoolers. Some will keep your records and provide transcripts when you provide documentation to support the records. Check Appendix D, "Independent Study Programs and Support Schools, Publications, and Vendors," for a listing of support schools.

Independent Study School Records

Correspondence schools generally send schoolwork to home-based students, who return the work for grading. Such schools keep on-going records of students' work, sending out reports at scheduled intervals.

Other independent study schools have a variety of policies. If you enroll with a full-service program, you may be required to use a specific curriculum, keep records in a certain way, and make reports on a regular basis. Some independent study schools have several programs, offering varying degrees of autonomy. Some turn as much responsibility back to the parent as the parent is willing to assume. Your choice of an independent study school and the program you enroll your child in will determine how many and what kinds of records you will be required to keep.

Learning Lookouts

Keep copies of all schoolwork that is sent to a correspondence school. Many homeschoolers have horror stories about the class their child had to re-create on paper because the original was lost in the mail or before grading at the office. Now you can't say you haven't been warned!

Government Agency Records

The rule of thumb for keeping records for government agencies is this: Be sure you understand exactly what is required, and don't provide anything more. Obtain record-keeping guidelines in writing, and check with local homeschoolers to find out what their experience has been in dealing with record keeping for the state. Some states have guidelines that they don't actually enforce; others are sticklers for receiving exactly what is required in the regulations. While you want to provide what is needed to keep your homeschooling program legal, don't go overboard. If regulations require documentation of subjects studied, don't send a photo collage for each subject area. Save the artsy craftsy stuff for personal records and to share with Grandma. Send the state a list of the subject areas studied. If you want it to look professional, use good quality typing paper (some homeschoolers have a homeschool letterhead, which is a nice touch but not necessary) and check for typos and spelling errors before submitting. This is not the place to use a wrinkled piece of notebook paper with one corner chewed off by the baby!

Purchased Record-Keeping Systems

Homeschooling is a marketing niche! Therefore, companies exist that cater to the needs of homeschoolers. There are a variety of planners and record-keeping systems available. See if anyone in your homeschool support group has a system he or she likes. Ask that person to show it to you, explain how it works, and why he or she likes it. If you find a record-keeping system that looks like it was tailor-made for you and you can justify the expense, go for it! Check Appendix B, "Curriculum Winners and Selected Resources, Including Dynamite Web Sites," for more record-keeping plans and programs.

Spotlight on Education

Gina uses Homeschool Easy Records, a computer program. She uses the weekly lesson plan function ... only in reverse! She records what her children already did, rather than make advance lesson plans. Gina says it's like having an electronic teacher's lesson plan book. She tells the program what subjects she is covering, then each time she opens the program she types in what her children did in each subject area that day. The program allows recording of time spent on each activity, prints up neat, organized reports, and keeps a record of test scores, among other things.

Do-It-Yourself Record Keeping

As you get acquainted with other homeschoolers, ask what works for them for keeping good records with a minimum of fuss. Veteran homeschoolers have usually worked out something that will do the job without costing a fortune or entailing a lot of effort.

Calendar Records and Cardboard Box Files

Most families have a calendar by the central phone or the back door that is used to track important appointments, everyone's schedule (soccer practice, piano lessons, and family events), and other things, such as birthdays, anniversaries, and special dates. Many homeschooling families use a calendar with very large blocks (a desk blotter works well), and include a running record of special events in the homeschool day. A very minimal record, to be sure, but it may be enough to jog your memory if you use the calendar to make up weekly, monthly, or even quarterly records. To supplement the calendar, use a file drawer or purchased cardboard file box, in which you keep folders for museum brochures, handouts from field trips, photos, and anything else that you might need later to supplement your record keeping.

Creating Units and Credits

You can use your calendar records, supplemented with the contents of the file drawer or box, when pulling together records. Noticing that your child has taken a field trip to the XYZ Natural History Museum, you can pull out the brochure and photographs, plus the report your child wrote about bison. Flip the calendar to the field trip to the Bison Ranch and note the date, checking the file for more information. Your child's reading list may include the names of several books he or she has read on the westward movement including some on buffalo hunters or Native Americans and how they used the buffalo for everything from shelter and clothing to food. As you gather information, you may see a pattern and pull the information into an after-the-fact unit study on bison that crosses all the curriculum areas.

When a high schooler is pulling together information to be transformed into *Carnegie credit units* or a traditional transcript, he or she may discover that certain activities grouped together add up to a credit. He or she may have initially labeled an activity one way, but it makes more sense to group it with other activities to form a different credit. Remember my theme song: Whatever works!

Folders by Activity, Student, or Subject

If you are a filer, or want to become one, determine the most practical way to keep records for your homeschool. Do you want to group your records by activity, pulling the information from

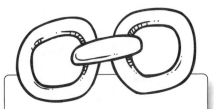

Learning Links

Keep a phone list of local homeschoolers and a small upright file near the calendar and the phone. You can check the upright file for details on class offerings from the YMCA, homeschool newsletter with support group meeting, field trip, and cooperative class dates, and even the reminder card for getting the kids' homeschool pictures taken. Having everything centralized is very helpful.

Speaking Educationese

Carnegie credit units is a system of timekeeping used by most institutional high schools. One Carnegie credit unit is equal to 180 clock hours. A good rule of thumb for translating real-life and textbook learning into Carnegie credit units for high school homeschoolers: Accumulate about 180 clock hours of study time for each high school credit required.

these folders as you write up records for your students? Or do you want to keep a folder for each student? Perhaps grouping files by subject area makes more sense to you. There is no one right way to keep records. Setting up a system and sticking to it is more important than duplicating what works for someone else. However, if filing is not your thing, you may want to talk to other homeschoolers and find out what has worked for them, try it, and decide if it might work for you. Any basic filing plan will work, and over time you can personalize it to fit your needs. Since everyone's homeschool is different, everyone's record-keeping system is unique.

Record Keeping Using Journals and Portfolios

Whether you're a nostalgia buff or not, keep a journal! You won't regret it. Not only will you have a detailed record of your homeschooling journey, you'll be modeling writing to your children, a good way to ensure that they will value the skill. Encourage your children to keep journals, too. Even pre-writers can draw in a blank book, and dictate entries to a scribe (you, your spouse, or an older sibling).

Portfolios make nice mementos for homeschoolers. Younger students enjoy making a book about themselves. Small photo journals make nice gifts for grandparents, and larger ones can remain at home as a record of the student's accomplishments for the year. See Chapter 16, "Other Assessments for Measuring Progress," for an in-depth discussion on the value of journals and portfolios for assessment and record keeping.

The Least You Need to Know

➤ Homeschooling records provide documentation for personal reference, to satisfy legal or support school requirements, and proof that learning is happening.

➤ Records kept for government agencies and support schools should follow reporting guidelines.

➤ Get creative when keeping records for personal use or portfolios.

➤ Your record-keeping style will reflect your lifestyle and the way you homeschool.

➤ You can use a commercial record-keeping system or you can design your own.

Part 6

Burnout Prevention

Burnout—giving up on homeschooling—is often caused by doing too much, setting your expectations too high, and separating learning from life. I'll help you schedule your homeschool experience to fit your family's lifestyle, analyze the everyday events of life as they relate to learning, and capitalize on the learning centers that already exist in your home.

I'll also share with you some homeschool success stories, pointing out the keys to success and how you can implement them to prevent burnout. You'll learn about using your records to encourage yourself, talking about your discouraging moments, and how to share your successes. Finally, I'll include tips on how to use the extended homeschool community (both real and virtual) to bolster your flagging efforts.

Schedule
5 AM- Get up
5:05- Shower
5:10- Breakfast
5:15: chores
8:00- School
12- Lunch
12:30-More School
3- School's out
3:05- Grade work
5:00- Do Freelance
~job
2 AM- Bed

Chapter 18

Getting a Grip: Keeping Burnout at Bay

In This Chapter

➤ Providing an open-ended schedule with enough flexibility to accommodate the unexpected

➤ Organizing your home to maximize learning

➤ Capitalizing on your resources at home

➤ Rolling with the punches when life is uncertain

➤ Using a home-based business as a learning tool

➤ How to be a model of lifelong learning for your children while taking care of your personal needs

---

Burnout—the experience of hitting the wall, getting to the end of your rope, or feeling like you can't homeschool any more because it's just too much, too hard, too *everything*—occurs most often among homeschoolers who try to duplicate the school environment at home. Parents who live in states with stringent homeschooling requirements either struggle to comply or become creative at providing an equivalent education.

Many new homeschoolers begin by setting aside a block of time which they devote to academic pursuits, squeezing the everyday events of life (dishes, laundry, cleaning, cooking, appointments, and other interruptions to the daily routine) into a separate sphere. While this works for some, the average person finds it difficult to keep two separate lives going in the same household. Adjusting to the new demands of home-schooling and attempting to continue to do everything you've done before can turn into a lose-lose situation. Your children may also experience burnout as a result of trying to keep up with unrealistic expectations and goals and your frustration when things don't go the way you envisioned them. Integrating academic and everyday activities, rethinking priorities, and realizing that life holds lessons that run parallel to educational objectives are helpful strategies for preventing burnout.

If you are considering homeschooling or trying to decide whether homeschooling is going to continue to be a part of your lifestyle, read on for some tips to help you get—and keep—it all together.

Scheduling Your Day: Learning to Go with the Flow

School-at-homers may have a planner or schedule dictating which subjects will be done at what time, using which materials, and by whom. If that works for you, go for it! If you want to find a different way, reconsider your homeschooling style, your priorities, and the information found between the covers of this book to make changes that will make life and learning happier for you and yours. Once you realize that the everyday experiences of life provide excellent opportunities for learning, you will understand that your children don't have to spend quite as much time on bookish pursuits.

Remember that we talked about using a curriculum as a guideline? Rather than focusing on the curriculum as the only route to the end, use it as a road map with many routes. For example, if you've spent the morning doing lessons and are en route to the library for a book on birds (your child's latest interest), be flexible enough to stop at a construction site, observe a parachutist, or feed the geese on the way. Although these activities aren't on your schedule for today, they may not be available at another time. Grasp the learning experiences that serendipitously come your way, record them under the appropriate topic headings wherever you keep records, and move the afternoon's planned activities to another day. Flexibility is a vital key to preventing burnout in both homeschooling parents and children.

Teaming Up to Tackle Cleaning and Other Chores

When learning comes home to stay, many parents wonder how they'll ever do it all! This is an excellent time to announce to your assembled progeny that everyone will be helping around the house so mom and dad can do the extra things that will be required by homeschooling. Learning to do the household chores is an important part of the learning and growing-up process. If your household hasn't already been including the children in chores around the house and yard, there's no time like the present. Daily chores are the first part of the homeschool day for many homeschoolers, regardless of approach.

Tracking Academic/Text Work

If your child is expected to complete specific assignments, be sure he or she is aware of exactly what you require. Have some sort of accountability system in place, whether it's as simple as a checklist you provide for your child to use, or part of a larger plan that you implement and check regularly. Whether you break up subjects into small fragments and do all subjects daily (typical of the institutional school) or use unit studies or interest-oriented learning, if you are required to keep records (see Chapter 17, "Keeping Records"), it's important to have some sort of system in place to keep track of what everyone is accomplishing. Start even the youngest learner with a checklist for which he or she is responsible; the first step toward independent learning. I'll talk more about the value of independent learning in preventing burnout in Chapter 19, "Self-Directed Learning: The Key to Motivation." Prereaders enjoy a chart on the wall with pictures to represent their assigned chores and academic lessons; stickers placed in the appropriate box correspond with each task completed. Transferring accountability to each family member is another way to prevent burnout.

Learning Lookouts

Simply adding homeschooling to your already busy life is a recipe for disaster. Every member of the family must make adjustments. Older children can incorporate cooking, cleaning, and laundry chores into their days, while younger children can begin to help with minor chores until they can take on larger tasks. Everyone needs to realize he or she is an integral part of a larger plan: the smooth running of the family.

Integrating Activities: Maximizing Learning Time

Children who are involved in project-oriented learning may be covering a number of curriculum areas throughout the course of the project. Discussion, taking photographs, journaling, and making lists of subject areas covered can help you keep track of what is being accomplished.

Activities that may have been considered extracurricular if your child were enrolled in an institutional school may become an integral part of his or her curriculum in the homeschool. Look at your child's involvement in organizations, sports, and hobbies with the eyes of a curriculum planner and ask ...

➤ Are any of the objectives for the child's grade level being met?

➤ What subject areas are being covered?

➤ What skills are being learned or reinforced?

Consider your child's solitary activities and how he or she spends time when with friends and ask yourself the same questions. Children are learning all the time;

recognize what is being learned, by whom, and what subject areas are being covered. Whether you are keeping records for a support school, to comply with regulations, or to assure yourself that your child is making appropriate progress, thinking outside the box is an essential key to preventing burnout.

Visits to the doctor, dentist, and other health care providers can be turned into educational experiences simply by asking a few well-thought-out questions while you are there. Homeschoolers can also make the most of such visits by taking along a book to read or some coursework to do in the waiting room. If you're caught unprepared, turn the outdated magazines into an on-the-spot unit study:

➤ **Health/nutrition:** Look for food ads and discuss the advertising strategies. Is the advertiser telling the whole story? Is the food good for you? What would be a better food to eat instead? Why?

➤ **Science:** Find pictures of animals and classify them by groups: mammals, vertebrates and invertebrates, warm-blooded and cold-blooded, carnivore and herbivore.

➤ **Math:** Find and count specified items throughout the magazines. If you have a paper and pencil you can graph your findings: Which item did you find the most pictures of? The least?

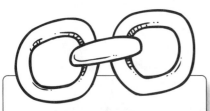

Learning Links

Repair people seldom mind being asked questions by children who show real interest in their activities. Questions about how he or she became a repair person, what training he needed, and what he likes most about his job can be part of a unit on career planning. Save questions for the worker's break times and be sure to ask if he minds spending time talking to your children.

Once you're back home, you don't have to fret about the wasted three hours. You know you spent the time profitably, your children were engaged in learning, and something you found in a magazine or learned while talking to the nurse or doctor may spark a new learning interest for your child.

Home visits by insurance representatives, investment counselors, and repair people can provide excellent lessons for your children, too. Keep accurate records of appointments on your calendar so you can include them as part of your child's records. Rather than regarding appointments as necessary but time-wasting, integrate each experience into your child's educational experience. Talk to your child ahead of time about what he or she is going to experience. Be on the lookout for new concepts and discuss the experience afterwards.

Reread the sample journal entries in Chapter 5, "Approaches to Home Education," for ideas on how the various curriculum areas can be covered by hands-on activities, involvement in community service, and everyday events such as appointments. Make the most of opportunities, don't bemoan what might have been, and move on; these strategies are key to preventing burnout.

Organization 101: Organizing Your Home

Rome wasn't built in a day, and you won't get your homeschool organized overnight, either. It's better to jump in and get started homeschooling even if you aren't completely organized, than it is to spend several months getting organized before bringing your children home. You will probably find that what you thought would be the perfect setting, isn't. All you really need to do to get started is bring home the kids, supply them with some library books, and spend time with them. You can get more organized later, unless you find, as many homeschoolers have, that you and your children like learning this way.

Dejunk

If you have time to do anything ahead of time get rid of nonessentials. Of course, when beginning to homeschool it's a little difficult to know what is nonessential. What seems to be junk now may turn out to be the exact item you need to build a model tornado. So use discretion when determining nonessentials. If you've been a pack rat until now you probably won't get rid of anything too vital! But if the things sitting around your house are truly junk and not likely to be used for any projects or as learning tools, it's time to fill the dumpster.

You're the only one who can determine how organized you need to be to be comfortable with your home and yourself. Most homeschoolers' houses have a comfortably lived-in look; you'll develop your own standards for what's acceptable as you go along. Organize and simplify are good rules of thumb for helping to prevent burnout.

Learning Links

Be prepared for your house having that lived-in look. Most homeschoolers, unless they reserve a special part of the house for homeschooling activities, find that they are overrun with science projects, crafts, and books. Organized confusion is the name of the game and the easiest way to cope is to accept it.

Keep Materials Accessible

Unless there are small children in the house, keeping homeschool materials accessible is the best way to go. Items that are within easy reach get used more often than those that are tucked away out of reach or out of sight. For homeschoolers with little ones, using see-through plastic bins with labels is a good way to store items you want to be within sight if not within reach. Keep items the little ones can use on low shelves, and keep items you don't want them to use up higher. Of course, toxic or dangerous items must be stored safely out of reach and perhaps under lock and key.

Consider providing learning centers, keeping materials that are used together in one place. Some examples of learning centers include:

➤ **Science:** A microscope, hand lens, nature guides (birds, trees, wildflowers, mammals), nature journals, displays of items found on nature walks

➤ **Art:** Large work area, containers to hold paints, brushes, chalks, markers, pastels, crayons, pencils and pens, an assortment of paper, newspaper, glues, glitter, drawing tools, erasers, rubber stamps, scissors, beads

➤ **Math:** A scale, base-10 blocks, counters, activity books, dice, math posters, calculator, ruler, protractor, triangle, compass, math games, puzzles

Having a place for everything not only makes pickup time more efficient, it helps everyone know where to look for a given item. Keeping materials accessible, visible, and organized helps prevent burnout for everyone in the household.

Rich Educational Environments

Rethink your household as a learning laboratory. Your everyday activities in the kitchen, garage or workshop, and garden or yard can be integrated into your child's curriculum. Including your child in necessary work in these areas melds the usual household requirements into a learning experience that teaches your child essential independent living skills. And balancing practical skills with academic pursuits helps to prevent burnout for everyone.

Let's take a closer look at some fun activities for different areas of the house.

What's Cooking in the Kitchen?

Children who have been helping in the kitchen all along will soon be able to take turns preparing meals, preserving foods, and baking. Children who haven't had kitchen experience can begin by helping and work their way up to self-sufficient kitchen tasks, all a part of a home learning experience. Regardless of homeschooling approach, your children should be learning to be helpers while honing skills that will lead to independence. If you're a gourmet cook, preserve most of your own garden produce, or decorate cakes, include your children so they can benefit from your expertise in these areas. Enlist the help of grandmothers, friends, or neighbors in teaching your children these skills if you don't have time or aren't much of a cook yourself.

Remember that many of the skills learned in the kitchen are taught in school as abstract concepts; doubling and halving recipes provides a concrete reason for learning to manipulate fractions! On days when your child practices such skills, he or she may not need to work as many problems in his or her math text, thus reducing stress caused by trying to fit too many activities into one day.

Gearing Up in the Garage or Workshop

Include your children in the chores and hobbies pursued by older family members in these vital and rich resource centers of the home. Learning wood working, automotive maintenance, repair of lawn equipment, and other skills are also part of developing a self-sufficient, independent child. Learning how to sharpen a lawn mower blade (including learning safety rules for handling the tools and protecting oneself with goggles), helping to change the oil in the mower, replace the string in a string-trimmer, or calculating the gas mileage for the last tank of gas in the family vehicle helps children feel a part of the everyday workings of the

Learning Lookouts

Don't devote all your child's time to academic pursuits while neglecting everyday skills that will be necessary for independent living. It's important for kids to know how to balance a budget, buy groceries, pay bills, care for a home, lawn, and home care equipment, and maintain a vehicle. Such things are best learned on the job rather than from a book.

family. If someone in the family is a woodworker, start children out with small projects to sand and finish; they can work up to learning to use the scroll saw to cut out their own projects. Dads often shine in this area, but grandfathers, neighbors, and friends can also play a vital role in providing instruction, encouragement, and mentorship in these areas.

How Does Your Garden (or Yard) Grow?

Most homeschoolers have outdoor maintenance and yard work to do, while some grow extensive gardens for enjoyment or to provide for the family. Whatever your family's motivation, teach your children the skills they will need to know to care for their own outdoor areas someday. Whether you grow an herb garden on the windowsill and tomatoes in pots on the patio or grow enough vegetables in your garden to provide canned and frozen food all winter long, your child can learn gardening as the plants flourish. Learning basic lawn care; seeing the results of mulching, fertilizing, watering, and caring for plants; and feeling the pride in a job well done are important parts of a child's balanced education. As homeschooled children grown up, they often take over some of the lawn care or gardening duties, learning responsibility and the satisfaction of being a contributing member of the family, while helping reduce burnout for their parents. Many of the lessons learned in the yard and garden can be expanded on during academic lessons and counted as part of a basic science curriculum.

Turning Life's Surprises into Learning Experiences

Whether the unplanned events of life are pleasant or distressing, uncertainty and being caught off guard are two of the most common starting points for stress, which can lead to burnout. Whenever something comes up that you're not prepared for, take a deep breath, do a little self-talk, and focus on acting, not reacting. Think before you jump in with both feet. If you have time to plan a strategy that will reduce stress, do so. One of the certainties of life is that life is uncertain. Take things one day at a time, one step at a time.

Visitors: Capitalize on Natural Socialization

Having house guests can seem overwhelming as you consider the entertaining and extra work required. It's easy to feel a little stressed as you try to be the perfect host or hostess. Rethinking house guests as resources to be used in your children's education can reduce the stress immediately. Plan to accept all offers of help from your guests around the house.

Learning Links

Involve your visitors in your homeschooling by having them teach your child new games, share information about their career or job, and talk about how they got the education or training to get that job.

The grandparents' annual visits can be stressful events as Grandpa quizzes the children on academic subjects and Grandma sniffs with disapproval when a child can't answer. If this is the case in your home, turn the tables and ask for their help. Ask them to share details on their recent cruise or vacation, to explain about their heart surgery, or share details of their hobbies. Make a list ahead of time and keep the conversation moving, making the grandparents the experts and center of attention, diverting attention from the children.

Relatives and other house guests delight in talking about themselves, and are often flattered to be asked to impart knowledge in the name of education. With both the difficult and the delightful house guest you may enjoy playing games, working on a craft project, cooking goodies in the kitchen together, and other simple but educational pursuits. Plan some field trips; take your visitors on a tour of local museums, the zoo, or other points of interest. The secret is initiating activity, diverting your guests from critiquing your child and your lifestyle choices. Make your guests feel important, needed, useful, and special by keeping them busy and occupied. Explain that these activities are all part of the child's education and you appreciate their help. Refuse to let the interruptions throw you. Instead, find the hidden educational opportunities in every situation.

When Life Gives You Lemons, Make Lemonade!

Homeschoolers have lived and learned through family illnesses, accidents, hospitalization, divorce, and deaths. Some have lost their jobs and transferred across country, leaving extended family and friends behind. Military homeschool families adjust to the constant moving and settling into new communities, churches, and finding new friends and support groups. Sometimes the stay-at-home partner has to take a job outside the home while the wage-earning spouse stays home to supervise the children's education and recuperate from a debilitating injury. Many homeschoolers' families include children with learning disabilities, physical or mental handicaps, or terminal illnesses. Rather than using such situations as a reason to give up, remember that you can prevent burnout by prioritizing and planning. Integrate the necessary activities of life, based on your family's unique situation, with curriculum basics to determine what your child will learn from what life has doled out.

Spotlight on Education

The year my nephew and some family friends were in automobile accidents just a month apart I was enrolled in a college course. My nephew and the 11-year-old son of the other family were in a rehabilitation center for several months. We learned to use the hour's drive in the car profitably by listening to audiotapes or doing schoolwork. During weekly visits, we participated in play therapy with our friend, cheered both boys on in rehab, and pulled out our books and studied during the times when our presence would be a distraction. We learned to appreciate our health and had the importance of wearing seatbelts engraved on our minds, as well as how quickly accidents can change a life forever.

Home-Based Business: Life Is a Great Teacher

Starting a business as well as homeschooling may seem like a good way to cause, rather than prevent, burnout. However, many homeschooling families have proven otherwise. Starting a home-based business is a financial necessity for some homeschooling families. If your household income is less due to changes made to juggle the responsibilities of wage earning with those of homeschooling, you'll understand how working from home has proved a stress-busting option for many homeschoolers. You can incorporate business-related activities into the general curriculum, relieve the pressure to do separate activities for business and education, and in effect, give yourself more hours in the day. Melding business-related activities into your child's lessons provides her with a purpose for learning, imparts a sense of responsibility and pride in a job well done, and builds self-worth as the child sees herself as an integral part of family and business. And while you may not have as much time to spend one-on-one with your child, you are there to supervise her activities, help with problems when they arise, and model a good work ethic. New homeschoolers who were already home-based entrepreneurs or home workers reap the same benefits when they include their home-educated children as employees or partners.

Don't look on starting a home business as the proverbial last straw; think of it as a way to encourage learning from life. Many home-based businesses provide across-the-curriculum experience and education in most subject areas. Running a business takes understanding of economics, entrepreneurship, customer relations, accounting, taxes, English, social studies, and more. Breaking down the various tasks a child must do to keep a business afloat, many homeschoolers are startled and delighted to realize that they don't need to provide textbook assignments; their children are learning what they need to know while doing something they enjoy, and are making a profit as well.

Spotlight on Education

Many homeschooling families have homeschool–related businesses, selling curriculum or other products and speaking at conferences. Others have found their niche by selling home–baked bread, specialty baskets, plants, or other products locally or by mail. Others sell booklets and brochures about homeschooling and other topics. Some provide services such as pet sitting, baby sitting, plant care, lawn care, excavation, house sitting, or house cleaning. Some have turned hobbies or newly learned skills into a lucrative income, such as designing Web sites, word processing, and quilting.

Homeschoolers are often asked, "How will your child function in the real world?" Running a business, or working for someone in a business, *is* the real world. Many homeschoolers use the home as a base for learning but find that real-life experience provides most of the education, especially when their child is running his or her own business, or working in the family business.

Some homeschooled youngsters have learned similar lessons while employed outside the home. Keep records of the child's work responsibilities and plug them into curricular areas for homeschooled credit. Kids who run a business, work in a family business, or work outside the home get a real-world experience that can't be duplicated in an institutional school setting. We all learn from life, whether homeschooled or not. Homeschoolers simply consider such essential lessons an integral part of the curriculum.

Are you beginning to realize that preventing burnout may be as simple as looking at things from another angle? It's all in your state of mind. Regard new experiences as opportunities to learn rather than as one more thing to squeeze into an already busy life.

Learning Links

One youngster, when asked what he wanted to be when he grew up, replied, "I am doing great just being who I am right now. I don't know who I'll be when I grow up." Perhaps he's on the right track. If your child can focus on being the best he or she can be right now, the future will take care of itself.

Model Lifelong Learning for Your Children

A picture is worth a thousand words, and an example is worth even more. Homeschoolers have learned that what they do speaks much more loudly to their children than anything they say. Although parents may be successful in home educating their child by assigning academic lessons and watching the soaps while their child completes his or her schoolwork, it is more likely that the child will get a well-rounded education when the parents model lifelong learning in the following ways:

➤ Pursuing hobbies

➤ Reading

➤ Taking care of themselves emotionally

➤ Performing community service

Share Your Hobby with Your Child

Whether you enjoy genealogical research, needlepoint, painting, or yoga, include your child and share your passion. Your child may not develop a matching passion but early exposure may produce an interest at a later date. Participating in the hobby you enjoy can also spark a related interest in your child. One mother's interest in genealogy inspired her daughter to learn to type so she could enter records into her mother's computer genealogy program. Difficulty finding frames for your needlework or paintings could lead to an interest in learning matting and framing. Each of these interests can be recorded in the corresponding curricular areas of your child's homeschooling records. If your child is learning while participating in some phase of your activities, there will be a lot less stress involved than if you are trying to get your child to complete seven workbook pages while practicing your latest yoga routine.

Reading and Using the Library

While you may not read an adult book to your child, sharing interesting tidbits from your current reading material may spark your child's interest in topics that you find fascinating. Find a book at your child's level on the topic you are researching and either read it to your child or suggest that your child read it him- or herself. Then you will be able to discuss it together. Model researching by pointing out times when you have a question and look up the answer in a reference book, at the library, or on the Internet.

Learning Links

If your child is interested in something, he or she will retain the information more readily than if you present a preplanned item of no interest. Substitute. Add. Deviate. The book that catches your child's eye this week may turn out to be the beginning of a year-long unit study.

The library should be familiar to your child from an early age. Browse the shelves with your child; allow him or her to choose books that catch the eye. Don't worry if it's something that is not in the curriculum. Children whose interest is engaged retain subject matter longer than those who are simply learning for the test or to please an instructor. Check with the children's librarian for children's programming and story hours; many of these are educational and give you a break from providing every aspect of your child's education. Some libraries have toys and games available for checkout, as well as videos, and books on audiotape; use these resources and integrate them into your child's curriculum. Be sure to ask what services are available through your local library and determine how you can use them in your homeschool. Prevent burnout by placing your child in the educational environment of the library, flexing the curriculum to follow your child's interests, providing varied resources to facilitate and engage learning, and teaching lifelong learning skills by example.

Take Care of Yourself First

Burnout is more common in homeschool parents who try to put their own needs on the back burner while devoting all their time and energy to homeschooling. Although it may seem impossible, make yourself your first priority. If an evening soaking in the tub with a novel is your idea of bliss, see what you can work out with your partner or a friend to make it possible occasionally. If intellectual stimulation is what you need, take a class in something of interest to you; and model researching, studying, and learning for your kids. If physical movement and a break from sticky little fingers are vital, take a yoga, aerobics or swimming class, or take a walk several times weekly. Make time to sustain your relationship with your partner. One of the smartest things my husband and I ever did was to establish a weekly date night; these vary from walks on the beach, fast-food sandwiches and an evening shopping, to dinners out at memorable restaurants. Get out, learn, move, and revitalize. Whatever works to keep you happy and healthy emotionally will reduce stress and help prevent burnout. Make it a priority!

Community Service

Many homeschoolers continue to perform community service while homeschooling. Those most successful at incorporating homeschooling into a lifestyle often start their children on the volunteer path at an early age. Homeschoolers unload the food cooperative truck and sort food with a young helper, deliver Meals on Wheels with the kids along to deliver hand-drawn greeting cards and a smile, and lead a La Leche League series meeting with older children along to baby-sit their own and others' toddlers, actively teaching their children the joys of serving others. Maintain the level of joy in your own life and you are less apt to burn out.

The Least You Need to Know

➤ A workable schedule based on your need for structure, integrating necessary daily routines into your academic schedule, helps prevent burnout.

➤ Organization is key but depends largely on personal preference.

➤ You need look no further than your home to provide a rich educational environment for everyday learning.

➤ Go with the flow when life gets difficult.

➤ Integrating activities necessary to home-based businesses with academics helps prevent burnout.

➤ Modeling lifelong learning for your children may be one of the most important lessons you teach them, and can reduce your stress level at the same time.

Chapter 19

Self-Directed Learning: The Key to Motivation

In This Chapter

➤ Some famous and not-so-famous self-directed learners

➤ Helping your child become an independent learner

➤ Providing the tools for independent living

➤ Giving credit for life experience

It doesn't take homeschooling parents long to see the advantages of their children becoming independent learners. The next step is determining how to motivate their children to think for themselves, initiate learning, and become an independent learner.

Institutional schools use a preplanned curriculum, lesson plans, and schedules as a way to implement education, depending on grades, class standing and status, rewards, or the approval of others to motivate students. Homeschoolers soon see that these factors don't motivate all students to learn, and begin to search for a way to help their student be inwardly, rather than externally motivated.

Having a self-directed, inwardly motivated learner is one of the best ways to guarantee that none of you will experience burnout. A child who is a self-directed learner frees the parent to focus energies on keeping up with the child's activities, rather than spending time pushing, prodding, and pressuring the child to learn something … anything! What can you do as a homeschooler to guide your child into becoming a self-directed learner? Let's find out!

The Essence of Self-Directed Learning

We can get some clues for developing independent learners from the lives of some *self-directed learners* in the past and present. Many famous self-taught individuals have similar traits and personalities. Quite a few followed their own interests in developing an educational plan that worked for them. Others learned from the experiences of life—the school of hard knocks.

Speaking Educationese

Self-directed learners tend to learn in their own way, in their own time, and at their own pace. Generally focused and in-wardly motivated when pursuing their passion, these individuals don't always fit into society's accepted mold.

By studying famous self-directed learners you can recognize similar character traits, types of experiences, and other factors shared by your own child and attempt to help your child cultivate them.

Here's a quick overview of some well-known self-directed learners. What similarities do you see in the following stories?

➤ Soichiro Honda left school at age 15 and headed to Tokyo to become an automobile mechanic who built his business into the Honda company.

➤ Ray Kroc, founder of McDonald's, dropped out of school after his sophomore year.

➤ Jimmy Lai, founder of Giordano International, a 350-million-dollar chain clothing store, attributes his success to never setting foot in a classroom, but learning everything by trial and error.

➤ Colonel Harland Sanders, founder of the Kentucky Fried Chicken chain, had no formal education beyond seventh grade.

➤ David Thomas, of Wendy's restaurant chain fame, dropped out of school because "School wasn't teaching me what I wanted to know." Already a successful entrepreneur, he earned his GED in 1993 at the age of 60.

➤ William F. Buckley, editor of the *National Review*, author, and well-known politically conservative columnist, was taught at home by tutors and his parents.

➤ Jill Ker Conway, former president of Smith College from 1975 to 1985, was raised on a sheep station in Australia and learned from life and correspondence lessons that she began at the age of eight.

➤ Gloria Steinem, leading advocate of women's liberation and editor of *Ms* magazine, didn't attend school regularly until age 12 because her family traveled extensively.

Spotlight on Education

According to Tom Peters, management guru, all history makers have 15 traits in common. Some of these traits include commitment, a determination to make a difference, focus, and passion. The history makers also made many people mad, flouted the chain of command, were irreverent and disrespectful, thrived on chaos, were always honest, and were good at what they did. Recognize anyone in your household? You might want to read Tom Peters' book, *The Brand You 50: Or: Fifty Ways to Transform Yourself from an "Employee" into a Brand That Shouts Distinction, Commitment, and Passion!* (Knopf, 1999) for more insights into what makes an independent thinker.

Famous self-directed learners who dropped out of school were not your typical dropouts. It appears that, on the contrary, these independent thinkers had the rise-out mentality advocated by Grace Llewellyn in her book *The Teenage Liberation Handbook: How to Quit School and Get a Real Life and Education* (see Appendix E, "Bibliography"). Leaving school and eschewing education isn't the answer; the secret is in becoming a life-long learner.

Vignettes of Home-Educated Kids Today

Chuck Dobson found a career as a fire fighter while participating in an Eagle Scout troop affiliated with the local fire department. Chuck, at 21, has seven years of hands-on experience in his chosen career and has served his community while doing something he loves. Read *Homeschooler's Success Stories* (see Appendix E) by Chuck's mother, Linda Dobson, for more exciting stories of the ways that home-educated kids today are making their mark in the world while pursuing education in unique ways.

Ryan Ransom, my oldest son, also 21, learned about engines by taking a correspondence course in small engine repair, working on our family vehicles, running a small engine repair business, working as a volunteer for an independent mechanic, taking classes at the intermediate school district's technologies center, working in a lube shop, apprenticing in automobile dealerships, and taking General Motors and Chrysler training. For a speech credit he volunteered as a docent at a local museum, which helped him develop confidence in public speaking, an asset in his current position. He teaches automotive technology at the same technology center where he took automotive classes just a few years ago.

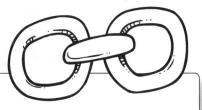

Learning Links

One component that crops up over and over again in the lives of successful independent thinkers is community spirit. We find these capable, talented young people volunteering their time and energy to help others in unique ways. Find local opportunities by visiting SERVEnet at www.servenet.org. Involve your whole family!

Learning Lookouts

If your child starts a business, the secret to fostering independence is allowing your child to have ownership of the business and all related activities. Don't run the business for your child. One of the hardest things a parent has to do is hand the phone over to a 9- or 12-year-old when the child gets a call from a customer requesting a bid on a job.

The Williams sisters, Venus and Serena, rocketed their way to tennis fame while homeschooling. The sisters began learning tennis at four, attending institutional schools until middle school. Their father rightly determined that the sisters needed a flexible education schedule so they could concentrate on their tennis; the girls started homeschooling in middle school. Both girls' homeschooling schedules included speaking at inner-city schools. Venus graduated from homeschool high school in 1997 with a 3.8 GPA. Serena is currently enrolled in the Art Institute of Florida and supports several tennis clinics. Against the advice of others, their father launched his daughters into the big leagues, skipping the Junior Championships; the girls' latest coup is winning the 2000 Wimbledon ladies' doubles championship!

Fostering Independent Learning

How can you, as a homeschooler, help your child become an independent learner? What are some of the trends that we see over and over in the lives of independent learners past and present? When should you begin letting go of the reins and allowing your child to make his or her own decisions?

Techniques That Work

Thomas Edison's mother allowed her son to follow his own interests early in his home-education experience. Tom was fascinated by how things worked and was an avid inventor. He was internally motivated to explore, experiment, and do things himself. It's also apparent that Tom was motivated by earning money; some of his earliest endeavors included selling snacks, writing a newspaper to sell, and learning to send Morse code so he could obtain a job. You can see from Edison's example that important factors in developing inner motivation include encouraging a child to follow his or her interests, to explore and study things in depth, and possibly run his or her own business.

Abraham Lincoln read avidly as a child and as an adult. One might say he read his education; he even learned how to be a lawyer by reading a law tome. From Abe's experience you can learn that it's important to provide a good supply of top-quality reading material, to teach your children how to use the library, and to provide an incentive for reading good books. Depending on the child, incentives might include having someone available to read to him or her, offering a reward program providing incentives for the completion of a certain number of books, or developing interest in reading the classics and other good literature by providing audio versions. Such tactics can help develop a love for reading good books which will in turn encourage the child to become a better reader. Abe, of course, didn't have the distractions of mindless video games and television programming to keep him from reading during his limited leisure time. Many families have found it helpful to place limits on such activities, or to eliminate them completely.

Pearl S. Buck had a Chinese tutor and a Chinese nanny, and enjoyed visiting with the other household help. Although these were not planned parts of her education, they had a direct and positive influence on her as she developed a love for things Asian. This immersion learning (learning from life) was instrumental in her future success as a writer. Her writing was strongly influenced by her early years spent in China, and her respect and love for the Chinese people and their culture flows through her writings. From Pearl Buck's experience you can learn to include your child in planning his or her own learning experiences. Build on your child's interests when searching for materials, activities, and programs to include in your curriculum plans.

Materials That Encourage Independence

Parents can encourage their children by providing self-teaching materials. If you are using texts, see if they include good explanations and can be used independently, or if the text is dependent on a teacher's manual to provide explanations. Look for texts that don't "dumb down" or trivialize the material presented. Many independent learners use texts only as a guideline or reference, and turn to living books from the library or bookstore to provide a more in-depth discussion of the same topics covered in the textbooks.

Many homeschoolers have learned that multi-age materials—books, educational games, and other materials that can be used year after year—are good investments. These materials also promote independence because they allow a child to move along at his or her own pace. Students can supplement multi-age materials with library books, hands-on projects, field trips, and other activities.

Real books, fiction or nonfiction, encourage independence because they don't impart the same expectations as texts: that the child will complete the reading assignment and answer a set of questions or take a test to prove that he or she learned the material contained within. Rather, living books tend to pull the reader in and capture his or her interest. Some parents find it helpful to read books with their child, or scan

Learning Links

All kinds of books can foster independent learning. "Just-for-fun" fiction can help develop reading skills. Historical fiction sparks an interest in a specific time period or event in history. A biography can help a child understand real people in a specific historical setting. Many books are available today on just about any topic, providing information in a colorful, interesting context, suitable for self-study.

them ahead of time and discuss them together after the child has completed the book. Others, knowing that their child is a fluent reader with good comprehension skills, consider reading to be a gateway to knowledge, and don't expect the child to regurgitate the information or prove that he or she learned it. Rather, as the child makes connections to other information, the content of such reading materials is brought forth and shared in conversation with others. More relaxed homeschoolers find this indicative of true learning.

Kids Can Learn to Find Their Own Resources

While homeschooling parents become masters at ferreting out resources, tutors, programs, and other activities that match up with their children's needs, it's also important to begin sharing these research skills with their children. Discuss the way you search for such things, and encourage your child to use the phone to inquire about volunteer opportunities, interview potential tutors or teachers, and follow up on newspaper articles about planned programs. Role play with your child, teach him or her to jot down questions he or she wants to ask, and encourage your child in every way to develop the confidence to do things independently.

Getting Acquainted with the Library

Most kids catch on quite quickly to finding their favorite authors or the latest series books on the library shelves! It's important to learn about all the resources the library offers; if you aren't sure yourself, plan a field trip to the library for your homeschool group or family, asking the librarian ahead of time to include how to find and use library resources in her presentation. You will probably learn or be reminded of some resources you didn't know about or had forgotten.

If taking a library tour isn't an option, at the very least spend time in the reference section of your library learning about the special books and materials included there. Teach your child how to use basic reference materials, such as the dictionary, encyclopedia, and thesaurus. Show your child the guide words at the top of the dictionary pages and how they help find words on the pages. Demonstrate the use of the encyclopedia; if there is a special index or guide volume, explore it together. Teach your child to scan the table of contents and index of nonfiction books to determine content and to get an overview of the material presented.

Spotlight on Education

Basic library skills are not used just during the school years but throughout a person's lifetime. At the very least, children should be familiar with the alphabetic and numeric arrangements of resources and where they are located. Manual and electronic catalog use should be demonstrated as soon as the child can read, including how to search by subject heading. Research and study skills can be taught as soon as the child can read and write, while information–seeking strategies can be modeled and explained even earlier to the child who shows an interest. If you have a research question, ask the librarian and have her explain it to both you and your child.

Show your child how the *Dewey decimal system* works in libraries everywhere to simplify the shelving and subsequent retrieval of books. Teach your child how to find information on the Internet. If you aren't computer-savvy, spend time together learning how to use this research option. You may learn something new from your child; most kids aren't afraid of pushing the wrong button and this learning experience may turn into an adventure for both of you.

Finding Tutors, Mentors, and Teachers in the Community

Speaking Educationese

The **Dewey decimal system** is a cataloging system developed by librarian Melvil Dewey to make it easier for library patrons to find books. A Web site that tells all about the development of the Dewey Decimal System is tqjunior.thinkquest.org/5002.

Tutors, mentors, and teachers are often as close as your own circle of friends and acquaintances. Children sometimes find their own mentors while talking to someone about their interests. You may occasionally find it necessary to network with everyone you know to start a search for people to work with your child. Ask the librarian, other homeschoolers, and people you come in contact with while shopping, running errands, or working out at the gym. Contact local community colleges, post notices on community bulletin boards, or run an ad in the homeschool newsletter. Be sure to include your child in the process of searching for a mentor. Your child will learn a lot about the networking process as you discuss developments with him or her.

Learning Lookouts

Do an informal background check before getting involved with private teachers and mentors. Interview the individual and check references. Have the teacher come to your home, or stay nearby if your child is working at a teacher's home or place of business. Once you feel comfortable, stop in now and then to keep an eye on things. You aren't being overly protective, just cautious.

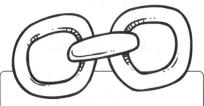

Learning Links

To find information on virtually any topic, search with meta search engines using keywords related to the subject you're researching; you will find Web sites packed with information, bulletin boards with archives to search for comments, suggestions, tips, and hints, and much more. Check Appendix B, "Curriculum Winners and Selected Resources, Including Dynamite Web Sites," for a list of search engines.

Using the Internet Constructively

The Internet provides a wealth of information that is constantly changing and rearranging. Occasionally frustrating, surfing the Net can help your child (and you!) find everything from other homeschoolers to classes offered online. There are bulletin boards and chats for an endless variety of interests. While we used to always head for the encyclopedia, now we quite often turn to the Internet for up-to-date information on many of the topics we want to research. Many homeschoolers install a software screening program, or make children's use of the Internet a supervised activity.

In many homeschooling families, the kids are far more computer-savvy than the parents, with the parents depending on the kids to keep their computers up and running, install software, or perform simple maintenance operations. Kids who are learning circles around us are definitely becoming independent learners!

Offering Your Children Choices

When encouraging independence, it's never too early to start offering choices. Children are often more motivated when they feel they have some autonomy. Depending on your family dynamics, your children's personalities and need for independence, it's wise to begin by allowing choices within your own boundaries. Rather than using a wide-open question like "What do you want to do?" you can offer choices such as "Do you want to use this computer game or your math video today?" or "Would you rather do your spelling or your reading first?"

When planning curriculum, include current interests as much as possible, and ask your child for input. You will have a much more productive year and a better chance of developing an independent learner when you study areas that are of interest to the child. Use an interest as a starting point and introduce side trips into areas that you believe are important. Even a short side trip may enable your child to make a connection that will encourage him or her to study that area at a later date.

Getting Credit for Life Experiences

Don't lose sight of the fact that when your child is following an interest or passion, many of the activities he or she becomes immersed in are learning experiences. Many homeschoolers call this learning from life. Although he or she isn't following a pre-planned curriculum, you can be an after-the-fact record keeper and jot down lists of things the child did, places he or she went, people he or she contacted or learned from. Such casual records can later be turned into permanent records; once you see where a project takes your child, you can begin to pigeonhole the activities into curriculum areas.

If your child's handwriting assignments include copying recipes for a personal recipe collection, rather than copying the alphabet from a handwriting workbook, the transcript will still read "Handwriting." Details aren't necessary. However, if you're required to use a handwriting curriculum and need to indicate what your child has done, you will have to look to your own conscience as to how much you actually use the curriculum, and how much your child does equivalent activities instead. In many cases, such details are unimportant; what is important is that your child has learned to write legibly. For an in-depth discussion on the need to give credit for life, review Chapter 18, "Getting a Grip: Keeping Burnout at Bay."

Spotlight on Education

When Ryan tinkered with his electronics kit at the age of 11, who would have guessed that in a few years he would have a job diagnosing problems with automobile computer systems? Aaron's passion for snowboarding helped him decide to major in marketing and management in college; he thought it would be awesome to work for his favorite snowboard company. Ervin spent hours transferring drawings to graphs on the computer drawing program; he recently announced that he wants to study commercial art. You won't always find such direct correlation, but it pays to keep alert for and capitalize on your child's interests. In each case a personal interest became part of a child's educational pursuits.

Kids can learn to think like homeschoolers (slotting life's learning experiences into curricular subject areas), keep their own records, and help prevent parental burnout by becoming not only an independent learner but an independent record keeper.

The Least You Need to Know

➤ Study the lives of self-directed learners for clues to use in motivating your homeschooled child.

➤ Foster independent study by providing appropriate materials and using proven techniques.

➤ To encourage self-directed learning, teach your child research skills, model life-long learning, and find others to work with your child in areas of interest.

➤ Once your child begins to follow his or her interests, stay attuned to the learning that is happening and give him or her credit for life.

Chapter 20

Dealing with Doubts

In This Chapter

➤ Is homeschooling working for you? Rethinking your homeschool program

➤ Analyzing success stories to find tips and techniques that will work for you

➤ Using your homeschool records to encourage yourself and improve your homeschool

➤ Realizing that you are on a learning curve and learning takes time

➤ Talking about your doubts and finding support for your efforts

---

When doubts about whether they are succeeding at homeschooling and whether their kids are learning begin to creep in, some homeschoolers throw in the towel. Doubts are one of the first steps on the road to burnout. If you feel yourself succumbing to doubts, give yourself a quick self-test. Why did you begin to homeschool? Do those reasons still exist? What will you accomplish by giving up? Can you change something within your home and family that will make homeschooling possible? Are you sticking with a curriculum that just isn't right for you and your child? Are you trying to do too much? Are your expectations for your child unrealistic? Has your child been given ample time to deschool and unwind from a previous negative school experience?

An unknown wise person once said, "If you always do what you always did, you'll always get what you always got." If putting your child into institutional school is the correct choice right now, don't feel like a failure. On the other hand, it's unlikely that you made the choice to home educate lightly: It's possible that you can tweak what is going on in your homeschool before you make another life-changing decision.

Are We Doing What We're Supposed to Be Doing?

What are you supposed to be doing? Who says so? Be sure your goals are really *your* goals and you aren't being influenced by the expectations of your children's grandparents, former teachers, and your neighbors. There are too many variables in families and homeschools for there to be only one right answer. Another key to continuing to homeschool is for you to be totally convinced that this is the best way to provide an education for your child. If you aren't convinced, doubts can overwhelm you. It's wise to remember that many homeschoolers have continued to homeschool through doubt for a few years, before being totally convinced that it was working. Why? Having made the choice to homeschool, they want to give it a working chance. And results aren't always immediately apparent. Your child will take a while to adjust to being home, to doing school differently, and to spending so much time with you. And face it, it's also a big change for you. If you need some encouragement, let's first look at some ways to help you determine if you are doing what you're supposed to be doing.

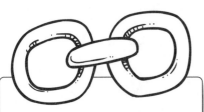

Learning Links

If you've read through the entire book up to this point, you know there is no one right answer to the question of what you should be doing. If you just turned to this chapter because you are having doubts, take time to read the book! You'll find plenty of ideas, questions, and tips to help you determine what you should be doing right now.

Scope and Sequence Critique

The schooled side of you may be agonizing over the fact that Johnny, 12, and Jenny, 6, haven't been keeping up with their schoolwork. Let's hypothesize that before you began homeschooling, you spent hours talking with homeschoolers and researching materials. Then you purchased a much-advertised writing program, several highly recommended textbooks, and a manipulative-based math program. When you purchased these materials you were convinced that you were providing Johnny and Jenny with the best possible educational materials for their grade levels.

However, since the school year began, Johnny and Jenny resist getting up in the morning, dawdle over breakfast, and aren't the least bit interested in the carefully chosen materials you've provided for their education. When you do get the children to sit down with their books, Johnny repeatedly tells you "This isn't the way my teacher did it," and Jenny, who was never in institutional school, echoes his words.

You feel like you are rapidly losing control of the situation. When the school bus goes by with the neighborhood kids aboard, homeward bound, your kids ask if they can go outside to play. But you feel that they have not learned a thing all day!

This story is a classic example of children and parents who need time to deschool. I know, Jenny was never in school, but she also isn't used to the idea of sitting down and doing schoolwork. Her idea of learning is fun stuff like watching educational videos, attending library story hour, and doing things with you. It also demonstrates that having a shelf full of wonderful materials does not an education make.

Look at your expectations. You thought Johnny would be so happy to be at home for learning that he would miraculously sit in his chair and complete pages and pages of school-type work. After all, he was in school every day for seven hours prior to coming home; shouldn't he be able to spend a few hours a day doing schoolwork without a problem? This is the schooled side of you thinking. Stop and consider one of the main reasons you decided to homeschool Johnny: He had difficulties with sitting still in class, remaining focused, and completing assignments. Perhaps Johnny needs a different approach. If his education were presented in a way that sparked his interest, would he be able to learn without being constantly nagged? If you could present educational concepts in a completely different way, would he quit dawdling and comparing everything to his school experience?

Learning Lookouts

Don't give up during the first year. The first year is the hardest, most fraught with new experiences and doubts. After the first year, things fall into place more readily. Give yourself time to adjust to all the changes homeschooling brings.

Look at Jenny for inspiration: She loves watching educational videos and doing hands-on and group activities. Is it possible that you could borrow some of these techniques with Johnny? Homeschooling can be very efficient, but when children who aren't visual/linguistic are assigned reams of textbook reading and writing assignments, it's amazing how long it can take them to get it done (if they ever do). See if you can tweak some of those educational materials and adapt them to your children's learning styles. Rather than assigning Johnny chapters and questions from the textbooks, find some interesting library books to cover the same material. Read out loud to both of the kids, discuss the material, and have them do some related hands-on projects as a way to show off their newly acquired knowledge. Use the materials you've already purchased as a guideline rather than letting them dictate a visual/linguistic approach.

You'll find that when you present materials in a format based on your child's learning style, focus on the subject matter rather than insist that learning happen in a particular manner, and combine learning projects for both children, learning will happen much more efficiently. Do some fun activities with your children, take day trips to educational places, and view videos of classic literature to help them (and you) make

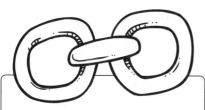

Learning Links

Spend the morning reading to your children about things they are interested in, and spend the afternoon observing nature while hiking and collecting some specimens. Include your children in the daily work of the household—baking and cooking, cleaning and laundry—and spend time interacting.

Speaking Educationese

The familiar **school-at-home mold** is based on the rather inflexible school model, complete with texts, tests, and a mandatory curriculum. The **home-school mold** is flexible. It considers the child's talents, interests, personality, and unique learning style to provide a learning environment that adapts as the child grows and learns.

the transition from institutional school to home-school. Then, when the school bus goes by with their little friends aboard, you'll feel free to say, "Sure, run and play with Nick and Reagan."

Quite often, parents find that their children learn much better this way than from texts and seat work. Such parents learn to incorporate many different learning activities into their program on a regular basis. You can, too.

Eye the Competition

What would your child be doing if he or she were in an institutional school? Would returning to institutional school solve Johnny's problems? Would enrolling Jenny in school bring her out of her shell or cause her to withdraw into it still more? Last year you were so certain that homeschooling was going to be the answer. But now Johnny won't cooperate. His bad feelings about learning seem to be transferring to Jenny. After three months into the school year you feel like you're trying to paddle upstream. Remember, if you always do what you always did, you'll always get what you always got—so what can you do differently?

First of all, try to relax. The events that led you to choose homeschooling didn't occur overnight and it will also take time to establish a successful home-school program. True learning happens on a child's own timetable. As I discussed in Chapter 15, "Testing, Testing, 1, 2, 3," much of the rote learning that takes place in school is short-term learning. That is, it's memorized for a test and then forgotten when there is no longer a need to use it. To ensure long-term retention, provide your child with projects and activities that are based on his or her interests. Connections will be made that will be retained for years.

Secondly, if the school model isn't working, forget it, at least temporarily. There are many other options. Put school on hold and focus on learning.

Success Stories

When you feel like a total failure, you may become even more discouraged when you read or hear about someone else's success story. Rather than comparing yourself negatively when you hear a success story, focus on it in a different way. Look for clues that you can use with your children. Find stories about kids who have personalities like your children. A shy child? Eleanor Roosevelt or Franklin Delano Roosevelt. Gabby, questioning, full of energy? Thomas Edison or Ben Franklin. What can you learn about the way these famous people learned? Don't try to fit your child into a *school-at-home mold*. Instead, make a *homeschool mold* that fits your child.

Talk to Other Homeschoolers

Rather than asking homeschoolers what materials they use, ask them about their children as individuals. Inquire about each child's personality, how he or she learns best, what learning experiences he or she enjoys, and what he or she is interested in. When you find someone with a child similar to yours, find out what materials that person uses and what he or she does. See if you can spend time with the person to observe the interaction with his or her children. Suggest getting together for a group learning activity, something you've planned that you know interests your children.

Where Were You This Time Last Year?

This is a reality check. Think about what was going on in the lives of you and your children at this time last year. Johnny already had three pink slips, had his name on the board for talking, lost his recess privileges for getting out of his seat, and lost most of his homework between home and school. Is putting him back in school going to lessen your anxiety and frustration? Think about how you felt then, the sleep you lost, and how difficult it was to deal with this situation from afar.

Spotlight on Education

Last year Ronnie was in school, but shy daydreamer Rachel stayed home an extra year because her parents planned to send her to kindergarten at age six. Ronnie was failing miserably, despite his questioning mind, ability to verbalize, and obvious intelligence. His teachers were frustrated with his wiggliness, the questions he blurted out in the middle of class, and his propensity for catching them in errors. When things came to a head with Ronnie, his parents decided to homeschool both Ronnie and Rachel this year. Ronnie's behavior has improved measurably with the implementation of a project- and interest-oriented approach, and Rachel is losing some of her shyness due to participation in a small study group of three other homeschoolers her age.

Last year Jenny was happy playing with dolls, working with modeling clay, drawing, singing along with her music tapes, and running errands with you. Jenny is still shy, enjoys one-on-one time with you better than being in a large group, and daydreams unless she's really interested in what she's doing. Will being in a large classroom setting provide her with what she needs? Think about it.

Read Your Records

Hopefully you have kept some records (see Chapter 17, "Keeping Records," for more). Even notes on the calendar will help you realize, at the lowest point in your own negativity, that you have accomplished something. You may not have covered the carefully planned lessons inscribed in your lesson plan book. But what have you been doing?

Learning Links

Make note of all your children's activities until it becomes second nature to you. Jot down anything your child asks about, any interest he or she shows, and whatever keeps his or her attention for a period of time. Plan to get some books from the library to continue to read up on or research that interest. Peruse the newspaper for related community activities or programs.

Focus on the Donut, Not the Hole!

Instead of thinking about what isn't happening, remind yourself of what *is* happening—the positive events. Remember the day you visited the planetarium and Johnny was so excited about the various stars that were identified? How can you pursue that interest? You might visit the library or the bookstore and get some books on the constellations and on being an astronomer. See if you can bring that excitement for learning alive again. Would a telescope make a good addition to your homeschool?

What clues can you get from your records to indicate that learning is, or could, happen just from the everyday occurrences of life? The calendar shows your parent's visit; remember the hours Johnny spent playing Boggle with his grandfather? That helped build his spelling skills. And remember how happy Jenny was baking cookies and decorating them with her grandmother? And what about the day you all spent at the zoo? Don't you wish you'd made some notes of the animals that sparked their interest and gotten some library books to read that would have expanded your children's interest and knowledge? Why not ask them what they remember and start that project now? Perhaps caring for a pet would be another good way to teach more about animals. Open your mind to the possibilities.

Determine What Needs to Change

Does your entire approach to homeschooling need to change? Perhaps. Does the money you've invested in materials make you feel locked into the program you have planned? Remember the bottom line here: Johnny and Jenny's education. Perhaps you can use some of those materials in a way that will engage interest better than following the original scope and sequence. Remember, you don't need to purchase a year's worth of materials in one fell swoop. It's better to start small and purchase things as your child develops interests. Don't feel bad. Most homeschoolers have made similar mistakes and lived to tell the story!

Spotlight on Education

Look at your history textbook. Is it dry, boring, hard to get excited about? Can you use it in a different way? Pick out the chapter headings or famous people and events, and find real books, television documentaries, videos, and museums to visit that will enhance learning the topics. If Johnny is stumbling over learning fractions, involve him in a project that requires measuring, such as woodworking or baking. Use the materials you've purchased as a starting point. After Johnny's mastered the concept in a hands-on way you may find that he can complete the lessons with ease. Don't bore him at that point by requiring every problem on every page.

Is your attitude about learning making things difficult? Even though you've read about relaxed homeschooling and different ways to do things, it may be hard to break away from the model that you're used to. Most homeschoolers, myself included, attended 12 or more years of institutional school. It seems natural to duplicate what we are familiar with. But is it natural? Was it true learning?

Think about some of the things you've learned since leaving school. How did you learn them? You may have learned by working with someone experienced. One-on-one tutorial learning is unmatched. You can duplicate it at home with Johnny and Jenny. Perhaps you got a book or pattern and learned by *trial and error*. You can do this in the homeschool, too. You don't have to worry about the time frame; the learning happens through the experience. There doesn't have to be a preplanned ending date or cutoff point. When the child has learned what he or she needs to know, the interest will dwindle or a new interest will take its place. That's your clue that the lesson is complete. Keep a journal during the period of the interest to remind yourself of all the things the child learned during the experience.

Speaking Educationese

Trial and error means learning a new skill or concept by trying a method, realizing it doesn't work, attempting another tactic, and so on, until you determine a method that will accomplish the task.

Learning Lookouts

Don't give up because there is something that you don't know how to teach. There are many self-teaching materials, videos, and computer programs available. You can hire a tutor or make use of cooperative classes to solve this homeschooling equation. Don't worry about keeping up to grade level; focus on your child's readiness and abilities.

Realize That Self-Doubt Goes with the Program

If I could get back all the hours of sleep that I lost staring at the ceiling and indulging in self-doubt, I'd be a well-rested woman. During the first few years of homeschooling, I can remember lying awake and fretting about whether my children would ever learn the multiplication tables, and whether they would all grow up and not be able to get into college or get a job. It's easier for me now, because two of my children have graduated from homeschool, been self-employed, held down other jobs, and attended college. But when you're at the beginning of the journey, you don't know the end of the story, and it's easy to slide into self-doubt.

You're Learning, Too!

The homeschooling journey is taken on a road with many curves, and we never know what's around the next bend. Homeschooling often involves our children much more directly in the everyday happenings of life. We don't have to present ourselves as the know-all and be-all. Children are capable of realizing that parents are people, too, with worries and fears. We don't have to share every nuance of our thoughts, but it can be very helpful to involve a child in the decision-making processes of homeschooling. For example, ask your child if he would rather attend a series of travelogues on various countries and points of interest along with doing research on those topics, or use a geography text. Find out if your child would rather read on his level about history, or have you read a more detailed book to him. Although you know your child better than anyone else, there's plenty you can learn about and from your child, too. Ask questions often.

There's no way you can learn everything about homeschooling overnight, or even in one school year. I read everything I could get my hands on, but when I look back I realize that when I read things that were in opposition to my own educational experience, they simply didn't sink in. I had to learn the hard way, from my own experience, that learning doesn't always happen in preplanned periods of time, in segments, or by being taught by someone else. It wasn't until I observed my children teaching themselves or learning in alternative ways that the message really got through.

Relearning Takes Time

It takes longer to relearn a skill than it does to learn it correctly the first time. Relearning how learning happens also takes time. Despite all the studies that have been done to prove that one-on-one tutorial learning is the optimal learning environment, the same flawed system is still being used in most of our schools and institutions of higher learning. While alternative schools and programming exist and are flourishing in some places, they aren't available to everyone. The educational system is such a huge entity that it will take a long time to revamp it to reflect the findings of educational research. It was my feeling that it wouldn't happen during my children's school years. During the six years my older children were enrolled in public schools, I worked as a parent volunteer and my children's advocate. I spent many late evenings tutoring and reteaching when my children were tired and frustrated from a day at school. It began to seem more sensible to me to start fresh each day and structure the children's education around their learning needs.

Spotlight on Education

During our early homeschool days, my older children were guinea pigs! Many times they learned what they needed or wanted to learn before I, copying the institutional system we had just left behind, could develop a lesson plan. My younger children were never institutionally schooled and I have learned some new ways to approach learning, so our days run a little more smoothly. They let me know when something I've suggested is redundant because they've already learned it while pursuing an interest. They can often spend the time more profitably building on their prior knowledge or learning something new, rather than reviewing something they are familiar with.

The familiar institutional school model—read the chapter, answer the questions, review, and take the test—is not the only path marked on the road map to producing a lifelong learner and independent thinker. In fact, it's not even the best path. Your child does not need to repeat that sequence for 13 years to capably accomplish that sequence in college.

Talk About Your Doubts with People Who Understand

It's tempting to pick up the phone and call your best friend or your Mom when you have a homeschool problem, just as you do when you have other kinds of problems. If your usual confidante doesn't understand or support homeschooling, it's better to save your homeschooling problems for someone who does. Send out your SOS to a fellow homeschooler.

Seasoned Homeschoolers

Whether you communicate online, by phone, or at a homeschool support meeting, one thing a homeschooler will not usually tell you right off the bat is, "Put them back in school." Homeschoolers are usually committed to their homeschooling choice, used to working through the tough times and problems that occur, and making it work. Thus, they will assume that you are also committed to making homeschooling work, and just need a little help getting over this bump in the road.

Learning Lookouts

If homeschooling isn't the best choice for your family right now, or for one or more of your children, it's okay to have some of your children at home, and some in institutional schools. Some parents homeschool for a number of years and later enroll their child in an institutional school for a while. Some states allow part-time enrollment in institutional schools. Remember, whatever works.

Sometimes just talking with someone who understands is enough to give you the lift you need to continue.

Homeschoolers have found that it helps to find like-minded homeschoolers to talk to. If you are a school-at-home person, and absolutely, positively sure that's the only route for you and your family, get your encouragement from someone who schools the way you do. If you're a school-at-homer who needs some new ideas and activities to make homeschooling work for you, finding someone who's worked through similar challenges will be helpful. If you're an unschooler, you'll probably find the most helpful advice from others who are using similar methods.

Supportive Friends

One of my most supportive friends shares my philosophies in a number of areas, but her children are institutionally schooled. She feels free to gripe to me about her children's problems in school, knowing that I understand (been there, done that, bought several T-shirts!) but won't say to her, "If you'd only homeschool, you wouldn't have to go through all this."

Likewise, I can grumble about days when nothing goes right, the kids are being uncooperative, and life seems really down, knowing that she will offer helpful suggestions that don't include, "Put your kids in school; then, you won't have to go through all this." If you have a friend like this, by all means use him or her as a sounding board. Just remember to let your friend know when the good stuff happens, too!

Understanding Relatives

If you have relatives who support your choice to homeschool, they may be able to offer suggestions that you wouldn't think of yourself. Quite often someone not immediately involved in a situation can see things from a different viewpoint. Sometimes we are too close to a situation to see the problem clearly, much less the solution! Ask for suggestions, knowing that you will use only the advice that seems right to you, but that you may receive some help that you wouldn't get otherwise.

Sharing Success Stories Helps You, Too!

Be sure to share your success stories with your understanding relatives and friends as well as the folks who don't support you! Pull out Johnny's scrapbook or Jenny's latest drawings to be admired. Tell about the day at the beach when you collected and identified 17 types of shells. Or the field trip where your Jenny asked the most interesting question the tour guide had ever heard. Let them know about the alternative methods that work, rather than trying to always tell them about the things they readily understand, like the math papers with "100%" at the top. Help them stretch their minds to a new idea. While you do so, you're stretching your own.

The Least You Need to Know

➤ You are the final word on what your children should be doing and how they should be doing it.

➤ Self-doubt goes with the territory, but it doesn't have to last forever.

➤ It's okay to stop what you're doing, tweak the existing program, or try a new route.

➤ When in doubt, talk to another homeschooler, or someone who supports your efforts.

➤ Share your successful moments with both supporters and nay-sayers.

Involvement in the Homeschooling Community

While some homeschoolers do it all on their own, many find it helpful to be part of a homeschooling community. The homeschooling community can be as small as a few local families working together cooperatively in various ways, or it can stretch to include several local groups of homeschoolers or regional groups in a specific state or province. The homeschooling community can be as large as national or international groups and individuals involved in homeschooling.

E-mail lists, Web sites, and chats help homeschoolers access the larger world of homeschooling. Read on to learn what each has to offer to you as a homeschooler.

Getting the Most from an Existing Support Group

Your local support group may have been in existence for a number of years. It may have morphed several times by the time you get involved. Or it might be a fledgling group. Either way, before trying to initiate changes, take some time to get a feel for the direction of the group, its strengths and weaknesses, and what it offers.

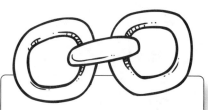

Learning Links

When thinking about how to get fellow homeschoolers together, working on educational projects comes to mind first. But why not organize a car wash, a bake sale, a curriculum swap, or a plain and simple potluck gathering to help members become acquainted? A jam session to toss out ideas and get a feel for the individual needs of the group can be scheduled toward the end of the activity.

Organizing a Group Project

If the group seems to be floundering, you might suggest a project that involves the membership and brings people together for a common purpose. If the group is agreeable to a project that meets your needs, you will be fulfilling two purposes at once. During the early years of my involvement with our local group, we had two globe projects, based on the National Geographic globe contest. The first one involved getting groups of mothers and kids together at a central point to work on an oversized model of the globe. The second was a smaller globe that traveled from house to house for the various steps.

Getting Other Parents Involved

Make an announcement about your proposed group project at a support group meeting and ask for suggestions and comments. If the support group meeting has other items on the agenda, set a date for a planning meeting. Have a clipboard and paper or notebook handy to jot down suggestions and comments to refer to later at the planning meeting. Ask if anyone is willing to help you head up a committee to plan the project.

If there is no longer an existing group, mail out a flier or call the homeschool parents you are aware of and announce a group project planning meeting. Ask the homeschoolers you contact to contact any other homeschoolers they know.

Lifting a Group Out of the Doldrums

Sometimes the support group leader is weary from years of organizing meetings, calling members with announcements, and providing a place for meetings and activities. Announce to the membership that in the future support group meetings will be rotated among a number of homes. Ask for volunteers to host such meetings. If meetings are currently held in a public place, take time to assess whether it's adequate for the size of the group and the activities that are being planned. If not, ask for suggestions of other places to meet. Let the newer (if not the newest) members know that their input and help are important and needed. Ask for suggestions and find out if they are willing to begin to be more involved with the group.

Spotlight on Education

The local homeschool group in Rita's area didn't meet her family's needs at all, due to differences in both homeschooling and religious beliefs. Although Rita would have preferred that the local group support all homeschoolers regardless of learning style or religious belief, the existing group had no intentions of doing so. Rita advertised in local newspapers, posted fliers on community bulletin boards, and began a new group with just three like-minded homeschooling families. Over time that group has grown to provide a variety of services for local homeschoolers, including cooperative classes, volunteer opportunities, and speakers on a number of topics. Last year the group sponsored a curriculum fair with workshops for adults and children.

Starting a Newsletter/Phone Chain

If the group doesn't have a newsletter, try to drum up some interest in one. Some groups thrive with a phone chain, but the drawback is that a phone chain is only as good as its weakest link. If several people don't make their phone calls, you may not get announcements out in a timely manner. Find out if there is interest in a newsletter, look for volunteers to edit and print it, and let people know that contributions are appreciated.

Parents' Night Out

Many homeschoolers find it helpful to get a night away once in a while. If you can arrange babysitting, a "date" with your partner may be the best boost available. If not, perhaps one of you will be kind enough to entertain and feed the kids occasionally while the other recharges his or her batteries by an evening with fellow homeschoolers or other good friends. Some homeschool groups sponsor special inspirational meetings, coffee klatches, and activities just for parents.

Learning Lookouts

Getting people to contribute to a newsletter can be difficult. Story starters, questionnaires, and mind-boggling questions included in the newsletter may spark an interest in contributing. Ask members to share outstanding essays, pictures, and photographs of special activities which can be included in the newsletter.

Daytime Playgroups/Activities

You'll welcome the diversion provided by organizing or participating in daytime activities with other homeschoolers. Get together with one or two other families on a regular basis for playtime for the kids and a chance to connect with other homeschoolers. Some homeschool groups have planned activities for toddlers. If local homeschooled teens are looking for volunteer opportunities, they might be willing to baby-sit the toddlers and infants while the parents do activities with the older children. Explore a variety of options for getting out and about, providing group activities for your children, as well as true socialization with children and adults.

Organizing Field Trips

If your group already has a field trip organizer, find out if he or she is looking for suggestions. Provide a list of events and sites for field trips you would like to attend. If field trips aren't a part of the existing group, you may have found your niche. Use your local yellow pages and chamber of commerce for ideas, and contact the chamber of commerce for towns in a radius that are easily accessible by the homeschool group's membership.

Learning Lookouts

New homeschoolers are sometimes wary of group meetings held in a church, believing that if they aren't religious homeschoolers they won't be welcome. If your new group holds meetings at a church but the focus is not religious, be sure your announcements indicate the real focus of the meetings to reassure newcomers.

Starting a New Group

If the existing group is not welcoming because of differences of philosophy, or doesn't fill your needs and won't change, or if there isn't a group, it's time to think about starting a new group.

Make a list of ideas. Do you know anyone who homeschools in the area? Where and when could you meet? How can you let people know about the new group? What would your mission be? Once you've gotten your facts in order, it's time to spring into action.

How to Let People Know

The most important part of any support group is … members! How can you let people know that there will to be a new support group in your area? Talk to anyone you know who homeschools and ask each one to let others know. Print up information sheets listing the meeting place, date, and time, and details on the reasons for the new group. Ask homeschoolers to pass on the sheets to others. Post the information sheets in the grocery store, library, Laundromat, and community center. Run an ad in a local newspaper.

Getting Your First Meeting Off the Ground

At the first meeting you will want to present yourself and your idea. Explain why you think there is a need for a group, and what you want to achieve. Ask for suggestions, comments, and ideas. Take notes or ask someone to take notes for you. Make plans for a date to have a follow-up meeting, and ask for volunteers to help with specific needs:

➤ Finding a meeting site, or organizing a rotation of members' homes for meetings

➤ Planning a questionnaire to solicit opinions about meeting dates, what each person wants the group to do for him or her, and so on

➤ Someone to organize a phone chain and/or newsletter

➤ Field trip organizer

Take an informal poll of those who attend to determine a date and time for a follow-up meeting that will work for the majority. Determine what you want to accomplish at the meetings:

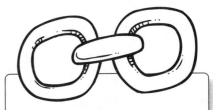

Learning Links

Provide drinks and ask attendees to bring finger foods to share. Refreshments help break the ice and make a meeting seem more informal and relaxed.

➤ Provide support for all homeschoolers, regardless of motivation or approach used

➤ Provide support for a specific group of homeschoolers, determined by a mission statement or statement of faith

➤ Provide nurturing support for homeschooling parents

➤ Share resources, sponsor swaps or sales

➤ Provide social time

➤ Bring in speakers

➤ Hold informal workshops

➤ Provide national programs such as Book-it

➤ Sponsor homeschooling sports leagues

➤ Offer group activities for the kids

➤ Plan field trips

➤ Organize a homeschooling cooperative

➤ Sponsor an end-of-the-year program and project sharing

Scheduling Activities

Take everyone's schedules into consideration as much as possible, but eventually dates must be settled on. Once a date is set for an activity, those who make it a priority will be there. If you're aware that a specific night of the week is not going to work for the majority, you will want to consider that when scheduling meetings, activities, field trips, and programs. Without participants all planned activities will flop.

Starting a Homeschool Cooperative

Many homeschoolers have found that involvement with a *homeschool cooperative* enhances their homeschooling experience. Some children thrive with the small group experience, so enrolling them in some group activities and classes will nurture that need.

Keeping classes and activities small enables families to reap the benefits of the classroom setting with none of the drawbacks. Volunteers can serve as helpers and aides, keeping the ratio of student to adult low, as recommended by educational research.

Speaking Educationese

A **homeschool cooperative** is a group of home educators who pool their resources and provide classes, activities, and, perhaps, a library of materials to be used for the benefit of the entire group. Everyone involved contributes in some way.

Getting the Word Out

Most homeschool cooperatives are sponsored by an existing support group. In that case, a mailing or call to a phone chain may be all that's needed to notify members that something new is in the air. If you are attempting to pull together a new support group and cooperative at one time, just include suggestions for a homeschool cooperative when talking about the plans for the new group.

Planning Meetings

A very large group can be unwieldy when planning a cooperative, so it may be wise to form a committee to do the planning for the co-op. If the support group has leadership in place, the leadership may be the ones to do the planning, taking into consideration the needs of the group. Or a committee may be composed of volunteers or appointed members. Start out by determining the purpose of the cooperative, the needs of the group, and what you want to achieve.

Spotlight on Education

The South Haven Area Homeschool Group's growth indicated a need for cooperative homeschool classes. Several of the parents met to plan the future focus of the group, and to organize a system that would, hopefully, provide a way to run cooperative classes effectively and fairly. Sign-up was held and each teacher provided materials and information about his or her planned classes. Parents asked questions and reviewed the texts, books, and materials to be used in the classes. Payment was required by a set date, allowing teachers to purchase materials well in advance of classes, at a discount rate through a cooperative buying service, and without using their own money.

Setting the Ground Rules

Every group will have its own ideas about what is most important, but that will change over time and with experience. All suggestions should be duly noted and discussed, keeping the end goal in view. A cooperative must have the cooperation of all members and participants in order for the plan to work. Compile a list of services that can be performed by parents whose children are participating in classes and activities. Some cooperatives have a monthly participation fee that is charged to those parents who aren't teaching classes or volunteering in any other capacity. During sign up, children of parents who are not active in the cooperative may be put on a waiting list until the sign-up cutoff, so children of active participants get priority. Fees for classes or workshops must be paid by a certain date so teachers have time before classes begin to purchase materials and books.

Who Teaches What, When, and Where?

Some potential teachers will volunteer to teach a specific class. They may know their children need to cover this subject and think it will be more fun for them to share it with a group. Others will teach certain topics just because they enjoy teaching them. Still others teach classes because they simply enjoy teaching. If a member has a talent in a certain area but doesn't volunteer, someone in the group may approach him or her and ask if he or she would be available to teach a class.

Schedule planning meetings to brainstorm about bringing in others to teach classes, such as a native speaker to teach a foreign language class, or a martial arts expert to teach a self-defense class. Such classes will usually be more costly than those taught by homeschool parent volunteers.

Don't overlook teens in the group who are looking for community service hours. They may serve as teachers' aides, teach toddler arts and crafts classes, or conduct workshops in their areas of expertise.

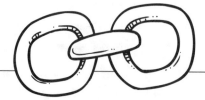

Learning Links

Take time to get acquainted with the volunteers who work with your child. Ask if there is anything that you can follow up with at home, or if your child needs any special help. Stay for class occasionally to observe how your child interacts with other students and the teacher. Ask your child how he or she feels about the class and the teacher. Keep communication open and respect your child's opinions about his or her experience.

Learning Lookouts

The record keeper must be someone who is willing to check up on people who don't keep current with their debts. Phone calls and reminders may be needed to keep the cooperative running smoothly. Although an ideal cooperative would include only members who pay their debts punctually, every group seems to have at least one person who must always be reminded.

A committee may be appointed to find a site for classes, or parents may teach in their own homes. Some cooperatives settle on one day of the week for all classes, while others schedule classes throughout the week.

Good Record Keeping Is a Must

Someone with good record-keeping skills and the ability to keep people current on their volunteer time and payments is vital to the success of a homeschooling cooperative. An initial plan for the group is essential, with fees, volunteer duties, and services rendered plainly outlined. Once this is in place, it should be a simple matter for someone to keep track of payments and donated time. If some members give the teachers the money for purchasing materials directly, it is imperative that the record keeper be notified promptly, to prevent confusion. Every transaction of money or time must be accounted for.

Volunteer Work Can Be Bartered for Services

Bartering provides families a way to enroll their children in classes without incurring a large financial obligation. A parent can teach a class, perform baby-sitting duties for a group of youngsters whose parents are teaching, clean the site afterwards, make photocopies for teachers, and a myriad of other duties that are necessary to make a cooperative run smoothly.

A More Relaxed Approach

If organizing a working cooperative sounds intimidating or isn't what you're looking for, consider some other options. Providing group experiences for your youngsters is possible in a number of ways:

➤ **Get together with another family to work on projects.** If you notice that you and your children seem to click well with another family at homeschool activities, approach the family with a suggestion to collaborate on a project or short unit study. If the other parent is agreeable, you might like to get together over coffee at one of your homes to plan the details, while the children play. This can be the start of many similar experiences, which can benefit both families.

➤ **Take turns teaching each other's kids.** If you have a child who enjoys being with a friend who also homeschools, you and the other parent may be able to take turns teaching each other's kids. Aside from play dates, your child may enjoy studying with someone else, putting together a project, or puzzle, or playing an educational game with a buddy. Since learning with someone else or in small groups is an essential part of some children's learning styles, such cooperative teaching may be a vital part of your children's education.

➤ **Plan short day trips with one or two compatible families.** If you or your child find large field trips overwhelming, speak with one or two other families and find out if they'd like to do small group field trips. Take turns planning the day trips and enjoy the advantages of having a small group.

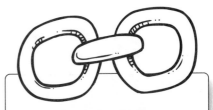

Learning Links

Although you may pay a little more for a smaller group tour, you'll soon notice that keeping track of a dozen people is much easier than keeping 30 people together. A smaller group makes pausing and perusing a specific exhibit possible, and interacting with the guide more personal. Quieter children may open up more readily in a small group, too.

Reaching Beyond Your Area

In addition to what's offered locally, you may find statewide support for homeschooling including field trips and other activities you can participate in if you are willing to go further afield. Some state groups have Web sites where you can access information, while others have printed newsletters that you can subscribe to by mail or e-mail.

Spotlight on Education

Jen felt most information on homeschooling was being influenced by a state group that wasn't taking into consideration the needs of all homeschoolers. Unable to enlist the cooperation of her state group, she began to make information available through a newsletter. Eventually she networked with small groups across the state, providing contact information on a Web site, and making telephone numbers available for homeschool group leaders in various parts of the state. Most recently, in her effort to help homeschoolers find information about homeschooling in her state, Jen has encouraged the leaders of all local support groups to list their contact information with the National Home Education Network, www.nhen.org, a grassroots organization dedicated to helping all homeschoolers.

Contact Other Support Groups

Ask members of your local group for names and addresses of other groups within driving distance, as well as the names of any statewide support groups they may be aware of. Sometimes groups swap newsletters as a way of keeping abreast of activities within a larger area. Homeschoolers who see an activity they are interested in may simply call the person in charge of responses and find out about signing up.

Plan Larger Field Trips with Several Groups

If your group is small and has a hard time mustering enough members to make up a group for minimum numbers required for group tours, collaborate with several other groups in planning field trips. Advertise activities and field days in all newsletters, with a central person taking responsibility for handling all responses. This way, everyone has a fair chance to sign up before the cutoff date.

Collaborate on Bringing in Speakers and Fundraising

Several small homeschool groups in a certain area may get acquainted well enough to get together for curriculum swaps, field days, activities, and trips. Such collaborations may also include pooling resources for fund raising (such as car washes, yard sales, and bake sales) to raise funds for a particular group project or a special, costly trip. Fundraising may also make it possible to start a centrally located homeschool book and resource library. One group alone may not be able to afford bringing in an inspirational or motivational speaker, while collaboration on the part of several groups may make it possible. The possibilities are endless: Put on your thinking cap and see what you can come up with!

The Least You Need to Know

➤ Join the local support group or organize your own if none exists or fits your needs.

➤ Once you've gotten acquainted, make suggestions and get involved with the local support group.

➤ Organization and good record keeping are essential to a successful homeschool cooperative.

➤ Small group projects and activities can be helpful to promote learning for some children.

➤ Your local support group can band together with other groups to implement a variety of projects.

Chapter 22

Cyber Learning

In This Chapter

➤ Finding what you're looking for online

➤ Using the Internet to develop curriculum

➤ Designing unit studies using online resources

➤ Locating cyber schools for every need

Whether you've been using a computer for quite a while or are just contemplating getting one, whether you consider yourself an Internet guru or a total newbie, read on to find some tips that will help you use the Internet as a useful tool for your home-school.

Mining the Internet

The World Wide Web is a bit like a gold mine. There are nuggets here and there, just waiting to be found, but it sometimes takes some digging and picking before you get to them. Occasionally you will run across a rich vein of information that will make you almost as happy as the old prospector who struck it rich. Maybe this chapter will serve as a map: X marks the spot!

What's There for Me?

What do you want to learn about? Does talk about the Internet intimidate you because it sounds like so much geek speak? What is a search engine, a *URL*, or a *browser?* Have you tried to find your way around, gotten lost and given up, totally frustrated? Found a super Web site but then couldn't locate it again? Is it really worth all the effort? Yes! Although there is a wealth of information available through traditional sources, such as encyclopedias and dictionaries (bound volumes or CD) and the library, with the World Wide Web you are a click away from the latest information on just about any topic.

Speaking Educationese

URL stands for **uniform resource locator,** the unique address of each Web page. A Web address usually starts with www. A web **browser** is a program that lets you explore and view information on the World Wide Web. Netscape and Microsoft Internet Explorer are two popular browsers.

Searching the Web Effectively

There are a number of ways to search for information on the World Wide Web. You can search the Web for free because many search tools sell advertising space on their Web sites. Most search tools let you search for information in newsgroups or discussion groups, storing information that has been posted to the groups for a number of weeks. Search tools store the information collected from Web sites in a database. When you initiate a search, the search tool searches the database for the information you requested. Directories, special databases that store information about Web sites that people have reviewed and organized, provide another source of information. Finally, search engines use a program, called a robot, to scan the Web for new and updated pages. How do you use all this information to find what you want quickly and effectively?

Using a *metasearch engine* can speed up your search, providing you with dozens or hundreds of hits, which you can scan rapidly, clicking on those that appear to be most closely related to your search. Try one or two of these excellent metasearch engines next time you do a search:

Speaking Educationese

A **metasearch engine** searches the databases of several search engines at one time, providing you with results much more quickly than you could get by searching with each individual search engine yourself.

➤ www.c4.com

➤ www.dogpile.com

➤ www.411.com

➤ www.800go.com

➤ www.Highway61.com

➤ www.infind.com

➤ www.metacrawler.com

➤ www.metafind.com

➤ www.savvysearch.com

➤ www.stpt.com

➤ www.37.com

You will probably find one search engine that you prefer using for most searches. When you strike out, try a different search engine for a change!

Friendly Online Communities

Newsgroups are like message boards. To access newsgroups, either use the news feature of your Web browser or install special software to read them. Access to newsgroups can be as simple as clicking on a link or can be very complicated. You may want to enlist the aid of a knowledgeable computer geek friend or contact your Internet service provider for information on subscribing to newsgroups.

A friendly online homeschooling community awaits you at www.kaleidoscapes.com, a message board Web site. Kaleidoscapes includes *clickable links* to many topics of interest to beginning and veteran homeschoolers, discussions of specific topics on a number of boards, and archives of older discussions. Each message board is moderated by veteran homeschoolers.

Message boards are also available through the National Home Education Network, Home Education Magazine, and other homeschool Web sites. A query posted to any of these boards will probably help you find just the resource you have been searching for.

Creating Internet Lesson Plans

When surfing the Web to find Web sites on topics of interest, keep in mind that you will find far

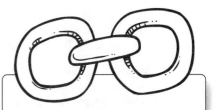

Learning Links

For some hints to help you get started subscribing to newgroups, check out www.geocities.com:0080/Athens/8259/news.html. Also see Appendix B, "Curriculum Winners and Selected Resources, Including Dynamite Web Sites," for a listing of homeschool newsgroups that cover such topics as general homeschooling, Christian homeschooling, and homeschooling children with disabilities.

Speaking Educationese

Clickable links are URLs embedded into the text or listed in the index of a Web site. To view the Web site, simply position your cursor over the link and click your left mouse button. Voilà! Depending upon the speed of your connection, you will soon be viewing the Web site.

more on any given topic than one child (or adult) can soak up. Use the Web sites that seem most promising, but supplement cyber learning using real books, hands-on experiences, and field trips to give the learning multiple dimensions.

As exciting as cyber learning may be, it's a good idea to provide a variety of learning experiences throughout a child's day, as computer use can become an addiction with some children. And although there is certainly enough information available on the Web to keep a child busy 24/7, be aware that using a computer exclusively may be detrimental to your child's general health. It's important that the child refocus his or her eyes frequently to avoid eyestrain and to take breaks that include active movement, such as taking a walk, riding a bike, and stretching.

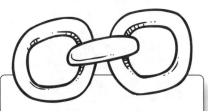

Learning Links

Have you ever wished you could take a class on homeschooling? Well, your wish is granted. Visit www.virtual-learning.ab.ca/ to sign up for classes on such topics as learning styles, teaching skills, homeschooling in high school and beyond, unschooling, and much more. Classes have been developed considering the wide variety of homeschooling styles and philosophies. Class facilitators are experienced homeschooling parents.

What Do You Want to Learn?

If you are looking for information on curriculum planning, creating your own lesson plans, or topics of interest to your child, you will find it all on the World Wide Web. Determine how your child's current interests can be used as a starting point for learning, and use newsgroups, message boards, homeschooling Web sites, and search engines to access the information you need.

Finding Online Scope and Sequences

A search on www.dogpile.com using scope-and-sequence as keywords (using dashes tells some search engine robots that you want only hits using all three words) came up with links to scope and sequences for technology, art, honors algebra, classic Christianity, math, Latin, grade-level appropriate links, and skills-based scope and sequence guides, as well as Web sites to help teachers design curricula. Check links on any homeschooling Web sites you visit for information on scope and sequence and curriculum design. World Book Encyclopedia has printable grade-level-appropriate curriculum plans on its Web site.

Most search Web sites include a link to a site with basic instructions for expediting your search. Follow the directions for optimal results.

As I mentioned in Chapter 9, "Out of the Box: Planning Your Own Curriculum," pre-planned scope and sequences or curriculum are someone else's idea of what a child of a certain age or grade level should cover in a given period of time. You can use a pre-planned curriculum as a guideline in planning an individualized program for your child, but be aware that most will not take into consideration your child's interests, personality, learning style, or preferences. You can utilize your knowledge of your child's individuality while customizing a preplanned scope and sequence or designing your own. See Chapter 9 for more on scope and sequence.

Creating Internet Unit Studies

A unit study is a collection of learning activities based on a theme. Unit studies can be as sedate or eclectic as you wish. Many unit studies are available free on Web sites; do a search to find some on your chosen topic. Then branch out! What do you know that would enhance this study? Do you know someone who is a storehouse of information? Make contact with him or her and pick his or her brain. Always consider your child's learning needs. If he or she learns best by experiencing things, make the larger portion of your chosen activities field trips, hands-on projects, and real-life activities. If your child learns best by reading, you will focus more on finding books, magazines, Web sites, and other printed matter to present the information, but use a variety of hands-on projects to diversify. You don't want to totally neglect whole modalities because your child learns best in one mode, but you do want to focus on the modality that gets the best results.

Pick Your Theme

For ease of understanding, let's choose a topic to use as an example. Let's say your child is interested in learning about wilderness survival techniques. Where to start? Begin with the Internet and branch out from there. Check your library for some likely books and read them together. Keep your eyes open for other resources that might be helpful. Search www.amazon.com for newer books that may not be available at your library, or request them through interlibrary loan. Here are just a few of the 340 books listed after an amazon.com search of wilderness survival:

➤ *Mountainman Crafts and Skills: A Fully Illustrated Guide to Wilderness Living and Survival* by David R. Montgomery

➤ *Native American Crafts and Skills: A Fully Illustrated Guide to Wilderness Living and Survival* by David Montgomery

➤ *The New Way of the Wilderness: The Classic Guide to Survival in the Wild* (Fesler-Lampert Minnesota Heritage Book Series) by Calvin Rutstrum

➤ *The New Wilderness Handbook* by Paul Petzoldt

If you search all products in an amazon.com search, you also get the names of videos that are available on this topic, both new and hard to locate, which may be available through auctions on the amazon.com site. All products will also link you to sites

Learning Links

A comprehensive guide to finding used books is *The Book Hunter's Bible* by David S. and Susan Siegel. Check out their Web site at www.bookhunterpress. com for a sample of their regional books, sample maps, and other information to help you search for used books online or on foot.

where you can buy out-of-print books. If you are interested in building a library of resources for a child with an unwavering interest, this can be a good resource for you. Many homeschoolers also enjoy finding and traveling to used bookstores and book sales to search for treasures themselves. Using online auctions such as eBay (www.ebay.com) can be quicker when you are anxious to find a book or resource on the spot.

Most encyclopedias have an index that will help you locate all articles on a particular topic. If you look up a specific topic, be sure to check to see if there is a list of related articles at the end. These can lead you on a circuitous route that may end up somewhere unexpected, but the search can be enlightening and fun!

Beyond books and tapes, where else can you find materials for your child? Returning to our wilderness survival example, camping and survival skills are taught at Boy and Girl Scouts, and Campfire. Joining such a group may be a good way for your child to learn some basic skills while providing a social experience at the same time.

Learning Lookouts

If you're interested in wilderness survival, for example, check with a local Boy Scout, Girl Scout, or Campfire group to see what its focus is and whether your local troop works on badges related to survival. Depending upon the leadership, the focus of local groups can vary. If the local troop doesn't provide what you want, look into the possibility of forming a homeschooling scout troop or club that will focus on the areas you feel are essential. Check Appendix B for national Web sites for groups such as Scouts, Campfire, and 4-H, which may lead you to local groups.

My sons have enjoyed borrowing Boy Scout books from the library and doing some of the projects on their own, or with each other or a friend, rather than in a large group. Check to see if there are any historical reenactment groups in your area, museums that have pertinent displays, or any pioneer crafts and antique arms shows scheduled in the near future. Finally, after you've done the research, gathered the materials and done some learning, why not try some of the skills as a family? Camp out in the backyard, cook in a Dutch oven or over a campfire, and lie outside to watch the stars. If your backyard isn't appropriate for these activities, join up with someone who has a backyard out in the country: another homeschooling family, relatives, or friends.

Don't Reinvent the Wheel

If all this searching and waiting sounds like too much work, search the World Wide Web for planned unit studies. Quite a few unit study sites have partial or complete unit studies available for printing or downloading. These same sites often include listings of more complete themed studies available for purchase. If you don't have the time or inclination to start from scratch, use a preplanned unit study. Just be ready for the side trips that will happen no matter what you plan or purchase!

List Your Subject Areas

Staying with our wilderness survival example, let's list the various subject areas and see what we can find online to cover the skills your child needs to learn, based on your student's interest in wilderness survival:

➤ **Math:** Navigation, including map reading (particularly topographical maps) and familiarity with latitude and longitude, teaches numerical skills; using landmarks to orient oneself teaches spatial relationships; and planning how many supplies are necessary for a certain number of days and under specific conditions reinforces basic math skills. Web sites: www.usgs.gov/education/learnweb/wwmaps.html;www.geocities.com/Yosemite/Falls/9200/navigation_map_compass.html.

➤ **Science:** Using the night sky, constellations, and moon phases for orientation; learning the daytime sky and suns phases for orientation; understanding magnetic declination for compass reading; becoming aware of edible and inedible plants, as well as those that can be used for first aid; being aware of signs that predict weather changes and how to cope with each; knowledge of geology to help find water, shelter, and even the location of certain edible plants. Web sites: www.astronomy.com/home.asp; www.northstar.k12.ak.us/NSFPIS/PC_Geology.html; www.egroups.com/group/TrackerSchool.

➤ **Social studies:** Knot tying, shelter building, fire making, and tool craft from civilizations and peoples of the past. Web sites: www.northnet.org/ropeworks/index.html; www.mistral.co.uk/42brghtn/knots/42ktmenu.html; www.gripclips.com/primitiveways/; www.nativetech.org/.

➤ **Language arts:** Writing on any of the topics studied, as well as writing to obtain more information from such sources as the Department of Natural Resources, state tourism centers, weather bureaus, and wilderness conservation groups. Reading materials pertaining to any of the many parts of wilderness survival. Web sites: members.tripod.com/~lklivingston/essay/; www.geocities.com:0080/ Athens/Parthenon/9502/essay.html.

➤ **Health/physical education:** Learning first aid and safety; loading and carrying a pack to prevent injury while hiking; using available plants for first aid; planning and preparing a basic first-aid kit. Web sites: www.geocities.com/ Yosemite/Falls/9200/backpacking_and_hiking.html; www.geocities.com/ Yosemite/Falls/9200/backpacking_and_hiking.html#Outdoor Safety.

➤ **Art and music:** Keeping nature notebooks with sketches of plants, animals, terrain, and anything of interest observed during the study; learning to identify bird songs and calls; becoming aware of the music of nature and training the ear to interpret the sounds of the wind, trees, plants, and animals. Web sites: members.aol. com/BeeME1/nature.html; members.truepath.com/Jody/nature.htm; www.pbs. org/lifeofbirds/; www.1000plus.com/BirdSong/; www.naturesongs.com/.

Learning Lookouts

Don't assume that your child's interest has no value. We learn from everything. Ask your child open-ended questions to determine what the attraction is to this particular topic. Do a little research yourself. See if you can find some educational value in your child's interest. Even playing video games has value if your child is interested in designing graphics.

Do a Search

When beginning a study, you will want to do a search for materials. Starting at the library usually provides instant access to some books, unless your subject is extremely obscure. Books often contain bibliographies that will lead you to more resources. Your local bookstores, new and used, are another source of books. Museum stores, catalogs, and the Internet provide kits for hands-on projects, instructions, and helpful tips. During the course of the study you will be surprised at how often you find yourself back at the library or in front of the computer searching for yet another resource. Most immersion studies take several unexpected side trips as new things excite your student along the way. Welcome the unexpected! Continue to search. Your anticipated six weeks may turn into six months, six years, or even a lifetime. And that's wonderful! Many homeschooled kids have turned a new interest into a career or a lifetime interest and hobby.

Cyber Schools

The Internet abounds with cyber classes and Internet schools. Where to begin in weeding out the best, the good, and the downright no good? If you know home-schoolers who are using a cyber school successfully, that's a good starting point. Ask them what they like about the school, its good and bad points, how problems are dealt with, whether they get timely feedback from someone at the school, and how long they've been using the program.

You'll find everything from Internet online classes to distance-learning companies, freebie classes to cyber schools with tuition schedules posted online. If you don't find what you're looking for, look again next week—by then someone may be providing it.

Elementary and Middle School

Although many youngsters enjoy using computers, it's important to provide variety. Doing all academic work via computer may not allow students enough time to move around, experiment, and experience tactile and kinesthetic learning. Younger elementary students shouldn't spend more than two or three hours per day on strictly academic pursuits; the larger part of their learning should include movement, interaction with others, and real-life experiences. Students in the upper elementary grades will also benefit from a program that includes plenty of hands-on learning, group or one-on-one tutorial learning, and activity. Perhaps elementary is a little early for the average child to do a cyber learning program in its entirety, unless the program includes breaks and suggestions for active learning as a part of regular learning activities.

Spotlight on Education

Ervin, 13, is interested in pursuing an education and career in commercial art/graphic design. He did research on the World Wide Web to determine which graphic arts program he wanted to purchase to begin his at-home learning. Online tutorials and demos, link pages, and other online resources helped him narrow his choices down to Bryce 4.0. While Ervin plans to attend the intermediate school district's technologies center in high school, using a graphic arts program now will provide him with hands-on experience and enable him to learn some basics upon which he can build at a later date.

Including cyber lessons or classes as part of an eclectic or traditional program is an excellent way to determine if distance learning works for your child. Some support schools provide programs that allow your child to enroll in one or two online programs along with other more traditional fare.

High School

Many extremely motivated young adults have turned to cyber learning as a way to locate the courses they want in order to obtain the education they need. Rather than attending zero hour at dawn and later sitting through required classes that are repetitions of topics already covered and digested, these young people have determined that they can have their cake and eat it, too! Such students have been able to fit their required classes into a schedule that includes full- or part-time jobs or running their own businesses. Quite often, their involvement with volunteer work or community service is an important part of their education, helping them to become well-rounded citizens, involved in the real world, who will continue to be contributors in the future. Such far-seeing students realize that by using cyber classes or a cyber school, they can fit their traditional studies more readily into their real life, enabling them to grow and mature in ways that aren't possible when they are locked into the traditional school schedule.

Spotlight on Education

Michelle found public high school stressful. Traveling extensively with her family, she often found herself doing assignments the class hadn't gotten around to, or missing a new concept. Working at her own pace was nearly impossible. Through AOL's search engine she found Core Curriculum of America, where she could take harder courses than offered by the local high school! Michelle likes the way Core Curriculum uses a phone interview to determine your level, and mixes and matches books from different companies, providing a personalized program. She plans to complete two years' worth of high school in one year, and loves learning by experience, travel, and through life, rather than being completely motivated by grades.

College

Since many homeschooled high school students efficiently complete their high school requirements at a relatively young age, they may be academically ready for college classes but, as yet, too young to leave and attend a college away from home. Cyber learning is just one way that determined homeschooling families have used to enable their young adult students to pursue college credit while continuing to enjoy the familiarity and security of family life. More than once, homeschooling parents have gotten in on the act and taken college courses right along with their high school students, earning degrees or simply building their own confidence by completing difficult coursework.

Whether your high school student chooses to complete his or her college degree via cyber school, or just takes a few courses to get the feel for doing college coursework, there are many options available. Check out Appendix D for a listing of cyber schools, Internet providers of cyber classes, and free online classes.

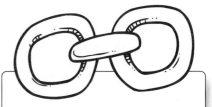

Learning Links

Core Curriculum of America (1-888-689-4626) provides its services for a yearly fee, with a payment plan for purchasing curriculum. Although text-based, Core Curriculum helps students determine how their life experiences (such as their job, community service, hobby, or an apprenticeship) can apply toward credit. Check out Core Curriculum's Web site at members.nbci.com/corecurric/ala.html.

The Least You Need to Know

➤ The Internet is a gold mine of information for homeschoolers.

➤ Metasearch engines make searching more efficient.

➤ You can plan an entire curriculum around Web sites.

➤ Supplement unit studies or traditional learning with information from the World Wide Web.

➤ Cyber schools provide entire programs and individual classes.

Glossary

ACT   The American College Testing Assessment, or ACT, is a test that is used as an assessment tool to determine the readiness of high schoolers for college.

browser   A Web browser is a program that lets you search for, explore, and view information on the World Wide Web.

burnout   The experience of hitting the wall, getting to the end of your rope, or, simply put, feeling like you can't homeschool any more because it's just too much, too hard, too everything.

Carnegie credit units   A system of timekeeping used by the majority of institutional high schools. One Carnegie credit unit is equal to 180 clock hours.

Charlotte Mason approach   Also known as the living books or real books method of homeschooling, this approach is based on the writings of British educator Charlotte Mason. With a focus on teaching good habits and the basics (reading, writing, and math), it exposes children to the best sources for each subject: nature walks for science, arts museums and concerts for the fine arts, and reading good literature.

classical homeschooling   An approach that uses a curriculum structured around three stages of childhood development called the Trivium. Verbal and written expression are emphasized, as well as ancient disciplines and the study of the classics and Latin.

clickable links   Web addresses embedded in the text or listed in the index of a Web site.

compulsory attendance   State-required attendance in an educational program between certain ages, which vary from state to state.

consumable text   A workbook or work text that the student writes in. Once it has been used, it cannot be reused.

criterion-referenced tests   Tests on which scores are based on whether or not one can perform up to a set standard.

curriculum   A course of study; also called scope and sequence.

curriculum fair   A homeschool conference on a small scale, usually including workshops, a vendor hall, and sometimes a used-curriculum swap.

deschooling   A decompression period for children who are taken out of an institutional school and placed in a homeschooling environment. This can take from six weeks to six months for every year a child has been institutionally schooled.

Dewey decimal system   A numerical system of library classification developed by librarian Melvil Dewey to make it easier for library patrons to find books.

distance-learning programs   Ranging from correspondence schools with pre-planned curriculum to home-based education programs of private schools that permit enrollee-designed curriculum, such programs provide a wide variety of services to homeschoolers and other alternative learners. Some full-service programs are available from private entities designed strictly to serve homeschoolers, some are available from curriculum vendors, and still others are implemented by universities and colleges.

docent   A tour guide, teacher, or lecturer.

dual enrollment   Taking a class at an institution other than the one you regularly attend and receiving credit for it in both places.

dumb down   To dilute, condense, and break down information into small increments.

dyslexia   A Specific Language Disability characterized by a severe difficulty in understanding or using one or more areas of language, including listening, speaking, reading, writing, and spelling, while skills in the other areas are age-appropriate.

eclectic homeschooling   This approach allows families to tailor a program to fit their needs, choosing what works best from a variety of approaches, while remaining flexible enough to bend with changes. This ensures a low-stress and high-retention style of learning.

educational philosophy   The set of beliefs you have about the way children learn. This may be determined by a combination of your own experiences and more recent observation, reading, and research.

educationese   A unique language used by teachers who perform evaluations, college recruiters, and admissions officers. As a homeschooler, you must take real-life learning experiences and translate them into a form that is easily understood by people in the academic community.

equivalency laws   Laws that exempt children from compulsory attendance if they are receiving virtually the same education elsewhere.

evaluation   Appraisal, judgment, or assessment. The evaluator will usually look over a portfolio or collection of materials provided by the homeschooler and submit a report to the necessary officials. In most cases, an evaluation includes speaking with the homeschooled child and the parent.

extracurricular   Of or relating to school-connected activities (such as sports) carrying no academic credit in traditional schools, but often an integral part of a homeschool curriculum.

FAQs   Frequently asked questions. On Web sites, this link leads you to a page that will help you understand the content or purpose of the Web site or how to use the Web site most efficiently.

filer   A person who is meticulous about filing every piece of paperwork as soon as it reaches his or her hands.

GED   General education diploma. This diploma is granted after the student has successfully passed a GED test. Classes and study guides are available to prepare students for the test.

grass roots organization   An organization of the common people, generally separate from official or established leadership.

hand-me-down education   The body of information learned by younger siblings from older ones.

homeschool   This word started out as two and is commonly accepted as one today. Synonyms include "home educate" and "home-based learning." Homeschooling includes families who teach their children at home, or do part of the teaching at home and use resources from the community as well.

homeschool conference   A gathering sponsored by a support school, a support group, or an individual to bring together potential, beginning, and veteran homeschoolers for mutual support, discussion, networking, and workshops. Some conferences include sessions especially for kids, both educational and just for fun.

homeschool cooperative   A group of home educators who pool their resources and provide classes, activities, and materials for the benefit of the entire group. Everyone involved contributes in some way to the common good.

homeschool mold   A flexible method that considers the child's talents, interests, personality, and unique learning style to provide a learning environment that adapts as the child grows and learns.

homeschool support group   Homeschoolers banding together to provide support in the form of resources, meetings, and activities on the national, state, or local level.

homeschooling community   May be comprised of a few local families working together cooperatively in various ways, of several groups of homeschoolers, or of homeschooling groups throughout the entire state or province. Or, it may refer to the national or international groups and individuals involved in homeschooling. E-mail lists, Web sites, and chat rooms help homeschoolers access the larger homeschooling community.

IEP   Individual education plan. Children enrolled in special education programs in institutional schools have IEPs. Some homeschooling umbrella schools and support programs will work with you to develop an IEP for your child with special needs.

independent study school   An institution that provides services to individuals who wish to homeschool or study on their own. Some, but not all, independent study schools have a campus school. These programs serve as umbrellas or covers to help homeschoolers meet legal requirements.

intramural   Occurring within the walls or confines of a school or institution.

kinesthetic learner   A person who needs to move about while learning.

LD   Learning disabled. This label encompasses a variety of special needs, including, but not limited to, attention deficit disorder, hyperactivity, dyslexia, dyscalculia, dysgraphia, dysnomia, and dyspraxia.

learning gaps   Areas not covered by the educational plan (curriculum or scope and sequence) or something the child didn't learn because his or her interest wasn't engaged.

literature-based approach   A homeschooling curriculum planned around a specific body of literature. *The Five In A Row* unit studies are based on children's literature, while many homeschoolers create their own literature-based curricula.

living books approach   See **Charlotte Mason approach.**

mastery   Possession or display of skill or knowledge.

metasearch engine   Searches the databases of several search engines at one time, providing you with the results much more quickly than you could search them all by yourself.

Montessori homeschooling   Based on the work of Dr. Maria Montessori, this method promotes preparing a natural and life-supporting environment for the child, observing the child living freely in this environment, and continually adapting the environment so the child may fulfill his or her greatest potential—physically, mentally, emotionally, and spiritually.

narration   Having a child tell back a story that has been read to him or her, which teaches a child to recall details of a story in order, and is a way to find out whether the child remembers and understands what has been taught or read.

natural learning   Occurs as a result of participating in the everyday experiences of life. Families who are involved in home business, are active in their communities, or have an interest that the whole family shares find this a workable choice. Sometimes called unschooling, child-led, or interest-oriented learning.

norm-referenced tests   Tests in which scores are derived by comparing the number of items answered correctly with the average performance of others.

objective   As an adjective, means treating or dealing with facts without distortion by personal feelings or prejudices; as a noun, it's an aim, goal, or end.

Orton-Gillingham approach   A language-based, multisensory, structured, sequential, cumulative, perceptive approach that utilizes the typically strong cognitive (thinking) skills of the student. It was named for Samuel Torrey Orton (1879–1948), who was a physician, a scientist, and an educator; and for Anna Gillingham, (1878–1963), a gifted educator with a mastery of the English language. Dr. Orton identified the syndrome of dyslexia as an educational problem in 1925.

phonetically   Learning by the sounds made by the letters when they are spoken.

piler   A person whose paperwork never seems to make it into a file folder but ends up in piles all over the house.

playgroup   An informal gathering of young children and their parents for the purpose of nurturing interaction between the children.

preschoolers   Institutional designation for children under the age of five.

preteen   A boy or girl who is not yet 13 years old, especially one between the ages of 10 and 13.

SAT   The SAT, formerly called the Scholastic Aptitude Test, is used as an assessment tool to determine the readiness of high schoolers for college. The PSAT is a preliminary SAT.

school-at-home approach   The homeschool approach most resembling the methods used in the traditional institutional school setting.

school-at-home mold   A traditional method based on the rather inflexible school model, complete with texts, tests, and a mandatory curriculum.

scope and sequence   Who learns what when. The scope is the total body of material that will be covered, while the sequence is the order in which the material will be covered. It is also known as a curriculum.

scrapbooking   A hobby in which collections of photos and related mementos are combined with attractive lettering, coordinating papers, stamping, and stickers to form pages in a memory book.

self-directed learners   People who tend to learn things in their own way, in their own time, and at their own pace. Generally focused and inwardly motivated when pursuing their passion, these individuals don't always fit into society's accepted mold.

self-educated   Taught by oneself. Unable or unwilling to attend school, many famous homeschoolers have educated themselves by seeking out resources, observing the world around them, and reading avidly. Many modern-day homeschoolers, especially teens, are doing the same today.

short-term learning   Learning and retaining information for a specific goal, such as a test. Such learning has a low long-term retention rate.

socialization   The ability to get along with people of all kinds in a variety of situations.

specific language disability   A severe difficulty in some aspect of listening, speaking, reading, writing, or spelling, while skills in the other areas are age-appropriate. Also called specific language learning disability (SLLD).

subjective   Influenced by an individual's state of mind.

support school   An institution that provides legal cover and services for a homeschooler. Some are private schools with a program for homeschoolers, while others exist solely to provide services for homeschoolers. Typical services provided are record keeping, curriculum counseling, and selling educational materials.

tactile learning   To learn or have concepts reinforced through the sense of touch.

teachable moment   The exact moment when a child's interest is engaged, and he or she is open and receptive to instruction.

teacher-directed materials   Materials that are structured to help the teacher give instructions and explanations prior to an assignment.

teaching to the test   Teaching only the material that will be included on a specific test while neglecting other areas of the curriculum. This practice is often criticized not only by parents but by the teachers who are required to implement the practice.

transcript   An official copy of a student's educational record.

trial-and-error learning   Learning a new skill or concept by trying a method, realizing it doesn't work, attempting another tactic, and so on, until you determine a method that will accomplish the task.

twaddle   A term coined by Charlotte Mason, referring to books that contain secondhand, distilled information, as opposed to books that bring a subject to life.

twenty-minute pickup   A planned or spontaneous period of time designated for picking up and putting away as many items as possible. Everyone in the household is included, the timer is set for 20 minutes, and bouncy music is played as an optional mood setter.

umbrella schools   Created to provide a way for homeschoolers to educate their children under the "umbrella" or protection of an institutional school.

unit studies   Integrated learning based on a chosen topic or theme.

unschooling   Learning that happens without the usual structure of schooling. Although some unschoolers use traditional methods when they find it appropriate, most prefer to learn from mentors, while doing volunteer work or holding a job, pursuing an interest or hobby, play, or reading and researching on their own. Sometimes called natural learning, child-led learning, or interest-oriented learning.

URL   Stands for uniform resource locator, the unique address of each Web page.

values training   Imparting specific ideals or principles. Many homeschooling families today base their curriculum on specific values or character traits.

Waldorf homeschooling   A holistic approach based on the educational philosophy of Rudolph Steiner, which considers the changing developmental stages of the child. Because Steiner attempted to achieve a homelike setting in his schools, his methods are easily adapted for the homeschool.

Curriculum Winners and Selected Resources, Including Dynamite Web Sites

The Charlotte Mason Approach

http://members.aol.com/BeeME1/monthly.html—subscribe to a free e-mail newsletter about Charlotte Mason homeschooling, order books, and link to related pages, including a reading list of living books.

http://members.xoom.com/CatholicCM—for those who want to pursue a "Catholic Charlotte Mason Method" lifestyle, subscribe to an e-mail list and link to other resources.

www.angelfire.com/journal/CharlotteMason/—join a Charlotte Mason study loop or link to related resources.

The Classical Education Approach

Trivium Pursuit, PMB 168, 139 Colorado Street, Muscatine, IA 62761; Web site: www.triviumpursuit.com—resources that apply Christian Classical Education to Homeschooling. Link to articles, an online catalog, homeschooling resources, or schedule a seminar for your homeschool conference.

The Well-Trained Mind Newsletter: Peace Hill Farm, 18101 The Glebe Lane, Charles City, VA 23030; Web site: www.welltrainedmind.com/newsletter.html—subscribe to the newsletter ($6 per year for four issues) or read articles from the current issue online.

www.classicalhomeschooling.org—dedicated to classical education and its practical application in grades K–12 for homeschooling families.

http://home.att.net/~MikeJaqua/news/index.html—back issues of the *ClassEd Newsletter*, the Classical Education Chat Room, information on Classical Christian Homeschooling, and an exclusively Classical Curriculum Swap list.

Core Knowledge Sequence

www.coreknowledge.org—link to lesson plans, articles, and a study on the effects of using the Core Knowledge sequence.

www.homestead.com/hmckcare/index1.html—includes links to Core Knowledge homeschooling chats.

Curriculum Planning

Classical Christian Homeschooling Curriculum, Escondido Tutorial Service, 2634 Bernardo Avenue, Escondido, CA, 92029; 760-746-0980; e-mail: gbt@gbt.org; Web site: www.classicalhomeschooling.org/curriculum/scope.html—sample classical curriculum planning guides online.

The Homeschool Academy, 334 Second Street, Catasauqua, PA 18032-2501; 1-800-863-1474; Web site: www.homeschoolacademy.com/academy/index.html— links to School of Tomorrow curriculum online.

Scholastic Inc., 555 Broadway, New York, NY 10012-3999, Web site: www.scholastic.com—click on "teachers" for thousands of free lesson plans, activities, and resources.

TeachersFirst Classroom Resource Finder (Lesson Plans): www.youthfirst.org/class-f.htm—searchable grade-level resource finder.

World Book's Scope and Sequence, World Book, Inc. Headquarters, 233 Michigan Avenue, Suite 2000, Chicago, IL 60601; 1-800-WORLDBK or 312-729-5800; e-mail: content@worldbook.com; Web site: www.worldbook.com/ptrc/html/curr.htm—call to request one print copy free or print grade-level scope and sequences online.

Discussion Boards and Chats

Kaleidoscapes Discussion Boards: www.kaleidoscapes.com—monitored inclusive discussion boards on general homeschooling questions, monthly topics, curricula, unit studies, compliance, high school and college, special needs, and a sidetracks board for everything else.

Home Education Magazine Networking and Discussion Boards: http://home-ed-magazine.com/DSC/discus/messages/board-topics.html—boards include home-schooling news and announcements, talk with writers and editors of HEM, Q&As and FAQs for new homeschoolers, support group network, specific interests, resources, general discussion (living and learning) and classified ads.

www.angelfire.com/mo/sasschool/BBs.html—links to many message boards and discussion forums.

http://eho.org/discussi.htm—links to homeschool discussion boards and chats.

http://learninfreedom.org/discussiongroups.html—links to several homeschooling and education reform chats and discussion boards.

www.geocities.com/Athens/8259/IRCchat.html—info on chats and other ways to connect online with homeschoolers.

Distance Learning

Atlapedia Online: www.atlapedia.com—map study, including stats on ethnic language, religion, economy, educational system, and history of each country.

Black History Museum: www.afroam.org/history/history.html—links to interactive exhibits.

ChildU: www.childu.com—free trial to The Learning Oddysey's interactive learning adventures.

Cobblestone Publishing: www.cobblestonepub.com—free articles, quizzes, hands-on projects, and more.

Culture, Diversity, and Multiculturalism: www.ncbe.gwu.edu/links/langcult/multi.htm—links to resources for multicultural education and cultural diversity.

The Franklin Institute Online: http://sln.fi.edu/tfi/hotlists—educational links by category (cover your whole curriculum right here).

Free Online Classes: www.blackboard.com (high school); www.free-ed.net (high school); www.sitesalive.com (K–12).

Free worksheets and downloadable education games: www.freeworksheets.com; www.schoolexpress.com/fws.

Freebies for educators: www.llg.freeyellow.com/curfree.html.

Global Online Adventure Learning Site: www.goals.com/—interactive, hands-on learning experience with curriculum guidelines.

Myths and Fables From Around the World: www.afroam.org/children/myths/myths.html—links to myths and fables.

The Nine Planets Homepage: www.seds.lpl.arizona.edu/nineplanets—tour of the solar system.

PBS OnLine: www.pbs.org/—activities and program discussions, links to PBS programming and other educational sites.

Smithsonian Institution: www.si.edu/—links to other museums, virtual Smithsonian, online videos.

Unit study on the United States (elementary): homeschooling.about.com/education/homeschooling.

The Village Learning Center www.snowcrest.net/villcen/vlchp.html—online classes based on the unit study approach.

Virtual anatomy: www.virtual-anatomy.com/—3-D Skeletal system.

Virtual frog: http://george.lbl.gov/vfrog/—dissection without the formaldehyde.

The Eclectic Approach

Eclectic Homeschool magazine: Eclectic Homeschool, P.O. Box 736, Bellevue, NE 68005-0736.

I Love Homeschool, a free online newsletter for people who love the wonderfully eclectic world of homeschooling: www.xmission.com/~clawson/clawacad.html.

Putting Together an Eclectic Curriculum: www.home-ed-press.com/INF/OH/oh_ecl.cur.html.

Chart & Compass' Eclectic Resources page: www.chartncompass.com/EclecticResources.html.

Eclectic Homeschool Online, the Magazine for Creative Homeschoolers: http://eho.org.

Extracurricular

Boy Scouts of America, 1325 West Walnut Hill Lane, P.O. Box 12079, Irving, TX 75015-2079; 972-580-2000; Web site: www.bsa.scouting.org.

Campfire Boys and Girls, 4601 Madison Avenue, Kansas City, MO 64112; 816-756-1950; Web site: www.campfire.org.

Families, 4-H and Nutrition, 1400 Independence Avenue South West, Washington, DC 20250; 202-720-2908; Web site: www.4-h.org.

Girl Scouts of the USA, 420 5th Avenue, New York, NY 10018-2798; 1-800-GSUSA 4U; Web site: www.GSUSA.org.

Frugal Homeschooling

ClassroomDirect.com, P.O. Box 830677, Birmingham, AL 35283-0677; 1-877-698-1988; Web site: www.ClassroomDirect.com—school supplies at a deep discount.

Creative Educational Surplus, 1000 Apollo Road, Eagan, MN 55121-2240; Web site: www.creativesurplus.com.

Homeschooling on a Shoestring: www.geocities.com/Athens/4663.

Used Book and Curriculum Web Sites

The Back Pack, P.O. Box 125, Ernul, NC 28527; Web site: www.thebackpack.com.

Book Hunter Press, P.O. Box 193, Yorktown Heights, NY 10598; 914-245-6608; fax: 914-245-2630; e-mail: bookhuntpr@aol.com; Web site: www.bookhunterpress.com/index.cgi/index.htmlCarty's Curriculum Corner: www.usedbookstore.net, or e-mail carty@reliable-net.net with your book request.

The Homeschool Publishing House, P.O. Box 19-I, Cherry Valley, MA 01611-0019; Web site: http://bravewc.com/hph/hss_main.html.

Newlife HS Books: www.angelfire.com/biz/newlife2.

Pam's Used Homeschool Books and More: http://members.tripod.com/~p_van/books.html.

RWD Used Book Search: 4724 Murphy Road #25, Franklin, NC 28734; e-mail: rwdmd@tcw.net; Web site: www.mail-archive.com/dia-list@lysator.liu.se/msg03090.html.

Homeschool Books: To shop, swap, or sell, go to http://communities.msn.com/HomeSchoolBooksShopSwaporSell.

Homeschooling (General)

A to Z Home's Cool: www.gomilpitas.com/homeschooling/index.html—links, articles, activities, resources, and a search.

Family Unschoolers Network: www.unschooling.org/index.htm—support for un-schooling, homeschooling, and self-directed learning.

Homeschool Zone: www.homeschoolzone.com/main.htm—links to resources, articles, freebies, book reviews, and interviews with homeschoolers and authors.

Jon's Homeschool Resource Page: www.midnightbeach.com/hs/—Links to articles, e-mail lists, support groups, more.

Learn in Freedom!: http://learninfreedom.org/—taking responsibility for your own learning, booklists, resource guides, articles, and links.

Home Business and Homeschooling

Bookswithoutborders.com, 10217 119th Avenue North East, Kirkland, WA 98033-5159; 1-888-840-2962; orders and payment, e-mail: sales@bookswithoutborders.com; customer service, e-mail: mail@bookswithoutborders.com; Web site: http://bookswithoutborders.com—opportunities selling books and resources.

Running a Daycare While Homeschooling: www.geocities.com/hughouse/both.html.

Home Biz—Top Ten Ways to Start Your Own Home Business: families-first.com/homebiz/news/sue-ten-ways.htm.

Educational Development Corporation, 10302 E. 55th Place, Tulsa, Oklahoma 74146-6515; 1-800-475-4522; fax 1-800-747-4509; e-mail: edc@edcpub.com or ubah@ubah.com; Web site: www.ubah.com—work as a sales consultant for Usborne Books At Home.

Language

Audio Forum Languages, Jeffrey Norton Publishers, 96 Broad Street, Guilford, CT 06437; 1-800-243-1234 or 203-453-9794; e-mail: info@audioforum.com; Web site: http://audioforum.com.

Dover Publications, 31 East 2nd Street, Mineola, NY 11501-38582—children's books in English and other languages.

The Learnables, International Linguistics Corporation, 3505 East Red Bridge Road, Kansas City, MO 64137; 1-800-237-1830; e-mail: info@learnables.com; Web site: www.learnables.com.

Power-Glide Foreign Language Courses, 1682 West 820 North, Provo, UT 84601; 1-800-596-0910; Web site: www.power-glide.com/home.

The Rosetta Stone Language Library, Fairfield Language Technologies, 165 South Main Street, Harrisonburg, VA 22801; 1-800-788-0822 or 540-432-6166; fax: 540-432-0953; e-mail: info@RosettaStone.com; Web site: www.RosettaStone.com.

Sign Language Dictionary Online: http://dww.deafworldweb.org/sl—interactive site.

Babel Fish—Web site that translates text from one language to another: http://babel.altavista.com/translate.dyn.

Language Arts

Alpha-Phonics Kit, available from Harvest Educational Products, 5 Mead Farm Road, Seymour, CT 06483; 203-888-0427; fax: 203-888-0413; Web site: www.HarvestEd.com/index.html—a complete phonics program; includes instructional video, seven audiotapes, workbooks, flashcards, teacher book, and student flip book.

Ball-Stick-Bird Publications, Inc.Renee Fuller, Ph.D., P.O. Box 592, Stony Brook, NY 11790; 860-738-8871.

Grammar Songs: Learning With Music by Kathy Troxel (workbook/songbook and audiocassette), Audio Memory, 501 Cliff Drive, Newport Beach, CA, 92663; e-mail: hq@audiomemory.com; Web site: www.audiomemory.com.

Knowledge Farm, Web site: www.knowledgefarm.co.uk—free study guides and lesson plans in support of literature, the arts, and humanities.

Learning Language Arts Through Literature, Common Sense Press, 8786 Highway 21, Melrose, FL 32666; 352-475-5757; e-mail: webmaster@cspress.com; Web site: www. cspress.com.

Pizza Hut, Inc. BOOK IT!, Reading Incentive Program, P.O. Box 2999, Wichita, KS 67201; 1-800-426-6548; Web site: www.bookitprogram.com.

Scholastic Book Clubs and Software Clubs, 1-800-724-6527 (Book Clubs) or 1-800-724-4811 (Software Clubs); Web site: http://teacher.scholastic.com/bookclubs/custsvcfaq.htm.

Sing, Spell, Read, and Write, Pearson Learning, 1-800-526-9907; e-mail: pearson.learning1@pearsonlearning.com; Web site: www.singspell.com—a comprehensive phonics program using audiotapes and music.

A.Word.A.Day: www.wordsmith.org/awad/index.html—subscribe to the mailing list, discuss words, read the FAQs.

Write Every Day by Evan-Moor Educational Publishers, 18 Lower Ragsdale Drive, Monterey, CA 93940-5746; 1-800-777-4362 (in North America), 1-831-649-5901 (outside North America); e-mail: sales@evan-moor.com; Web site: www.evan-moor.com.

Writing in Narrative, WIN, The Seven Sentence Story: A Simplified Introduction to Story Writing, The Elijah Company, Route 2, Box 100B, Crossville, TN 38555-9600; 1-888-2-ELIJAH or 615-456-6284; e-mail: elijahco@elijahco.com; Web site: www.elijahco.com.

Writing Strands, National Writing Institute, 1746 Wright Road, Niles, MI 49120—a unique approach to learning to write.

Learning Styles

Multiple Intelligences survey: Print free at http://surfaquarium.com/MIinvent.htm, or send a check for $10 to Walter McKenzie, c/o Creative Classroom Consulting, 10808 Seven Oaks Court, Spotsylvania, PA 22553.

MIDAS: Multiple Intelligences Development Assessment Scales and Howard Gardner's books available for purchase: M.I. Research and Consulting, Attn: C. Branton Shearer, 1316 S. Lincoln Street, Kent, OH 44240; 330-677-8534; Web site: www.miresearch.org.

Reflective Educational Perspectives Learning Style Assessment available from Creative Home Teaching, P.O. Box 152581, San Diego, CA 92195; 619-263-8633 (phone and fax).

Math Resources

Cuisenaire Materials: Dale Seymour Publications, Pearson Learning, 299 Jefferson Road, P.O. Box 480, Parsippany, NJ 07054; 1-800-526-9907; Web site: www.pearsonlearning.com/dsp-publications/index.htm.

Geo-boards: ETA/Cuisenaire, 500 Greenview Court, Vernon Hills, IL 60061; 1-800-445-5985 or 847-816-5050; Fax: 800-382-9326; Web site: www.cuisenaire.com.

Harvest Educational Products, 5 Mead Farm Road, Seymour, CT 06483; 203-888-0427, Fax: 203-888-0413; for catalog, e-mail: catalog@HarvestEd.com; for other comments, e-mail: Harvest@harvested.com; Web site: www.HarvestEd.com—math resources and more.

Learning Wrap-ups, 1660 West Gordon Avenue #4, Layton, UT 84041; 1-800-992-4966, local: 801-497-0050; fax: 801-497-0063; e-mail: info@learningwrapups.com; Web site: www.learningwrapups.com—fun, hands-on, self-correcting method of learning basic math facts and more.

Math Games: Math War card game, S'Math (similar to Scrabble), Yahtzee, Monopoly, Alien Hotshots: The War of the Numbers by Gamewright, Star Wars Math by Lucas Learning (software), Chutes and Ladders, Hi Ho Cherri-O.

Mega Mathematics: www.c3.lanl.gov/mega-math—colorful site introduces advanced math concepts to youngsters through stories and puzzles encouraging the use of a wide range of reasoning skills.

Mortenson Math, VJ Mortensen Company, Mortensen Math World Headquarters, 2600A E Seltice Way #179, Post Falls, ID 83854-7977; 1-800-475-8748.

Professor Weissman's Software, 246 Crafton Avenue, Staten Island, NY 10314; 718-698-5219; e-mail: mathprof@hotmail.com; Web sites: http://math911.com and http://themathprof.com—algebra and pre-calculus software, books, free downloads, and tutorials.

Math-It, from Moore Foundation Curriculum Services, Box 1, Camas, WA 98607; 360-835-2736; e-mail: moorefnd@pacifier.com; Web site:www. moorefoundation.com—audiotape math drills.

Math-U-See, 1-888-854-6284, in Canada 1-800-255-6654; e-mail: mathusee@epix.net; Web site: www.mathusee.com—video/manipulative/workbook math approach.

Miquon Math, Key Curriculum Press, 1150 65th Street, Emeryville, CA 94608; 1-800-995-MATH; fax: 1-800-541-2442; Web site: www.keypress.com/catalog/products/supplementals/Prod_Miquon.html—math workbooks using Cuisenaire rods.

Nasco Math, 901 Janesville Avenue, P.O. Box 901, Fort Atkinson, WI 53538-0901; 920-568-2446; fax: 920-563-8296, Order phone:1-800-558-9595—catalog of unique math resources.

Saxon Publishers, Inc., 1320 W. Lindsey, Norman, OK 73069; 405-329-7071; Web site: www.saxonpub.com—math texts with home study packets.

Tangrams, Kaidy Educational Resources, P.O. Box 831853, Richardson, TX 75083-1853; 1-800-365-2439 (order hotline) or 972-234-6161; fax: 972-234-5626; e-mail: Service@Kaidy.com; Web site: www.kaidy.com.

Miscellaneous

Cobblestone Publishing, 300 Grove Street, Suite C, Peterborough, NH 03458; 1-800-821-0115; fax: 603-924-7380; e-mail: custsvc@cobblestone.mv.com; Web site: www.cobblestonepub.com—educational magazines.

The Montessori Approach

Michael Olaf, 65 Ericson Court, Arcata, CA 95521; Order: 1-888-880-9235, regular phone: 707-826-1557; e-mail: Michaelola@aol.com; Web site: www.michaelolaf. net—materials and information about the Montessori method, including an e-mail list and catalog.

Montessori Homeschooling Web site: www.montessori.edu/homeschooling.html— includes links to related Montessori sites, questions and answers.

www.saber.net/~mearth/edbooks.htm—Montessori and homeschool books and materials, free e-mail newsletter, many links to related and unrelated sites.

www.gomilpitas.com/homeschooling/methods/Montessori.htm—many links to Montessori sites.

Multimedia

A Beka Video Home School, P.O. Box 18000, Pansacola, FL 32523-9160; 1-800-874-3592; Web site: www.abeka.org—Christian school video programs for K5–12.

The Annenberg/CPB Collection, P.O. Box 2345, South Burlington, VT 05407-2345; 1-800-LEARNER, fax: 802-864-9846.

The Complete National Geographic (all 100 years) on CD with free video: www.softwareandstuff.com/s_ref_other_nationalgeog.html.

Gateway Films/Vision Video, P.O. Box 540, Worcester, PA 19490-0540; 1-800-523-0226; e-mail: visionvide@aol.com; Web site: www.gatewayfilms.com.

National Geographic Store, 1-800-437 5521; Web site: www.shop.nationalgeographic. com/v2.0-img/operations/ngsstore/desc/index.html.

NYLink Discount Service, send orders to: Mrs. Suzanne Farrell, PBS Video, 3 Horicon Avenue, Glens Falls, NY 12801-2616; 1-800-215-7306; e-mail: sfarrell@capital.netto. To request a PBS catalog, ask for Kari at PBS Customer Service at 1-800-424-7963, ext. 5388; Web site: www.nylink.suny.edu/coop/PBSVideo.htm.

Reader's Digest Video, Order Department, Pleasantville, NY 10470; 1-800-846-2100; Web site: www.readersdigest.com/entertain/videos2.asp.

The Robinson Self-Teaching Curriculum, RC Internet, 2887 Berkshire Dr. Troy, MI 48083; 248-740-2697; fax: 248-740-2782; e-mail: support@robinsoncurriculum.com; Web site: www.robinsoncurriculum.com/view/rc/s31p42.htm—CD-ROM curriculum.

Schoolhouse Videos & CDs, 4205 Grove Ridge Drive, Durham, NC 27703; 1-908-229-0608; e-mail: sales@totalmarketing.com; Web site: www.totalmarketing.com.

Switched-On Schoolhouse, Bridgestone Multimedia Group, 300 North McKemy Avenue, Chandler, AZ 85226-2618; 1-800-622-3070; Web site: www.switched-on-schoolhouse.com—Bible-based CD-ROM curriculum with grading, record keeping, review, and tutoring options.

Newsgroups

Homeschooling Newsgroups, www.geocities.com/Athens/8259/news.html—links to many newsgroups and other homeschool sites.

Physical Education

U Can Do, Can Do Kids videotapes to meet the gaps in Christian homeschooling, 17900 Dolores Lane, Sonora, CA 95370; 1-800-286-8585; e-mail: Laura@candokids. com; Web site: http://candokids.com—these videotapes combine math and movement.

Physical Education lesson plans: www.lessonplanspage.com/PE.htm.

The President's Challenge, 400 E. 7th Street, Bloomington, IN 47405-3085; 1-800-258-8146; special homeschool packet available, e-mail: preschal@indiana.edu; Web site: www.indiana.edu/~preschal.

Preschool and Kindergarten

www.preschoolathome.com/links/pages/—links to theme ideas, articles on preschool at home, support, inspiration, sharing, and exploration.

www.mcg.net/nelson/pscoop.htm—ideas for organizing your own preschool co-operative.

http://geocities.com/Heartland/Valley/8004/preschool.html—year-round preschool and Bible themes.

Record Keeping

HomeSchool Easy Records, DataPlus Solutions, 1067 Camp Eden Road, Golden, CO 80403; 1-888-328-7587; Web site: http://home.earthlink.net/~vdugar/features.htm.

Living Is Learning Curriculum Guides (double as record-keepers) by Nancy Plent, available from John Holt's Bookstore, 2380 Massachusetts Avenue, Suite 104, Cambridge, MA 02140-1226; 617-864-3100, toll-free order line: 888-925-9298; fax: 617-864-9235; Web site: www.holtgws.com/gws.htm.

The following (plus more) are available from Rainbow Resource Center, Route 1, Box 159A, 50 North 500 East Road, Toulon, IL 61483; 1-888-841-3456; e-mail: rainbowr@cin.net; Web site: www.rainbowresource.com: Modern Plan Book series—includes the No. 4 Plan Book, the Page Per Day Plan Book No. 8, and Rules 6 Period and 8-Period Planbooks.

T.I.P.S. Planners—two versions, one for teachers and one for students.

The Home Schooler's Journal—weekly lesson layout, instructions, two-year calendar, year-at-a-glance summary, planning, and more.

Homeschooler's High School Journal—same as above for grades 7–12.

Lesson Planner by Soteria—each page is a weekly lesson planning guide, journal, attendance and grading chart, and an envelope in which you can file papers.

Student Weekly Assignment Book—40 week-at-a-glance assignment pages plus class schedule, special projects, schedule of "school events," directory, and more.

Student Planbooks—standard-format student assignment books in two versions, both with weekly pages with room for daily assignments, notes, and ideas plus reference information in back.

Organized Kid Daily Planner (grades 2 through 8)—includes space for personal information, reference materials, weekly planner pages, daily assignment space, goals, monthly events, reading chart, and stickers.

Science Resources

Dacta, Pitsco; 1-800-362-4308; Web site: www.pitsco-legodacta.com—innovative hands-on projects and activities, plus curriculum for K–6.

Earth and space science lessons: www.electricstudyguide.com—free earth and space science lessons.

Edmund Scientific, 101 East Gloucester Pike, Barrington, NJ 08007-1380; 1-800-728-6999; fax: 856-547-4826; Web site: www.edmundscientific.com/scientifics/scientifics.cfm—online catalog, tech tips, and events.

Gears, Gears, Gears!, Learning Resources: We Make Learning Fun, e-mail: info@learningresources.com; Web site: www.learningresources.com—online catalog, educational toys, classroom materials, and links to other resources.

Great Scopes, P.O. Box 1948, Jamestown, NC 27282; toll free: 1-877-454-6364, or 336-454-6361; e-mail: scopemaster@greatscopes.com; Web site: http://greatscopes.com/index.html—microscopes, experiments and activities, and bookstore.

How Stuff Works: 5625 Dillard Drive, Suite 217, Cary, NC 27511; 919-882-5000; e-mail: brain@howstuffworks; Web site: www.howstuffworks.com—newsletter, articles about how things work, and daily interactive activities.

NASA Spacelink: http://spacelink.msfc.nasa.gov/—the latest info about the space program.

Nature's Workshop Plus!, P.O. Box 220, Pittsboro, IN 46167-0220; orders: 1-888-393-5663, inquiries and fax: 317-892-5791; e-mail: naturesworkshopplus@ juno.com—homeschool resource catalog specializing in science materials, including *Nature Friend* magazine, a nature periodical for children ages 4–14.

Robert Krampf's Science Education Company (free e-mail experiment of the week and much more), P.O. Box 60982, Jacksonville, FL 32236-0982; 904-471-4578; e-mail: krampf@aol.com; Web site: www.krampf.com—experiment of the week e-mail list, information about booking shows on electricity, and links to fun and useful sites.

Science Toys: www.scitoys.com/cgi-bin/shop.cgi/page=contents.html—online directions for toys you can make from common household items to demonstrate scientific principles, online catalog for science kits.

Tobin's Lab, P.O. Box 725, Culpeper, VA 22701; 1-800-522-4776 or 540-547-2959; Web site: www.tobinlab.com—online science catalog carries science kits, microscopes, owl pellets, and resources for teaching chemistry, dissection, and about living things.

Search Engines

SearchMe: Web site: www.net-comber.com/—a fast and simple search engine resource center, many links.

www.c4.com—ask a question or enter a keyword or phrase.

www.dogpile.com—keyword search and links.

www.highway61.com—search with many options and features.

www.infind.com—fast parallel web search.

www.metacrawler.com—search, power search, and links.

www.savvysearch.com—links to specialized searches.

Special Needs

Autism Recovery through Medicine, Education and Diet (ARMED) Contact: Elizabeth Bowers, 8601 Redbud Lane, Lenexa, KS 66220, (913) 422-8666, Web site: Rx4autism. org—consultations, lectures, presentations, and more.

At Our Own Pace, 102 Willow Drive, Waukegan, IL 60087; e-mail editor Jean Kulczyk: yukko5@aol.com—free newsletter on homeschooling children with special needs.

Americans with Disabilities Act (ADA), http://search.usdoj.gov/compass?scope= ADA&ui=sr&view-template=dojsimple—search the Department of Justice Web site for links and information about your child's rights under this act.

Aut-2B-Home: maelstrom.stjohns.edu/archives/aut-2b-home.html—support for homeschooling autistic kids.

Coaching for Learning Success, Reflective Educational Perspectives, 1451 E. Main Street, Suite 200, Ventura, CA 93001; Web site: www.redp.com—tips for using your child's learning style to plan a curriculum.

Dreamms for Kids: Assistive Technology Solutions, e-mail: janet@dreamms.org; Web site: www.dreamms.org/link.htm—newsletter, links, and resources.

The Dyslexic Reader newsletter; 1-888-999-3324; Web site: www.dyslexia.com.

ECL (Education, Communication, Language) Publications, P.O. Box 26, 11121 West Michigan Avenue, Suite A, Youngtown, AZ 85363; 623-974-4560; Web site: www. eclpublications—speech and language materials, auditory materials.

Educators Publishing Service, Inc., 31 Smith Place, Cambridge, MA 02138-1089; 1-800-225-5750; Web site: www.epsbooks.com—*Explode the Code* phonics workbook series and more.

Gallaudet University, 800 Florida Avenue NE, Washington D.C., 20002-3695; Web site: www.gallaudet.edu—undergraduate and graduate programs for deaf, hard-of-hearing, and hearing students.

Great Plains Laboratory, 9335 West 75th Street, Overland Park, KS 66204; 913-341-8949; fax: 913-341-6207; e-mail: gpl4u@aol.com; Web site: www. greatplainslaboratory.com—testing for learning disorders, book and audiotape catalog online, and links to information about autism and PDD conferences.

The Handle Institute, 1530 Eastlake Avenue East, Suite 100, Seattle, WA 98102; 206-860-2665; fax: 206-860-3505; Web site: www.handle.org—offers an effective, drug-free alternative for diagnosing and treating most neuro-developmental disorders.

Harris Communications, Inc., 15159 Technology Drive, Eden Prairie, MN 55344; 612-906-1198; Web site: http://harriscomm.com/acb/index.cfm?ncp=yes&DID=7—assistive products designed for deaf and hard-of-hearing people, including books, videos, equipment, and novelties.

Heartsong Communications, P.O. Box 2455, Glenview, IL 60025; Web site: http://members.aol.com/hrtsngComm/Gaia.html—links to resources, kidsign club, signs for songs, song demos, video demos, catalog.

The Hyperlexia Association, 195 West Spangler, Elmhurst, IL 60126; 630-530-5909; Web site: www.hyperlexia.org—info on hyperlexia, mailing list, links to sister sites, catalog.

Special Kids Company, P.O. Box 462, Muskego, WI 53150; 1-800-543-7153; Web site: www.specialkids1.com—educational videotapes for special kids.

Tin Man Press, P.O. Box 219, Stanwood, WA 98292; voice and fax: 1-800-676-0459; e-mail: tinman@tinmanpress.com; Web site: www.tinmanpress.com—thinking skills materials for the elementary grades, for use in enrichment and gifted programs, free sample sheets.

T.J. Publishers Inc., 817 Silver Spring Avenue, Silver Spring, MD 20910; 301-585-4440; fax: 301-585-5930; e-mail: TJPubinc@aol.com; Web site: www.bowker.com/lrg/home/entries/t.j._publishers_inc%2Cbook_publishers.html—books, videotapes, and other materials related to American sign language and deafness.

Turning Challenges into Opportunities, by Sharon Hensley, RR #1, Box 188, Atwood, IL 61913; 217-578-2530—a quarterly newsletter for $12 a year.

Testing

ACT: www.act.org—learn about, register, and prepare for the ACT assessment test.

Assessment Software: www.smarterkids.com—discover the best products for your child by using the State Test Prep Center, Early Development Checklists, Grade Expectations! Guide, or Learning Styles Survey; online catalog, many links.

The College Board: www.collegeboard.org—learn about, register, and prepare for the PSAT, SAT, CLEP.

Online Training Institute: www.oltraining.com/be_ged/basic-ae.html—learn about, register, and prepare for the GED.

PASS Test, available for Grades 3–8,from Hewitt Homeschooling Resources, P.O. Box 9, Washougal, WA 98671; 360-835-8708; Web site: www.hewitthomeschooling.com.

Scoring High (standardized test specific) and Spectrum (grade-level-appropriate prep for any of the five major standardized tests) test preparation books available from Rainbow Resource Center, Route 1, Box 159A, 50 North 500 East Road, Touton, IL 61483; 888-841-3456; Web site: www.rainbowresource.com.

Scoring High and Spectrum test preparation software available from TeachChildren. com, 26537 Bouquet Canyon, Saugus, CA 91350; 661-263-0756; Web site: http:// teachchildren.com/index.html.

Test Ready, subject test preparation available from Curriculum Associates, Inc., P.O. Box 2001, North Billerica, MA 01862-0901; 1-800-255-0248; Web site: www. cahomeschool.com.

Textbook Publishers

A Beka Book: 1-800-877-5226; Web site: www.abeka.com—Christian textbooks and workbooks.

Bob Jones University Press, Greenville, SC 29614; 1-800-845-5731; Web site: www. bjup.com—Christian textbooks.

Christian Liberty Press, 502 West Euclid Avenue, Arlington Heights, IL 60004; 1-800-832-2741; Web site: www.class-homeschool.org/clpress/clpress.htm—curriculum materials with a Biblical worldview.

Pearson Learning (imprints include Celebration Press, Dale Seymour Publications, Good Year Books, and Modern Curriculum Press); 1-800-526-9907; Web site: www. pearsonlearning.com—assessment testing, bilingual/ESL (English as a second language), developmental reading resources, teacher materials, textbooks, and manipulative-based math resources.

Rod and Staff Publishers, Inc., P.O. Box 3, Hwy. 172, Crockett, KY 41413-0003; 606-522-4348—Bible-based textbooks and literature.

Saxon Publishers, Inc., 1320 W. Lindsey, Norman, OK 73069; 405-329-7071; Web site: www.saxonpub.com—textbooks with home study packets for K through 12 phonics and math.

Scholastic Inc., 555 Broadway, New York, NY 10012-3999; Web site: http://teacher. scholastic.com/products/index.htm—online catalog of up-to-date teaching resources.

Unit Studies

A to Z Home's Cool Unit Study Method: www.gomilpitas.com/homeschooling/
methods/Units.htm—links to free unit studies, and learning about unit studies;
www.gomilpitas.com/homeschooling/methods/OwnUnits.htm—links to sites about
creating your own unit studies.

Design-A-Study Guides, 408 Victoria Avenue, Wilmington, DE 19804-2124;
302-998-3889; Web site: www.designastudy.com—everything you need to design
your own unit study or create a custom curriculum.

Five In A Row, P.O. Box 707, Grandview, MO 64030-0707; 816-331-5769; Fax:
816-322-8150; e-mail: lamberts@fiveinarow.com; Web site: www.fiveinarow.com—
literature-based unit studies for ages 2–12, online bookstore for related resources.

Theme Units and Unit Study Idea Kit for World Book: available from The Sycamore
Tree, 2179 Meyer Place, Costa Mesa, CA 92627; 1-800-779-6750; Web site: www.
sycamoretree.com—kit with ideas and preplanned units, tips for creating your own
unit studies using the *World Book Encyclopedia,* Childcraft, and Early World of
Learning.

The Weaver Curriculum: 1-888-367-9871; Web site: http://weaverinc.com—a
unit-based home education for children from preschool through high school that
teaches fundamental knowledge and learning within the larger context of the
Scriptures.

Merit Badge.com: www.meritbadge.com—e-mail newsletter, links; use this site to
develop unit studies for personal use, or the use of a homeschool cooperative or
homeschooling scout troop.

Unschooling

Autodidactic Press, P.O. Box 872749, Wasilla, AK 99687; voice and fax: 907-376-2932;
e-mail: info@autodidactic.com; Web site: www.autodidactic.com/selfnews.htm—
Self-University Newsletter, links to alternative education sites, essays, and bookstore.

Growing Without Schooling available from John Holt's Bookstore: www.holtgws. com—
magazine by and for unschoolers, based on John Holt's philosophies.

Libertarian Unschooling: www.geocities.com:0080/Athens/6529/index2.html—links
to John Holt's writings, articles by unschoolers, and the Separation of School and
Web site.

Karl M. Bunday's Learn in Freedom page: learninfreedom.org—all the information
you need to take responsibility for your own learning.

Grace Llewellyn's Not Back to School Camp, P.O. Box 1014, Eugene, OR 97440;
541-686-2315; Web site: www.nbtsc.org—an annual gathering of teen unschoolers.

Workbook Publishers

Alpha Omega Publications, Life-Pacs, 300 North McKemy Avenue, Chandler, AZ 85226-2618; 1-800-622-3070; Web site: www.home-schooling.com—Christian curriculum.

Christian Light Publications, Inc., P.O. Box 1212, Harrisonburg, VA 22801-1212; 540-434-0768; e-mail: office@clp.org; Web site: www.clp.org—Anabaptist Christian curriculum.

Continental Press, Elizabethtown, PA 17022-2299; 1-800-233-0759; Web site: www.continentalpress.com—instructional materials for K–12.

Educators Publishing Service, Inc., 31 Smith Place, Cambridge, MA 02138-1089; 1-800-435-7728; Web site: www.epsbooks.com—workbooks to help you teach, including special needs.

School of Tomorrow, P.O. Box 299000, Lewisville, TX 75029-9000; 972-315-1776 (general), 1-800-925-7777 (orders); Web site: www.schooloftomorrow.com/homesch.htm—theistic character-building individualized curriculum.

Key Curriculum Press, 1150 65th Street, Emeryville, CA 94608-1109; 1-800-995-MATH; Web site: www.keypress.com—unique mathematics workbooks.

Milliken Publishing, 1100 Research Blvd., P.O. Box 21579, St. Louis, MO 63132; 1-800-325-4136; Web site: www.millikenpub.com—supplementary products for K–12, including workbooks.

Modern Curriculum Press, division of Pearson Learning, 1-800-526-9907; Web site: www.pearsonlearning.com—workbooks and much more.

Scott Foresman Educational Publishers, 1900 East Lake Avenue, Glenview, IL 60025; 1-800-552-2259; Web site: www.sf.aw.com/—workbooks for K–6.

The Waldorf Approach

Anthroposophic Press, P.O. Box 960, Herndon, VA 20172-0960; order line 1-800-856-8664; fax order line: 1-800-277-7947; Web site: 222.anthropress.org—catalog of books related to Rudolph Steiner's philosophy of holistic learning.

A to Z Home's Cool Waldorf Method: Web site: www.gomilpitas.com/homeschooling/methods/Waldorf.htm—links to help you learn about the Waldorf method, discussion boards, chats, e-mail lists, resources, publications, and more.

Magic Cabin Dolls: Childhood's Purest Treasures, 1950 Waldorf NW, Grand Rapids, MI 49550-7000; 1-888-623-6557; Web site: www.magiccabin.com—catalog of doll and craft kits, many using natural materials, books, and toys to encourage imaginative play.

Homeschooling Support Organizations

The following resources will help you locate local support in your area. I've done my best to make this listing as up-to-date as possible, but be aware that local support groups change and regroup, Web sites disappear, and contact information may change.

About.com includes state-by-state listings of homeschooling support groups: http://homeschooling.about.com/education/homeschooling/mbody.htm.

Growing Without Schooling, 2380 Massachusetts Avenue, Suite 104, Cambridge, MA 02140; 617-864-3100; e-mail: HoltGWS@erols.com; Web site: www.holtgws.com; publishes an annual issue with a listing of national, state, and local homeschool support groups, resource centers, and organizations.

Home Education magazine, P.O. Box 1083, Tonasket WA, 98855-1083; 1-800-236-3278 or 509-486-0453; e-mail: HEM@home-ed-magazine.com; Web site: www.home-ed-press.com/HEM/HEM_gninfo.html; publishes an annual issue with a listing of support groups.

Home School Legal Defense Association, P.O. Box 3000, Purcellville, VA 20134; 540-338-5600; Web site: www.hslda.org; lists affiliated Christian homeschool support groups.

Jon's Homeschool Resource Web site: www.midnightbeach.com/hs; has some support groups listed and suggestions for finding others.

National Home Education Network's Web site: www.nhen.org; provides voluntarily listed local support groups as well as state liaison volunteers to help you find a support group in your area.

National Home Education Research Institute, Dr. Brian D. Ray, President, P.O. Box 13939, Salem, OR 97309; 503-364-1490; fax: 503-364-2827; e-mail: mail@nheri.org; Web site: www.nheri.org.

National and Special Interest Support

The Adventist Home Educator
P.O. Box 836, Camino, CA 95709
916-647-2110

American Homeschool Association
P.O. Box 218
Tonasket, WA 98855
E-mail: AHA@americanhomeschool
association.org
www.home-ed-magazine.com/
AHA/aha.html

**Catholic Homeschool Network
of America**
Contact: Katie Moran
P.O. Box 6343
River Forest, IL 60305-6343
Fax: 330-652-3380, 708-386-3380,
or 608-592-5893
330-652-4923
E-mail: moran@netdotcom.com
or ekgtampa@juno.com
www.geocities.com/Heartland/8579/
chsna.html

Family Unschoolers Network
1688 Belhaven Woods Court
Pasadena, MD 21122-3727
Voice mail/fax: 410-360-7330
E-mail: FUNNews@MCImail.com

**Homeschool Association for
Christian Science Families**
445 Airport Road
Tioga, TX 76271

**Homeschooling Widows/Widowers
e-mail list**
www.egroups.com/group/homeschool-
widow

Homeschoolers for Peace
P.O. Box 74
Midpines, CA 95345

**Homeschoolers of Latter Days
(HOLD)**
Contact: Erin Harisay
702-437-6006
E-mail: HOLD@about.com
pages.about.com/HOLD

**Homeschooling Unitarian
Universalists
and Humanists and Friends**
Contact: Joyce Dowling
E-mail: jdowling@drix.net
www.drix.net/jdowling/HUUH.html

**Islamic Homeschool Association
of North America**
1312 Plymouth Court
Raleigh, NC 27610

Jewish Home Educator's Network
Contact: Lisa Kander
2122 Houser
Holly, MI 48442
E-mail: jhen@snj.com
http://snj.com/jhen

**Latter-Day Saint Home Educators
Association (LDS-HEA)**
2770 South 1000 West
Perry, UT 84302
www.ldshea.org

The Moore Foundation
P.O. Box 1
Camas, WA 98607
360-835-2736
E-mail: moorefnd@pacifier.com
www.moorefoundation.com

**Muslim Homeschool Network and
Resources**
P.O. Box 803
Attleboro, MA 02703
E-mail: MHSNR@aol.com
www.muslimhomeschool.com

326

National Association for Mormon Home Educators
2770 South 1000 West
Perry, UT 84302

National Association of Catholic Home Educators
6102 Saints Hill Lane
Broad Run, VA 22014
540-349-4314

Native American Home School Association
P.O. Box 979
Fries, VA 24330
expage.com/page/nahomeschool

Pagan Homeschoolers
E-mail:
Paganhomeschool@egroups.com
http://members.nbci.com/trtlgrrl/
PaganHomeschool.htm

Rose Rock Inclusive Global Homeschool Network
805-942-4465
E-mail: RoseRockHSG@bigfoot.com
www.bigfoot.com/~RoseRockHSG

Single Parents Educating Children in Alternative Learning
2 Pineview Drive #5
Amelia, OH 45102

Special Needs

At Our Own Pace
Contact: Jean Kulczyk
102 Willow Drive
Waukegan, IL 60087
847-662-5432

National Challenged Homeschoolers Association (NATHHAN)
P.O. Box 39
Porthill, ID 83853
208-267-6246
E-mail: nathanews@aol.com
www.nathhan.com

National Handicapped Homeschoolers Association
814 Shavertown Road
Boothwyn, PA 19061
215-459-2035

State Organizations

Alabama

Alabama Home Educators
P.O. Box 16091
Mobile, AL 36116

Alabama Home Educators Network (AHEN)
605 Mountain Gap Drive
Huntsville, AL 35803
256-882-0208
E-mail: KaeKaeB@aol.com

Home Educators of Alabama Round Table (HEART)
Contact: Donna DePaolo
P.O. Box 1091
Huntsville, AL 35807
P.O. Box 55182
Birmingham, AL 35255
205-933-2571
E-mail: mirator@mindspring.com
www.educationalfreedom.com/heart

Alaska

Alaska Homeschool Network
Networking, e-mail discussion list
E-mail: AHN@akhomeschool.net.com
www.akhomeschool.net

Alaska Private and Home Educators Association (APHEA)
Contact: Bob or Robin Parsons
1328 Kinnikinnick Street
Anchorage, AK 99508
E-mail: rjp@alaska.net
www.aphea.org

Alaska Homespun Educators
Contact: Annie Gibbs (907-783-2127)
or Gini McDonagh (907-346-1776)
P.O. Box 798
Girdwood, AK 99587907-346-1776
E-mail: HomeSpunEd@aol.com
or Gini@compuserve.com
http://members.aol.com/
homespuned/webpage.html

Arizona

Arizona Families for Home Education
P.O. Box 2035
Chandler, AZ 85244-2035
E-mail: kingskids@integrity.com
http://members.aol.com/ajunschl

SPICE
10414 West Mulberry Drive
Avondale, AZ 85323
Contact: Susan Taniguchi
602-877-3642

Arkansas

Coalition of Arkansas Parents (CAP)
P.O. Box 192455
Little Rock, AR 72219

Home Educators of Arkansas (HEAR)
P.O. Box 192455
Little Rock, AR 72219
501-847-4942
E-mail: HEAREPORT@juno.com
www.geocities,com/heartland/
garden/4555/hear.html

Home Educators of Arkansas Voicing Excellence Now (HEAVEN)
8 Glenbrook Place
Sherwood, AR 72120

California

California Homeschool Network (CHN)
P.O. Box 55485
Hayward, CA 94545-0485
1-800-327-5339
E-mail CHNMAIL@aol.com
www.cahomeschoolnet.org

E-mail discussion of all legal issues that affect California homeschoolers
www.egroups.com/group/CA-HS-Law

Home School Association of California
P.O. Box 2442
Atascadero, CA 93434-2442
1-888-HSC-4440
www.hsc.org

**Homeschooling Co-op of
Sacramento**
15 Moses Court
Sacramento, CA 95823-6368

**Legal Reference Desk for California
Homeschoolers**
http://members.aol.com/cotter1225/
hslaws.htm

Colorado

**Colorado Home Educators'
Association**
3043 South Laredo Circle
Aurora, CO 80013
303-441-9938
E-mail: chea@tms-co.com

Colorado Home Schooling Network
74990 West Apache,
Sedalia, CO 80135
303-688-4136

Concerned Parents of Colorado
P.O. Box 547
Florissant, CO 80816
719-748-8360

West River Unschoolers
Contact: Peggy Nishikawa
2420 North 1 Street
Grand Junction, CO 80501
970-241-4137

Connecticut

**Connecticut Home Educators
Association**
Contact: Dale Schneider
10 Ellen Lane
Deep River, CT 06417
E-mail: Daleas@juno.com
www.cthomeschoolers.com

**Connecticut's Citizens to Uphold
the Right to Educate (Connecticut's
CURE)**
Contact: Alison Brion
P.O. Box 597
Sherman, CT 06784
203-355-4724

Unschoolers' Unlimited
Contact: Luz Shoshie
22 Wildrose Avenue
Guilford, CT 06437
203-458-7402

Delaware

**Delaware Home Education
Association**
P.O. Box 1003
Dover, DE 19903

**Delaware Homeschool Information
Home Page**
http://home-educate.com/DE

Tri State Homeschool Network
P.O. Box 7193
Newark, DE 19714-7193
302-322-2018

Florida

**Florida Association for Schools
at Home**
1000 Devil's Dip
Tallahassee, FL 32308
850-878-2793

**Florida Parent-Educators Association
(FPEA)**
P.O. Box 50685
Jacksonville Beach, FL 32240
1-877-ASK-FPEA
E-mail: office@fpea.com
www.fpea.com

329

Georgia

Georgians for Freedom in Education
7180 Cane Leaf Drive
Fairburn, GA 30213
770-463-1563

**Home Education Information
Resource Center**
P.O. Box 2111
Rosewell, GA 30077-2111
404-681-HEIR
http://info@heir.org

Lifetime Learners of Georgia
c/o Lara Kimber
861 Franklin Road, Bldg. 2, Apt. 14
Marietta, GA 30067
770-419-8680
E-mail: mrslarak@yahoo.com
http://llg.freeyellow.com

Hawaii

Christian Homeschoolers of Hawaii
Contact: John and Arleen Alejado
91-824 Oama Street
Ewa Beach, HI 96706
808-689-6398
E-mail: oamastpro@aol.com

**Hawaii Homeschool Association
(HHA)**
P.O. Box 893476
Mililani, HI 96789
Voice mail: 808-944-3339
E-mail: TGthrngplc@aol.com
www.geocities.com/Heartland/Hollow/
4239

Idaho

Idaho Coalition of Home Educators
Contact: Larry and Kathy Reitz
5415 Kendall Street

Boise, ID 83706
E-mail: ritzbitz@juno.com
www.homeschoolwatch.com/
id/iche.htm

Family Unschooling Network
Contact: Neysa Jensen
1809 North 7th Street
Boise, ID 83702
208-345-2703
E-mail:
NeysaJensen@CompuServe.com

Home Educators of Idaho
3618 Pine Hill Drive
Coeur d'Alene, ID 83814
208-667-2778

Illinois

Christian Home Educators of Illinois
P.O. Box 47322
Chicago, IL 60647-0322
E-mail: ilchec@aol.com
http://members.aol.com/ilchec

Homeschooling Families of Illinois
1924 Crossing Court
Naperville, IL 60540
630-548-4349

**Home Oriented Unique Schooling
Experience (HOUSE)**
9508 Springfield Avenue
Evanston, IL 60203
Information line: 847-604-3541
www.geocities.com/illinoishouse

Illinois Christian Home Educators
P.O. Box 775
Harvard, Illinois 60033
815-943-7882
Fax: 815-943-7883
E-mail: ICHE83@juno.com
www.iche.org

Indiana

Indiana Association of Home Educators (AHE)
8106 Madison Avenue
Indianapolis, IN 46227
317-859-1202
Fax: 317-859-1204
E-mail: iahe@inhomeeducators.org
www.inhomeeducators.org

Life Education and Resource Network (LEARN)
Contact: Barbara McKinney
P.O. Box 452
Bloomington, IN 47402
www.bloomington.in.us/~learn

Discussion of a new inclusive state-wide organization
IndianaHomeschoolers@egroups.com

Iowa

Iowa Home Educators' Association
P.O. Box 213
Des Moines, IA 50301

Iowa Families for Christian Education
Rural Route 3
Box 143
Missouri Valley, IA 51555

Iowans Dedicated to Educational Alternatives (IDEA)
c/o Katy Diltz
3298 Linn-Buchanan Road
Coggon, IA 52218
319-224-3675
E-mail: hsinfo@juno.com
home.plutonium.net/~pdiltz/idea

Network of Iowa Christian Home Educators (NICHE)
P.O. Box 158
Dexter, Iowa 50070
1-800-723-0438 (within Iowa)
or 515-830-1614
E-mail: niche@netins.net
showcase.netins.net/web/niche

Kansas

Christian Home Educators Confederation of Kansas (CHECK)
P.O. Box 3564
Shawnee Mission, KS 66201
316-945-0810
E-mail: info@kansashomeschool.org
www.kansashomeschool.org

Kentucky

Kentucky Home Education Association
P.O. Box 81
Winchester, KY 40392

Kentucky Independent Learners Network
Contact: Meg McClory
P.O. Box 275
Somerset, KY 42501
606-678-2527

Louisiana

Louisiana Citizens for Home Education
3404 Van Buren
Baker, LA 70714

Louisiana Home Education Network (LAHEN)
PMB 700
Lake Charles, LA 70601
www.la-home-education.com

Louisiana Homeschoolers
Contact: Lauren Brenner-Katz
or Maryann Clair
E-mail: CopyKatz@aol.com
or ofy-matt@hotmail.com

Maine

Homeschoolers of Maine
337 Hatchet Mountain Road
Hope, Maine 04847
www.homeschool-maine.org

Maine Homeschool Association
P.O. Box 421
Topsham, ME 04086
1-800-520-0577

Maryland

Christian Home Educators Network (CHEN)
P.O. Box 2010
Ellicott City, Maryland 21043
301-474-9055
E-mail: chenmaster@chenmd.org
www.chenmd.org

Maryland Association of Christian Home Educators (MACHE)
P.O. Box 247
Point of Rocks, MD 21777-0247
Phone/Fax: 301-607-4284
E-mail: info@machemd.org
www.machemd.org

Maryland Home Education Association
Contact: M. Smith
9085 Flamepool Way
Columbia, MD 21045
410-730-0073

Maryland-Pennsylvania Home Educators
P.O. Box 67
Shrewsbury, PA 17361
717-993-3603

Massachusetts

Massachusetts Home Learning Association (MHLA)
Contact: Elisa Wood
P.O. Box 1558
Marstons Mills MA 02648
E-mail: subscribe@mhla.org
www.mhla.org

Massachusetts Homeschool Organization of Parent Educators (Mass Hope)
Contact: Wendy Orth
5 Atwood Road
Cherry Valley, MA 01611
978-544-7948
E-mail: info@masshope.org
www.masshope.org

Massachusetts Homeschoolers Organization of Parent Education
15 Ohio Street
Wilmington, MA 01887
508-658-8970

Michigan

Upper Peninsula Home Education League of Parents (HELP) Michigan
125 East Lincoln
Negaunee, MI 49866
906-475-5508
E-mail: UP4hmsklrs@aol.com

The Homeschool Support Network
Contact: Jackie Beattie
P.O. Box 2457
Riverview, MI 48192
734-284-1249

Information Network for Christian Homes (INCH)
4150 Ambrose North East
Grand Rapids, MI 49505
www.inch.org

Michigan Homeschoolers
E-mail: Home2Teach@homestead.com
michiganhomeschoolers.homestead.com

Minnesota

Minnesota Association of Christian Home Educators (MACHE)
P.O. Box 32308
Fridley, MN 55432-0308
E-mail: mache@isd.net
www.mache.org

Minnesota Home School Network
9669 E 123rd
Hastings, MN 55033
651-437-3049

Minnesota Homeschoolers Alliance
P.O. Box 23072
Richfield, MN 55423
612-288-9662, 1-888-346-7622
E-mail: mha@homeschoolers.org
www.homeschoolers.org

Mississippi

Byram-Terry Mississippi Homeschoolers e-mail list
www2.netdoor.com/~vannoys/Byram-Terry-MS.htm

Mississippi Home Educators Association
Rural Route 9
P.O. Box 350
Laurel, MS 39440-8720

Missouri

Families for Home Education in Missouri
E-mail: fhe@microlink.net
www.microlink.net/~fhe

Let Education Always Remain Natural (LEARN)
Contact: Kelly Wilson
E-mail: learn-info@kclearn.org
www.kclearn.org

Missouri Association of Teaching Christian Homes, Inc. (MATCH)
Contact: Michael and Orilla Crider
2203 Rhonda Drive
West Plains, MO 65775-1615
Phone/fax: 417-255-2824
E-mail: match@match-inc.org
www.match-inc.org

Montana

Montana Coalition of Home Educators
P.O. Box 43
Gallatin Gateway, MT 59730
406-587-616
http://222.mtche.org

Montana Homeschoolers
www.egroups.com/group/MontanaHomeschoolers

333

Nebraska

LEARN
Contact: Rose Yonekura
7741 East Avon Lane
Lincoln, NE 68505
402-488-7741

Nevada

Homeschool Melting Pot
Contact: Nancy Barcus
1778 Antelope Valley Avenue
Henderson, NV 89012
702-269-9101
E-mail barcus@lvcm.com
www.angelfire.com/nv/
homeschoolmeltingpot

Homeschools United
P.O. Box 26811
Las Vegas, NV 89126
702-870-9566

**Parent Activists Committed
to Education**
P.O. Box 13587
Las Vegas, NV 89112
702-457-1509

New Hampshire

**New Hampshire Alliance for Home
Education**
Contact: Betsy Westgate
17 Preserve Drive
Nashua, New Hampshire 03060
603-880-8629

**New Hampshire Home School
Coalition**
P.O. Box 2224
Concord, NH 03302
603-539-7233

E-mail: webmaster@
nhhomeschooling.org
www.nhhomeschooling.org/
index.html

New Jersey

Families Learning Together
P.O. Box 8051
Piscataway NJ, 08855
732-968-5143
E-mail: debbie.henderson@erols.com

**New Jersey Family Schools
Association**
RD 2
P.O. Box 208
Washington, NJ 07882

Unschooler's Network
Contact: Nancy Plent
2 Smith Street
Farmingdale, NJ 07727
732-938-2473

New Mexico

**Christian Association of Parent
Educators**
P.O. Box 25046
Albuquerque, NM 87125
505-898-8548
E-mail: cape-nm@juno.com
www.cape-nm.org

**New Mexico Family Educators
(NMFE)**
P.O. Box 92276
Albuquerque, NM 87199
505-275-7053

New York

New York Home Educators' Network
Contact: Anne Hodge
39 North Street
Saratoga Springs, NY 12866
518-584-9110

New York State Home Education News
Contact: Seth Rockmuller or Katharine Houk
P.O. Box 59
East Chatham, NY 12060
518-392-6900
E-mail: allpie@taconic.net

North Carolina

Families Learning Together
1670 NC 33 West
Chocowinity, NC 27817
E-mail: cn2464@abaco.coastalnet.com
www.mindspring.com/~flt-nc

North Carolinians for Home Education (NCHE)
Contact: Susan Van Dyke
419 North Boylan Avenue
Raleigh, NC 27603-1211
919-834-NCHE
Fax: 919-834-6241
E-mail: nche@mindspring.com
www.nche.com

North Dakota

North Dakota Home School Association (NDHSA)
P.O. Box 7400
Bismarck, ND 58507-7400
E-mail: ndhsa@wdata.com
701-223-4080

Ohio

Association of Ohio Homeschoolers
3636 Paris Boulevard
Westerville, OH 43081

Christian Home Educators of Ohio
P.O. Box 1224
Kent, OH 44240

Home Education Resource Organization
170 West Main Street
Norwalk, OH 44857
419-663-1064

Ohio Home Educators Network (O-HEN)
P.O. Box 38132
Olmsted Falls, OH 44138-8132
330-274-0542
E-mail: mardavnix@surfree.com
grafixbynix.com/ohen

Oklahoma

Home Educators' Resource Organization (HERO of Oklahoma)
302 N. Coolidge
Enid, OK 73703-3819
E-mail: HERO@OklahomaHomeschooling.org
OklahomaHomeschooling.org/oklahoma.htm

Oklahoma Christian Home Educators Association
P.O. Box 471032
Tulsa, OK 74147-1032

Oklahoma Home Educators' Network
P.O. Box 1420
Blanchard, OK 73010
www.telepath.com/ohenet

335

Oregon

Homeschool Information and Service Network
1044 Bismark
Klamath Falls, OR 97601

Homeschooler's Educational Resources of Oregon
E-mail: askstaff@heroweb.org
www.heroweb.org

Online Inclusive Support Group for Oregon Homeschools (ORSig)
Contact: Christine Webb
E-mail: Retromom@aol.com

Oregon Christian Home Education Association
2515 North East 37th Avenue
Portland, OR 97212
E-mail: oceanet@oceanetwork.org
www.oceanetwork.org

Oregon Home Education Network (OHEN)
Contact: Jeanne Biggerstaff
P.O. Box 218
Beaverton, OR 97075
503-321-5166
E-mail: ohen@teleport.com
www.teleport.com/~ohen

Pennsylvania

Maryland-Pennsylvania Home Educators
P.O. Box 67
Shrewsbury, PA 17361
717-993-3603 or 717-993-2962

Pennsylvania Home Education Network
Contact: Kathy Terleski
285 Allegheny Street
Meadville, PA 16335
412-561-5288
http://dmoz.org/Reference/Education

Pennsylvania Home Education News
P.O. Box 305
Summerhill, PA 14948
Contact: Karen Levantry
814-495-5651
E-mail: Karenleven@aol.com

Pennsylvania Homeschool Connection
Home School Headlines
650 Company Farm Road
Aspers, PA 17304
717-528-8850
Fax: 717-528-8124
E-mail: homesh@cvn.net
www.homeschoolheadlines.com/hspa.htm

A listing of local Pennsylvania support groups
www.barbpage.tripod.com/index.html

Rhode Island

Parent Educators of Rhode Island
P.O. Box 782
Glendale, RI 02826

Rhode Island Guild of Home Teachers
P.O. Box 11
Hope, RI 02831
401-821-7700
E-mail: right_right@mail.excite.com
members.tripod.com/righthome

South Carolina

Home Organization of Parent Educators (HOPE)
c/o Griesemer
1697 Dotterer's Run
Charleston, SC 29414

South Carolina Association of Independent Home Schools
P.O. Box 2104
Irmo, SC 29063-2104

South Carolina Home Educators Association (SCHEA)
P.O. Box 3221
Columbia, SC 29230
803-772-2330
E-mail: schea1@aol.com
www.christianity.com/schea

South Carolina Homeschool Alliance
1679 Memorial Park Road
Suite 179
Lancaster, SC 29720

South Carolina Homeschool Support Group
Contact: Sherry Huston
242 Weathers Farm Road
Bowman, SC 29018
803-563-9322

A South Carolina Members Association of Home Schoolers (ASCMAHS)
9 Byerly Lane
Gilbert; SC 29054-8566
E-mail:
sc-homeschool@worldnet.att.net
sc-homeschool.home.att.net

South Dakota

South Dakota Christian Home Educators
P.O. Box 528
Black Hawk, SD 57718
605-923-1893

South Dakota Home School Association
Contact: Kim Liedtke
P.O. Box 882
Sioux Falls, SD 57101
605-338-9689
E-mail: lafrance3@juno.com

South Dakota Homeschoolers
beta.communities.msn.com/
southdakotahomeschoolers

Tennessee

Eclectic Homeschoolers of Tennessee (EHT)
Contact: Jacki Willard
E-mail: LearningHappens@home.com

Home Education Association of Tennessee (HEAT)
3677 Richbriar Court
Nashville, TN 37211

Tennessee Home Education Association (THEA)
615-834-3529
E-mail: jcthornton3@earthlink.net

Tennessee Homeschooling Families
Contact: Lin Kemper Wallace
214 Park Lane
Oliver Springs, TN 37840
615-435-4375

Tennessee's Homeschooling Information Site
TNHomeEd.homestead.com

Texas

**Home Education Association
of Texas**
9625 Exter Road
Houston, TX 77093
713-695-8109
E-mail: homeschool@lobbyist.com

**Learning and Education Alternatives
Resource Network**
P.O. Box 176
Arlington, TX 76004-0176
E-mail: deblewis@fastlane.net

**Texas Advocates for Freedom in
Education (TAFFIE)**
Contact: Beth Jackson
13635 Greenridge Street
Sugar Land, TX 77478
713-242-7994
E-mail: taffie-request@jsoft.com
www.jsoft.com/archive.taffie

Texas Homeschool Coalition
P.O. Box 6982
Lubbock, TX 79493
806-797-4927

Utah

**Utah Christian Home School
Association
(UTCH or U-Teach)**
P.O. Box 3942
Salt Lake City, UT 84110-3942
801-394-4156

**Utah Home Educators Association
(UHEA)**
P.O. Box 167
Roy, Utah 84067
1-888-887-UHEA
E-mail: uhea@itsnet.com
www.itsnet.com/~uhea

Vermont

**Christian Home Educators
of Vermont**
214 North Prospect #105
Burlington, VT 05401
802-658-4561

**Vermont Homeschoolers'
Association**
Rural Route 2
Box 4440
Bristol, VT 05443
802-453-5460

Virginia

**Home Education Association
of Virginia**
P.O. Box 1810
Front Royal, VA 22630
703-635-9322

**Home Educators Association
of Virginia**
1900 Byrd Avenue, Suite 201
Richmond, VA 23230
804-288-1608
E-mail: HEAV33@aol.com
www.heav.org

**The Virginia Home Education
Association**
P.O. Box 5131
Charlottesville, VA 22905
540-832-3578 after 1:00 P.M.
E-mail vhea@juno.edu
www.poe.acc.virginia.edu/~pm6f/
vhea.html

**Virginia's state-wide eclectic
homeschool discussion list**
E-mail: VaEclecticHomeschool-
subscribe@onelist.com
expage.com/page/folcfolks

Washington

Family Learning Organization
Contact: Kathleen McCurdy
P.O. Box 7247
Spokane, WA 99207
509-924-3760
E-mail:
homeschool@familylearning.org
www.familylearning.org

Teaching Parents Association
Contact: Laurie McDonald
P.O. Box 1934
Woodinville, WA 98072
206-505-1561, ext. 1274
E-mail: info@washtpa.org
www.washtpa.org

Washington Association of Teaching Christian Homes (WATCH)
1026 224th Avenue NE
Sammamish, WA 98074
206-729-4889
E-mail: Info@WATCHhome.org
www.WATCHhome.org

Washington Homeschool Organization
6632 South 191st Place, Suite E100
Kent, WA 98032-2117
425-251-0439
E-mail: WHOoffice@juno.com

Washington DC

Bolling Area Home Educators
P.O. Box 8401
BAFB, Washington, DC 20336-8401
202-561-0234
E-mail: Tjensen718@aol.com

West Virginia

Christian Home Educators of West Virginia (CHEWV)
Contact: Melody Sheppard
Route 1
P.O. Box 122A
Buckhannon, WV 26201
E-mail: chewvadm@aol.com
www.geocities.com/Athens/Forum/8045

West Virginia Home Educators Association
P.O. Box 3707
Charleston, WV 25337
1-800-736-9843
E-mail: wvhea@bigfoot.com
members.tripod.com/~WVHEA

Wisconsin

Wisconsin Christian Home Educators Association (CHEA)
262-637-5127
E-mail: jang@execpc.com
www.execpc.com/~jang

Wisconsin Parents Association
P.O. Box 2502
Madison, WI 53701-2502
Voice mail: 608-283-3131
www.homeschooling-WPA.org

Wyoming

Homeschoolers of Wyoming
P.O. Box 3151
Jackson County, WY 83001
307-733-2834
E-mail: mungermtrr@compuserve.com

Unschoolers of Wyoming
Contact: Chris Anderson-Sprecher
429 Hwy 230 #20
Laramie, WY 82010

Independent Study Programs and Support Schools, Publications, and Vendors

Independent Study Programs and Support Schools

A Beka Home School
Station HE
Pensacola, FL 32523-6030
1-800-874-BEKA (3592)
www.abeka.com/ABB/
ContactInfo.html

Active Learning Academy
14949 South Tamiami Trail #112
North Port, Florida 34287
941-948-1658
http://members.nbci.com/
corecurric/ala.html

Alger Learning Center
Independence High School
121 Alder Drive
Sedro-Woolley, WA 98284
1-800-595-2630
www.independent-learning.com/
distanceprogram.html

American School
850 E. 58th Street
Chicago, IL 60637
1-800-228-5600

Basic Christian Education, Inc.
P.O. Box D
Nottawa, MI 49075
616-467-7017
Fax: 616-467-1885

Calvert School
Dept. 2CAT
105 Tuscany Road
Baltimore, MD 21210
410-243-6030
Fax: 410-366-0674
www.calvertschool.org

Cambridge Academy
3855 South East Lake Weir Avenue
Ocala, FL 34480
1-800-252-3777
www.cambridgeacademy.com

Center for Talent Development
Northwestern University
617 Dartmouth Place
Evanston, IL 60208-4175
847-491-3782
E-mail: ctd@nwu.edu
www.ctd.northwestern.edu

ChildU
316 NE Fourth Street, Suite 200
Fort Lauderdale, FL 33301
877-4-CHILDU
www.childu.com

Christian Liberty Academy Satellite Schools
502 West Euclid Avenue
Arlington Heights, IL 60004-5495
1-800-348-0899
www.homeschools.org

Citizens High School
P.O. Box 1929
Orange Park, FL 32067-9944

Clonlara Home Based Education Program
1289 Jewett, Ann Arbor, MI 48104
734-769-4511
www.clonlara.org

Foley-Belsaw Institute
6301 Equitable Road
Kansas City, MO 64120-9957
1-800-487-2100

The Foundation for American Christian Education
P.O. Box 9588, Chesapeake, VA 23321
1-800-352-FACE
www.face.net

Harcourt Learning Direct
925 Oak Street
Scranton, PA 18540-9889

Home Education & Family Services
Royal Academy, Inc.
P.O. Box 1056
51 West Gray Road
Gray, ME 04039
207-657-2800
www.HomeEducator.com/HEFS/
royalacademy.htm

Home Study International
12501 Old Columbia Pike
Silver Spring, MD 20904
301- 680-6570
www.hsi.edu

Homeschool Associates
25 Willow Street
Lewiston, ME 04240
207-777-0077
www.homeschoolassociates.com

InternetHomeSchool.com
915 East Gurley Street, Suite 101
Prescott, AZ 86301
520-708-9404
Contact: Christina Moody, Director of Business Administration
E-mail: clm@internethomeschool.com
internethomeschool.com

Keystone National High School School House Station
420 West 5th Street
Bloomsburg, PA 17815-1564
717-784-5220
Fax: 717-784-2129
E-mail: kschool@mail.prolog.net

Laurel Springs School
P.O. Box 1440
1002 East Ojai Avenue
Ojai, CA 93024
1-800-377-5890

Moore Foundation
P.O. Box 1
Camas, WA 98607
360-835-2736
www.moorefoundation.com

North Atlantic Regional Schools
25 Adams Avenue
Lewiston, ME 04240
207-753-1522
Fax: 207-777-1776
E-mail: Diploma@NARSonline.com
www.NARSonline.com

Oak Meadow School
P.O. Box 740
Putney, VT 05346
www.oakmeadow.com/IndexFlash.htm

Pennsylvania Homeschoolers
RR 2 Box 117
Kittanning PA 16201-9311
E-mail:
richmans@pahomeschoolers.com
www.pahomeschoolers.com/
oldindex.html

The Sycamore Tree Center for Home Education
2179 Meyer Place
Costa Mesa, CA 92627
949-650-4466
www.sycamoretree.com

The University of Arizona Extended University
P.O. Box 210158
888 North Euclid Avenue
Tucson, AZ 85721-0158
1-800-772-7480 or 520-626-4222
Fax: 520-621-3269
E-mail: ldykstra@ccit.arizona.edu
www.eu.arizona.edu/~uaextend

University of Alabama College of Continuing Studies
Division of Distance Education
127 Marhta Parham West
P.O. Box 870388
Tuscaloosa, AL 35487-0388
1-800-452-5971 or 205-238-9278
E-mail: disted@ccs.ua.edu
http://bama.disted.ua.edu

University of Nebraska—Lincoln
Independent Study High School
Clifford Hardin Nebraska Center for
Continuing Education, Rm. 269
Lincoln, NE 68583-9800
1-877-243-4747 or 402-472-4321
E-mail: unlishs2@unl.edu
www.unl.edu/ishs

The University of Texas at Austin
Continuing and Extended Education
1-888-BE-A-GRAD
www.utexas.edu/conted/

West River Academy
2420 North First Street
Grand Junction, CO 81501
970-241-4137
E-mail: WRU2420@aol.com

Publications

Gentle Spirit, All Things Home, All Things Natural, All Things Neighborly
P.O. Box 246
Wauna, WA 98395
425-747-7703
www.gentlespirit.com

Growing Without Schooling
John Holt's Bookstore
2269 Massachusetts Avenue
Cambridge, MA 02140-1226
617-864-3100
www.holtgws.com/holtbkst.htm

HELM (Home Education Learning Magazine)
P.O. Box 1159
Tallevast, FL 34270
E-mail: helm@helmonline.com
www.helmonline.com

Home Education magazine
P.O. Box 1083
Tonasket, WA 98855
509-486-1351
www.home-ed-magazine.com

343

Home Educator's Family Times
P.O. Box 708
51 West Gray Road
Gray, ME 04039

Homeschooling Today
S Squared Productions
P.O. Box 1608
Fort Collins, CO 80522-1608
954-962-1930
www.homeschooltoday.com

The Link: A Homeschool Newspaper
PMB 911
587 N. Ventu Park Road, Suite F
Newbury Park, CA 91230
805-492-1373
Fax: 805-493-9216
E-mail: hompaper@gte.net
www.homeschoolnewslink.com

*Paths of Learning: Options for Families
and Communities*
P.O. Box 328
Brandon, VT 05733-0328
www.great-ideas.org

Practical Homeschooling
Home Life, Inc.
P.O. Box 1250
Fenton, MO 63026
1-800-346-6322
www.home-school.com/
Catalog/PHS.html

*The Teaching Home: A Christian
Magazine for Home Educators*
P.O. Box 20219
Portland, OR 97294
503-25309633
www.TeachingHome.com

*Voices: The Journal of the National Home
Education Network*
P.O. Box 41067
Long Beach, CA 90853
www.nhen.org

Vendors

Audio Forum: The Language Source
Jeffrey Norton Publishers
96 Broad Street
Guilford, CT 06437
1-800-243-1234 or 203-453-9794
E-mail: in\fo@audioforum.com
http://audioforum.com

Blackstone Audiobooks
P.O. Box 969
Ashland, OR 97520
1-800-729-2665
www.blackstoneaudio.com

Bluestocking Press
P.O. Box 2030
Shingle Springs, CA 95682-2030
1-800-959-8586 or 530-621-1123

Chinaberry Books
2780 Via Orange Way, Suite B
Spring Valley, CA 91978
1-800-776-2242

Davidsons Music
6727 Metcalf
Shawnee Mission, KS 66204
913-262-4982

**Delta Education: Because Children
Learn by Doing**
80 Northwest Boulevard
P.O. Box 3000
Nashua, NH 03061-3000
E-mail: mbacon@delta-edu.com
www.delta-education.com

Eagle's Wings Educational Materials
P.O. Box 502
Duncan, OK 73534
580-252-1555
E-mail: info@eagleswingsed.com
www.EaglesWingsEd.com

The Elijah Company
1053 Eldridge Loop
Crossville, TN 38558
1-888-2-ELIJAH or 1-800-258-1302
E-mail: elijahcoWalijahco.com
www.elijahco.com

Emmanuel Center
4061 Holt Road
Holt, MI 48842-1843
Questions: 517-699-2728
Orders: 1-800-256-5044
E-mail: emmanuel@tir.com
www.homeschoolcenter.com

Family Things
19363 Willamette Drive, #237
West Linn, OR 97068
503-727-5473
E-mail: customerservice@
singaporemath.com
www.sales@singaporemath.com

Farm Country General Store
412 North Fork Road
Metamora, IL 61548
Orders: 1-800-551-FARM;
other calls 309-367-2844
E-mail: fcgs@homeschoolfcgs.com
www.homeschoolfcgs.com

Franklin Learning Resources
One Franklin Plaza
Burlington, NJ 08016-4907
1-800-525-9673
www.franklin.com

Friendship House
29313 Clemens Road #2-G
P.O. Box 450978
Cleveland, OH 44145-0623
1-800-791-9876
www.friendshiphouse.com

Gariel Screen Printing
1-800-442-7435
Fax: 856-384-8549
E-mail: info@gariel.com
www.gariel.com/homeschool/
homeschool.html

God's World Book Club
P.O. Box 2330
Asheville, NC 28802
www.gwbc.com

Great Products Online.com
2813 59th Avenue
St. Petersburg, FL 33714
727-403-2772
E-mail: admin@jctproducts.com
www.jctproducts.com/
HomeschoolShirts.htm

Greenleaf Press Catalog
3761 Highway 109N, Unit D
Lebanon, TN 37087
615-449-1617
www.greenleafpress.com

Harvest Educational Products
5 Mead Farm Road
Seymour, CT 06483
203-888-0427
Fax: 203-888-0413
www.harvested.com

Hearthsong
1950 Waldorf North West
Grand Rapids, MI 49550-7100
1-800-325-2502
www.hearthsong.com

The Helping Hand
P.O. Box 496316
Garland, TX 75049-6316
1-800-460-7171
E-mail:
helpinghand@classicshome.com
www.classicshome.com

Home Education and Family Services Bookstore Catalog
P.O. Box 1056
Gray, ME 04039
207-657-2800
www.chfweb.com/hefs

The Home School Catalog
P.O. Box 308
North Chemlsford, MA 01863-0308
1-800-788-1221
www.thehomeschool.com

Home School Discount Warehouse
229 South Bridge Street
P.O. Box 8000
Elkton, MD 21922-8000
1-800-775-5422

Integri-Tee
Attn: Cindy Clark
5102 West 126th Street
Hawthorne, CA 90250

Knowledge Products
The Audio Classics Series
772 Rundle Avenue, Suite A-13
Nashville, TN 37210
1-800-876-4332 or 615-742-3852

LibertyTree
134 98th Avenue
Oakland, CA 94603-1004
1-800-927-8733

Love to Learn
741 North State Road 198
Salem, UT 84653-9299
1-888-771-1034
E-mail: info@LoveToLearn.net
www.LoveToLearn.net

Magic Cabin Dolls
1950 Waldorf North West
Grand Rapids, MI 49550-7000
1-888-623-6557

Mastery Publications
90 Hillside Lane
Arden, NC 28704-9709
828-684-0429
http://members.aol.com/masterypub

Meridian Creative Group
5178 Station Road
Erie, PA 16510
1-800-695-9427
http://home.meridiancg.com

MindWare: Brainy Toys for Kids of All Ages
121 5th Avenue North West
New Brighton, MN, 55112
Orders: 1-800-999-0938
Customer service: 1-800-274-6123
Fax: 1-888-299-9273
www.MINDWAREonline.com

Music for Little People
P.O. Box 757
Greenland, NH 03840
1-800-409-2457
www.mflp.com

Professor Weissman's Software and Laugh With Math
246 Crafton Avenue
Staten Island, NY 10314
718-698-5219
E-mail: mathprof@hotmail.com
http://themathprof.com or
http://math911.com

The Providence Project
Dept. CTS
14566 North West 110th Street
Whitewater, KS 67154
1-888-776-8776

Rainbow Resource Center
Route 1
P.O. Box 159A
Toulon, IL 60483
1-888-841-3456
www.rainbowresource.com

Recorded Books, Inc.
270 Skipjack Road
Prince Frederick, MD 20678
1-800-638-1304
E-mail: recordedbooks
@recordedbooks.com

R.O.C.K. Solid
376 New Berlin Road
Jacksonville, FL 32218
1-800-705-3452 or 904-751-3569
www.rocksolidinc.com

Roots & Wings
P.O. Box 19678
Boulder, CO 80308-2678
1-800-833-1787 or 303-776-4796

Shekinah Curriculum Cellar
101 Meador Road
Kilgore, TX 75662
903-643-2760
24-hour fax/order line: 903-643-2796
E-mail: customerservice
@shekinahcc.com
www.shekinahcc.com

Sing 'n Learn
2626 Club Meadow
Garland, TX 75043-1102
1-800-460-1973 or 972-278-1973
www.singnlearn.com

Sonlight
8042 South Grant Way
Littleton, Co 80122
303-795-8668
E-mail: main@sonlight.com
www.sonlight.com

Tabletop Press
P.O. Box 2064
Orinda, CA 94563

Timberdoodle Company
1510 East Spencer Lake Road
Shelton, WA 98584
360-426-0672
www.timberdoodle.com

Usborne Books
Lynne Urso, Supervisor and
Educational Consultant
1-800-558-7449
E-mail: info@usbornebks.com
www.usbornebks.com/

The Vision Forum, Inc.
32335 U.S. Highway 281 North
Bulverde, TX 78163-3158
1-800-440-0022
www.visionforum.com

Bibliography

The Charlotte Mason Approach

Andreola, Karen. *A Charlotte Mason Companion: Personal Reflections on the Gentle Art of Learning* (Charlotte Mason Research & Supply Company, 1998).

Gardner, Penny. *The Charlotte Mason Study Guide* (Penny Gardner, 1997).

Levison, Catherine. *A Charlotte Mason Education* (Champion Press, 1999).

Macaulay, Susan Schaeffer. *For the Children's Sake* (Good News Publishing, 1984).

Trelease, Jim. *The Read Aloud Handbook* (Penguin, 1995).

Wilson, Edith. *Books Children Love: A Guide to the Best Children's Literature* (Crossway Books, 1987).

The Classical Education Approach

Berquist, Laura M. *Designing Your Own Classical Curriculum: A Guide to Catholic Home Education* (Ignatius Press, 1988).

Wilson, Douglas. *Recovering the Lost Tools of Learning: An Approach to Distinctively Christian Education* (Good News Pub, 1991). Includes the original essay "The Lost Tools of Learning," by Dorothy Sayers.

Wise, Jessie, and Susan Wise Bauer. *The Well-Trained Mind: A Guide to Classical Education at Home* (W.W. Norton & Co., 1999).

College and Career Planning

Barron's *Profiles of American Colleges* (Barron's Educational Series, 2000).

Bear, Mariah P., and John Bear, Ph.D., *Bears' Guide to Earning Degrees Nontraditionally* (13th Ed.) (Ten Speed Press, 1999).

Cohen, Cafi. *And What About College?: How Homeschooling Leads to Admissions to the Best Colleges and Universities* (Holt Associates, 2000).

Lamdin, Lois S. *Earn College Credit for What You Know* (Kendall/Hunt Publishing Co., 1997).

Lee, Linda. *Success Without College: College May Not Be Right for Your Child, or Right Just Now* (Doubleday, 2000).

Bolles, Richard Nelson. *What Color is Your Parachute? 2001: A Practical Manual for Job-Hunters and Career-Changers* (Ten Speed Press, 2000).

Core Knowledge Sequence

Hirsch, E.D. *Cultural Literacy: What Every American Needs to Know* (Vintage Books, 1988).

——. *What Your Kindergartner Needs to Know* (Delta, 1997).

——. *What Your First Grader Needs to Know* (Delta, 1998).

——. *What Your Second Grader Needs to Know* (Delta, 1999).

——. *What Your Third Grader Needs to Know* (Delta, 1994).

——. *What Your Fourth Grader Needs to Know* (Delta, 1994).

——. *What Your Fifth Grader Needs to Know* (Delta, 1995).

——. What Your Sixth Grader Needs to Know (Delta, 1995).

Curriculum Planning and Record Keeping

Berquist, Laura M. *Designing Your Own Classical Curriculum: A Guide to Catholic Home Education* (Ignatius Press, 1998).

Duffy, Cathy. *Christian Home Educators' Curriculum Manual: Elementary Grades* (Grove Pub., 2000).

——. *Christian Home Educators' Curriculum Manual: Junior/Senior High* (Grove Pub., 2000).

Hendrickson. Borg. *Home School: Taking the First Step—The Complete Home-School Program Planning Guide* (Mountain Meadow Press, 1994).

——. *How To Write a Low Cost/No Cost Curriculum for Your Homeschool Child* (Mountain Meadow Press, 1998).

Heuer, Loretta, M.Ed. *The Homeschooler's Guide to Portfolios and Transcripts* (IDG Books Worldwide, 2000).

Reed, Donn. *The Home School Source Book: A Comprehensive Catalog and Directory of Learning Materials That Are Challenging, Constructive, and Fun; with Commentaries, Notes, and Essays About a "Liberal Arts" Education at Home, from Birth Through Adulthood* (Brook Farm Books, 1994).

Rupp, Rebecca. *How to Design a Homeschool Curriculum: What Your Child Needs to Know from Preschool Through High School* (Three Rivers Press, 2000).

Scarlata, Robin. *What Your Child Needs to Know When* (Heart of Wisdom Publishing, 1996).

Willis, Mariaemma, M.S., and Victoria Kindle Hodson, M.A. *Discover Your Child's Learning Style* (Prima Publishing, 1999).

Educational Philosophy

Appleton. Matthew. *A Free Range Childhood: Self-Regulation at Summerhill School* (Foundation for Educational Renewal, 2000).

Gardner, Howard. *Frames of Mind: The Theory of Multiple Intelligences* (Basic Books, 1993).

——. *The Unschooled Mind: How Children Think and How Schools Should Teach* (Basic Books, 1993).

Gatto, John Taylor. *Dumbing Us Down: The Hidden Curriculum of Compulsory Schooling* (New Society Publishers, 1992).

——. *The Underground History of American Education* (The Oxford Village Press, 2001).

Holt, John. *How Children Fail* (Dell, 1964).

——. *How Children Learn* (Dell, 1967).

——. *Learning All The Time* (Perseum Press, 1990).

——. *What Do I Do Monday?* (E.P. Dutton & Co., 1970).

Mercogliano, Chris. *Making It Up As We Go Along: The Story of the Albany Free School* (Heinneman, 1998).

Miller, Ron, ed. *Creating Learning Communities: Models, Resources, and New Ways of Thinking About Teaching and Learning* by *A Coalition for Self Learning* (Foundation for Educational Renewal, 2000).

Neil, A.S. *Summerhill: A Radical Approach to Child Rearing* (St. Martin's Press, 1995).

Tobias, Cynthia. *The Way They Learn* (Focus on the Family Publishing, 1998).

Famous Homeschoolers

Goyer, Tricia. "From Hollywood to Homeschooling (Lisa Whelchel's Journey of Success)," (*Homeschooling Today,* January/February 1999).

Plent, Max, and Nancy Plent. *An A in Life: Famous Homeschoolers* (Unschooler's Network, 1999).

Seefeldt, Susan McMinn. "Add These Woman to Your List! (Famous People Who Didn't Go to School), (*Home Education* magazine, May/June 1997).

Frugal Homeschooling

Farrow, Elvira. *Montessori on a Limited Budget: A Manual for the Amateur Craftsman* (Education Systems Pub., 1975).

Gold, Lauramaery, and Joan M. Zielinski. *Homeschool Your Child for Free: More Than 1,200 Smart, Effective, and Practical Resources for Home Education on the Internet and Beyond* (Prima Publishing, 2000).

Morgan, Melissa L., and Judith Waite Allee. *Homeschooling on a Shoestring: A Jam-Packed Guide* (Harold Shaw Pub., 1999).

Siegel, David S., and Susan Siegel. *Used Book Lover's Guide to Canada* (Book Hunter Press, 1999, updated 2000).

——. *Used Book Lover's Guide to the Central States* (Book Hunter Press, 1996, updated 2000).

——. *Used Book Lover's Guide to the Mid-Atlantic States* (Book Hunter Press, 1997 (updated 2000).

——. *Used Book Lover's Guide to the Midwest* (Book Hunter Press, 1999 (updated 2000).

——. *Used Book Lover's Guide to the New England States* (Book Hunter Press, 2nd Rev Ed, 2000).

——. *Used Book Lover's Guide to the Pacific Coast States* (Book Hunter Press, Rev Ed 2000).

——. *Used Book Lover's Guide to the South Atlantic States* (Book Hunter Press, Rev Ed 1997, updated 2000).

Home Business

Berg, Adriane G., and Arthur Berg Bochner. *The Totally Awesome Business Book for Kids: With Twenty Super Businesses You Can Start Right Now!* (Newmarket Press, 1995).

Bernstein, Daryl. *Better Than a Lemonade Stand: Small Business Ideas for Kids (Kid's Books by Kids)* (Beyond Words Publishing Company, 1992).

Edwards, Paul, and Sarah Edwards. *The Best Home Businesses for the 21st Century: The Inside Information You Need to Know to Select a Home-Based Business That's Right for You* (J.P. Tarcher, 1999).

Kushell, Jennifer. *The Young Entrepreneur's Edge: Using Your Ambition, Independence, and Youth to Launch a Successful Business* (Princeton Review Series) (Random House, 1999).

Mariotti, Steve. *The Young Entrepreneur's Guide to Starting and Running a Business* (Times Books, 2000).

Weltman, Barbara, and Beverly Williams. *The Complete Idiot's Guide to Starting a Home-Based Business* (Alpha Books, 2000).

Homeschooling in General

Beechick, Ruth. *You Can Teach Your Child Successfully* (Arrow Press, 1992).

Cohen, Cafi. *Homeschooling: The Teen Years* (Prima Publishing, 2000).

Colfax, David, and Mary Colfax. *Homeschooling for Excellence: How to Take Charge of Your Child's Education—and Why You Absolutely Must* (Warner Books, 1988).

Dobson, Linda. *The Art of Education: Reclaiming Your Family, Community, and Self* (Holt Associates, 1997).

——. *The Homeschooling Book of Answers: The 88 Most Important Questions Answered by Homeschooling's Most Respected Voices* (Prima Publishing, 1998).

——. *Homeschoolers' Success Stories: 15 Adults and 12 Young People Share the Impact That Homeschooling Has Made on Their Lives* (Prima Publishing, 2000).

Graham, Gayle. *How to Home School: A Practical Approach* (Common Sense Press, 1992).

Guterson, David. *Family Matters: Why Homeschooling Makes Sense* (Harvest Books, 1993).

Holt, John. *Teach Your Own: A Hopeful Path for Education* (Dell Pub., 1981).

Layne, Marty. *Learning at Home: A Mother's Guide to Homeschooling* (Sea Change Publications, 2000).

Llewellyn, Grace. *Real Lives: Eleven Teenagers Who Don't Go to School* (Lowry House Pub., 1993).

——. *The Teenage Liberation Handbook: How to Quit School and Get a Real Life and Education* (Lowry House Pub., 1998).

Macaulay, Susan Schaeffer. *For the Children's Sake* (Good News Pub., 1984).

McAlister, Diana, and Candice Oneschak. *Homeschooling the High Schooler* (Family Academy Publications, 1993).

Moore, Raymond S., and Dorothy N. Moore. *The Successful Homeschool Family Handbook: A Creative and Stress-Free Approach to Homeschooling* (Thomas Nelson, 1994).

Language Arts

Andreola, Karen. *Simply Grammar: An Illustrated Primer (A Revised and Expanded Edition of First Grammar Lessons by Charlotte Mason, Founder of the Homeschooling Movement)* (Charlotte Mason Research & Supply Company, 1993).

Engelmann, Siegfried; Haddox, Phyllis; and Bruner, Elaine, *Teach Your Child to Read in 100 Easy Lessons* (Simon & Schuster, 1986).

Frank, Marjorie, *Complete Writing Lessons for the Primary Grades* (Incentive Publications, 1987).

——. *Complete Writing Lessons for the Middle Grades* (Incentive Publications, 1987).

——. *If You're Trying to Teach Kids How to Write, You've Gotta Have This Book* (Incentive Publications, 1995).

Hyde, Mary. *English for the Thoughtful Child* (Greenleaf Press, 1990).

Von der Porten, Edward. *The Short Report: An Introduction to the Term Paper* (Perfection Form Company, 1980).

Weiner, Harvey S. *Any Child Can Write* (Oxford University Press, 1994).

Legal Issues

Duffy, Cathy. *Government Nannies: The Cradle-to-Grave Agenda of Goals 2000 and Outcome Based Education* (Noble Pub Assoc/Noble Books, 1995).

Klicka, Christopher J. "Can Homeschoolers Participate in Public School Programs?" (*Practical Homeschooling,* Jan/Feb 2000).

Kaseman, Larry, and Susan Kaseman. "Why the Question of Homeschoolers' Playing Public School Sports Affects All Homeschoolers," (*Home Education Magazine,* May/June 2000).

Whitehead, John W., and Alexis Irene Crow. *Home Education: Rights and Reasons* (Crossway Books, 1993).

Math

Baratta-Lorton, Robert. *Mathematics: A Way of Thinking* (Addison Wesley Publishing Company, 1977).

Burns, Marilyn. *About Teaching Mathematics: A K–8 Resource* (Math Solutions Publications, 2000).

——. *The Book of Think: Or, How to Solve a Problem Twice Your Size (A Brown Paper School Book)* (Little Brown & Company, 1976).

——. *Math for Smarty Pants (Brown Paper School Book)* (Little Brown & Company, 1982).

Hansen, Jaye. *Grocery Cart Math* (Common Sense Press, 1994).

Kenda, Margaret, and Phyllis S. Williams. *Math Wizardry for Kids* (Barrons Juvenile, 1995).

Stenmark, Jean Kerr, Thompson, Virginia, and Ruth Cossey. *Family Math* (Equals, 1986).

Weissman, Professor. *Laugh With Math* (Laugh and Learn, 1995).

Miscellaneous

Ellis, David. *Becoming a Master Student* Houghton Mifflin Company, 1998).

Lines, Patricia M., Homeschooling Comes of Age, *The Public Interest,* July 1, 2000. (Read article on The Discovery Institute's Web site at www.discovery.org).

Ray, Brian D., Ph.D., *Home Schooling on the Threshold: A Survey of Research at the Dawn of the New Millennium* (Read page 3 online, print fact sheets from links, or order the study).

"A Profile of Home Schooling in Canada," *Education Quarterly Review,* Catalogue No. 81-003-XPB, Winter 1997, Vol. 4, No. 4 from Culture, Tourism & the Centre of Education Statistics, Ottawa, Ontario, Canada KIA 0T6.

The Montessori Approach

Hainstock, Elizabeth G. *Teaching Montessori in the Home: The School Years* (Plume, 1997).

Montessori, Maria, and J. McV Hunt (contributor). *The Montessori Method* (Schocken Books, 1989).

Spietz, Heidi Anne. *Montessori Resources in the 1990s: A Complete Guide to Finding Montessori Resources for Parents and Teachers* (American Montessori Consulting, 1999).

Parenting

Campbell, Ross, Dr. *How to Really Love Your Child* (Chariot Victor Books, 1992).

——. *How to Really Love Your Teenager* (Chariot Victor Books, 1993).

McCullough, Bonnie Runyan, and Susan Mon. *401 Ways to Get Your Kids to Work at Home* (St. Martin's Press, 1982).

Rich, Dorothy. *Megaskills: Building Children's Achievement for the Information Age* (Houghton Mifflin Co., 1998).

Preschool and Kindergarten

Engelhardt, Anne, and Cheryl Sullivan. *Playful Learning: An Alternate Approach to Preschool* (La Leche League International, 1986).

Gettman, David. *Basic Montessori: Learning Activities for Under-Fives* (St. Martin's Press, 1988).

Milord, Susan. *Hands Around the World: 365 Creative Ways to Encourage Cultural Awareness and Global Respect* (Williamson Publishing, 1992).

Oberlander, June. *Slow and Steady, Get Me Ready: A Parents' Handbook for Children from Birth to Age 5* (Bio Alpha, 1992).

Spietz, Heidi Anne. *Montessori at Home: A Complete Guide to Teaching Your Preschooler at Home Using the Montessori Method* (American Montessori Consulting, 1991).

Record Keeping

Heuer, Loretta. *The Homeschooler's Guide to Portfolios and Transcripts* (IDG Books Worldwide, Inc., 2000).

Kimeldorf, Martin. *Creating Portfolios: For Success in School, Work, and Life* (Free Spirit Publishing, 1994).

——. *A Teacher's Guide to Creating Portfolios: For Success in School, Work, and Life* (Free Spirit Publishing, 1994).

Science

Cassidy, John. *The Explorabook: A Kid's Science Museum in a Book/Book and Magnet* (Klutz, Inc., 1992).

Cole, Joanna. *The Magic Schoolbus on the Ocean Floor* (Scholastic, 1994).

Heddle, Rebecca, and K. Woodward. *Science in the Kitchen: Usborne Science Activities* (EDC Publications, 1992).

McCauley, David. *The New Way Things Work* (Houghton Mifflin Company, 1998).

——. *The Way Things Work Kit* (DK Publishing, 2000).

Milord, Susan. *The Kids' Nature Book: 365 Indoor/Outdoor Activities and Experiences* (Williamson Publishing, 1996).

VanCleave, Janice. *Janice Vancleave's Guide to the Best Science Fair Projects* (John Wiley & Sons, 1997).

——. *Astronomy, Chemistry, Physics for Every Kid* (John Wiley & Sons, 1992).

Special Needs

Armstrong, Thomas. *In Their Own Way: Discovering and Encouraging Your Child's Multiple Intelligences* (J.P. Tarcher, 2000).

Boyles, Nancy S., M.Ed., and Darlene Contadino, M.S.W. *The Learning Differences Sourcebook* (Lowell House, 1997).

Freed, Jeffrey, and Laurie Parsons. *Right-Brained Children in a Left-Brained World: Unlocking the Potential of Your ADD Child* (Fireside, 1998).

Gray, Carol. *The New Social Stories: Illustrated Edition* (Future Horizons, 2000).

Hartmann, Thom. *Attention Deficit Disorder: A Different Perception* (Underwood Books, 1997).

Hensley, Sharon, M.A. *Homeschooling Children with Special Needs* (Noble Publ. Assoc., 1995).

Herzog, Joyce. *Learning in Spite of Labels* (Greenleaf Press, 1994).

National Association of the Deaf. *Legal Rights: The Guide for Deaf and Hard of Hearing People* (Gallaudet University Press, 2000).

Testing and Assessment

Berger, Larry. *Up Your Score 2001–2002: The Underground Guide to the SAT* (Workman Publishing Company, 2000).

College Board. *Clep Official Study Guide 2001 Edition* (College Entrance Examination Board, 2001).

Jasmine, Julia. *How To Prepare Your Students for Standardized Tests* (Teacher Created Materials, 1997).

Lazear, David. *Multiple Intelligence Approaches to Assessment: Solving the Assessment Conundrum* (Zephyr Press, 1998).

Miller, Wilma H. *Alternative Assessment Techniques for Reading and Writing* (Center for Applied Research in Education, 1995).

Weber, Karl. *Insider's Guide to the Act Assessment* (Petersons Guides, 2001).

Unschooling

Colfax, David, and Mary Colfax. *Hard Times in Paradise: An American Family's Struggle to Carve Out a Homestead in California's Redwood Mountains* (Warner Books, 1992).

Farenga, Patrick, *The Beginner's Guide to Homeschooling* (Holt Associates, 2000).

Griffith, Mary. *The Unschooling Handbook: How to Use the Whole World As Your Child's Classroom* (Prima Publishing, 1998).

Holt, John. *Growing Without Schooling: A Record of a Grassroots Movement* (Holt Associates, 1997).

Hood, Mary. *The Relaxed Home School* (Ambleside Educational Press, 1994).

Leistico, Agnes. *I Learn Better by Teaching Myself* and *Still Teaching Ourselves* (Holt Associates, 1997).

Index

C

M

N

S

381